Rohan Bi[signature]

Praise for *102 Minutes*

"An astounding reconstruction of what happened inside the World Trade Center. . . . These are stories, after all, you have to share."
—*Newsweek*

"There have been many 9/11 books, but the sheer volume of detail about individuals and their acts of heroism and humanity puts this one in a class by itself." —*Reader's Digest* (editor's choice)

"It's just one of those great books of reporting, and you read it almost at one sitting with your hair on end. . . . There have been 50 different preachy books and 10,000 op-ed pieces, but this is one that really takes you back to that beautiful morning in New York."
—Garrison Keillor, *Hartford Courant*

"A masterpiece of reporting. . . . [*102 Minutes*] is a remarkably comprehensive account of what went on inside the trade center that day, distilled to an amazingly coherent 261 pages of text. The authors have added charts and drawings to help readers keep track of the dozens of individuals whose plights they follow, but so vivid are their characterizations that one hardly needs to refer to such aids. Their style is invariably succinct and understated; like all the best reporters, they let the story they have dug out speak for itself. . . . Mr. Dwyer and Mr. Flynn's story is an intensely human, personal one. And yet it also draws them inevitably into the question of whether or not some part of this calamity might have been ameliorated. . . . Brilliant and troubling." —Kevin Baker, *The New York Times*

"The chief virtue of *102 Minutes*, Jim Dwyer and Kevin Flynn's unsparing, eloquent history of the struggle to survive inside the World Trade Center, is the authors' insistence that truth supplant myth. However comforting myths may be after a defeat, they're useless in assessing what went wrong and may actually be impediments to preventing future disasters. . . . With its consistently clear prose, *102 Minutes* does an admirable job of conveying this chaos without replicating it."
—John Farmer (senior counsel to the 9/11 Commission, former New Jersey attorney general), *The Washington Post Book World*

"The writing—sometimes searing, sometimes factual but always appropriate—brings the human experience of disaster into focus. . . . Thanks to this volume, those voices have not been silenced."

—*Boston Herald*

"Riveting human drama."

—*The Columbus Dispatch*

"A powerful account of the disaster that hesitates neither to confer laurels nor point fingers. . . . [Dwyer and Flynn] celebrate the extraordinary capacities of ordinary folk. Swift, photographic prose defines the dimensions of hell—and of humanity."

—*Kirkus Reviews* (starred review)

"Superb reporting. . . . The book vividly captures the stories of those struggling to survive. Heartbreaking and heroic."

—*The Dallas Morning News*

"A masterful account."

—*Entertainment Weekly*

"This is a heart-stopping, heartbreaking book. It is also an infuriating one. Jim Dwyer and Kevin Flynn give us vivid examples of uncommon valor in the face of approaching doom. Nobody can read those pages without feeling a chilly surge of fear. But they also give us—in lucid, understated prose—explanations for the immensity of the calamity. In short, this is an essential document about New York's worst human tragedy. And it's a terrific book."

—Pete Hamill, author of
Forever and *Downtown: My Manhattan*

"A triumph of ground level reporting. Dwyer and Flynn deliver us inside a day the world has seen only from the outside looking in, and in the process show what happens in the first moments when human beings collide with the impossible."

—Robert Kurson, author of *Shadow Divers*

"*102 Minutes* does for the September 11 catastrophe at New York's World Trade Center what Walter Lord did for the *Titanic* in his masterpiece, *A Night to Remember*. Jim Dwyer and Kevin Flynn have written a book that is searing, poignant, and utterly compelling."

—Rick Atkinson, author of *An Army at Dawn*
and *In the Company of Soldiers*

102 Minutes

TIMES BOOKS
Henry Holt and Company   New York

102 Minutes

*The Unforgettable Story of the Fight
to Survive inside the Twin Towers*

Jim Dwyer and Kevin Flynn

Times Books
Henry Holt and Company, LLC
Publishers since 1866
175 Fifth Avenue
New York, New York 10010
www.henryholt.com

Henry Holt® is a registered trademark of
Henry Holt and Company, LLC.

Library of Congress Cataloging-in-Publication Data

Dwyer, Jim, 1957–
    102 minutes : the unforgettable story of the fight to survive inside
the Twin Towers / Jim Dwyer and Kevin Flynn. — 2nd paperback ed.
        p. cm.
    Originally published: New York : Times Books, 2005.
    Includes bibliographical references and index.
    ISBN 978-0-8050-9421-3
    1. September 11 Terrorist Attacks, 2001.   2. Victims of terrorism—
New York (State)—New York.   3. Buildings—Evacuation—New York
(State)—New York.   4. Rescue work—New York (State)—New York.
5. Self-preservation—New York (State)—New York.   6. World Trade
Center (New York, N.Y.)   I. Flynn, Kevin, 1956–   II. Title.   III. Title:
One hundred two minutes.
    HV6432.7.D89 2011
  ·974.7'1044—dc23
                                                        2011026055

Henry Holt books are available for special promotions and
premiums. For details contact: Director, Special Markets.

First published in hardcover in 2005 by Times Books

First Paperback Edition 2006
Second Paperback Edition 2011

Designed by Paula Szafranski

Printed in the United States of America
3   5   7   9   10   8   6   4

Contents

Contents

Illustrations

Graphics edited by Steve Duenes

367 People at the World Trade Center

1 WORLD TRADE CENTER (NORTH TOWER)

The 89th floor

Rick Bryan
Raffaele Cava
Dianne DeFontes
Nathan Goldwasser
Akane Ito
Stephanie Manning

Harold Martin
Tirsa Moya
Walter Pilipiak
Rob Sibarium
Lynn Simpson

Beast Financial Systems

Susan Fredericks

Sharon Premoli

Cantor Fitzgerald

Stephen Cherry
Charles Heeran
David Kravette

Andrew Rosenblum
Martin Wortley

Carr Futures

Brendan Dolan
Joe Holland
Tom McGinnis
Damian Meehan

Jeffrey Nussbaum
Jim Paul
Elkin Yuen

Clearstream Banking

Anne Prosser

Empire Blue Cross and Blue Shield

Ed Beyea
Irma Fuller

Abe Zelmanowitz

Julian Studley

James Gartenberg

Patricia Puma

Marsh & McLennan

Dana Coulthurst
Judith Martin
Patricia Massari
Keith Meerholz

Ian Robb
Gerry Wertz
Chris Young

May Davis Group

Steve Charest

Mike Jacobs

Network Plus

Michael Benfante

John Cerquiera

Port Authority of New York and New Jersey, 88th floor

Jim Connors
Patricia Cullen
Carlos DaCosta
Frank De Martini
Nicole De Martini, *guest*
Elaine Duch
Gerry Gaeta
Jeff Gertler

Mak Hanna
Moe Lipson
Pete Negron
Pablo Ortiz
Judith Reese
Anita Serpe
Dorene Smith
Frank Varriano

Port Authority of New York and New Jersey, elsewhere in building

Ana Abelians
John Abruzzo
Michael Ambrosio
Lenny Ardizzone
Ezra Aviles
Peter Bitwinski
Frank Bucaretti
Pasquale Buzzelli
Phillip Caffrey
Richard Capriotti
Nelson Chanfrau
Michael Curci
Frank DiMola
Gerry Drohan
Bob Eisenstadt
Michael Fabiano
Ken Greene
Genelle Guzman
Tina Hansen
Josephine Harris

Mark Jakubek
Patrick Hoey
Michael Hurley
Shivam Iyer
Vickie Cross Kelly
John Labriola
Louis Lesce
Cecilia Lillo
Wilson Pacheco
John Paczkowski
Tony Pecora
George Phoenix
John Rappa
Alan Reiss
Colin Richardson
Tony Savas
Gerald Simpkins
George Tabeek
Greg Trevor
Peggy Zoch

Silverstein Properties

John Griffin

Windows on the World guests

Peter Alderman
Caleb Arron Dack
Garth Feeney
Christopher Hanley
Emeric Harvey
William Kelly
Stuart Lee

Neil Levin
Peter Mardikian
Michael Nestor
Liz Thompson
Richard Tierney
Stephen Tompsett
Geoffrey Wharton

Windows on the World staff

Ivhan Carpio
Doris Eng
Howard Kane

Jan Maciejewski
Christine Olender

WPIX-TV
Steve Jacobson

Others
Keith Ensler
David Frank
Norma Hessic
Michael Hingson
Bill Hult

Vanessa Lawrence
Theresa Leone
Jules Naudet
Al Smith
Richard Wright

Building staff
Jan Demczur
Anthony Giardina
Mike McQuaid
Marie Refuse

Tony Segarra
Lloyd Thompson
Greg Trapp

2 WORLD TRADE CENTER (SOUTH TOWER)

Aon Insurance
Mary Jo Arrowsmith
Kevin Cosgrove
Keating Crown
Sarah Dechalus
Eric Eisenberg
Tamitha Freeman
Richard Gabrielle
Karen Hagerty
Gary Herold
Howard Kestenbaum
Alan Mann

Greg Milanowycz
Ed Nicholls
Marissa Panigrosso
Vijay Paramsothy
Robert Radomsky
Kelly Reyher
Sean Rooney
Gigi Singer
Donna Spera
Judy Wein

Euro Brokers
Brett Bailey
Brian Clark
Bobby Coll

Dennis Coughlin
Ron DiFrancesco
Richard Fern

Edward Keslo
Ed Mardovich
Jose Marrero
Ann McHugh
Steven Salovich
Andy Soloway

Thomas Sparacio
Michael Stabile
Patty Troxell
Dave Vera
Karen Yagos
Kevin York

Fiduciary Trust
Shimmy Biegeleisen
Elsie Castellanos
Donovan Cowan
Ed Emery
Anne Foodim
Alayne Gentul

Elnora Hutton
Stephanie Koskuba
Bob Mattson
Ed McNally
Paul Rizza
Doris Torres

Garban ICAP
George Nemeth

Michael Sheehan

Keefe, Bruyette & Woods
J. J. Aguiar
Joseph Berry
Will DeRiso
Frank Doyle
Bradley Fetchet
Scott Johnson

Stephen Mulderry
Bob Planer
Linda Rothemund
Lauren Smith
Rick Thorpe
Brad Vadas

Kemper Insurance
Terence McCormick

Mizuho Capital Markets/Fuji Bank
Jack Andreacchio
Manny Gomez
Yuji Goya
Richard Jacobs
Bobby McMurray
Stephen Miller

Michael Otten
Stanley Praimnath
Silvion Ramsundar
Christine Sasser
Keiji Takahashi
Brian Thompson

Morgan Stanley

Nat Alcamo
Ed Ciffone
Kristen Farrell
Sean Pierce

Rick Rescorla
Al Roxo
Louis A. Torres

New York State Department of Taxation and Finance

Dianne Gladstone
Mary Jos
Yeshavant Tembe

Diane Urban
Sankara Velamuri
Ling Young

Oppenheimer Management Corp.

Edgardo Villegas

Sandler O'Neill & Partners

Jace Day
Jennifer Gorsuch

Herman Sandler

Others

Katherine Hachinski
Eric Johnson

John Mongello

Building staff/Port Authority

Roselyn Braud
Ed Calderon
Roko Camaj
James Flores
Phil Hayes

Ron Hoerner
Robert Gabriel Martinez
Francis Riccardelli
Esmerlin Salcedo

3 WORLD TRADE CENTER (MARRIOTT HOTEL)

Reverend Paul Engel
Rich Fetter

Joe Keller
Abdu A. Malahi

Fire Department of New York

Commissioner Thomas Von
    Essen

Deputy Commissioner
    Tom Fitzpatrick

Chief of Department Peter Ganci
Assistant Chief Joseph Callan
Deputy Assistant Chief Al Turi
Deputy Chief Donald Burns
Deputy Chief Tom Galvin
Deputy Chief Peter Hayden
Battalion Chief Ed Geraghty
Battalion Chief Orio J. Palmer
Battalion Chief John Paolillo
Battalion Chief Joseph Pfeifer
Battalion Chief Richard Picciotto
Fire Marshal Ron Bucca
Fire Marshal Jim Devery
Fire Marshal Steve Mosiello
Captain William Burke Jr.
Captain Fred Ill
Captain Jay Jonas
Lieutenant Raymond Brown
Lieutenant Joseph Chiafari
Lieutenant John Fischer
Lieutenant Gregg Hansson
Lieutenant Mickey Kross
Lieutenant Joseph Leavey
Lieutenant Steve Modica
Lieutenant Bob Nagel
Lieutenant Kevin Pfeifer
Lieutenant Richard Smiouskas
Lieutenant Warren Smith
Lieutenant William Walsh
Lieutenant Mike Warchola
Reverend John Delendick
Reverend Mychal Judge
David Arce

Rich Billy
Michael Boyle
Billy Butler
Robert Byrne
Sal D'Agostino
Dennis Dowdican
Robert Evans
Tommy Falco
Tom Feaser
Mike Fitzpatrick
Liam Flaherty
Sean Halper
Pat Kelly
Tom Kelly
Robert King Jr.
Matt Komorowski
Scott Kopytko
Scott Larsen
Joseph Maffeo
Keithroy Maynard
Michael Meldrum
Bill Morris
Rich Nogan
Douglas Oelschlager
Michael Otten
Bob Pino
Christian Regenhard
Willie Roberts
Bill Spade
Danny Suhr
David Weiss
John Wilson

New York Police Department

Chief of Department Joseph
  Esposito
Captain Tim Pearson

Lieutenant Steve Reardon
Sergeant Michael Curtin
Detective Timothy Hayes

Detective Greg Semendinger
Detective Patrick Walsh
Detective Ken Winkler
James Ciccone
John D'Allara
Yvonne Kelhetter

Paddy McGee
Dave Norman
John Perry
Moira Smith
Scott Strauss

Port Authority Police Department
Inspector James Romito
Captain Anthony Whitaker
Sergeant Al DeVona
Sergeant John Mariano
   (via phone)
Sergeant John McLoughlin
Sergeant Robert Vargas
Christopher Amoroso
Greg Brady *(via phone)*
Thomas Grogan *(via phone)*
James Hall
Will Jimeno

Sue Keane
David Leclaire
David Lim
Patrick Lucas
Steve Maggett *(via phone)*
Ray Murray *(via phone)*
Richie Paugh
Dominick Pezzulo
Barry Pikaard
Stephen Prospero
Antonio Rodriguez

New York State Court Officers
Captain Joseph Baccellieri
Sergeant Al Moscola

Sergeant Andrew Wender

New York City Emergency Medical Services
Division Chief John Peruggia
Paramedic Joseph Cahill
Paramedic Manuel Delgado

Paramedic Carlos Lillo
EMT Richard Erdey
EMT Soraya O'Donnell

New York City Office of Emergency Management
Director Richard Sheirer

Rich Zarillo

United States Marine Corps
Staff Sergeant David Karnes

Others
Sister Cynthia Mahoney
Deborah Mardenfeld

Chuck Sereika

Authors' Note

For 102 minutes on the morning of September 11, 2001, 14,000 men and women fought for life at the World Trade Center. This book aims to tell what happened solely from the perspective of the people inside the twin towers—office workers, visitors, and the rescuers who rushed to help them. Their accounts are drawn from 200 interviews with survivors and witnesses, thousands of pages of transcribed radio transmissions, phone messages, e-mails, and oral histories. All sources are named and enumerated.

No single voice can describe scenes that unfolded at terrible velocities in so many places. Taken together, though, the words, witnesses, and records provide not only a broad and chilling view of the devastation, but also a singularly revealing window onto acts of grace at a brutal hour.

The immediate challenges these people faced were not geopolitical but intensely local: how, for instance, to open a jammed door, or navigate a flaming hallway, or climb dozens of flights of stairs. Civilians or rescuers, they had to take care of themselves and those around them. Their words inevitably trace a narrative of excruciating loss; they also describe how the simplest gestures and tools were put to transcendent use—everything from a squeegee in a stuck elevator to a squeeze on the shoulder, from a voice booming an order to get out to a crowbar smashing Sheetrock around a jammed door. As chapters in the history of human valor and frailty and struggle, these are matters of first importance. They brought us to this book.

That the crises in the two buildings had identical beginnings and endings—suicidal attacks by terrorists in airliners, followed by raging fire and total collapses—evokes the parallel shape and size of the buildings, suggesting one more way in which the towers were twins. Yet the events in each tower ran on different clocks and took different courses, each separately instructive. The north tower was hit first, at 8:46:31, sixteen minutes and twenty-eight seconds before the strike against the south tower at 9:02:59; this gap between crashes afforded some opportunity to begin an evacuation in the south building before the second plane flew into it. Conversely, the south tower, though hit second, was the first to fall, collapsing at 9:58:59, twenty-nine minutes and twenty-six seconds before the north tower, which fell at 10:28:25—in effect, giving notice that total calamity was not only possible but also imminent, and thus providing a chance for rescuers to pull out of the north building.

In heartbreaking measure, many people could not take hold of those fleeting opportunities. During those two intervals, and ultimately, across the entire 102 minutes, decades of struggle over safety in skyscrapers and over the sensible operation of New York's emergency services would come to shattering ends.

Nothing can diminish the culpability of the hijackers and their masters in the murders of September 11, 2001, which stand beyond mitigation as the defining historical truth of the day. The ferocity of the attacks meant that innocent people lived or died because they stepped back from a doorway, or hopped onto a closing elevator, or simply shifted their weight from one foot to another. That said, simply to declare that the hijackers alone killed all those people gives them far more credit as tacticians than they are due. The buildings themselves became weapons, apparently well beyond the designs of the hijackers, if not their hopes; so, too, did a sclerotic emergency response culture in New York that resisted reform, even when confronted again and again with the dangers of business as usual.

At least 1,500 people in the trade center—and possibly many more—survived the initial crashes but died because they were unable to escape from their floors or elevators while the buildings stood. Those people were not killed by the planes alone any more than passengers on the *Titanic* were killed by the iceberg. With 102 minutes in the north tower, and 57 minutes in the south, thousands of people had time to evacuate, and did. Those who did not escape were trapped by circumstances that had been the subject of debates that began before the first shovelful of earth was turned for the trade center, and that continued, at a low volume, through the entire existence of the towers. Could the buildings withstand the direct impact of an airplane? Was the fireproofing adequate? Were there enough exits?

The willingness of firefighters, police officers, and medical workers to serve others, never in question, was indelibly established on September 11. Stark and towering as their sacrifices are, they do not stand alone in history. We have now obtained many records documenting the emergency response that both the City of New York and the Port Authority of New York and New Jersey have tried to keep secret. These records show that for all the aggressiveness of the response, emergency workers suffered the same failures of communication, coordination, and command that they had experienced on February 26, 1993, when terrorists first tried to knock down the trade center. This time, those failures came at terrible cost. Indeed, for 102 minutes, success and failure, life and death, ran parallel courses—as did effort and selflessness, infighting and shortsightedness.

Finally, the fate of all the men and women inside the towers during those 102 minutes was specifically, and intimately, linked to decisions about the planning and construction of, and faith in, colossally tall buildings. Approximately 12,000 people—nearly everyone below the crash zones—got out, creating an encyclopedia of survival: the towers stood long enough, the office workers formed a mass of civility, the responders helped steer and steady them.

And then there is the brutal calculus of death. The Office of the Chief Medical Examiner of New York City reports that 2,753 people died in the attacks on New York. Of these, 147 were passengers or crew members on the two flights; in the buildings, no more than 600 people were on floors where the planes hit, close enough to be killed immediately. Another 412 of the dead were rescue workers who came to help. The rest, more than 1,500 men and women, survived the plane crashes, but were trapped as far as twenty floors from the impact. Like the passengers on the unsinkable *Titanic*, many of the individuals inside the World Trade Center simply did not have the means to escape towers that were promised not to sink, even if struck by airplanes. In the struggle to live, those who survived and those who did not sent out hundreds of messages. They gave us the history of those 102 minutes.

Jim Dwyer and Kevin Flynn

September 2004
New York City

102 Minutes

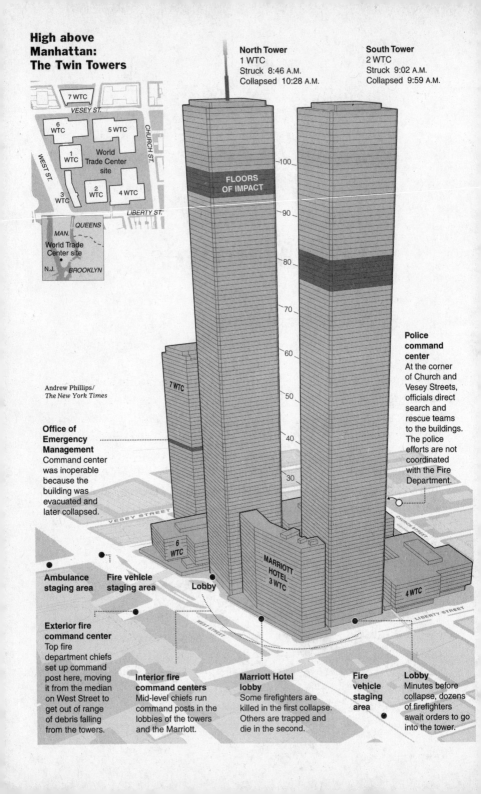

High above Manhattan: The Twin Towers

7 WTC
VESEY ST.
6 WTC
5 WTC
1 WTC
World Trade Center site
CHURCH ST.
WEST ST.
3 WTC
2 WTC
4 WTC
LIBERTY ST.

QUEENS
MAN.
World Trade Center site
N.J.
BROOKLYN

North Tower
1 WTC
Struck 8:46 A.M.
Collapsed 10:28 A.M.

South Tower
2 WTC
Struck 9:02 A.M.
Collapsed 9:59 A.M.

FLOORS OF IMPACT

—100—
—90—
—80—
—70—
—60—
—50—
—40—
—30—

Andrew Phillips/
The New York Times

7 WTC

Police command center
At the corner of Church and Vesey Streets, officials direct search and rescue teams to the buildings. The police efforts are not coordinated with the Fire Department.

Office of Emergency Management
Command center was inoperable because the building was evacuated and later collapsed.

VESEY STREET

6 WTC

MARRIOTT HOTEL 3 WTC

4 WTC

LIBERTY STREET

Ambulance staging area

Fire vehicle staging area

Lobby

WEST STREET

Exterior fire command center
Top fire department chiefs set up command post here, moving it from the median on West Street to get out of range of debris falling from the towers.

Interior fire command centers
Mid-level chiefs run command posts in the lobbies of the towers and the Marriott.

Marriott Hotel lobby
Some firefighters are killed in the first collapse. Others are trapped and die in the second.

Fire vehicle staging area

Lobby
Minutes before collapse, dozens of firefighters await orders to go into the tower.

Prologue

First into the office on the 89th floor of 1 World Trade Center, as always, Dianne DeFontes shut the door behind her, then locked it with a bolt that slid up and down, into floor and ceiling. The lawyers were unlikely to arrive at the office of Drinker Biddle & Reath for another thirty minutes. Until then, DeFontes, the fifty-one-year-old receptionist, would serve as the early voice of a humming, busy law firm engaged in global-trade litigation. Atop the world—or near enough, more than 1,000 feet above New York Harbor—she settled into a solitary bubble. She sipped coffee, spooned yogurt, answered the phone. *He's not at his desk right now; may I have him call you?* She swapped the easy-on-the-feet running shoes she wore to commute for the easy-on-the-eyes dress shoes stashed in a desk drawer.

The conference room behind her stood empty. The hallway walls were lined with bookshelves, a law library for this satellite office of a firm based in Philadelphia. The 89th floor in the north tower of the World Trade Center gave the lawyers an office where they could see, and be seen, for miles. It had taken DeFontes a long time to get used to life at the trade center, but now, after thirteen years, she at

1

last felt that she had her arms around it. She had a few friends on the floor—Tirsa Moya, her girlfriend at the insurance company down the hall, and Raffaele Cava, the older gentleman at the freight company who always wore a hat, no matter what the weather. DeFontes may have been the earliest arrival in her office, but Cava, at eighty years old, was always the first person on the 89th floor, at his desk by 6:30. To DeFontes, Tirsa and Raffaele were fixtures.

On the way to work, as her morning train rolled across Brooklyn, the towers grabbed hold of the sky ahead, staying in view until the train sank into the tunnel that crossed the harbor. From a distance, the sight surged through her with . . . well, she found it hard to define the feeling. Familiarity. Maybe a kind of pride, a tiny fraction of ownership, or simply the pleasant jolt of seeing the familiar with fresh eyes, like glancing down from an airplane and spotting a particular house or a park. Of course, the view from the train was pretty much the only way the world at large saw the twin towers: two silver streams running in a blue sky. To DeFontes, they were all that. But they were also the place where she worked and ate and spent half her waking hours. The winter before, the building operators had set up a rink in the plaza, and she had finally learned to ice-skate. During the summer, she lolled over lunch in that same plaza, catching free concerts. In fact, a concert was scheduled for the afternoon; when she arrived that morning, the chairs were in place. As iconic structures, the towers could be seen for miles and miles; their human pulse was palpable only from the inside out. For DeFontes, the geography of the World Trade Center began in a desk drawer in room 8961 of the north tower, where she stashed her dress shoes.

With her door locked, Dianne DeFontes felt safe, if alone, in this colossus.

At 8:30 on Tuesday, September 11, 2001, she was one of the 14,154 people who typically arrived between midnight and 8:47 A.M. in the 110-story towers known as 1 and 2 World Trade Center. Another 940 were registered in the Marriott Hotel nestled between them, at 3 World Trade Center. Yet DeFontes' sense of solitude, while an illusion, should hardly count as a delusion. This small city of people was spread across more than 220 vertical acres: each of the 110 floors per tower was its own acre of space, not to mention the hotel, and a basement that gave the trade center more space below the street than the majestic Empire State Building had above it.

Vast as the whole physical place seemed from afar, people inside naturally experienced it on a far more human scale. Each floor provided a little more room than a football field. The count of 14,154 people in the towers worked out to about 64 per floor—or 64 spread across a football field, including the end zones. On the 89th floor, where Dianne DeFontes sat, 25 people were also arriving for work; her solitude actually was just a spatial illusion, from the low density of the place. This spaciousness made it easy to feel that each floor was its own island, part of an archipelago in an ocean of sky. A person in the south tower, sitting 131 feet away from DeFontes, might as well have been in the Bronx. For that matter, someone on the floor below, a mere 12 feet under her, was not only invisible but also inaudible.

All around Dianne DeFontes' corner of the sky, people she could not see were, like herself, poised on the brink of the workday. On 88, Frank and Nicole De Martini sipped coffee and chatted with Frank's staff and colleagues. The couple had driven in from Brooklyn that morning after dropping their children at a new school, and traffic had been light. Nicole worked in the south tower, but with a few extra minutes, she decided to visit Frank's office in the north tower to say hello. Frank worked for the Port Authority of New York and New Jersey, which built and owned the trade center. The agency had just completed a deal to lease the entire complex to Larry Silverstein, a private real estate operator, and down the hall from Frank's office, his colleague Jim Connors, a member of the Port Authority's real estate department, awaited a messenger who was bringing a flatbed trolley stacked with the indentures and documents that described the transaction in excruciating detail. The change in control had, inevitably, led to anxiety among members of the Port Authority staff who served as de facto mayors of the complex, masters of its byways, keepers of its lore. For the most part, they were being transferred to new departments within the Port Authority. Alan Reiss, who had run the world trade department, including the trade center, was downstairs on this Tuesday morning, in a delicatessen at street level, part of his own shift to new work. He was transferring to the post of deputy director of the Port Authority's aviation department, so he was having a cup of coffee and an English muffin with the deputy directors from some of the agency's other departments.

The 90th floor, directly above Dianne DeFontes, was not quite vacant, but close; Anne Prosser was just arriving for her job at Clearstream, an international bank. She would be getting married in a month. On this floor, some artists had studios because the Port Authority gave them unused space. They kept irregular hours and none had arrived yet for the day. Most of the 91st floor also was empty, but Mike McQuaid, an electrician, was there, installing fire alarms in vacant space that would soon be used by Silverstein Properties, the new operators of the trade center. McQuaid stopped at the office of the American Bureau of Shipping, the only business currently on the floor, to chat with someone he knew.

Above him, on a quiet corner of the 92nd floor, a sculptor named Michael Richards was in his studio space, having worked through the night, as he often did. The rest of the floor was unusually busy, and tense. Carr Futures, a division of a French company, Crédit Agricole Indosuez, had summoned about forty of its brokers for a meeting on commission rates. The brokers, most of them men, led daily lives of wallet-to-wallet combat on the floors of exchanges that traded commodities; many of them had become wealthy through a combination of guile, charm, and pure nerve, without having stopped at the more prestigious universities or, for some, at any college at all. Tom McGinnis, who normally worked at the Mercantile Exchange trading natural gas for Carr, had told his wife that he expected the meeting to run from 8:00 until 8:30, when their boss, Jim Paul, had to join a conference call. The meeting would resume after the market closed at four o'clock. Instead, the schedule had slipped, which was not surprising, given the contentious topic of commissions for people who earned their living by thinking and acting quickly.

Carr Futures was hardly the only business in the trade center where many people came to work unsure of how much money they would go home with at day's end. And few companies in the trade center had more people, with more money at stake, than Cantor Fitzgerald, a bond-trading company famed for its aggressiveness. Yet the firm also encouraged its employees to recommend family members for jobs, so that it was not uncommon for a father to be working a few steps from a son, or for a brother to have an office just a flight of stairs away from a sister. The firm's founders had been art collectors, and Rodin sculptures were arrayed in well-lit displays around the office. Cantor occupied four floors near the top of the building—101, 103, 104, and 105—and they were far busier than most at this hour. Some 659 people were already at work.

One of them, the firm's managing director, David Kravette, stood by his desk, talking on the phone with his wife. She wanted to cancel their newspaper delivery. The paper was being thrown into the driveway, their kids were running out to the street to get it, so she wanted to put a stop to the problem.

Kravette listened impatiently. Clients were waiting for him in the lobby, nearly a quarter mile below his offices. They had just called from downstairs, more than a half hour late for an appointment. And despite Kravette's specific reminders, one had forgotten to bring a picture ID. So now they would have to be personally escorted through the lobby checkpoint. His assistant, heavily pregnant, was busy. He would fetch them himself. Just as he was departing for this irritating errand, his wife called to report on the newspaper-in-the-driveway crisis.

"Janice, I got people downstairs," Kravette said. "Let me talk to you later about this."

"Let's talk now," she responded. "I'm out all day."

And so it went, on the 101st floor and every other floor in the complex. Life simmered at 14,154 different temperatures, in the log-on ritual for e-mail, as men and women lined up the day's tasks, or as they unloaded some fraction of life at home that had been carried into the world of work. One woman called her husband to report that she had stopped at a drugstore to pick up a second home pregnancy test, still not quite able to accept the results of the one she had taken earlier that morning. A window washer, bucket dangling on his arm, waited at the 44th floor of the north tower, having just grabbed a bite of breakfast in the Port Authority cafeteria on 43. In the health club atop the Marriott Hotel, a Roman Catholic priest with clogged arteries had just climbed down from the stationary bicycle, and was weighing a decision to complete his workout with a few laps in the pool. In the north tower lobby, Judith Martin, a secretary with Marsh & McLennan, had just hopped on an express elevator after finishing a final cigarette outside before work. On the 27th floor of the north tower, Ed Beyea rolled his wheelchair to his desk in the office of Empire Blue Cross and Blue Shield, his aide having set him up with the head pointer that he used to operate his computer. At the top of it all, Christine Olender called home from Windows on the World, the restaurant on the 106th and 107th floors of the north tower, where she worked as the assistant general manager. She had lived in New York City for twenty years, but still checked in most mornings with her mom and dad back in Chicago. Christine and her mother were organizing a visit by her parents to the city, no doubt one that would include a stop at Windows. Still, she had a busy morning ahead of her—besides the regulars having breakfast in the dining area called Wild Blue, a conference was about to begin in the ballroom, sponsored by Risk Waters, a big financial publishing firm. Mother and daughter agreed to talk again later.

As Dianne DeFontes was settling in for the day, the passengers on American Airlines Flight 11 from Boston were seated for their flight to California. The crew chief would have recited the procedures for an emergency evacuation—lights on the floors, locations of the exits, life vests under every seat. Among those who would have been listening, perhaps with the glaze of repetition, was Linda George, a buyer for the apparel retailer TJX who was on her way to Los Angeles for a buying trip. She was to be married at the end of October to a man she had met while playing volleyball. Their first date had been to see the movie *Titanic*.

As it happened, the safety rituals of modern airline travel—the instructions on the location of doors, life vests, emergency masks—were all the residue of seagoing laws enacted after the *Titanic* brushed against an iceberg and foundered in the North Atlantic in 1912. Perhaps the most famous safety inquiries of the twentieth century had examined the catastrophe. The goal had been to learn how such a mighty and supposedly unsinkable ship had been lost. Why had 1,522 of the ship's 2,227 passengers perished, even though the vessel remained afloat for nearly three hours after the collision? In the end, the deaths turned out to be not much of a mystery. The casualties were a result of poor preparations, communication failures and confusion, and a woefully inadequate inventory of lifeboats. If the hearings on the *Titanic* did not answer precisely why the unsinkable ship had sunk, they provided a clear explanation of why so many died and an agenda for reforms.

Moments after the American Airlines crew demonstrated the evacuation protocols that evolved from those revelations, Flight 11 turned unexpectedly south, toward the World Trade Center. It was a journey that had started some twelve years earlier.

In the summer of 1989, a group of mujahideen warriors, fresh from the triumph of turning back the Soviet invasion of Afghanistan, migrated from Central Asia and the Middle East to the United States. A battlefield formed in slow motion. One group of the mujahideen took over a mosque in Brooklyn, installing Sheikh Omar Abdel Rahman, a blind fundamentalist cleric from Egypt, as spiritual leader. In November 1990, the group made its first strike in the United States, targeting Meir Kahane, a radical rabbi and Israeli politician who had made himself into a human megaphone of Jewish empowerment and anti-Arab views. Kahane was assassinated after giving a speech at a hotel in midtown Manhattan. A member of the gang was arrested fleeing the hotel, smoking gun in hand. Inside a locker at his job, and in boxes at his home, police found stashes of ammunition and tracts in Arabic calling for destruction of the "edifices of capitalism." They also found pictures of American landmarks, including the Statue of Liberty and the World Trade Center. The gunman was quickly written off as a lone nut. City and federal officials overlooked blunt evidence that he had associated with quite a few men of similar ideological bent. In fact, most of the written material in his possession would not get translated for a long time.

The gunman's accomplices in the Kahane assassination—followers of Sheikh Rahman—were not arrested until three years later, after they drove a yellow Ford Econoline van into the basement of one of those edifices of capitalism, the World Trade Center. At midday on Friday, February 26, 1993, a bomb in that van killed six people: Wilfredo Mercado, Bob Kirkpatrick, Steve Knapp, Bill Macko, John DiGiovanni, and Monica Rodriguez Smith. All had been in the basement, a few yards away, when the van exploded. The electricity mains failed. Then the backup generators were flooded. Dozens of cars caught fire, and the burning tires released waves of filthy smoke. For thousands of people in the towers, the loss of power meant a slow, labored evacuation down dark and smoky stairs, with no guidance from public-address systems. It took ten hours to get everyone out. Yasyuka Shibata had arrived that morning in February from Japan and was sitting down to lunch at Windows on the World when the explosion shook the china on his table. He walked down 106 flights in thick smoke. His face was covered with soot. He swiped at his face with a handkerchief as he spoke to a reporter. "I went from Windows on the World," he said, "to a window on hell."

The pursuit of the bombers, the farcical manner in which the plot unraveled—one of the conspirators went back to the truck rental agency and demanded a refund for his deposit on the van that he had just blown up—overshadowed deeper, more disturbing matters that emerged long after public attention in the crime had waned. The FBI, it developed, had had an informant inside the cell that carried out the bombing, but had fired him eight months before, in a dispute over his $500-a-week stipend. Afterward, the agency quietly hired him back—for $1.5 million—to penetrate other groups of Islamic radicals. The only person to be disciplined for the fiasco was the agent who had championed the informant.

In the eyes of the Fire Department's senior commanders, the 1993 attack brought chilling lessons in what could go wrong when multiple emergency agencies respond to a disaster. The fire chiefs, while proud of having helped thousands evacuate, believed that their efforts at a coordinated response with the Police Department had simply collapsed. The next eight years appeared to be a golden era of public safety in New York, with crime dropping and the number of fires shrinking. Yet the rifts between the two agencies only deepened. In 1996, the Fire Department took charge of emergency medical response, and promptly stripped paramedics and emergency medical technicians of the ability to listen to police communications. In 1997 and 1998, the city spent thousands of dollars for brand-new radios that would allow police and fire commanders to communicate with each other, but these state-of-the-art devices sat unused, on the shelves in police offices, and in the trunks of fire chiefs' cars. And just as the two departments had not worked together on February 26, 1993, they never returned to the trade center to drill together.

At the Port Authority, the 1993 attack had a revolutionary effect, at least compared with the reactions of other public agencies. The bombing shifted power in an argument that had gone on for the lifetime of the towers, a struggle that pitted safety against space. The stairs were crowded and dark; while it would have been very difficult to squeeze more stairways into the towers, the Port Authority marked the ones it did have with photoluminescent paint, and provided emergency lights with backup batteries. None of the tenants had known where to go, or whether to go, so a new sound system was installed, and a long-dormant fire warden program was awakened and revitalized. In the concourse shopping mall beneath the trade center, a half-dozen stores were torn out and replaced with corridors, so that the exits would comply with city codes. One of the deepest secrets of the two buildings was that their structural steel—webbed together in a novel, lightweight design—had never been fireproofed to the satisfaction of the trade center's engineers or architects. No one had ever tested the fireproofing of the steel in two of the tallest buildings in the world. In fact, it was crumbling off. Not long after the bombing, the Port Authority began to replace the fireproofing, and by the morning of September 11, had completed about 30 floors of the 220 in the towers.

And yet for those present on that blustery February day in 1993, the lasting image was of skyscrapers that appeared, from the outside, to be not only unmolested but Herculean in their indifference to an enormous bomb. The structural engineer explained that not even a Boeing 707, the largest airplane flying at the time they were built, could knock them over. The dead were buried, the basement rebuilt, a memorial erected, the buildings reopened. Over time, nearly all the 1993 bombers were caught and sent to prison. The Port Authority closed the garage to public parking. Ferocious-looking truck stoppers were set around the driveway entrances. No one would ever again be able simply to roll a truck bomb up to the base of the towers. Any person who entered the buildings had to clear a battalion of blue-blazered guards in the lobbies before boarding the elevators. The bottom twenty feet of the towers were as secure as any public space in the world. Every morning, Dianne DeFontes swiped her identification card at the turnstiles. The want of proper identification had held up the clients of David Kravette, stuck on the phone with his wife in the Cantor Fitzgerald office as they discussed the newspaper delivery problem.

By the morning of September 11, 2001, the 1993 bombing seemed to have been the work of another age. The towers had been hit with what the FBI described at the time as "the largest improvised explosive device" in the history of American crime. And yet the bones of the buildings stood with no visible scratches.

Nonetheless, the memories lingered in the soft tissue. Their potency ran in uneven currents across the archipelago of the trade center, where people came and went as businesses moved or

floundered. The memory of that Friday in 1993 slumbered just out
of sight, below the gloss and demands of work life, freeing the habi-
tants of the trade center to savor the glories of a morning like September 11, 2001. With the sky bright, the wind mild, a late summer
day in New York had begun to unfurl its soft promises.

As Liz Thompson arrived that Tuesday morning for breakfast atop
the tallest building in New York, she would mark the greeting that
Doris Eng gave to her as particularly sunny in tone, if ordinary in
language. Windows on the World relied not only on the charms of
its views, but also on the welcome of its staff.

"Good morning, Ms. Thompson," Eng had said.

Bright as the day, it seemed to Thompson. Glorious weather: a
rich September sky flooded through the windows.

Familiar faces filled many of the tables in Wild Blue, the inti-
mate adjunct aerie to Windows that Eng helped manage. As much
as any one place, that single room captured the sweep of humanity
that worked and played in the trade center.

Thompson, the president of the Lower Manhattan Cultural
Council, was having breakfast with Geoffrey Wharton, an executive
with Silverstein Properties. At the next table sat Michael Nestor, the
deputy inspector general of the Port Authority, and one of his investigators, Richard Tierney. They ate there nearly every morning.

At a third table were six stockbrokers, several of whom came
every Tuesday. For one of them, Emeric Harvey, Eng had a special
treat. The night before, another manager at the restaurant had
given her two impossible-to-get tickets to *The Producers* and asked
her to pass them along to Harvey.

Sitting by himself at a window table, overlooking the Statue of
Liberty, was a relative newcomer, Neil Levin, who had become the
executive director of the Port Authority in April. No one could
recall seeing him at Windows for breakfast before this morning.
His secretary had requested a table a few days earlier and now he
sat waiting for a companion, a banker friend.

Every other minute or so, a waiter, Jan Maciejewski, swept through the room, refilling coffee cups and taking orders. Maciejewski was one of the handful of restaurant staff workers on the 107th floor. Most of the seventy-nine employees were on 106, at the Risk Waters conference.

Already eighty-one people had arrived for the conference, including top executives from Merrill Lynch and UBS Warburg. They sipped coffee, chewed pastries, and speared slices of smoked salmon in the restaurant's ballroom, which overlooked the East River. In the Horizon Suite, just across the hall from the ballroom, two exhibitors from Bloomberg L.P., Peter Alderman and William Kelly, had set up a booth and chatted amiably with a former colleague, Christopher Hanley of Radianz. As they stood beside a multi-screened computer display, a photographer from Bloomberg snapped their picture. Across the way, Stuart Lee and Garth Feeney, vice presidents for Data Synapse, were hosts for a similar showcase of their company's software platform.

In the lobby, 105 floors below, an assistant to Neil Levin was waiting for the boss's breakfast guest. When the guest arrived, they boarded an elevator, bound for the restaurant. But it was the wrong car, so they had to go back down to the lobby to start over again.

Upstairs, Levin patiently read his newspaper, watched carefully by Nestor and Tierney. Who, they wondered, was their boss meeting for breakfast? When it came to gossip, the Port Authority had the insatiability of most bureaucracies, but Nestor and Tierney couldn't stick around to satisfy their curiosity, because Nestor had a meeting downstairs. Instead, they stopped briefly at Levin's table to say good-bye. Then they walked to the restaurant's lobby and caught a waiting elevator.

A few strides behind them, Liz Thompson and Geoffrey Wharton hurried to get on board. Nestor held the car open for them. Quickly, they stepped in. Then the doors closed and the last people ever to leave Windows on the World began their descent. It was 8:44 A.M.

1

*"It's a bomb,
let's get out of here."*

A bomb, Dianne DeFontes thought, when thinking became possible again. At 8:46:30, an impact had knocked her off a chair in the law office on the 89th floor of the north tower, 1 World Trade Center. The door swung free, even though she had bolted it shut. In another part of the floor, Walter Pilipiak had just pushed open the door to the offices of Cosmos International, an insurance brokerage where he was president. Akane Ito heard him coming and looked up from her desk to greet him. Before Pilipiak could get the words "Good morning" out of his mouth, he felt something smack the back of his head, and he was hurled into a wall. Ceiling tiles collapsed on Ito. A bomb, they decided, several breaths later.

On the southwest end of the 89th floor, the insurance company MetLife had 10,000 square feet of space. After the initial slam, Rob Sibarium could feel every one of those square feet tilting as the tower bent south, so far that it seemed as if it would never recoil. It did, slowly returning to center. Something had happened in the other building, Sibarium thought. An explosion.

Mike McQuaid, the electrician installing fire alarms, was sure he knew what he was feeling: an exploding transformer, from a

13

machine room somewhere below the 91st floor. Nothing else could rock the place with such power.

In the lobby, Dave Kravette had just ridden down from the Cantor Fitzgerald office to meet his guests, after ending the conversation with his wife about the newspaper delivery. Just a few steps out of the elevator, he heard a tremendous crash and what sounded like elevator cars free-falling. Then he saw a fireball blow out of a shaft. Around him, people dived to the ground. Kravette froze and watched the fireball fold back on itself.

She dropped the phone, Louis Massari would remember thinking. His wife, Patricia, had been reporting to him that she had bought a second home pregnancy test. The first one, that morning, had been positive, a surprise. Patricia worked as a capital analyst on the 98th floor of the north tower for Marsh & McLennan, an insurance and financial services concern; at night she took college courses. The pregnancy test was on her mind; it trumped, naturally, the test she was due to take that evening in her class and had been fretting over. So they had plenty to talk about.

"Oh, my God—" she said, and then Louis heard nothing. She had slipped, somehow, he was sure, and had pulled the cord out of the jack.

Higher still in the building, on the 106th floor, Howard Kane, the controller for Windows on the World, was speaking by phone with his wife, Lori. Kane dropped the receiver, or so it seemed to his wife, because the sounds of clamor and alarm, the high notes of anxiety if not the exact words, filled her ear. Maybe he was having a heart attack. Then she could hear a woman screaming, "Oh, my God, we're trapped," and her husband calling out, "Lori!"

Then another man picked up the phone, and spoke. "There's a fire," he said. "We have to call 911."

From the Risk Waters conference in Windows on the World, Caleb Arron Dack, a computer consultant, called his wife, Abigail Carter, on a cell phone. "We're at Windows on the World," Dack said. "There was a bomb." He could not get through to the police emergency line. He needed Abigail to call 911 for him. The bomb may have been in the bathroom.

At another breakfast, in a delicatessen a quarter mile below Windows on the World, the former director of the world trade department, Alan Reiss, had not heard, felt, or seen a thing. He sat with his back to the window that overlooked the plaza. Suddenly, one of the other Port Authority managers, Vickie Cross Kelly, looking past Reiss's shoulder to the window, called out.

"Something must have happened," she said. "People are running around on the mall." Reiss turned. He saw terrified people, sprinting in every direction. A person with a gun had set off the chaos, he guessed.

"I've got to go," Reiss said, tossing a five-dollar bill on the table, then headed for the trade center police office, one floor above them, in the low-rise building known as 5 World Trade Center. Through big plate-glass windows that faced east toward Church Street, he could see a blizzard of burning confetti. This was not as straightforward as someone with a gun. Another bomb?

In 1993, Reiss had just opened the door to his basement office when the terrorists' truck bomb exploded 150 feet away. Afterward, he had been part of the team that refitted the towers for better evacuation. As a matter of doctrine at the trade center, bombs were seen as a threat that could cause harrowing but local damage. They were unlikely to bring cataclysm.

In the weeks and months following the 1993 attack, the danger from a powerful bomb attack on the trade center, especially the two towers, had been considered by the Port Authority and its security consultants. Most experts agreed that while the towers could be hurt by a bomb, they could not be destroyed. Anyone might, in theory, sneak a bomb onto a floor, but the damage would largely be confined to 1 floor out of 110—or looked at another way, 1 acre out of 110. In general, bombs are as powerful as they are big. The larger the bomb, the bigger the explosion, the greater the damage. The 1993 terrorists had driven 1,200 pounds of explosive into the basement. Even so, the base of the towers, the strongest part of the buildings, easily deflected the explosion. Compared with the powerful load absorbed by the face of the towers from winds that blew every hour of every day, the truck bomb in the basement was puny.

Moreover, there was no simple way of getting 1,200 pounds of explosive to the upper floors, where the structure was not as dense as the base. If the monumentalism of the towers made them a natural target, their very height added protection, not vulnerability. Gravity was part of the built-in defense to the devastation of a big bomb.

From what Reiss could see, he was sure that someone had set off a big bomb. While it is true that small bombs—explosives fitted into a tape recorder or hidden inside a suitcase—can blow an airplane out of the sky, that destructiveness has less to do with the bomb than with the altitude. What rips apart the aircraft is not the size of the bomb but a rupture in the fuselage at 35,000 feet, with the lethal force coming from the difference between the cabin pressure and the atmosphere. Those forces are not present even at the top of skyscrapers as tall as the twin towers, limiting the destructive energy of a conventional bomb to its size.

By the time Reiss had run up one flight on the escalator, he guessed that a truck bomb must have blown up somewhere around the trade center.

Reiss no longer worked in the basement, as he had in 1993, and he wondered, fleetingly, who in his old department had arrived for work on the 88th floor of the north tower. Up there, no one had illusions about a truck bomb. The moment arrived as a powerful fist rocking the building. As soon as Gerry Gaeta, a member of the team that oversaw construction projects at the trade center, could find his words, he hollered, "It's a bomb, let's get out of here." And he was sure he knew how it had gotten up there. Moments earlier, a messenger had arrived with a trolley of documents for Jim Connors in the real estate department. Surely that was how the bomb had been wheeled in, Gaeta thought; the boxes of "documents" had been a Trojan horse.

Down the hall, Nicole De Martini had just drawn the last sip of her coffee and had risen to leave her husband's office to go to hers, in the south tower, when she and Frank heard a boom from overhead and felt the building lurch. Nicole watched a river of fire spill past the window in Frank's office. It was a bomb, they both thought.

Or maybe the machine room had exploded, burning diesel fuel. Nothing else could explain the force they felt, one that seemed directly above them.

The elevators had rocked, swinging like pendulums. Pasquale Buzzelli, a Port Authority engineer going to his office on 64, felt the car right itself, then slowly descend to the 44th floor, where he had started from. Smoke began to pump through the shaft. No one seemed to understand what was happening, so he got back on the elevator, which now was working just fine, and rode up to the 64th floor. There he met his boss, Patrick Hoey, the engineer in charge of the Port Authority's bridges and tunnels, who was just as puzzled.

"What happened, Pat?" Buzzelli asked.

"I don't know, but it near knocked me out of my chair," Hoey replied.

The tower had miles of elevator shafts. In one that served the middle of the building, six men were in a car bound for the upper floors. They felt the jolt, then a swoop. A window washer named Jan Demczur punched the emergency stop button. In a moment, fingers of smoke crept into the car, rising past the cuffs of the men in the car, pushing down from the roof. They rang the intercom. No one answered. On board another elevator, which had just left the north tower lobby, was Judith Martin, the secretary who had lingered outside for a cigarette. She and six other people were now stuck, pressing the alarm and calling for help.

In the Marriott Hotel, tucked between the two towers, the Rev. Paul Engel, naked except for a cross dangling on a chain around his neck, had just gone to the lockers after working out when he heard an impossibly loud screech of metal on metal, like the squeal of train brakes. A Catholic priest, Engel went every morning to the health club atop the hotel. Normally, he finished his exercise with some laps in the pool, but had skipped that part of his routine today. Now he quickly pulled on the nearest garment, his swimming trunks, and peeked at the pool. It was on fire.

From a window on the 61st floor in the north tower, Ezra Aviles had seen everything. He knew it was no bomb. His window faced north, and he saw the plane tearing through the skies, heading straight for the tower. It had crashed into the building over his head—how far, he was not sure. In fact, its lower wing cut the ceiling of the 93rd floor, and its right wing had ripped across the 98th floor, at the very moment that Patricia Massari was speaking to her husband about her home pregnancy test.

Aviles worked for the Port Authority. He dialed five numbers, leaving identical messages, describing what he saw, and telling everyone up the chain of command to begin the evacuation. He called one colleague, John Paczkowski, but reached his voice mail. "It seems to be an American Airlines jetliner came in from the northern direction, toward—from the Empire State Building, toward us," Aviles said. He ticked through a list of notifications—he had called the police and the public affairs office, and had beeped the chief operating officer for the agency. "Smoke is beginning to come, so I think I'm gonna start bailing outta here, man. . . . Don't come near the building if you're outside. Pieces are coming down, man. Bye."

Then he phoned his wife, Mildred, who was at home with two of their three children. "Millie, a plane hit the building," he said. "It's going to be on the news."

By then, the havoc was escalating, even if the cause was not apparent. In the police bureau at the base, Alan Reiss heard talk of a missile having been fired from the roof of the Woolworth Building, just a couple of blocks east of the trade center.

As Reiss was listening to this, a Port Authority detective, Richie Paugh, arrived.

"We're going out onto the plaza to let you know what's going on," Reiss told the desk. He and Paugh walked down the hallway from the plaza, past an airline ticket counter. A revolving door put them under a soffit, an overhang sheltering the entrance to 5 World Trade Center. They peered out. Debris had rained onto the plaza—steel and concrete and fragments of offices and glass. Above them, they could see the east side of the north tower, and also its northern face. Instead of the waffle gridding of the building's face, they now saw a wall of fire spread across ten or fifteen floors. Then they saw the people coming out the windows, driven toward air, and into air. The plane had struck not two minutes earlier.

North Tower: The Impact

By tipping its wings just before impact, Flight 11 cut a swath through seven floors, severely damaging all three escape staircases. The three staircases were clustered in the central core of the building as the building code permitted.

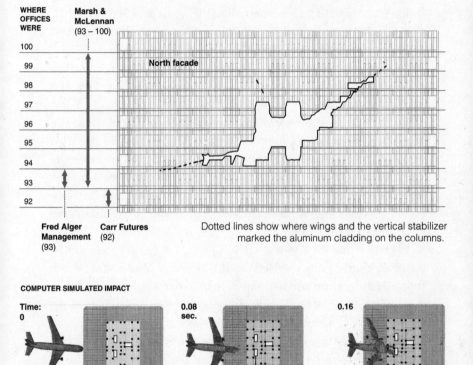

WHERE OFFICES WERE

Marsh & McLennan (93 – 100)

North facade

100
99
98
97
96
95
94
93
92

Fred Alger Management (93)

Carr Futures (92)

Dotted lines show where wings and the vertical stabilizer marked the aluminum cladding on the columns.

COMPUTER SIMULATED IMPACT

Time: 0

North facade

0.08 sec.

Stairwells

0.16

Core columns

0.24

0.32

Severed or significantly damaged columns

Damaged columns

0.40

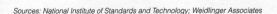

Sources: National Institute of Standards and Technology; Weidlinger Associates

The New York Times

On the ground, they saw an odd shape. Reiss looked closer. It was the nose gear of an airplane, missing the rubber tire, but with its wheel still connected to the hydraulic elbow that retracts into the bottom of the plane. Paugh began to take notes on its shape and location. Reiss protested. "There's crap falling on us," he said. "I don't have a hard hat on or anything, let's just drag it in."

He and Paugh lugged the part into the police office. "It's evidence, put a sticker on it," Reiss said.

"A plane hit the building," Paugh said.

"It's a big plane," Reiss added. "It's not a Piper Cub. This is a bi-i-i-g fucking wheel."

For hundreds of people on the upper floors of the north tower, death had come in a thunderous instant. The remains of one man who worked for Marsh & McLennan, which occupied space on the 93rd to 100th floors, would later be found five blocks from the tower. American Airlines Flight 11 had flown directly into the company's offices. The impact killed scores of people who could never have known what hit them.

Flight 11 had hit 1 World Trade Center, the north tower, at 450 miles an hour, having traveled the full length of Manhattan Island, fourteen miles from north to south, in less than two minutes. When it slammed into the north side of the building, the plane's forward motion came to a halt. The plane itself was fractionalized. Hunks of it erupted from the south side of the tower, opposite to where it had entered. A part of the landing gear landed five blocks south. The jet fuel ignited and roared across the sky, as if the fuel continued to fly on course, even without its jet. Much of the energy deflected from the speeding plane shot in waves down the skeleton of the north tower. The waves pulsed into the bedrock, rolled out to the Atlantic Ocean, and along the bed of the Hudson River. The impact registered on instruments in Columbia University's Lamont-Doherty Earth Observatory in Palisades, New York, twenty-two miles to the north, generating signals for twelve seconds. The earth shook.

2

"It's going to be the top story of the day."

In the south tower, the one that had not been hit, the explosion brought Michael Sheehan to his feet. New Yorkers love the fable of their own imperturbability, to boast of how unflappable they remain whether confronted with a rooster that has gotten loose in the subway or a prime minister crossing Lexington Avenue. Yet no one could be blasé about explosions at the trade center. Not only height, mass, and population distinguished that patch of land and sky. The 1993 bombing marked it as an icon and target. Even if the memory of that attack had lost some of its vigor, it still slept fitfully in every pore of the place. Terrorists had already tried to kill these buildings and all in them. With the first bloom of fire on September 11, 2001, that history welled from memory into the moment. The force of Flight 11's impact not only registered on seismographs miles away, it also jolted the people moored to the trade center workday.

Sheehan normally sat with his back to a window that faced west, overlooking the Hudson River. Now he was peering out the window, unable to see much. The glass was just twenty-two inches across, no more than the width of a magazine spread open, plus six inches. To see south or north was impossible. The towers had been designed by an architect who feared heights, and his antidote to acrophobia in the world's tallest building had been skinny windows. That way, anyone unnerved by the unnatural height could look out while gripping both sides of the window.

Halfway up one of the highest human-made structures on earth, the stunted view permitted Sheehan to see west, but in no other direction. He glanced toward the street, saw nothing that could explain the blast, then pulled his head back and spotted confetti blowing overhead, in a blizzard. The same drafts carried billows of smoke. That was enough for Sheehan. He spun around.

He faced a room full of people who might have been dressed for work in construction, or an outing to the gym, or a day of golf. Brokers for Garban ICAP, they worked elbow to elbow along a line of desks fitted with telephones and computer screens, part of a company that handled $200 billion a day in transactions among commercial banks and institutions that dealt in bonds. Sheehan, forty years old, wore running shoes—his father was the late Dr. George Sheehan, the cardiologist and running guru of the 1970s—and he put them to immediate use. He raced for the exit.

Another broker, George Nemeth, stood between him and the door. Sheehan did not notice him. He ran Nemeth down and kept going. Less than a minute after the explosion, Sheehan was heading down the stairway. He sized up the crowd—maybe twenty or thirty people from his office of about two hundred. What were the rest of them waiting for? he wondered. That George Nemeth was still picking himself off the floor, Sheehan had no idea. That Sheehan himself had accidentally knocked Nemeth clear off his feet, he did not have the faintest notion. And he knew nothing about an airplane.

For a long moment, Sarah Dechalus thought the fire was trying to leap the 131 feet from the north tower to the south tower. Holding a fax that she had just picked off the machine, she watched from a window on the 98th floor of the south tower as orbs of fire blew from the north tower. In minutes, the television cameras of the world would be pointing at the same scene. Now Dechalus stood at the precise altitude where Flight 11 had struck the other tower. On the same floor, Marissa Panigrosso had been at her desk listening to Donna Summer music on headphones, so she felt the explosion as much as heard it. A hot blast slapped her in the face, as if the door of an oven had suddenly been thrown open. So intense was the heat that papers on desks were singed. Whatever had happened in the north tower, waves of anxiety were now moving through the south tower.

In their offices—Dechalus and Panigrosso worked for Aon, an insurance company—the steady, regular momentum of a workday suddenly slumped. In its place came the clatter of alarm. Panigrosso rose. All around her, people stood. Some screamed. Dechalus ran for the elevator. Panigrosso was stuck in place. She sat one desk from the window, but feared going any closer. Others edged forward, because they had to know.

"Get away from the windows," a New York–accented voice commanded. "Everybody get away. Stay calm. Go to the stairs."

It was Eric Eisenberg, one of the bosses at Aon. A new element was shaping the day: not ritual, not shock, but instructions. Panigrosso snapped out of her fog. "Let's get moving," Eisenberg hollered. She followed him and another supervisor, Gary Herold, toward the stairway.

Dechalus, waiting at the elevators, did not hear these directions. She carried an ID card, but not her Palm Pilot, or money, or even her handbag. Maybe she should get them. Suddenly, Eisenberg turned up in the elevator lobby. "Start going down the stairs," he ordered. Dechalus turned for the stairway, along with others who had been waiting for the elevator. She ran into Panigrosso. Eisenberg, meanwhile, continued his rounds.

At that hour, thirty-two Aon employees had arrived at work on the 98th floor. On the other side of the building, Sean Rooney also had gotten a glimpse at the devastation. He called his wife, Beverly Eckert, at her job in Connecticut, but she had not yet arrived. He left a voice-mail message for her shortly before nine.

"Hey, Beverly, this is Sean, in case you get this message. There has been an explosion in World Trade One—that's the other building. It looks like a plane struck it. It's on fire at about the 90th floor.

"And it's, it's—it's horrible. Bye."

Deep inside the 84th floor of the south tower, surrounded by the hushing of air-conditioners that cooled the computer equipment, Richard Fern neither heard nor saw anything. His alert came when the lights flickered—a power waver—which he knew could cause problems with the systems he ran for Euro Brokers, a trading operation. He rose to investigate. On the trading floor, where many of the brokers began their day at seven in the morning, they now watched at the windows, appalled and frightened, discussing how a bomb must have gone off in the other tower. The place was crammed with computer screens, keyboards, digital displays. Tiny fans were clipped onto many of the computer screens to provide some relief from the heat of all that hardware.

At her desk in the "repo trading pit"—an area specializing in repurchase agreements involving currency trades—Patty Troxell heard the thump. She stayed at her desk, but the areas around the windows quickly became crowded. The faces that turned away were billboards of distress. Seated next to Troxell, her friend Karen Yagos spoke. "Grab your bag," Yagos said. "We're going." Next to them, Ann McHugh also rose to leave. She had recently joined Euro Brokers from Cantor Fitzgerald, which operated in the other tower—and where she had been working in 1993. As the women headed toward the stairways, McHugh tried to calm Troxell. And Troxell's boss, Ed Mardovich, well regarded for his cool temperament, did not even leave their cluster of desks. He told Edward Keslo, who had just begun work at Euro Brokers the day before, that the disruption probably involved the automatic window-washing gadget that ran on tracks along the outside of the building. Keslo decided to leave anyway, prodded by the alarm in the deportment of Jose Marrero, a jack-of-all-trades who worked for Euro Brokers' facilities department. Marrero, who served as one of the fire wardens for the floor, was anxious, but could not persuade many people to leave. Mardovich and nine others on the repurchase desk—half of the twenty people working there that morning—stayed. Nearly fifty of Euro Brokers' traders also remained.

All of them were seated or standing in the southeast corner of the tower, trying to look out the windows. Rich Fern had emerged from the computer room and got his first view of papers and flames drifting across the sky. He went to another office, and took in an even more distressing view of flames shooting from gashes in the other tower. More fire wardens appeared and started to usher people toward the stairs. These wardens, like Jose Marrero, were Euro Brokers employees who had volunteered to clear the floor during fires or provide guidance in a crisis in which evacuation might be required. The program had been given fresh emphasis at the trade center after the 1993 bombing, although wardens had been required for most skyscrapers long before then. In effect, they were a human measure meant to make up for what the Fire Department saw as the safety deficiencies in tall buildings like the trade center that had been erected under the 1968 building code. That code, championed by the real estate industry, had made it cheaper to build tall buildings and more profitable to own them. It had been enacted over numerous objections from the Fire Department, which complained that fire safety was being compromised. After fires in two new skyscrapers had killed five people in 1970, the city required owners of private skyscrapers to operate a fire warden program as part of Local Law 5, a package of safety measures enacted at the request of the fire commissioner, John T. O'Hagan.

As for the trade center, executives of the Port Authority of New York and New Jersey often boasted that the agency had voluntarily used the 1968 code in the construction of the towers, even though it was not required to do so because it was not bound by the laws of either of the two states that had created the agency. But when it came to complying with Local Law 5, the Port Authority was sporadic; the real estate industry had challenged the legality of the new requirements, and not until the New York courts finally dismissed the case did the Port Authority move to install sprinklers, which were generally regarded by fire-safety experts as the most critical of the new requirements, not to mention the costliest. Many of the other features of the law received nominal attention, if any. There was little the Fire Department could do about it. Private landlords caught slacking on Local Law 5 were forced to publish mea culpas in big display advertisements that explained the provisions of the law and their importance. The Port Authority, however, existed beyond the requirements of Local Law 5, and the all-but-invisible warden program was an example of the fitful role fire-safety issues had played in the daily life of the towers before the 1993 bombing. Now, Marrero and the other wardens were taking a powerful role in clearing out people who hesitated. Even so, they were having a hard time with some of their colleagues—particularly the ones who conducted financial trades.

As the evacuation from Euro Brokers began, a television was tuned to CNN, which reported that a plane had crashed into the trade center. The report made it clear that the problem was confined to the north tower. Given that they were in the south tower, many on Euro Brokers' trading floor were not prepared to bail out just then.

Under the Port Authority's safety program, tenants could turn to the fire command desks in the lobbies for guidance in a crisis. These desks were staffed by fire-safety directors, positions that required training and certification, another requirement of Local Law 5. A single button permitted them to deliver public-address-system announcements; other equipment on the consoles enabled them to adjust ventilation systems and monitor elevators. A private contractor, OCS Security, provided the staff who manned them. The Port Authority had cut their numbers in 1997, eliminating positions in the "sky lobbies"—the 44th and 78th floors—that were not required by code after the installation of a new automated fire alarm system. In the south tower, the deputy fire-safety director on duty at the moment the crisis began was Phil Hayes, a retired firefighter who had worked for many years in Brooklyn. In the earliest moments after the impact on the north tower, Hayes did not have any information or guidance for the tenants of the south tower; from his position in the lobby, he had no view of the blaze high above him, nor did he have the benefit of hearing from a fire safety director on the 44th and 78th floors who would have been able to see from those sky lobby windows, or would have heard from tenants on the high floors that the papers on their desks were singed by the heat of the fireball. Instead, he contacted his counterpart at the lobby desk in the north tower.

> *Phil Hayes:* Yeah, this is the, uh, fire command over at B tower.
> *Male A:* Yeah, we got, uh, a major explosion over at the trade center here. It might be an aircraft.
> *Phil Hayes:* Okay, yeah, we just wanted to get some direction on evacuation. But I'm not going to do anything until we hear the boss from the Fire Department or somebody.
> *Male A:* Okay.
> *Phil Hayes:* Okay?
> *Male A:* Okay.
> *Phil Hayes:* Because we don't know what it is yet.
> *Male A:* Okay.
> *Phil Hayes:* Okay.

With no clear understanding of what was happening, Hayes was being cautious about giving instructions to the people in the building. And upstairs, the tenants were proceeding by habit or instinct.

The messages had been delivered three or four times a year, and they could not have been more emphatic: In an emergency, do not go back to your desk to pick up anything. Just get up and go down the stairs. For eight years, Michael Otten had stood in the corridors of the 80th floor during those quarterly drills. They usually turned into schmooze sessions with friends from his company, Mizuho Capital Markets, and its corporate affiliate, Fuji Bank. Under one name or another, the bank had space on every floor between 78 and 83. Not a few people, Otten included, would inch back toward work, if there was more pressing business and if the drills dragged on. Still, he had managed to absorb the instructions about getting out, fast. Despite all that training, and even with his boss, Yuji Goya, hollering that it was time to leave, Otten had turned back for the soft leather bag his wife had given him for Christmas, with the minidisk player and his cell phone and medical information for managing his son's diabetes.

"Just forget it," Goya shouted. "Go!"

For Stephen Miller, it was the shoes. Miller, a computer systems administrator for Mizuho, had to go back for the new brown pair under his desk. He normally sat in front of two computer monitors, decorated with a picture of Britney Spears and a newspaper headline proclaiming, DIE YOU VILE SCUM. When the strange, high-pitched noise interrupted his morning reverie—he had been reading a story online about a woman who had climbed Mount Everest—he got out of his chair and walked over to the window. The sky was swirling with paper and soot. Then someone burst onto the bank's trading floor and hollered, "It is a bomb! Get out!" His boss, Keiji Takahashi, came through, repeating the order to leave. Miller had to go back to his desk, where he had taken off the shoes he was still breaking in. He was newly married, and his wife liked the shoes, and although they hurt, he expected that he would get used to them, sooner or later. He slipped them on and headed for the door.

Many of the people working for the bank had been in the building in 1993, so the memory of calamity ran just beneath the surface. The lesson had not been pleasant, but it could not be forgotten: They were very high in a building where the path to safety was narrow and most likely would be crowded. That experience had helped turn emergency preparations into a near-religion among the bank's staff. Clipped to the back of every chair was a plastic bag filled with tools to help in an evacuation—a glow stick, a breathing hood, and a flashlight. The employees learned where the real staircases were, so they would not mistake the interior stairs that just carried people between the bank's floors.

Perhaps more important than the drills, or the mechanics of stairwells, or the emergency kits, was the corporate culture of the bank, which also operated in Tokyo, Hong Kong, and London. In 1996, not long after Michael Otten had arrived at the trade center, the Provisional Irish Republican Army set off a colossal bomb at the Canary Wharf development in the City of London. After that, one of the bank's leaders sent out a memo to make its policy clear. The bank's assets, the memo said, were its people—more valuable than any reports that were being written, more important than tickets for trades that were outstanding, more vital than any project that would be disrupted. In an emergency, they were to drop their work and go.

Now, less than a minute after some vague but plainly serious problem had struck the north tower, bank managers were ordering people out of its south tower offices. Miller obeyed, as did nearly all his colleagues. Just when he stepped into the stairway, he realized he had forgotten the evacuation pack. So had Otten. In fact, it seemed hardly anyone from the bank remembered to bring along the kit.

One floor up from Miller and Otten, Stanley Praimnath, an assistant vice president for the bank, had walked out with a woman working as a temporary assistant. They immediately caught a local elevator that took them to the 78th floor. There, they boarded an express for the lobby.

When the trade center had opened in 1973, and for years after, few private concerns took up space there. The tenant rolls were dominated by public agencies, like the Port Authority—the building's owner—and the downstate office for the governor of New York, and those of other state agencies that had little say in the matter. Not only were the towers two of the tallest buildings in the world, but they also amounted to the largest collection of government offices ever built. In time, though, the market for office space in lower Manhattan evolved. Beginning in 1980 with the deregulation of the banking industry, a new breed of financial services company emerged, often leaner and faster than the traditional Wall Street investment banking firms. The revised laws and more flexible regulatory postures freed small regional banks, once fairly staid businesses, to deal in a much broader range of investments, and to operate across state lines. One collateral effect was an increase in the need for floor space in lower Manhattan, near Wall Street.

Another effect was that dowdy smaller banks suddenly became glamorous candidates for acquisition. That created an opening spotted by, among others, Herman Sandler, a senior executive with Bear, Stearns. He saw that the task of bringing the stock shares of small banks to the market, and of analyzing that market, did not get the full attention of the large investment banking concerns that served as midwives to expanding businesses. In 1988, Sandler left Bear, Stearns in a dispute over compensation. Joined by a group of five friends and colleagues, he started Sandler O'Neill & Partners to cater to medium- and smaller-sized banks. Some of the partners had known each other since childhood. They began operations in ramshackle space on lower Broadway, and joked that to run the copying machine, they had to unplug the coffeepot. As the business grew, the prospect of more space and cheap rents at the World Trade Center led them to the 104th floor of the south tower. They arrived on a Monday, February 22, 1993. On Friday, the bomb exploded in the basement. In company lore, the people who left endured an agonizingly slow walk down 104 flights, in the dark, with choking smoke belching from the car tires ignited in the garage. Another group went to the roof and shivered in the February cold, with the wind off the harbor even more biting at that altitude. Most of those on the roof eventually turned back and headed downstairs. Those who had the easiest time of all waited in their offices until rescuers reached them hours later, after the smoke had cleared.

On the morning of September 11, eighty-three people had arrived for work in Sandler O'Neill's office when the north tower was struck. Jennifer Gorsuch came out of the women's bathroom in time to see Sandler—the balding, six-foot-two-inch founder—step from his office exclaiming "Holy shit!" Another Sandler employee told Gorsuch about the stairway she had used in 1993, and the two women set off. The company had no special plan for an emergency, other than trying to use common sense. So the employees turned to Sandler—a man prized for his counsel, who had made a fortune by listening and then offering advice that seemed to make solid-gold sense. He told an investment banker that he thought the safest place to be was right in the office. But one of his partners, Jace Day, heard Sandler say that anyone who wanted to leave should go, and Day decided to do just that. Of the eighty-three people in the office, seventeen left immediately. The bond traders and most of the people working on the equity desk remained.

They began to call home, to alert their families that they were okay. For people outside the trade center, it was hard to keep track of which tower was 1—the north building—and which was 2, the south tower. To these outsiders, any commotion in the complex automatically became a pandemic, afflicting everyone, since the whole place could seem like a blur of aluminum and glass. The Sandler people wanted to make it clear to their families that the problem was in the other building.

Nearly 200 feet below, in a company very much like Sandler O'Neill, similar conversations were unfolding on the 88th- and 89th-floor office of Keefe, Bruyette & Woods, another small firm founded by partners who had seen an opportunity serving the finance needs of the banking industry. KBW hired circles of friends and family, giving them demanding jobs. They worked and played hard. The custom at many Wall Street firms was to bring in lunch for the traders, so that they would be able to eat without missing a sale. At KBW, lunch was served for the entire company, not just the traders, every day. On Junk Food Fridays, the meals were entirely built around Whoppers and Big Macs and Kentucky Fried Chicken, huge orders sent up from fast-food joints in the neighborhood. A fair number of the people at work had played college football, basketball, baseball, and not surprisingly, remained competitive weekend athletes. One of these was Rick Thorpe, a star quarterback who had led his high school team to an undefeated season. He called home from KBW immediately after the plane hit.

"I'm sick to my stomach," he told his wife, Linda Perry Thorpe. The board of KBW had been having merger discussions with Banque Nationale de Paris/Paribas, and Linda thought the deal had fallen through.

"What happened with the deal?" she asked.

"No, no," Thorpe said. "I just wanted you to know that a plane hit the other tower. I'm okay—but here we go again."

A veteran of the 1993 bombing, Thorpe was looking at a long, disruptive haul. "I want you to turn on the TV, because it's going to be the top story of the day," he said. They hung up.

"You wouldn't believe what I'm watching," Brad Vadas said from a desk nearby. "I just saw a guy rip his shirt off because it was on fire and jump."

Vadas had just called his fiancée, Kris McFerren, to report that he was okay, and to tell her what he was seeing. He and McFerren had been dating for nine years, and after going to a friend's wedding on Labor Day weekend, they had finally decided it was their turn. They would marry in May. McFerren was a physical therapist; Vadas had graduated from Boston College, a fine athlete, a competitive baseball player, and by age thirty-nine had gotten himself a waterfront home in Westport, Connecticut, and an apartment in Manhattan. Like his colleague Rick Thorpe, he too had been working at the trade center in 1993. The events of this morning were fresh horrors.

"Don't watch," McFerren pleaded.

"Listen, I really got to go. Could you call my mom?" Vadas asked.

McFerren would. Even though Vadas's title was senior vice president, he worked on a trading desk—a position that afforded little privacy, a world of the heavily armored humor of men, hardly the venue for expressions of tenderness. This morning, though, he had more to say to McFerren.

"Let me tell you something," Vadas said. "I just want you to know how much you mean to me."

Across the two floors of KBW, decisions to go or stay were made one at a time. Virtually the entire 88th floor cleared out, mostly people from the investment banking and research departments. A particularly loud voice came from J. J. Aguiar, an investment banker, who swept across the floor yelling at people to leave. On the 89th floor, where the KBW trading desk was located, there was less certainty. Will DeRiso, a salesman, had always been anxious about working in the trade center, though his colleagues would often rib him for his worries. The night before, he had switched desks, moving to one near the door. A few moments after the explosion, he heard pounding on the door. Two women from the information technology department stood outside, frozen with fear. DeRiso decided it was time to go.

Joseph Berry, the chief executive of the firm, stood outside his office, trying to figure out the best next move. He was yet another veteran of the 1993 attack, having spent hours trapped in an elevator when the electricity failed, and he knew about the painfully slow and sloppy descent of those who had gone down the stairs. Moreover, another reality kept KBW staff in their chairs. The traders made their money by staying on the phone, by being ready to move quickly. They did not leave for lunch. They barely stopped to go to the bathroom. Now Bob Planer, a vice president in sales, saw that some of the traders were peering out the windows. He heard other traders holler at them to get back to their seats. Planer left for the stairs. Bradley Fetchet, a twenty-four-year-old equities trader, called his father at work, then his mother, getting her answering machine.

"Hi, Mom, it's Brad. Just wanted to call and let you know. I'm sure that you heard there was . . . or maybe you haven't heard that a plane crashed into World Trade Center 1. We're fine. We're in World Trade Center 2. I'm obviously alive and well over here. But obviously . . . a pretty scary experience. I saw a guy fall out of probably the 91st story . . . ah . . . all the way down . . . so"—he paused and cleared his throat—"you're welcome to give a call here. I think we'll be here all day. I'm not sure if the firm is going to shut down for the day or what. But . . . ah . . . give me a call back later. I called Dad to let him know. Love you."

One of those who got back to the KBW trading desk was Stephen Mulderry. Of the eight Mulderry children, Stephen was the sixth, an All-American basketball player at the Division 3 level for the University of Albany. He took a call from his brother Peter, who had seen the news on TV at his own office.

"What's up, brother?" Stephen said, giving Peter his usual salutation.

"Are you all right?" Peter asked.

"Yeah, I was just over at the window, but, my God, I don't know if people were falling or jumping, but I saw people falling to their death," Stephen said.

"Oh, my God," Peter said.

"They're human beings," Stephen said. As he spoke, a public-address announcement was coming over. Stephen was being summoned, less noisily, but just as insistently, by his telephone on the trading desk. Since the traders all worked elbow to elbow, the phones lit up, rather than rang, to signal an incoming call.

"I gotta go," Stephen declared. "The lights are ringing and the market is going to open."

All of KBW's New York traders were at or near their chairs, ready for the 9:00 opening.

3

"Mom, I'm not calling to chat."

On the 91st floor of the north tower, Mike McQuaid and his crew of five electricians hunted for a stairway. They were two floors below the bottom of the impact zone of Flight 11, in a wholly ordinary space that had been transformed in the last two minutes into a warren of collapsed ceiling tiles and fallen walls. Even so, the materials that made up the rubble were light and the corridors to the exits in the center of the building remained passable. The stairwells, though, were another story entirely. Two of them had been reduced to smithereens. The remaining one, toward the northwest side of the building, was open. So they would be able to get out, after all. One of the electricians forgot his cell phone, and he hustled back to get it. As the others waited, McQuaid stuck his head into the offices of the American Bureau of Shipping, and hollered, "Anybody there?"

Most of 91 was empty—the American Bureau of Shipping was the only commercial tenant on the floor, occupying about a quarter of the space—and it happened to be on the northwest side, near the open stairway. Already, most of the eleven people in that office had collected themselves and started down.

Now a woman in a red hat came their way.

"I'm the last one," she declared.

Then they heard two other people from an area near the elevators. Vanessa Lawrence, a Scottish-born artist who worked on the floor, had just had taken one step out of the elevator when the concussion ran through the shaft. Gerry Wertz, a purchasing manager for Marsh & McLennan, was still in the elevator, on his way to the 93rd floor for a meeting. Someone had dropped a hand grenade on the roof of the car, he thought. He pitched forward and jumped from the car onto the ground. The ceiling and wallboards had collapsed. Behind them, the elevator seemed to disintegrate. At the height of the shock, Wertz could not quite understand what Lawrence was saying through her Scottish burr.

A moment later, the electricians hollered to them, leading them by voice toward a center corridor. One of the electricians was trying to make a two-way radio work, but could not get through.

"We've just got to get down," Wertz said, and the electricians led them toward the open stairwell.

The worker in McQuaid's crew returned with his phone, and they were ready to go, the last of the eighteen people on the 91st floor. As they stepped into the dark, surviving staircase, they were at a borderline. Three or four inches of drywall had been blasted off the stairwell walls above them, exposing the structural steel, and plugging the stairs that led up. Every single person had gotten off the 91st floor, but no one from the higher floors was coming down: the stairs to the 92nd floor were blocked tight, just like the stairs that Gerry Wertz would have encountered in the Marsh & McLennan office on the 93rd floor, had he not leapt and been thrown from the elevator on 91.

Just above them, on the 92nd floor, Damian Meehan of Carr Futures was discovering the same boundary, from the other side. He called his brother Eugene, a firefighter in the Bronx.

"It's really bad here," Damian said. "The elevators are gone."

"Get to the front door. See if there is smoke there," Eugene told him.

Eugene heard his brother put down the phone, then followed the sounds drifting into his ear. Yelling. Commotion, but not panic. Damian reported back a moment or two later. Yes, there was smoke.

"Get to the stairs," Eugene said. "See where the smoke is coming from. Go the other way."

Damian did not linger. "We've got to go," Eugene heard his brother say. Or maybe, "We're going." Whatever he said, none of the seventy people on the 92nd floor had access to an open staircase.

Garth Feeney did not work in the trade center but had gone there to attend the Risk Waters breakfast at Windows on the World. He phoned his mother, Judy, in Florida, who was just watching the first broadcasts about the crash.

"Hi, what's new?" she said, when she heard her son's voice.

"Mom, I'm not calling to chat," Feeney said. "I'm in the World Trade Center and it's been hit by a plane."

"Please tell me you are below it," his mother said.

"No, I'm above it. I'm on the top floor," he said. "There are seventy of us in one room. They have closed the doors and they are trying to keep the smoke out."

The building had barely stopped shuddering when smoke first appeared in Windows on the World, so thick and noxious that one man told his wife a bomb had gone off in the bathroom. Actually, the restaurant was well above the impact zone in the north tower: The fuselage of Flight 11 had entered between the 95th and 97th floors, and the tip of its right wing—the highest point of impact because the aircraft had banked—cut into the 99th floor. That was still seven stories, about eighty-five feet, beneath the restaurant. As easily as the roaring jet had knifed through the steel face of the tower, smoke now relentlessly, swiftly, seeped into the top of the building, finding paths through and around the concrete floors, emerging in billowing, ghastly clouds. Doris Eng, who had spent the first part of the morning welcoming people to the 106th and 107th floors, now was trying to figure out how to save their lives. In the restaurant were 170 men and women—diners, restaurant workers, and people attending the breakfast conference sponsored by Risk Waters. She kept calling emergency numbers, unsure where the damage was, but that almost did not matter. People in the restaurant could barely see or breathe.

In theory, any one of the floors between Windows on the World and the crash site should have stopped the spread of the fire and smoke. Each floor was designed as a fire-tight compartment able to contain a surge of flames and smoke, just as the hull of an ocean liner is divided into multiple chambers, so that if the ship springs a leak, the water will be trapped in a single chamber, blocked from flooding the entire hull and sinking the ship. In a thousand voices, the word came loud and clear that fire containment was not working. During the first ten minutes after the crash, the 911 system would log some 3,000 calls, many of them from people on the upper floors of the north tower. They would report the explosion, and that the stairs were cut off—destroyed outright, or blocked with rubble, or filled with smoke or fire. Downstairs, at the Port Authority police command desk for the trade center, the phone never stopped ringing. Officer Steve Maggett answered one of the lines, and heard from Christine Olender at Windows on the World.

"Hi, this is Christine, assistant GM of Windows. We're getting no direction up here. We're having a smoke condition."

Only a few minutes before, she had been chatting on the phone with her mother in Chicago to plan her parents' visit. Now she was trying to organize an escape.

"We have most people on the 106th floor; the 107th floor is way too smoky," she continued. "We need direction as to where we need to direct our guests and our employees, as soon as possible."

Maggett was 1,300 feet below Windows on the World. No one could get to the restaurant now other than by climbing the stairs. It would take hours.

"Okay," said Maggett. "We're doing our best, we've got the Fire Department, everybody, we're trying to get up to you, dear. All right, call back in about two or three minutes, and I'll find out what direction you should try to get down."

Olender started to speak: "Because our . . . our—"

"Are the stairways, A, B, and C all blocked off and smoky?" asked the policeman.

"The stairways are full of smoke, A, B, and C," Olender reported. "And my . . . and my electric . . . my fire phones are out."

"Oh, yeah, they're . . . all . . . all the lines are blown out right now," Maggett said. "But everybody is on their way, the Fire Department—"

Olender would not take that as reassurance.

"The condition up on 106 is getting worse," she said.

"Okay, dear," Maggett said. "All right, we are doing our best to get up to you right now. All right, dear?"

"But where . . . where do you want to [*inaudible*] can you at least . . . can you at least direct us to a certain tower in the building?"

"Uh . . ." Maggett said.

"Like what tower . . . like what area . . . what quadrant of the building can we go into, where we are not going to get all this smoke?" she asked.

"Unless we find out what exactly . . . area is the smoke . . . where most . . . most of the smoke is coming up there, and we can kind of direct that," Maggett said. "As I said, call back in about two minutes, dear."

"Call back in two minutes," Olender said. "Great."

"About two minutes, all right?" he said.

Two minutes, no time at all, except in a tower that raged with fires, where poisonous smoke was billowing through channels and ducts, and where the sprinklers were unable to suppress the flames. In two minutes, hundreds of people in the north tower would get word out, or try to. Their immediate worry was their own ability to elude the heat and smoke; they had not yet begun to doubt that the tower would survive the crash.

The building had easily absorbed the impact of the jetliner. The pinstripe columns that gave the towers their distinctive look—and kept the windows a mere twenty-two inches wide, comforting their height-fearing architect—were not simply ornamentation, or panic handles for acrophobiacs. They actually held the buildings up. The towers had columns in the central core, but most of every floor was open space. Those external pinstripes made the open floors possible by carrying the great weight of the building, running it down to the foundation, into the bedrock, and doing it with strength to spare. Gravity was actually a lesser force to be reckoned with than the wind. The towers stood like huge sails at the foot of Manhattan Island, with each face built to absorb a hurricane of 140 miles per hour. The wind load on an ordinary day was thirty times greater than the force of the airplane that would hit it on September 11. The mass of the tower was 1,000 times greater than the jet's. Given the sheer bulk of the towers, it was not surprising that the building continued to stand after the plane hit.

Indeed, that very assurance had been offered by the Port Authority more than three decades earlier, when private developers warned that planes would inevitably strike the towers. Now that the catastrophe had been realized, the surviving pinstripe columns on the north face of the north tower formed an arch around the wound in the building, creating new paths for the weight of the building to travel. In the instant after the plane struck, the everyday physical demands on skyscrapers, gravity and wind, were instantly passed along the arch to those unscathed columns. It looked as if the structural engineers had been correct back in the 1960s: the building was robust enough to stand up to the impact from an airplane.

No one had designs, however, for the people inside, perhaps 1,000 of whom were alive but marooned on the upper floors of the north tower. So they did what humans do: they talked. Just as arches had formed in the surviving structural steel columns and prevented an immediate collapse of the tower, the men and women stranded on the upper floors dialed cell phones, tapped the miniature keyboards on their pagers, and spoke into two-way radios, fashioning a bridge of voices.

Many in the crowd made their living providing information or the equipment that carried it, communications experts taking part in the morning's conference in the Windows on the World ballroom. They scrambled across their virtual bridge for bits of news. During the early minutes of the crisis, at least forty-one people in the restaurant sent word outside the building.

"Watch CNN," Stephen Tompsett, a computer scientist at the Risk Waters conference, e-mailed his wife, Dorry, using his Black-Berry communicator. "Need updates."

Pete Alderman and William Kelly, the two Bloomberg L.P. employees who had had their photograph taken before the breakfast conference began, sent e-mails to their offices and family, in hurried spelling and typography.

A friend of Kelly's sent around a group e-mail about the plane crash, not realizing that one of the recipients was in the building. Kelly replied, "I'm stuck on the 106th floor . . . stuck."

Alderman heard from a colleague who knew that he was scheduled to be in the trade center. "Pete, if you get this please let me know that you're okay," the colleague wrote.

"THERE IS A lot of SMOKE," Alderman replied.

"Are they telling you what to do?" the colleague asked.

"No its a mess."

"Are you still in the building."

"Yes cant move."

At the same time, Alderman was swapping messages with his sister Jane.

"I'm SCARED," he wrote. "THERE IS A lot OF SMOKE"

"can you get out of there?"

"No we are stuck."

Lower in the north tower, people could breathe. They could see the stairs. The mood was calmer, but still charged with urgency. At the Port Authority's public-relations office on the 68th floor, the phones started ringing just minutes after the plane shook the building. News reporters were calling. Greg Trevor, an authority spokesman paid to answer those calls, was still shaken from the impact. He had been nearly knocked to the floor and was as mystified as anyone dialing in about what was going on. All he knew was that something, an explosion, a bomb, had sent the building swinging back and forth like a car antenna. Fire, glass, and paper were falling past the windows, and everyone had to get out. The staff collected files and threw them into bags. They fielded a few calls, grabbed note-books, then forwarded their phones to the central Port Authority police desk in Jersey City. Just as they were ready to depart, one of Trevor's colleagues, Ana Abelians, told him that two more media calls were holding. The reflexes of a man who answers questions for a living kicked in.

"You get one, I'll get the other one," he told her. "We'll get rid of them and get the hell out of here."

He picked up the phone. "Greg Trevor here."

"Hi, I'm with NBC national news. If you could hold on for about five minutes, we're going to put you on for a live phone interview."

"I'm sorry, I can't. We're evacuating the building."

"But this will only take a minute."

"I'm sorry, you don't understand. We're leaving the building right now."

The caller seemed stunned. "But, but, this is NBC national news."

Apparently, Trevor thought to himself, it was okay to save your-self from a burning building if only a local affiliate was calling. But this was The Network.

He politely hung up and headed for the stairwell. Even now, as they started down, Trevor and his colleagues knew only that a plane had hit the building. And even that didn't make sense. How could a plane hit a 110-story building on such a clear day? He tried to call his wife, Allison, several times by cell phone, but couldn't get through. He reached a colleague, Pasquale DiFulco, through his BlackBerry communicator.

DiFulco had started the day on vacation and was home watching CNN. He began to give Trevor updates using digital haiku. His first message flashed: "AA 676 from boston crashed into 1wtc. fbi reporting plane was hijacked moments before crash." He had mis-typed the 767's model number, but Trevor understood.

At a stairway landing on the 27th floor, Ed Beyea watched the people streaming past him, a fixed point in a river of humanity. He was going nowhere, for now. Nothing below his neck moved. He had broken his neck twenty years earlier in a diving accident in upstate New York, where he grew up, and had come to the city for rehabilitation shortly thereafter. He never left. Now forty-two years old, he lived in an apartment on Roosevelt Island, a spit of land in the middle of the East River that was covered with high-rise buildings and was home to a hospital that served people with spinal cord injuries. The island's subway station had a modern elevator, making it possible for him to commute to the trade center without a car. He worked as a computer analyst for Empire Blue Cross and Blue Shield, traveling to and from the office with his aide, Irma Fuller. She had accompanied him on the elevator up to 27, hung up his jacket, and set him up with the mouth stick that he used to type. When the first plane hit, she had been upstairs ordering breakfast at a 43rd floor cafeteria. By the time she came down, Beyea had already gone onto the stairwell landing.

With Beyea was Abe Zelmanowitz, another Blue Cross computer analyst who worked one cubicle over, separated by an aisle on the south end of the floor. Considering the distances between them—physical, cultural, religious—that they were now inches from each other in the stairwell might have seemed peculiar.

Beyea came from a small town in upstate New York and had converted to Catholicism as an adult; Zelmanowitz, thirteen years his senior, was an Orthodox Jew from Brooklyn. Beyea laughed from a capacious belly, swollen by kidney problems and years of inactivity. He weighed 280 pounds. Zelmanowitz was soft-spoken and slim.

They had worked together for twelve years and had become close friends. Zelmanowitz made a reading stand that Beyea could use in bed. Beyea shot jokes that were irresistible to Zelmanowitz. Once or twice a month they went to a restaurant after work, always with Fuller, often with others from their office. If Beyea picked, he made sure the restaurant was kosher. If Zelmanowitz selected, he made sure it was wheelchair accessible. One favorite was Mr. Broadway, a kosher restaurant in midtown that served a nice rib-eye steak. Zelmanowitz lived with his older brother and his brother's family. Beyea, who had been briefly married and was separated, lived by himself. The two men had built a friendship on the solid footings of the everyday: joking, eating, and the minutiae of work in a small office, drawing them from the cloisters of their own lives.

The two men knew right away that their situation was serious. They had felt the jolt when the plane hit and had watched the debris fall past their windows. Still, the building had survived a bombing before and there was little smoke on their floor. Moreover, both of them knew that friendship alone would not carry Beyea down the stairs. They needed three or four strong men to do it safely, so they were waiting for help. In the meantime, Zelmanowitz told Fuller that she should go ahead and leave the building.

"I'll stay with Ed," he told her. Beyea also told her to go. Find someone downstairs, they told her, and tell them where we are. As Fuller started down, Zelmanowitz yelled a final note down the stairs: "Irma, we are on 27C."

A few minutes later, he called his brother, Jack, at home, who was watching the tower burn on TV. Zelmanowitz spoke calmly. The fire was above them.

"We're getting ready to go," he said. "We're just waiting for assistance."

"Is everything okay?" Jack asked. "You know, you have to get out of there."

"Don't worry," Zelmanowitz responded. "I'm here with Ed. We're just waiting for medical help, and firemen will come and help us go down. Don't worry. Everything looks like it's going to be okay."

Zelmanowitz then held the cell phone while Beyea called his mother, Janet, in Bath, New York, the town in the Finger Lakes where, as a young man, Beyea had tended bar at the Moose Club and waterskied on Keuka Lake. The conversation was short. Beyea told his mother that they were still in the building but they would be leaving soon.

"Mom," he said, "I'm all right."

4

"We have no communication established up there yet."

In the lobby of the north tower, Lloyd Thompson stood at a console, answering calls on the building's intercom system and trying to make sense of what people and the console were telling him about the smoke and fire on the upper floors. As the deputy fire safety director for the building, Thompson had often stood at the same spot during an emergency, and the console would quickly show him where trouble was: a red light, one for each floor, lit up when someone called for help. It was rare for more than one light to come on. Now Thompson faced a board of red lights.

Though the shape of the disaster was barely forming in his mind, Thompson knew enough about its scale to pick up the public-address microphone and order an immediate evacuation of the building. His message went nowhere: the plane had destroyed the building's public-address system.

At the police desk in 5 World Trade Center, the low-rise building just northeast of the north tower, Alan Reiss, the former director of the world trade department, was also answering a flood of calls for help. Reiss had run straight from his breakfast meeting in the concourse to the police desk to help answer the phones. He knew the people who worked in Windows—he had a membership in a club there, and a meal in the restaurant was one of the pleasures in his routine. He, too, could do little but tell them to hold on. Rescue workers were on their way. Even the simplest advice, to wet towels and stuff them in the doorsills, became another avenue of frustration. The plane had severed the pipes, so there was no water pressure upstairs, for drinking, putting out fires, or dampening cloths. When Jan Maciejewski, the waiter, called his wife from a cell phone, he told her that he would check the flower vases for water.

In trucks and cars and commandeered buses, on foot and by air, a fresh wave of men and women—on duty, off-duty, and no duty— were heading straight toward a catastrophe from which thousands of others were fleeing. The urge to help was powerful. Several blocks away at the Court Officers Academy, Capt. Joseph Baccellieri grabbed two of his sergeants, Al Moscola and Andrew Wender, and began running toward the trade center. They sprinted west across Fulton Street, weaving through crowds running east. Baccellieri, who was forty-one, had been sorting through a new shipment of uniforms when he heard the shattering noise of the plane's impact. He understood that he had no official role as a rescuer at a crash, or whatever this was. His job at the academy was to train the court officers who kept order in New York State's courts. But he had training as a first responder and a simple moral precept that he clung to: "You want people to come for you, you've got to help them." He also had a good deal of experience with the World Trade Center.

As a younger man, Baccellieri had driven a truck for his father's company, JLB Transport, which made deliveries once a month to the trade center, many of them loads of paper used by printing businesses in the towers. Baccellieri would have to navigate the subterranean maze of the garage to figure out which of the freight elevators served the north tower, the south, and the five other buildings that made up the garden of high-rises. Along sharp corners and dead ends, he would steer the big truck, known as a straight-through, struggling to bring it close to the tight delivery bays.

It was always confusing, he recalled, though nothing like the mayhem he was witnessing now as he ran toward the complex. People streamed from the buildings. The gash where the plane had entered the north tower was clearly visible. Already, just minutes after the crash, people were falling from the building while others screamed. Two police officers held open the doors into 5 World Trade Center, where the complex's police desk was located, and urged people to keep moving, to get away. As Baccellieri and his two colleagues walked in, one of the cops told him he was crazy.

Chief Joseph Pfeifer took a mental snapshot of the damage as he strode into the north tower lobby in his thick rubber boots. Shattered windows. Tan marble cracked and collapsed from the wall. Severely burned people being helped from the building. The fireball of exploding jet fuel had shot down the elevator shafts, reaching as far as four levels below the lobby. It had announced itself in the lobby with an explosion that had blackened a stretch of wall near one of the elevator banks, and blown the doors off the cars.

Pfeifer, a battalion chief, was the first fire commander to arrive at the scene, getting there at 8:50 A.M., just four minutes after the plane hit. He had heard Flight 11 screeching directly overhead as he stood on Lispenard Street in lower Manhattan, where he and firefighters from Engine 7 were investigating a gas leak. They watched as the plane blew into the upper floors of the north tower. Jules Naudet, a French documentary maker, was taping Pfeifer that day, and he pulled his camera up to record the plane as it burst into the north face of the north tower. They rushed into Pfeifer's battalion car, and sped south with Engine 7. "That looked like a direct attack," Pfeifer said in the car.

As they drove, Chief Pfeifer used his car radio to call in the first and second alarms simultaneously, alerting dispatchers to send nineteen fire trucks to the building. His first message began at 8:46:43, twelve seconds after the impact.

"We just had a plane crash into upper floors of the World Trade Center. Transmit a second alarm and start relocating companies into the area."

Not enough, he knew. Ninety seconds after the plane struck, he added a third alarm.

> **Battalion 1 to Manhattan.**
> We have a number of floors on fire. It looked like the plane was aiming toward the building. Transmit a third alarm throughout; the staging area at Vesey and West Street. As the third alarm assignment goes into that area, the second alarm assignment report to the building.

By having the firefighters responding to the third alarm go to Vesey and West Streets, the northwestern boundary of the trade center, Pfeifer was trying to manage the flood of arriving troops. It was good to have manpower, but not if it all showed up at once.

Standing on the sidewalk outside the north tower, the chief pulled his black-and-yellow turnout coat over his white shirt and tie. He tossed his white chief's hat on the dashboard, picked up his fire helmet, and tugged on his boots. He glanced at the high side of the building before he entered. It belched white smoke, but no flames were visible yet. That would be Pfeifer's last good look at the job he and hundreds would be taking on.

Trailing him throughout was the filmmaker, Jules Naudet, who rarely shifted the camera off Pfeifer even as the flames roared above them. For months, Naudet and his brother, Gedeon, had been making a documentary about the progress of a rookie firefighter as he grew into the job. The brothers had become regulars at the firehouse, even pitching in with kitchen chores. The preparation and consumption of meals was a central event on many a day at the firehouse, particularly since there were far more big dinners than big fires. The routine made for hearty fellowship, though not necessarily gripping documentary film. "By the end of August," Gedeon would say in an interview, "we knew that we had a great cooking show."

Now Jules Naudet recorded the first arrivals at what would become the largest rescue operation in New York City history. More than 225 fire units would go to the trade center, half of all the companies working that day. So many trucks showed up that parking became difficult. The trucks themselves were crowded with off-duty firefighters, most of whom had just gotten off the overnight shift and felt compelled to go along. Other firefighters heard the news at home or at their second jobs, grabbed their car keys, and headed in. In the brave, pell-mell rush to help, more than 1,000 firefighters would report. Among them were seventeen rookies, people like Christian Regenhard from Engine 279 in Brooklyn, a former Marine just six weeks out of the Fire Academy. Also there was Chief Pfeifer's brother, Kevin, a lieutenant who was on duty with Engine 33. The brothers spotted each other in the north tower lobby when Kevin's company arrived. They were both low-key commanders whose slow-to-ignite temperaments served them well in the high-octane situations they encountered. They lived only a few blocks apart in Middle Village, Queens, a neighborly patch of the city with small, tidy lawns, and little resemblance to the vertical clamor of Manhattan. Joe, a slim man with a thin mustache and the fact-driven manner of an accountant, was older by three years. He had spent two decades in the department and, as a chief in Battalion 1, was responsible for lower Manhattan. Calls to the trade center were part of his routine, and he knew the safety staff at the complex. Kevin was adventurous, without being loud. Unmarried, he was the uncle in the family who flew a Cessna, sailed a catamaran, and gave parties by the beach in Queens. Quickly, without ceremony, Joe, senior to Kevin not only in age but also in rank, ran down what he knew. Kevin didn't say much in reply, but Joe noticed the concerned look on his face. Then Kevin turned and took his company, David Arce, Michael Boyle, Robert Evans, Robert King Jr., and Keithroy Maynard, up the stairs.

From the first view of the gaping hole and flames, many fire officials would later say, they knew that they would not be able to put out the fire. It would be strictly a rescue operation. The FDNY could fight a fire on one floor, maybe two. They could not handle what confronted them now—at least five floors fully engulfed. The limitation was a matter not of bravery or skill or brawn, but of simple physics. Each hose could shoot 250 gallons of water a minute, enough to douse a fire spread across 2,500 square feet. With multiple hose lines, they might be able to battle a fire that stretched across a single trade center floor of 40,000 square feet, but not five floors, and certainly not, as it turned out, without water. So the three chiefs in charge at the lobby—Pfeifer, joined by Deputy Chief Peter Hayden and Assistant Chief Joseph Callan—decided that the companies would not extinguish the fire, but would concentrate on helping people evacuate. If they needed to knock down a patch of flames to open a stretch of stairs, that was OK, but otherwise they would just let the fire burn itself out. Whatever their eyes told them about the scale of the blaze, they would follow the fundamentals of high-rise firefighting doctrine, first by setting up a command post near the fire. But where was this fire? No one in the lobby knew. The building fire-detection system had been badly damaged. Pfeifer would remember hearing speculation by members of the building staff that the fire was at the 78th floor, which was actually twenty stories below the center of the impact. Small fires burned on many floors below the main conflagration, including 78. Pfeifer told his first units to head for the 70th floor, a spot safely beneath the fire, the customary position for setting up forward operations. If all went as expected, the fire would burn upward, not downward. Other companies were assigned to respond to specific distress calls. Still others were assigned floors and told to make sure everyone had gotten out.

The next task for the chiefs was transporting the companies upstairs. They discovered that nearly all the building's ninety-nine elevators were out of service. Many were stuck between floors with people trapped inside. At least two that had descended to the lobby were shut tight. The people inside were screaming, just a few yards from the fire command desk, but no one could hear them in the din.

The lack of working elevators meant the fires high in the tower would have a galloping, destructive head start. To get to the upper floors, the companies would be walking. Among the most experienced chiefs to arrive was Donald Burns, who had been a commander at the 1993 bombing and had written a thoughtful commentary on the event. "Without elevators," he had noted, "sending companies to upper floors in large high-rise buildings is measured in hours, not minutes."

In the stairwells, gravity ruled. A firefighter's turnout coat, pants, boots, and helmet weigh twenty-nine and a half pounds. The mask and oxygen tank add another twenty-seven pounds, bringing the basic load to fifty-six and a half pounds. Firefighters in engine companies also carry fifty feet of hose, called a roll-up, with aluminum fittings on each end. That weighs thirty pounds, increasing the load to eighty-six and a half pounds. Even though fighting the fire was out of the question, the reflex to bring the gear held: many companies lugged the bulky hose roll-ups into the stairs, already packed with people trying to flee.

In the ladder companies, some firefighters carried an extinguisher and hook, thirty-eight pounds, while others toted an ax and the Halligan tool, an all-purpose pry bar, with a weight of twenty-five pounds. One firefighter from each unit also carried a lifesaving rope, 150 feet long and weighing twenty-two pounds.

They all carried one more piece of equipment: a radio, the Motorola Saber, which weighs one pound, seven ounces.

Traveling through the ventilation system the smoke from the fire ten stories below was taking over both floors of Windows on the World. With the guests herded onto the lower floor, the 106th floor, Doris Eng, Christine Olender, and the rest of the staff were following their emergency-training instructions—to assemble everyone in a corridor near the stairs and to call the fire safety director in the lobby. The evacuation policy for the towers, which had been redrafted several years earlier, relied on assurances that a fire on one floor could be contained for a period of hours. The first priority was to evacuate the floor on fire and the one above it. People farther away were to leave only when directed by the command center or, as the training brochure blandly put it, "when conditions dictate such actions."

The operators for the 911 system were giving callers similar instructions: Stay put. The firemen are coming to get you.

Ivhan Carpio, a worker at the restaurant, left a message on his cousin's answering machine. "I can't go anywhere because they told us not to move," he said. It was Carpio's twenty-fourth birthday and his day off, but his extended family in Peru depended on Carpio's paycheck, and he had agreed to cover someone else's shift to earn extra money. "I have to wait for the firefighters," he told his cousin's machine.

Christine Olender now called the police desk again, as instructed.

"Right now," she told Officer Ray Murray, "we need to find a safe haven on 106, where the smoke condition isn't bad. Can you direct us to a certain quadrant?"

"All right," Murray responded. "We're sending . . . we're sending people up there as soon as possible."

"What's your ETA?" she asked.

"As soon as possible. As soon as it's humanly possible."

To do any good for the people upstairs, Chief Pfeifer needed a quick way to reach them, and reliable information from the high floors. Neither was available. Even as the firefighters ascended single file, the shape of the situation upstairs remained a mystery, if one with increasingly desperate overtones. The messages from Christine Olender had been relayed from the Port Authority police desk in 5 World Trade Center to Sergeant Al DeVona, a Port Authority police officer who had gone to the lobby of the north tower to coordinate his department's work with the firefighters. DeVona passed word to Pfeifer that people at Windows were trapped. The chiefs at the command post were sent word of other calls for help that had gone to the 911 system or to the building staff, who were answering the intercom phones.

The console at the fire command desk held few of the answers that Chief Pfeifer needed. Where was the fire? How fast was it spreading and where? Which stairwells were clear? The chief, it turned out, knew less than the people he was trying to rescue. They were being briefed on the phone by family and friends who were watching TV. He had no TV and the fire chiefs were getting only snatches of information from colleagues who walked outside and craned their heads, trying to fathom what was happening 1,200 feet in the sky. Few departments equal the rigor of New York City's basic firefighter training, but its commanders went through little formal planning for complex events. The concept of "situational awareness"—using modern tools to provide information needed by people making life-and-death decisions in fast-moving environments—had become a foundation for military maneuvers, air-traffic control, power-plant operation, and advanced manufacturing. That concept had not taken hold at many fire departments, including New York's. Though the FDNY rarely lacked for resources—indeed, it had prospered over the previous ten years, as its budget increased by $253 million above the inflation rate, even as the number of fires was dropping by 46 percent—it operated without video feeds, computer laptops with building plans, or strong communication links. Battalion Chief Pfeifer was junior to other arriving commanders, including his boss, Deputy Chief Hayden, and Assistant Chief Callan. (In the Fire Department's nomenclature, a hybrid glossary of civil service and tradition, a battalion chief is outranked by a deputy chief, who is in turn subordinate to an assistant chief.) The chiefs hoped to get better information when firefighters reached the upper floors and sent back reports, or when tenants from those floors started reaching the lower floors and could pass along their firsthand observations. Whether the intelligence came from descending civilians or ascending firefighters, the radios had to work. In high-rises, fire radios had a poor record because the mass of the building often prevented radio signals from penetrating, and chiefs lost touch with firefighters on upper floors. One of the more infamous episodes had occurred after the trade center bombing in 1993. Hundreds of firefighters had responded, overloading the radio frequencies. Messages were lost. Commanders had to rely on human messengers to transmit critical information. Afterward, in a report on the attack and the response, Anthony L. Fusco, the chief of department, said: "A major detriment to our ability to strengthen control of the incident was Fire Department on-scene communications."

In the days before portable radio technology, New York City firefighters used hand signals to communicate or sent runners to carry messages. Often they just shouted. By the mid-1940s, the department was using shortwave pack sets, similar to the ones employed by soldiers on the battlefields of Europe. In the 1960s, individual firefighters were given their own radios. Four decades after that innovation, however, and thirty years after men on the moon beamed live television pictures across the cosmos, firefighters were still having a hard time using their radios in high-rise buildings.

To communicate consistently in a tall building, an emergency agency needed two things: a reliable handheld radio and an amplifier to boost the radio's signal so that it could reach the upper floors. No matter how hardy a handheld radio was—Motorola salesmen used to drop the Saber radios on the floor in a cocky demonstration of their ruggedness—its signal was generally too weak to reliably penetrate multiple floors without a booster.

The New York Police Department had figured this out many years earlier. Its officers could communicate effectively in high-rise buildings even though a police officer's radio, the one that dangled from the belt, was much like a firefighter's radio. The difference was that, unlike the Fire Department, the police had installed boosters in 350 locations across the city to amplify their signals. The Fire Department had only a handful of boosters in place.

Part of the disparity in the use of boosters was found in how the two agencies used their radios on a daily basis. Police officers needed to be in touch with a distant central base or dispatcher, requiring a system designed to communicate over great distances. The situation was reversed for firefighters, who were more concerned with keeping track of a colleague lost in the smoke of an adjoining room. Amplification was generally not needed to talk at the scene of the average house fire. And though tourist postcards portrayed New York City as a forest of skyscrapers, most of its tall buildings really were in two pockets, lower Manhattan and midtown. The chiefs in those two neighborhoods complained long and hard when their radios malfunctioned inside office towers. For the rest of the department, working in neighborhoods where buildings seldom topped six stories, the problem of high-rise radio reception did not outrank other issues facing the FDNY.

Moreover, to install a booster system would have represented an entirely new way of doing things—never an easy sell in a department that resisted technological change. At the Fire Department, the loyalty of one firefighter to another, a soldierly bond, was at times extended to an attachment to gear and the old way of doing things. Technological ruts became enshrined as customs. Still, over the years, the Fire Department had boosters installed in a few critical buildings like train terminals and the trade center. In a city with a signature skyline, where more than 2,000 buildings in Manhattan alone rise higher than twenty stories, this was not a major achievement. But it was better than nothing, which was what many urban fire departments had when it came to such boosters.

At the trade center, the booster, also known as the repeater, had been part of $80 million in safety improvements made by the Port Authority after the 1993 bombing. The repeater—and its antenna—were installed at 5 World Trade Center, but it was turned on and operated from consoles at the fire command desks in both of the twin towers, across the plaza. When it was on, the device could capture messages from the firefighters' handheld radios and rebroadcast them at greater strength. That would allow fire commanders in a lobby to stay in touch with their troops working on the upper floors.

Earlier in 2001, the Fire Department had also issued new handheld radios, the Motorola XTS3500R. It employed the latest in digital technology, fire officials said, an improvement over the existing, aging, analog Motorola Saber radios, and would be better able to penetrate multiple layers of concrete and steel at high-rises.

Just days after the new radios were introduced, however, a fire-fighter lost in a house fire called for help and could not be heard by his colleagues outside. Other complaints soon surfaced, and the new radios were pulled from service amid a debate over whether the problem was a hardware glitch or a lack of training on how to use the new equipment.

As a result, the department was forced to reissue the Motorola Saber radios it had just withdrawn, some of them fifteen years old. On September 11, many of the firefighters marched into the towers with these old radios, the identical ones they had carried eight years earlier when the bomb went off. This time, though, they had the powerful repeater. It had been tested only a few months earlier and had worked well. Even with the old radios, the prospects for communicating within the tower looked brighter than they had in 1993.

Truck 1, an elite team of rescue specialists from the Emergency Service Unit of the New York Police Department, arrived at 8:52 A.M. and set up a command post at the corner of Church and Vesey Streets, about two blocks from the lobby where Pfeifer and the fire chiefs were directing their operation. The ESU cops, forty or so officers organized in six teams, were trained to help people who had been taken hostage, or were dangling from bridges or, as was the case here, trapped by fire. They were followed to the scene by hundreds of fellow New York police officers summoned at 8:56 A.M. by the chief of the department, Joseph Esposito.

"Car three," Esposito said on the radio. "We've got a level three and you might want to go to a level four here, Central, all right?"

A Level 4 mobilization was the department's highest, rarest state of alert, the police equivalent of a war footing. It meant that about 1,000 officers would be responding. As they arrived, most of the officers were given assignments outside the buildings. Some directed people leaving the trade center away from the perimeter of the complex and the streets around it. Others controlled the crowd or tried to direct the congealing traffic. The ESU cops were sent inside the building. On paper, they would work under Fire Department direction. The city had a protocol that established who did what at emergencies, which was supposed to avoid duplication of effort and to keep the chain of command clear. The Fire Department was in charge at fires, so technically the ESU teams were supposed to check in with fire officials at the lobby before they rushed to help in the building.

Some teams did check in, others didn't, and one that did felt rebuffed by the fire chiefs to whom they spoke. That was not a surprise. The Finest, as the police were called, and the Bravest, the nickname for the firefighters, did not like each other. The saying went that the only thing the two departments could ever agree on was the date of their annual boxing match. Sometimes, they didn't wait for that date, and fistfights broke out at rescue scenes. The corrosive nature of the relationship had far more serious consequences than a fat lip. To be completely effective, firefighters and police officers needed to share information, to act in concert, to anticipate what the other force might do as a disaster evolved. The decisions that commanders made were influenced by how quickly and accurately they sized up a situation based on what they learned both from their troops and their putative allies. But these two agencies didn't train together often or well. They couldn't talk to each other by radio because their frequencies did not match. And they didn't share equipment.

The police, for example, flew helicopters, and the city had drafted a plan to let firefighters ride in them at high-rise fires. This plan was revised after the 1993 bombing, but it was rarely used and infrequently rehearsed. And on this day the cooperation was no different. The Police and Fire Departments ran brave but completely independent rescue operations. They did not bicker; they simply did not communicate. No one from the Fire Department called up to request the use of a helicopter, as envisioned by the protocol. No one from the Police Department called to find out if they were coming. And so the police helicopters lifted off without any firefighters, leaving Chief Pfeifer to wonder about the spread of fire on the upper floors 1,200 feet above him, even though, from 8:52 on, a police helicopter had a clear view of the damage. Indeed, a few minutes later, the pilot of Aviation 14 sent in a grim bird's-eye report.

"Be advised at this time," Detective Timothy Hayes said. "Be advised we do have people confirmed falling out of the building at this time. It looks like four sides are cut open. A lot of flames."

That word did not get down to the fire commanders in the lobby of the north tower, not in an act of specific hostility, but because of a long-standing malaise that ran from the top of each department to the bottom. Mayors had tried for years to forge a peaceful, working relationship so that in the event of a big disaster, all the resources of the city would be coordinated. After a series of plane crashes, Mayor David N. Dinkins formed an Aviation Emergency Preparedness Working Group in 1990, with representatives from the Fire and Police Departments and Emergency Medical Services, as well as others. In a report, the group concluded that the agencies needed to practice working together and to arrange for a single radio frequency that commanders could share during emergencies. After a couple of years of drills, the group was disbanded in 1994, when a new mayor, Rudolph W. Giuliani, took office. Giuliani made public safety the signature cause of his administration. In 1996, he created the Office of Emergency Management (OEM), which ran a series of mock disaster drills, though none that involved an airliner crashing into a skyscraper, whether by accident or design. Indeed, despite the trade center's status as the city's leading terrorist target, coordinated disaster drills were extremely rare events in the life of the complex.

The consequences of a plane's striking one of the towers had been envisioned many years earlier, even before the towers were built, by opponents of their construction who ran an ad in *The New York Times* with a lurid—and, as it turned out, prescient—illustration of an airliner striking the north face of the north tower. The Port Authority quickly responded: calculations by its engineers and computer simulations showed that an airplane crash would wreak destruction across seven floors, but the building itself would stand. On Sunday, November 7, 1982, officials replicated a plane crash high in one of the towers, a "disaster" to which city Police and Fire Departments, Emergency Medical Services, and the Port Authority all responded. The drill followed a real near-disaster that had made news the year before: an Argentine airliner came within ninety seconds of hitting the north tower when it had problems communicating with air traffic controllers. No terrorism was involved.

After the 1993 bombing, a retired director of the World Trade Center, Guy Tozzoli, told a legislative hearing that the city should probably prepare for such a catastrophe, citing the drill from 1982. His suggestion was ignored. None of the city newspapers gave the idea even a sentence of coverage, and it did not appear in the legislative committee's report. A new administration took over the city government, and Mayor Giuliani, in the classic fashion of New York mayors, attacked the Port Authority for shortchanging the city on various financial arrangements. Giuliani raised the temperature on the customary mayoral critiques, decrying everything from the salaries the Port Authority paid to its police officers—higher than what the city paid to NYPD officers—and what he claimed was poor airport snow removal. For all the spears launched, however, the city did not organize a single joint drill involving all the emergency responders at the trade center in the eight years after the 1993 attack. The last joint drill appears to have been the one held in 1982, preparations for a plane crash that did not come for nineteen years.

If the city's Office of Emergency Management did not have the history or clout to forge an effective partnership between the Fire and Police Departments before September 11, as some critics believed, it certainly had no opportunity that morning. Just minutes after Flight 11 hit the north tower, the agency was forced to evacuate its own offices, a $13 million emergency "bunker" at 7 World Trade Center, a forty-seven-story building at the northern edge of the complex. The bunker had been conceived a few years earlier as a place where emergency officials and Mayor Giuliani could preside during a crisis, coordinating the response. Some emergency-response experts and politicians suggested that the location of the bunker was unwise, given the trade center's status as a terrorist target, but the mayor brushed off the critics as people mired in the "old ways" of thinking. His aides described the bunker as state of the art and imagined it as impregnable. A defiant response to the 1993 terrorist attack, the bunker was, intentionally or not, a barely veiled monument to the iron will of the mayor, and during his brief campaign for the United States Senate in 2000, it served as an occasional backdrop for Giuliani's meetings with the press.

Now, the first time the bunker was truly needed, the agency and its officials were homeless. They arranged to relocate to a specially outfitted command bus that had been prepared as a backup head-quarters. The redundancy in the planning, however—to use a phrase popular in emergency-management circles—only served to reinforce the misjudgment of the original arrangement.

Indeed, the arrangements were being made by OEM over radios broadcasting at 800 megahertz. In 1996 and 1997, dozens of these radios had been distributed to select police and fire commanders so the agencies could communicate, an important recommendation from the 1990 Aviation Emergency Preparedness Working Group. There was a hitch, though. Who would be in control of the inter-agency frequency? Who would decide when it should be used and how? Representatives of the Police and Fire Departments had met for months to settle these questions, but the talks had broken down over unresolved issues of protocol. The radios were new and ready to use. It was just that no one outside OEM was willing to talk on them yet. The fire chiefs kept them in the trunks of their cars. As for the police chiefs, the radios never left the shelves.

A few minutes before 9:00, after getting his bearings in the lobby of the north tower, Chief Pfeifer turned to Lloyd Thompson, the civilian safety director at the fire command desk for the building. "Turn the repeater on," he said. Thompson began fiddling with something on the desk in front of him. Then he looked over to his left, he would recall later, and saw that the repeater was already on. The repeater was controlled by a console that looked like a phone set with several buttons. One button, when depressed, turned it on. A second button activated a handset that looked like a telephone. It was supposed to carry the voice of the chief to all the radios that had been tuned to the repeater channel, channel 7. Pfeifer was depending on the repeater to keep him connected to the companies he was sending upstairs, to make sure it amplified the radio signal so that the firefighters could hear his words, so they wouldn't get trapped like the people they were trying to save. But before being used, the chief thought, the repeater should be double-checked.

Pfeifer and another chief, Orio J. Palmer, stood several yards apart in the lobby and began trying to talk to each other over the repeater channel. Palmer could not hear Pfeifer. Pfeifer could hear Palmer over the radio, but not through the handset, as he was supposed to. "I don't think we have the repeater," Pfeifer said aloud. "I pick you up on my radio, but not on the hard wire," he said, referring to the handset.

When it came to radio communication, Orio Palmer was among the most knowledgeable people in the department. A chief in Battalion 7 in Manhattan, he also held an associate's degree in electrical technology and had written a training article for the department on how to use repeaters to boost radio reception at high-rise fires. On this morning, though, he did not have any magic answers. The repeater, which previously had worked so well, did not seem to be working properly, and the chiefs decided there was no time to start fussing with it.

Palmer went outside to a battalion car and turned on a portable repeater. It did not seem to work, either. The fire chiefs concluded they would have to muddle through with the same, unaided normal channels they always used when fighting fires in smaller buildings. For all the talk and effort at improving things, it might as well have been 1993 all over again. Armed only with his handheld radio, Pfeifer resumed trying to make contact with units making their way upstairs. The moment was charged, and the north tower lobby was loud, with shouting, the crackle of competing radios, the wailing sirens of arriving trucks—an ambience that, while not deafening, was relentless, stressful, jarring. Worst of all were the thunderous, percussive claps as bodies hit the building canopy. So many people from the upper floors were jumping, even now, just minutes after the crash, that the chief went over to the public-address system, not realizing it had been rendered inoperable by the plane.

"Please don't jump," he spoke into the dead microphone. "We're coming up for you."

The handheld radios were at least working, but communications were still very much hit-and-miss. Pfeifer held his two-way radio to his ear. He tried to edge away from the louder talkers. Still no good. Company after company was trudging up the stairs, where some people awaited their arrival, like Ivhan Carpio at Windows on the World, trapped above acres of flaming offices. Already Pfeifer and his boss, Deputy Chief Hayden, were losing touch with the ascending companies.

"We have no communication established up there yet," Hayden told one of the other chiefs as he arrived in the lobby.

Some messages got through. Many went unanswered. After a while it became frustrating to keep calling out the names of the companies, one by one, and getting little response. Finally Chief Callan, the assistant chief who was Hayden's boss, tried to establish a baseline. Just how bad was this communication gap? He got on the radio, using code to identify his rank.

"Four David to any unit Tower 1, upper floor," he called out. "Four David to any unit Tower 1, upper floor."

If there was an answer, he could not hear it.

5

"Should we be staying here,
or should we evacuate?"

Like a black hole, the gaping, blazing wound in the north tower had a gravitational pull, absorbing the attention of pedestrians, rescuers, and camera crews for miles. That left the people in the south tower largely on their own. Thanks to all those drills, a group from the Fuji/Mizuho offices on the 80th and 81st floors had made it to the lobby of the south tower nearly as fast as anyone in that building. Stanley Praimnath and seventeen others, most of them the senior executives, had dutifully gotten off their floors, just as they had been taught. Praimnath, for instance, boarded a local elevator at the 81st floor, then switched to the express at 78. That floor was a "sky lobby," a way station that allowed elevators to whisk passengers for the upper floors past the intermediate stops, and where they could catch local shuttle elevators to their floors. The sky lobby normally was a crowded place during the morning and evening rush hours, but the Fuji/Mizuho folks had responded so quickly to the emergency that they had little competition for space on the elevators. On his way down, Praimnath ran into most of the bank's high-ranking executives. They made it downstairs in no more than ten minutes after the plane had struck the other building.

As they approached the security turnstiles in the south tower, a guard waylaid them.

"Where're you guys going?" the guard asked.

"We saw fireballs coming down," Praimnath said.

"No, no," the guard said. "All is well here. You can go back to your office. This building is secure."

For most of the group from the Japanese bank, the authoritative voice of the guard reversed the momentum of the drills that had brought them so quickly to the lobby. The same dutiful, responsive approach to emergencies was simply being flipped around. The group turned to go upstairs as fast as they had come down. Still, Praimnath was uncertain. He spoke, for a moment, to the temporary employee he had brought downstairs.

"Delise, why don't we take the rest of the day off?" he suggested. Delise agreed and went on her way, but Praimnath and the others headed back upstairs. Praimnath felt that some of the bosses gave him odd looks for his suggestion to Delise, as though he had exercised poor judgment. During the ride up, he turned to one colleague, the company's human resources director, Brian Thompson, and said, "It's a good time to take relocation." The others ribbed him about his anxiety. The bank president got off at 80. Praimnath got off at 81. Thompson continued to 82.

So quickly had they left their desks, gotten downstairs, and been sent back that they were well settled while hundreds of people were still approaching the sky lobby on 78, or shuffling down the stairways, trying to figure out which way to go. During the uncertain moments after the north tower was struck, the tenants of the south tower relied on habits, if they had any, or training, if they had taken any, or on the instructions of the authorities who had responsibility for safety in the towers.

For decades, firefighters and others responding to a high-rise fire trusted the building itself to protect the occupants. As the strategic thinking went, evacuation posed greater hazards than remaining on a floor that was free of fire and smoke. All the technical literature on high-rise fires stressed that most of those inside should stay put. "As soon as possible," said the Fire Department's manual, "begin the process of controlling evacuation." It warned, "Occupants of numerous floors may have self-initiated evacuation, causing almost a mob scene or near panic in stair shafts or building lobby." The overall cause of safety would be served if departing crowds did not get in the way of emergency workers. And among the lessons of the 1993 bombing, when the emergency-communications and public-address systems failed, was that an uncontrolled evacuation could create a huge amount of work. People had cleared out of the trade center of their own accord, and the firefighters ended up having to search some 10 million square feet of office space to see if everyone had indeed left.

Moreover, the World Trade Center was not built for total evacuation. Few modern American high-rise towers are. There would never be a need for everyone to leave at the same time. A fire or similar emergency would be contained on its floor by sprinklers and the fire-resistant materials. So the escape structures in the buildings—the number of staircases, their placement, their width—reflected the view that in the event of a fire, the building would be able to put the fire out itself, or certainly contain it. This was not simply a whim adopted in New York for the trade center. The major fire departments and the National Fire Protection Association, an organization funded by the insurance industry to study fire safety, all advocated a strategy called "defend in place." In general terms, this meant that only people on the same floor as the fire, or on the floor directly above it, should evacuate. The Port Authority had adopted this strategy as part of its official, published fire plan.

Indeed, the prospect of a total evacuation in a high-rise seemed so remote that in the months before September 11, two of the most influential design groups—a national association of code officers and the insurance industry's fire-safety group—suggested that stairways actually could be made narrower than some codes required. Stairs are not rentable space. By squeezing a few inches out of them, developers could add several thousand rentable square feet.

At the moment Stanley Praimnath and his colleagues were sent back upstairs by the security guard at the lobby turnstile, not ten minutes after Flight 11 struck, the official map of the crisis did not yet include a single foot of the south tower. The massive explosion and the giant fireballs all had emerged from the other building, the north tower. So they should go back to their desks. The problem was contained.

The dogma of Fuji/Mizuho—get out, go quickly—was overcome by the assurances of the security guard that no evacuation was needed. Perhaps that instruction was a reflexive reaction, or maybe it was the doctrine of high-rise firefighting—stay put, stand by—being applied at a moment of a bewildering and fast-moving crisis. In either case, it reflected the belief that high-rise buildings were bigger and more resilient than just about any problem that might beset them, including the crash of a commercial airliner next door. Encoded in all the plans for the trade center—the original architecture, the structural engineering, the day-to-day operations—was confidence that the towers would be able to stop their own fires. Without that faith, the complex never could have opened its doors. And yet at the trade center, fire resistance had been a matter of intense doubt, going back nearly four decades.

Long before September 11, the Port Authority's promotional literature for the trade center had boasted: "This is a building project like no other—in size, in complexity, in revolutionary concepts." From its earliest days, though, serious questions were raised about the prudence of constructing such behemoths with untested technology. A founding principle of the modern skyscraper is the presumption that it will resist and contain fire. No one can stream a hose of water at the 60th floor of a tower, more than 700 feet above the ground. Tall buildings have to be capable of putting any fires out, or at least come close to it. The lives of the people inside rely on that principle. The continued existence of the structure depends on it. Flames must not move from floor to floor, but be stopped by the fireproofing; the steel structure of the building must be protected from the distorting effects of fire for at least two hours; the floors, for three hours.

Here was a rich and not at all fanciful source of anxiety for the engineers and architects working for the Port Authority in the 1960s. They did not know if the innovative floors proposed for the towers—thin, lightweight webs of steel built into trusses—would survive a fire. Those floors helped hold the walls of the tower in place. That they weighed so little, compared with traditional beam-and-column construction, and did not cut into tenant space, helped make the towers economically feasible to build to such heights. Yet no one had experience in fireproofing those webbed trusses, known as "bar joists," with the techniques proposed and ultimately used in the trade center—a spray-on mixture of mineral fibers and adhesive. Both the architect and the structural engineer for the project refused to vouch for the ability of the floors to withstand fire. The Port Authority has no records of any tests to determine if the lightweight structural steel was adequately protected, an assurance the city code requires. While not legally bound by the code, the agency had announced that it would "meet or exceed" the code's requirements. The reasons the agency never did the fireproofing tests can only be guessed at, since the principal figures had died long before September 11, but negative results could have forced a new design—one that might have increased the construction costs so much that the towers could not have been built, at least on the scale that was planned.

Yet these were issues of prime concern during design and construction. In 1966, Emery Roth & Sons, the New York architecture firm that was the local representative for Minoru Yamasaki, the lead architect, stated that the fire rating of the floor system could not be determined without testing. Even so, a federal investigation found no evidence that such tests were done—not in 1966, when the buildings were still being planned, or in 1975, when the towers' structural engineering firm, Skilling Helle Christiansen Robertson, made similar statements. By that time, the towers had already opened, and small fires set by an arsonist in February 1975 had caused parts of floors to buckle. The fire damaged sections of the ninth through sixteenth floors.

In 1969, a Port Authority executive had ordered that the steel be protected by the sprayed-on fireproofing materials, a half inch thick. Why a half inch? No one can say. Would it be possible to apply the material to such skinny parts and make it stick in buildings that would be in constant motion from the wind? Again, the records are bereft of any tests.

Also in 1969, an architect from Emery Roth noted that Port Authority officials had deleted a requirement that the steel in the towers be able to stand up for three or four hours of fire, depending on the part of the structure. That deletion had turned the carefully drawn specifications for the buildings into a "meaningless document," the architects complained, for which they renounced responsibility.

Once the towers were open, the Port Authority refused to permit natural gas lines in the building, concerned for what a fire supplied with potent fuel might do to the structure. The chefs at Windows on the World, one of the nation's highest grossing restaurants, had to cook using electricity.

Over the three decades that the towers stood, endless rounds of remedial, if not penitential, reconstruction took place to address fire-safety vulnerabilities, some of them endemic to buildings that rose under the 1968 building code, others—most prominently, the fireproofing—unique to the trade center.

In a breathtakingly dense litigation, the Port Authority sued the manufacturer of one of its fireproofing products because it contained asbestos, viewed as a serious health hazard. Expert witnesses reported that hunks of the fireproofing, whether asbestos based or not, had fallen off the steel, leaving it exposed. In some cases, they said, it appeared never to have been applied at all. The Port Authority received a judgment of $66 million for its claim that asbestos was an unsafe product.

With the lawsuit over, the Port Authority was forced to confront the documentary evidence that large sections of its structural steel were not protected against fire. In 1995, Frank Lombardi, who had recently become the agency's chief engineer, began to consider how to improve the situation. By 1999, he had ordered the density of the fireproofing tripled, increasing it from a half inch of coating to an inch and a half. The work would be done only as tenants renovated their floors, when the floors and ceilings could be exposed for the messy work. The Port Authority would pick up the cost, about $1 million per floor. Just as in the 1960s, however, the adequacy of the new fireproofing for the trusses was not tested, a federal investigation found in 2003. Few people could have imagined that the fire-resistance system of two of the world's tallest buildings had never undergone a trial by fire.

Despite the gravity of these doubts, the evacuation policies at the trade center assumed that the towers were sturdy and fire-resistant. And now the towers and the people inside were going to be tested by a fire greater than what any building code had anticipated.

Among the buildings that hovered around the two towers, like pilot fish around a pair of whales, was 5 World Trade Center, where the Port Authority Police Department fielded hundreds of calls from the tenants of the towers. Within minutes of the attack on the north tower, the people in the south tower got drastically different instructions, depending on which police officer answered the phone. To one officer, who understood that the trouble was entirely in the north tower, that meant people in the south tower would be better off staying put.

> *Male Caller, 92nd Floor:* Hello?
> *PAPD Officer Greg Brady:* Yeah, Port Authority Police.
> *Male Caller, 92nd Floor:* This is . . . yeah, we're on 92, World Trade Center, Two World Trade.
> *PAPD Officer Greg Brady:* Two World Trade?
> *Male Caller, 92nd Floor:* We need to know if we need to get out of here, because we know there's an explosion, I don't know which building.
> *PAPD Officer Greg Brady:* Do you have any smoke . . . smoke conditions up in your location at two?
> *Male Caller, 92nd Floor:* No, we just smell it, though.

PAPD Officer Greg Brady: Okay.

Male Caller, 92nd Floor: Should we be staying here, or should we evacuate?

[*simultaneous conversations and other noise heard in background*]

Male Caller, 92nd Floor: I'm . . . I'm waiting . . .

Officer Brady was apparently distracted by another conversation, parts of which the caller from the 92nd floor heard. The policeman returned to his conversation with the man from the 92nd floor.

Male Caller, 92nd Floor: We're on 92, uh, we don't . . . I don't know if the elevators are working.

PAPD Officer Greg Brady: What building are you in?

Male Caller, 92nd Floor: Two World Trade.

PAPD Officer Greg Brady: Two World Trade.

Male Caller, 92nd Floor: Should we stay or should we not?

PAPD Officer Greg Brady: I would wait till further notice, we have . . . Building 1, they have people that can't get out of [*overlap*] floor.

Male Caller, 92nd Floor: Okay, all right [*overlap*]. Don't evacuate. [*Hangs up.*]

The doctrine—or reflex—of telling people to stay put during evacuations was not universally applied. Seated next to Officer Brady was another policeman, Officer Steve Maggett, who was receiving calls at the same moment. His advice was entirely different.

PAPD Officer Steve Maggett: Port Authority Police, Officer Maggett.

Female Caller, 2 WTC: Yes, I'm in 2 World Trade, what's going on?

PAPD Officer Steve Maggett: Uh, there was some kind of either accident or explosion in Building 1. Everybody get out.

Female Caller, 2 WTC: It's . . . shall we take the elevator?

PAPD Officer Steve Maggett: Everybody . . . no, try to take the stairs if you can, just in case.

Female Caller, 2 WTC: Okay.

Meanwhile, Officer Brady continued to receive calls from the south tower and advised the tenants to stay put.

> *PAPD Officer Greg Brady:* Port Authority Police, World Trade Center, Officer Brady.
>
> *Male Caller, 87th Floor:* Yes, we're trying to figure . . . we are up on the 87th floor. We're trying to figure out what's going on.
>
> *PAPD Officer Greg Brady:* One World Trade or—
>
> *Male Caller, 87th Floor:* Two.
>
> *PAPD Officer Greg Brady:* Two. Just stand by, there's no cond— . . . the incident happened at 1 World Trade Center. And we have the . . . that's the first . . . the first incident, the first emergency, as far as rescue. Just stand by.
>
> *Male Caller, 87th Floor:* Okay, thank you.
>
> *PAPD Officer Greg Brady:* Okay, thank you.

Around the same time, Officer Maggett received another call from the south tower—in this case, from Morgan Stanley, which had several thousand employees based at the trade center, though not all of them were on the scene.

> *PAPD Officer Steve Maggett:* Port Authority Police, Officer Maggett.
>
> *Al Roxo, Morgan Stanley:* Yeah, this is Al Roxo, Securities Department, from Morgan Stanley.
>
> *PAPD Officer Steve Maggett:* Uh-huh?
>
> *Al Roxo, Morgan Stanley:* Uh, what's the status right now as far as [*overlap*]?
>
> *PAPD Officer Steve Maggett:* We're still checking. Everybody just get out of the building, right now.
>
> *Al Roxo, Morgan Stanley:* All right. Have you guys announced an evacuation of two?
>
> *PAPD Officer Steve Maggett:* We are trying to do that right now.
>
> *Al Roxo, Morgan Stanley:* All right, thank you.

PAPD Officer Steve Maggett: All right? We are just advising
everybody to get out of the building.
Al Roxo, Morgan Stanley: All right, thank you, bye-bye.

The instruction to the caller from Morgan Stanley was especially
important. Morgan Stanley occupied twenty-two floors in the south
tower, and over 2,000 people worked for the company. An executive
for the bank, Ed Ciffone, had overseen years of intense evacuation
programs, and one of his deputies, Rick Rescorla, had led the drills
with a zeal that seemed near-evangelical, certainly on the eccentric
side. Now it made sense. Their wardens pulled out megaphones
and began to drive the Morgan staff out of the building.

Telephone calls were hardly the best way to provide guidance to
large numbers of people, however. Around 8:55, nine minutes after
Flight 11 had struck the north tower, the strobe lights flashed in
the south tower, and the wall siren gave a few whoops. On the
84th floor, Brian Clark, an executive with Euro Brokers who also
served as a fire warden, heard a familiar voice over the public-
address system.

> Your attention please, ladies and gentlemen. Building 2 is
> secure. There is no need to evacuate Building 2. If you are in
> the midst of evacuation, you may use the reentry doors and
> the elevators to return to your office. Repeat, Building 2 is
> secure.

The announcement was most likely made by Phil Hayes, the
retired city firefighter who worked at the trade center as a deputy
fire-safety director, and who was manning the control station in the
south tower. At 8:49, three minutes after the attack, he had been
recorded on a phone call to the north tower saying that he was going
to await orders before giving any instructions to the tenants of the
south tower. The reasons he ended up making the announcement a
few minutes later can only be guessed: the policy at the trade center,
and of the Fire Department, was to reserve the stairs and lobbies for
people who were in immediate danger, or for the rescuers who were
going to provide help. Under prevailing theories about the modern,

"fireproof" building, the tenants on other floors were in no danger, and did not need to leave. At this moment, no floors in the south tower were on fire. Moreover, people and flaming metal were dropping onto the plaza between the two towers, a common exit point, and the crisis appeared to be confined to the north tower.

The people at the fire-command desk in the south tower lobby had no view whatsoever of the fire that raged in the north tower. They could not look directly into the gaping holes of the north tower, as tenants on the upper floor of the south tower could; they did not see people step up to the windows in the north tower and jump, some holding hands; the papers on their desks were not singed, as they were in offices on the 98th floor. And even after the crash, the air-traffic controllers at La Guardia Airport in Queens did not know about the hijacking of Flight 11, or that three other planes had been seized by terrorists, or that one of them was flying toward New York—much less Phil Hayes in the lobby of the south tower, who was trying to keep people out of harm's way.

At the 55th floor, Stephen Miller hit a logjam in the stairs of the south tower. Until then, despite his stiff new shoes, he had made reasonable progress in his departure from the 80th-floor offices of Mizuho. Now the crowds joining the exodus from the lower floors fell in ahead of them. The delay gnawed at him, so he stepped out of the stairway. He would call home. He would use the men's room. Then he heard the announcement: There was no danger to tower two. The problem is localized in tower one. You can return to your desks.

Some of the people who had gotten out of the stairwell with him headed for the elevators. Keiji Takahashi, the boss who had swept him out of the office, was at the elevator bank. Miller boarded a different elevator, but felt uneasy. He had a muscular skepticism about most official pronouncements, a trait he felt had been cultivated by having grown up during the Watergate political scandals in the early 1970s. He didn't buy into a lot that came over public-address systems.

Something about staying in this elevator headed back up to the

78th floor did not sit well with Miller. He saw a friend from the office, told her that he was afraid. As more people boarded the elevator, the space seemed to shrink. He was sweating. He couldn't stay on. He jumped off. Keiji and three other bosses went up, although not on that elevator.

Then he went off in search of a phone. While he was hunting around the floor, he could hear the people at the windows. "Oh, my God, no—they're jumping."

As Miller was scouting the 55th floor, another of his colleagues from the 80th floor, Michael Otten, had already gotten down to 44, where he heard something about an airplane having hit the north tower. The announcement suggested that people could go to the cafeteria or return to their desks. Like Otten and Miller, many of the people from the upper floors who had gotten down quickly were driven more by the orders of their bosses and fear of what they didn't know than by any frightful thing they had seen. Before he had left his desk, Otten had seen the ugly gaping hole in one side of the other tower and had figured it was some kind of explosion. Now he was hearing it had been a plane crash. He assumed it was a twin engine, maybe a Cessna. The problem was taking a shape, still disturbing, but less fearsome. Now the public-address system was broadcasting that there was no problem in this tower, so Michael Otten turned back for the 80th floor.

He was delayed. The elevator doors would not shut. Otten eyeballed a man with a backpack who had pushed onto the elevator. Like people in elevators everywhere, he stared blankly ahead, waiting to reclaim his interrupted day.

In the minutes just after Flight 11 struck the north tower, a vortex had formed in the south tower, not from any precise understanding of what had happened across the plaza, but from the power of sounds and memories and sights. The voices of people like Eric Eisenberg in the offices of Aon on the 98th floor, who boomed orders to get out; the recollection of the 1993 attack; the sight of people leaping or falling from the north tower—all these forces wrenched thousands of people from their routines. Along the upper floors, they were drawn as if in a funnel toward the 78th and 44th floors—the points of embarkation, where express elevators dropped passengers in sky lobbies.

That they came to those particular spots owed to a paradox in the construction of skyscrapers. The taller the building, the more elevators are needed to move people to the higher floors in a reasonable amount of time. Adding more elevators—with shafts, machine rooms, lobby areas—meant subtracting rentable space. The arithmetic was inescapable: as buildings rose higher, the elevator infrastructure needed to support the height actually squeezed out profitable space. When the trade center was being designed, a solution was borrowed from another New York institution, one that had decades of experience in moving large numbers of people across distances near and far—the subways. The New York underground system used two tracks, one for express trains, the other for locals, to cover longer- and shorter-haul trips. Each tower was divided into three zones: up to the 44th floor; up to the 78th; and up to the 110th. Banks of express elevators, with each car able to hold fifty-five people, ran directly to the staging points on 44 and 78. There, the passengers could catch shuttle elevators to the intermediate floors. A single passenger car in each building ran all the way from the bottom to the top, serving the restaurant in the north tower and the observatory in the south; in addition, a freight elevator also had a clear run from the ground to the top.

In all, each tower had ninety-nine elevators, all of them built and installed by Otis Elevators, the company that made the modern skyscraper into a practical reality. The project manager for Otis during the construction was a man named Harry Friedenreich. On the morning of September 11, as Friedenreich was watching reports of the airplane crash on the *Today* show, his daughter, Alayne Gentul, was on the 90th floor of the south tower, herding people down to the 78th-floor express elevators. She was among the forces that began driving people out of their offices at Fiduciary Trust as soon as the plane hit the north tower, the vortex of instinct and duty that dragged people toward the exit.

It was Gentul's voice, in fact, that lodged in the head of Elnora Hutton, a Fiduciary employee who worked for her on the 90th floor. Shortly after the impact in the other building, Gentul ended a debate on the prudence of waiting for clear instructions. "Nora, let everyone go downstairs very quietly," Gentul said. Hutton counted about ten people who went down to 78 and immediately got on the elevators built by Gentul's father.

Ed Emery, another of the voices shepherding Fiduciary Trust employees out of their offices on the 90th floor, reached the 78th floor with Anne Foodim. Along the way, Foodim had tired—she had just finished a chemotherapy series for cancer, and was about to start radiation—but Emery, her boss, nudged her along. "If you can finish chemo, then you can get down those steps," Emery said. The week before, he had given Foodim a book on tranquility to soothe the rough patches of her cancer treatment. Stephanie Koskuba, another colleague, was passing her cell phone around. Emery tapped Koskuba on the shoulder and asked to borrow the phone, drifting toward a window to make his call.

The crowd in the sky lobby continued to grow. Some were intent on leaving; others wanted to touch base with the desk that had been set up there as a combination concierge, security, and satellite command post. Around 8:55, a member of the sky lobby security staff made a local announcement—he just raised his voice, not using the PA system—advising the crowd that the fire was in the other building, and that this tower was secure. If they wanted, they could go down.

The Fiduciary group huddled. Anne Foodim was afraid to get on the elevator. Elsie Castellanos, who had gone through the 1993 bombing, was shattered; Emery rubbed her shoulder, told her it would be all right. Were they staying, or should they go? The Fiduciary group looked to Emery.

"Go on down," Emery declared. "Go home. Everything's going to be fine. I'll see you tomorrow." They squeezed into a car, the five women from Fiduciary the last to board. Stephanie Koskuba turned to look for Emery, but could not see him. He must have been hidden in the crowded car, she would remember thinking. In fact,

Emery had not gotten on. He had already headed back upstairs to Fiduciary's office on the 90th floor, where he would meet up with Alayne Gentul. They agreed to check on the technology consultants who had come from California for disaster backup preparations and who were working on the 97th floor.

For some coming from the highest floors in the south tower, the long descent to 78 drained the moment of its urgent steam. Scores of people waited for elevators in moods and mind-sets that ran from terrified to annoyed. Dreadful as the big fire next door was, did it really make sense to shut down the entire south tower? With the announcements that all was well in their building, the human tides now ran in contrary directions. It became harder to know what was the right thing to do. Marissa Panigrosso and Sarah Dechalus, who had been shooed out of the Aon offices on 98 when Eric Eisenberg started rounding up people, walked down the twenty flights to the 78th floor. They met a colleague, Mary Jo Arrowsmith, who was crying. Panigrosso took her hand. She also met Tamitha Freeman, another Aon employee, the mother of a toddler, who had just returned from a trip to North Carolina.

Dechalus considered going upstairs to get her bag. She saw people turning back, but the truth was, you never could run right in or out. She pondered for a couple of minutes, then got on the elevator going down. Freeman, however, was bothered about her own bag.

"Forget it, you don't need it," Panigrosso said.

"My baby's pictures are in it," Freeman insisted. She turned back upstairs.

Panigrosso, with Arrowsmith in tow, kept going. Her elevator, which could hold fifty-five people, was half-empty. It was not yet 9:00.

On the ground, the entire emergency operation was being run from the lobby of the north tower, and the question of evacuating the south tower had stayed well in the background of what seemed like more pressing issues: locating the floors in the north tower that were on fire. Mustering the firefighters. Wrangling elevators.

As 9:00 approached, the ranking Port Authority police officers on the scene decided to empty the buildings. It was, after all, their complex—the trade center was a Port Authority property, meaning it was patrolled by the Port Authority's independent police agency, whose members responded to thefts, injuries, fires, all species of crisis large and small, almost always more quickly than the city emergency responders could get there. By plan, the PAPD checked out every report of fire; its officers were trained in at least rudimentary firefighting. In fact, one of the first people into the north tower had been Sgt. Al DeVona, who within three minutes of the plane's impact had ordered the building evacuated. DeVona had also relayed the calls to the Port Authority police from Windows on the World to the Fire Department's first chief on the scene, Joe Pfeifer.

At 8:59, thirteen minutes after Flight 11 struck, DeVona issued another order. "As soon as we are able, I want to start the building evacuation, Building 1 and Building 2, until we find out what caused it," DeVona said. As Pfeifer and the other fire chiefs were trying to size up the situation, Capt. Anthony Whitaker, the commander of the Port Authority police assigned to the trade center, had already done a quick survey of the complex. When Flight 11 hit, he had been standing in front of a Banana Republic store in the enclosed shopping mall and concourse beneath the two towers, a spot he occupied four mornings a week and where thousands of people exiting the subways could see him. Whitaker had been stunned by a fireball that ran down an elevator shaft in the north tower. He made his way to Liberty Street at the south end of the complex, which allowed him to see the damage in the north tower. A moment after DeVona issued his order to evacuate both buildings, Whitaker radioed the same instruction to DeVona: "I want to start a building evacuation, Building 1 and Building 2. [*Overlap/inaudible.*] I want you to report this."

In telling DeVona to "report this," Whitaker was giving yet another instruction, but also making a declaration. "Reporting" it meant that DeVona would enter the captain's order into the log of the day's events, so that it would be clear who had shut down the World Trade Center. Whitaker would take the weight for declaring a complete evacuation. He was closing not only the two towers, with 14,000 people already at their daily business, but also the five other buildings throughout the sixteen-acre complex—the mercantile exchange, offices of major investment banking concerns and government agencies, including the FBI, the Secret Service, and the CIA. The consequences of such a decision would surely rattle through the highest levels of government and of the American free-market system. A few hours after the 1993 attack had left the towers without power and forced all the businesses out, Charles Maikish, then the director of the trade center, heard, loud and clear, from an executive at Cantor Fitzgerald. The firm had a $5 billion bond trade that had not been entered onto its books when the bomb went off. Was Maikish prepared to take responsibility for the consequences of disrupting the debt market for the United States of America? Then someone from the White House called Maikish's boss at the Port Authority, just to make sure that he got the plain-English meaning of what they were saying. Another caller reminded him that the commodities market urgently needed to reopen—otherwise the price of oil globally would be subject to dangerous fluctuation. One of the lower-tier reasons for the "defend in place" strategy, according to the National Fire Protection Agency, was to avoid disruption to businesses. Closing the trade center was not something anyone would dare order casually, as Maikish had discovered in 1993.

Then, as now, though, there could be no argument as to the necessity of the evacuation order. The gash in the north tower, the smoke belching from the building, the people falling from impossible heights, all showed that this was a crisis new to every eye that saw it. Whitaker's order became part of the record, but its effect was uncertain, and it was never clear if his instruction was transmitted to any tenants. The authority to order an evacuation during a fire normally rests with the Fire Department, acting through the building's fire-safety directors. Around the time that Whitaker issued his order, the fire-safety director for the trade center, Michael Hurley, caught the attention of Chief Pfeifer.

"Do you want me to evacuate the whole place?" Hurley asked.

"Yeah," Pfeifer said. "Everyone goes."

6

"Get away from the door!"

9:01 A.M.
NORTH TOWER

The fuel on Flight 11, some 10,000 gallons, had ignited into giant fireballs, the biggest with a girth of 200 feet, wider than the building itself. The jet fuel probably was spent within a few minutes, much of it outside the building, but also traveling through the tower via the elevator shafts. The calamity was only beginning to ripen.

In the north tower, close to 1,000 people had survived the impact on the uppermost floors but were marooned in a distant sky without stairs or elevators. The structural engineers of the trade center had anticipated that the towers would be able to respond to the stress of an impact from the airplane. No one had designs, however, for the people inside. A strict border had formed between survival and entrapment.

Of all the people on the border territory in the north tower—the floors nearest but below the impact zone on the 93rd through 99th floors—none had been in the trade center longer than Raffaele Cava, the old man with the hat, for whom Tirsa Moya and Dianne DeFontes had such fondness. At eighty years old, he had passed lengths of his life in Egypt as the son of a Jewish Italian civil servant, in Milan as a printer, and now in a tiny office on the 89th floor of the north tower, working for his nephew's shipping company, Mutual International Forwarding. He arrived every morning at 6:30, after a plodding ride across New York Harbor on the Staten Island ferry. His nephew had moved the company into the north tower of the trade center in 1971, two years before the tower was officially opened, and before the upper floors were ready for occupancy. Now Raffaele Cava was in the territory just below where the plane had struck, picking himself off the ground, surveying the blown-out windows, and collecting his briefcase. He fixed his hat on his head and walked out. A few doors away, Dianne DeFontes was hoisting herself to her feet in the office of Drinker Biddle & Reath. Across the 89th floor were twenty-five other people, scattered in small numbers in the offices of a brokerage called Cosmos Insurance, a public-relations company, another law firm, and MetLife insurance.

Above and below Raffaele Cava and the tenants of the 89th floor in this borderland, the demands on people of all ages were to make sense of places that once had been so familiar that they had long ago stopped looking at them. The hallways where they walked to the restrooms. The windows they glanced through to see the weather below. Even the lobbies for the elevators. All of these were now utterly changed. Damian Meehan, a half century younger than Cava, was on the 92nd floor at Carr Futures; his whole work life was set among friends he knew from the streets of northern Manhattan, and the playing fields of Gaelic football, and who had come to work at the trade center. He could not get through the front door of his office now.

The people on the 91st floor had all been able to go directly to a staircase. One floor down, on 90, Anne Prosser had crawled from the elevator, which had just opened when the plane hit, to her office at Clearstream Banking. She had graduated in 1994 from Penn State with a degree in international studies and French and was due to get married in a month. The smoke was so thick that she dared not raise her head. In her office, about ten other people had arrived.

In the encapsulated existence of the modern office tower, few of these people knew anyone outside their own offices, even though they may have been riding a quarter mile every day in the same elevators. Yet everyone on the 88th floor knew Frank De Martini, the manager of construction in the trade center. Part of the reason was that a single organization, the Port Authority, occupied the entire 88th floor. More, though, because De Martini had a gift for arguing with the universe. If someone dropped a napkin on the sidewalk, he would break every law of New York nature and point out the nearest trash can to the person—"Excuse me? Excuse me! Did you know you dropped that? And that there's a can right there?"—unafraid of confronting a potential madman. He once chased down an armed mugger. And then there was the time firemen had gone to a house fire in Brooklyn, and radioed down: "There's some crazy guy on the roof next door who won't let us up." It was De Martini, protecting his lovingly restored brownstone from the risk of a less-than-fastidious firefighting effort in the adjacent building. He thrived in chaos, a trait his Swiss-born wife, Nicole, attributed to his being reared in a family of five children. In the weeks before September 11, the Port Authority staff on the 88th floor had been roiled over the lease of the entire trade center to the private developer Larry Silverstein. What would become of their jobs, making sure that the building was kept up? Did they have to turn over all their work to the Silverstein people? Who would go with Silverstein, what about their government pensions and benefits, could they find a new niche in the Port Authority's empire? One afternoon that summer, at the height of the anxiety, the children of two colleagues visited the 88th floor and wound up napping on the couch in De Martini's office. Their peace inspired him to write to his colleagues, urging them to keep their cool—in a way, another of his arguments with the universe.

> Guys, we have done and are doing a great job. Keep it up. Do not let rumors get you down. They are just rumors.
>
> Alan is trying to resolve the Code Compliance office issue. Not knowing is difficult but it should not stop us from doing our jobs. We have a lot to be proud of.
>
> Earlier this week tempers flared with several people. Don't feel badly about that. We are all human and this is a

stressful time. There is no getting around it. Redouble your efforts at patience. With yourself and your colleagues.

A prayer or a moment of silence for Jennifer's mother and our thoughts & prayers for Tom's wife's recovery.

Yesterday, Jennifer and Abdel's daughters took a nap on the couch in my office. There, in front of me, lay the hopes of humanity. Don't let this net lease keep us from seeing a much, much bigger and more important picture.

—Frank

Now, a few seconds after the plane's impact, Elaine Duch, a member of the Port Authority staff, wandered the 88th floor, dazed, charred, her clothes nearly burnt off her. She had been getting off the elevator when the fireball of fuel blew through the shaft, the flames shooting out of any opening to gulp oxygen. The ceilings had collapsed in the hallways. Out of their offices and cubicles, men and women were swarming. Where the elevators had been were now gaping holes. At least two of the three stairways were either in flames or filled with smoke. Who was in charge of salvaging them from this roaring hell?

De Martini emerged from his office with Nicole. Flames were shooting along one wall. He led the rattled, the shocked, and the frightened toward an office in the southwest corner, the farthest point from the impact, though no one realized yet that an airplane had hit the building. The suspicion that it was a bomb rose when a few people remembered the man who had just wheeled cartons of documents to the real estate department, the details of the leasing arrangement that bedeviled so many of the Port Authority employees. Whatever the cause, the result was chaos. De Martini was calm as a rock.

"Who needs medical help?" he called out.

One woman, his secretary, Judith Reese, had severe asthma. A colleague, Jeff Gertler, went to help her. A few others stood with Elaine Duch, who was still smoldering and in shock. De Martini had a walkie-talkie. At 8:54, about eight minutes after the explosion, this exchange was taped, though the speakers were not identified.

Male: Uh, we're on the 88th floor. We're kind of trapped up
   here and the smoke is, uh, is—
Male: What's your location?
Male: The 88th floor.
Male: Eighty-eighth floor, A tower?
Male: Seven-seven [the code for the dispatcher], we also
   have a person that needs medical attention immediately.
Male: What's the location?
Male: Eighty-eighth floor, badly burned.
Male: Eighty-eight?
Male: Tower A, south [side of] the 88th floor.
Male: Eighty-eighth floor, A tower, copy that.

For a moment or two, some people discussed waiting for help to
come, invoking the refrain being heard in many offices across the
two towers: the stairways had gotten so smoky in 1993, staying on
the floors actually was a smarter move. De Martini and one of his
managers, Mak Hanna, began to scout for an exit. During their
search of the floor, they spotted the flames and smoke. There was
no question now of waiting. When they got back to the southwest
corner office, De Martini's eyes were red; his hair and his eyelashes
were covered with soot. "Okay, I found a stairway," he said. Of the
three stairways in the building, stairway C, the one farthest south,
seemed to be the best route, although to get to it, people would have
to climb over a foot or more of broken walls and ceilings that had
dropped onto the floor. Hanna and two others—Frank Varriano and
Pablo Ortiz—were sent ahead to try to move some of the debris.

"If anyone needs medical attention, or suffers from asthma, they
should go first," De Martini announced.

Judith Reese, accompanied by Jeff Gertler, moved first, to get
her quickly away from the advancing smoke. They were followed
by Elaine Duch, escorted by another Port Authority colleague,
Dorene Smith. Someone had given Elaine a sweater because her
clothes had been burnt. Gerry Gaeta ran down a flight of stairs to
look over the condition of stairway C, as De Martini was worried

that the source of the explosion had been a nearby mechanical room. The stairway below was fine, Gaeta yelled back.

Anita Serpe, an administrative assistant, walked toward the stairs. De Martini squeezed her shoulder. They were going to be fine. Nicole De Martini also headed down, with her husband promising that he would be right behind her. Between twenty-five and forty people had found their way to what seemed the only passable stairwell.

Then Frank De Martini, Mak Hanna, Pablo Ortiz, and Frank Varriano swept across the floor to make sure everyone was out of the Port Authority office. Near the end of the line was Moe Lipson, eighty-nine years old, a member of an inspection team that certified renovation projects done by tenants of the building. That morning, the group was due to make the final checks of a big retail clothing store in the concourse being opened by Thomas Pink, and Lipson would check out the electrical work. The construction team sent Lipson down the stairs and grabbed hard hats. De Martini borrowed Hanna's walkie-talkie. Ortiz had a crowbar.

As they stepped into the stairway, they could hear pounding from above.

One floor up, on 89, the doors were jammed or unreachable. The occupants of that floor could not climb over rubble and get out the way their counterparts on 88 had. Raffaele Cava had been led into the lawyer's office down the hall and sat on a chair with his hat in his lap. Dianne DeFontes watched in slight amazement as most of the people from MetLife migrated into her space. In the office of Cosmos Insurance, another group formed. Walter Pilipiak, the company's president, opened the office door to stuff his jacket underneath, and the sudden shaft of light fell into the dark, smoky hallway. There, Lynn Simpson had been trying to find somewhere to go, away from the office of her public-relations firm, where the conference table had burst into flames after the plane hit. She followed the dash of light from Pilipiak's office, then led her staff toward it. No one seemed to know one another. Everyone began making calls, both there and in the law office, where DeFontes, alone a moment earlier, now had more than a dozen people with her. Stephanie Manning from MetLife hung up the phone and reported: "They're aware of the situation."

"Situation? What *situation?*" retorted Rob Sibarium, the president of MetLife's branch in the trade center. With more phone calls, word of the crash filtered through the room from friends and family members who were watching television. Someone switched on the radio, and a disk jockey was making jokes about how drunk the pilot must have been to crash into the trade center.

Rick Bryan, a lawyer who worked for MetLife, and others, had gone outside to investigate escape routes. They found that of the three stairways, the two closer to the north side were all but impossible to get to. The floor itself felt as if it were melting and buckling. The stairway door nearest them was wedged tightly into the frame.

"Do you have a fire extinguisher?" Bryan asked DeFontes, and she found one in the office. He took it out to the cavity where the elevator shafts had been. Ridiculous, he thought. He was sprinkling a few drops into an ocean of flame. A group of the men began throwing their shoulders and all their strength at the jammed stairway door, but had no luck. A few pounded on it, frustrated.

Back in Drinker Biddle & Reath's office, Bryan stood with his fire extinguisher, explaining that it was useless. The smoke was advancing; more and more of the floor was burning.

"We've got to get out of here," Sibarium said.

"Well, do you have any other bright ideas?" Bryan asked.

People began to make phone calls home, this time to say that the situation was desperate, and to bring up matters that had been left unsaid, or to affirm what was already part of their lives. Bryan called his father. DeFontes called her boyfriend, but couldn't reach him; then she called a girlfriend, to say she loved her and her child.

The men and women of the 89th floor had taken the small, protective steps of sensible people in smoke. They had moistened clothing to use as a filter, called for help, stuck jackets into the crevices at the bottom of office doors. Breathing through damp paper towels, men and women banged on the metal stairway door, but the act had an air of futility. Nathan Goldwasser from MetLife stood in the hallway, wondering if the world was unraveling. Suddenly, a muffled voice called out: "Get away from the door!"

A moment later, the claw tooth of a crowbar burst through the drywall, tearing around the frame. Pablo Ortiz pushed the door open. Behind him, in the stairs, were Frank De Martini and Mak Hanna. Ortiz walked to the law office and told Raffaele Cava and the other people there to move quickly to the stairs. Then he opened the door to the offices of Cosmos Insurance, where Tirsa Moya, Walter Pilipiak, and the others were huddled.

"Let's go," Ortiz announced.

As Walter Pilipiak entered the stairwell, De Martini and Ortiz were behind him. He thought he saw them continue up the stairs.

Having crawled away from the 90th-floor elevators just after the plane's impact, Anne Prosser had gotten to her office and called her mother, Vi, in Nashville. One of her knees had been burned. Her mother heard a determined voice. "I'm okay," she said. "We can't get out. We're all right. We're going to get out. I'll call you."

The group in the office made calls but could not figure a way to escape. After twenty-five minutes, a flashlight bobbed into the room. Help had arrived and almost certainly it was Ortiz and De Martini; any official rescue parties were still mustering in the lobby. With the path to the stairway now clearly marked by the man with the flashlight, Prosser made her way to the exit and started down.

On the 86th floor, Louis Lesce had been preparing to give a career-change seminar to a group of Port Authority employees when the plane hit. He had made such a fuss about punctuality that he had set his own watch ten minutes fast. Now Lesce and the early arrivals felt the conditions in the hall were too unsafe to navigate. They would wait for a rescue, but the smoke was making breathing unpleasant, so they decided to break a window, not in the room where they had gathered, but in the next one. By their thinking, if the fresh air were to draw fire, at least it would not be into their haven. The plan worked. The gusts were so powerful that they lifted paper off Lesce's desk in the next room, so high that he was practically able to read a résumé that had been on top of the pile. Lesce called home, as did the others. These were conversations meant to last. Then they looked up. A man in a hard hat appeared in the doorway, a Port Authority worker. He led them toward the stairs. Almost certainly, it was one of Frank De Martini's crew.

That the people in Louis Lesce's office expected a rescue was a most unwarranted assumption for someone on the 86th floor in a building ablaze and with no working elevators. It was hardly the job of Frank De Martini and Pablo Ortiz and the others from 88 to go around prying open doors. Their responsibilities at the trade center during an emergency were to get themselves out of the building. The sprinklers, the fireproofing, the smoke venting systems were all supposed to kick in automatically. This network of emergency systems succumbed, one by one, on September 11, replaced by a lethal web of obstacles. Only when people like De Martini and his crew took it upon themselves to attack those barriers—broken rubble, stuck doors, disorientation—could people go free.

Above the 91st floor, the stairways were plugged solid, the collapsed drywall forming an impermeable membrane, a border line that could not be crossed, even for people on the 92nd and 93rd floors, most of which had not been touched by the plane impact. And below 92, across all or parts of ten floors, dozens of people had been unable to open doors, or walk through burning corridors to the stairs and find their way past the rubble. Then help appeared. With crowbar, flashlight, hardhat, and big mouths, De Martini and Ortiz and their colleagues had pushed back the boundary line between life and death.

7

"If the conditions warrant on your floor, you may wish to start an orderly evacuation."

9:02 A.M.
SOUTH TOWER

From the office of Aon Insurance on the 98th floor of the south tower, Sean Rooney made a second call to his wife. The first time he called, at 8:59, was to tell her about the early moments of the crisis in the other building. Once again, he reached her voice mail. This time, as he spoke, an announcement could be heard in the background. The instructions from the lobby fire desk were changing. Twelve minutes earlier, at 8:50, the people from Mizuho/Fuji were told to go back to their office. Now a different message was being broadcast.

> *Rooney:* Yeah, honey, this is Sean again.
> *P.A. Voice: May I have your attention, please.*
> *Rooney:* Uh, looks like we'll be—
> *P.A. Voice: Repeating this message:*
> *Rooney:*—in this tower for a while. Um, it's—
> *P.A. Voice: The situation occurred in building one. If the—*
> *Rooney:* It's, it's secure here.

*P.A. Voice:—conditions warrant on your floor, you may wish
to start an orderly evacuation.*
Rooney: I'll talk to you later. Bye.

Scott Johnson, an analyst at Keefe, Bruyette & Woods, also was
on the phone when that announcement was made. It could be
heard in the background as he left a message on the answering
machine of his mother, Ann.

"Like I said, a different tower," Johnson said. "Uh, we don't know
too much info. We may be leaving the building. As of now, we're
not."

The announcer was starting to give an instruction about the exit
route, mentioning "the concourse at the base," as Scott signed off.

The time stamped on the calls from both Johnson and Rooney
was 9:02 A.M., sixteen minutes after the attack on the north tower.

The single-minded abandon of Michael Sheehan's departure—he
had blindly run down a colleague as he fled Garban ICAP's office on
the 55th floor of the south tower—should have carried him well
clear of the trade center by 9:02, but several developments managed to slow him down. In the stairs, someone had passed on a
report that a private plane had hit the other building, a disturbing
but not terrifying event, and a somewhat benign explanation for
the smoke he had seen. Then he heard fragments of the early
announcements assuring tenants that the south tower was all right.
Still, he was not impressed. When he came across a heavy woman
in the throes of panic at the 10th floor, Sheehan, no longer running
like a football halfback, walked down with her, the woman's anxiety
replacing his own. By the time other tenants were advised by the
lobby fire director that they could begin an orderly evacuation,
Sheehan and the woman had made their way out of the south end
of the tower, through an exit onto Liberty Street. In the riot of
papers and debris scattered by the first airplane strike, Sheehan
spotted a single sheet that looked interesting. He picked it up. It
was an itinerary for someone traveling to Los Angeles.

The realization slammed into his mind. That had not been the crash of a little Cessna.

"Oh, my God," Sheehan said. "It was a commercial plane." At that moment, he and the woman he had been helping heard the roar of yet another one.

At the south tower's 44th-floor sky lobby, Michael Otten waited for the elevator doors to close so he could get back up to his office on the 80th floor. They had all but closed when suddenly the electronic sensor read an obstruction, and the doors slid open. And then shut again—almost. And reopened again, in yet another maddening cycle. This is ridiculous, Otten thought, watching from the rear of the car. What's with this guy with the backpack? The guy had slipped into the elevator at the last moment, his back to the doors, unaware that his luggage was jutting into the light beam and holding everyone up. The people on the elevator were not panicked, just impatient. The morning had already been frazzled enough. Now some bozo with a backpack was holding them up. Otten began to lean over. A little verbal nudge had formed on his lips, and he was just about to launch it: *Hey, could you step in? It's your bag that's making the doors open.*

At the 78th-floor sky lobby, the tides crisscrossed and swirled, as some people were returning to their desks and others deciding to go ahead and leave. Between fifty and two hundred people waited at the elevator, a figure that shifted as elevators arrived and left. A big group from the New York State Department of Taxation and Finance had lingered on the 86th floor—several of them had once been docked a day's pay for leaving the office during a blackout, a traumatic memory for people living on civil-service salaries. Finally, many of them—particularly those with views that showed the raging fire in the north tower—decided to work their way down. At 9:02 they were on the 78th floor, waiting for the next express ride to the lobby.

Heading in the opposite direction were Donovan Cowan and Doris Torres from Fiduciary Trust, who felt encouraged by the announcements to go back up to their desks, call home, tell their folks they were okay. They stepped into a car at 78, and Cowan pushed the button for the 97th floor.

Silvion Ramsundar and Christine Sasser, both from the Mizuho/Fuji offices on 80, had come to the 78th floor, and as they waited for the express elevator to the street, were trying to call home on their cell phones, with no success.

Kelly Reyher, a lawyer with Aon, had walked down past the 78th floor, then climbed back up after hearing the announcements. About ten or twenty other people near him had done the same. He would ride up to the office, he decided, as did Donna Spera, who worked on the 100th floor, also for Aon. She was with five friends.

This assembly of people had heard three announcements since the explosion in the north tower, two encouraging them not to leave, one suggesting that they could leave if they wanted. Was this really all that serious? What about their purses and PalmPilots and briefcases? How long would they be out of the building? Judy Wein and Gigi Singer of Aon discussed going back to get their things from the 103rd floor. If they were leaving, Wein realized, she would need her pocketbook. How else would she get home? Howard Kestenbaum, another Aon colleague, told her to forget about it, that he would give her the carfare. "Let's just go," Kestenbaum said.

In the swarms outside the elevator doors, a number of people mentioned their eagerness to report home and check in on kids or spouses, suggesting that this entitled them to a spot on crowded elevators. One elevator was packed so tightly that Karen Hagerty, another Aon employee, had to step back, squeezed out of a spot.

"I have a horse and two cats," Hagerty joked to her colleague Ed Nicholls.

By 9:02, the boomerang of alarm and assurance had driven Stanley Praimnath from the 81st floor to the lobby, then back again to his office. The phone was ringing as he returned, and he picked it up to hear the voice of a colleague from Chicago, urgently inquiring after his well-being.

"Are you okay?" the woman asked Praimnath.

"Yes, I'm fine," he assured her.

"Stan, are you watching the monitor—are you watching the news to see what is going on?" she asked.

"Yes," he assured her again. "I'm fine."

As he spoke, Praimnath spun his seat around so he was facing in the direction of the window, though he was not staring out. His window looked south over New York Harbor and the Statue of Liberty, the light trails of froth cut in the slate-colored water by the steady traffic of ships and tugs and ferries. From the corner of his eye, he glimpsed an unfamiliar shape on the horizon. Praimnath turned slightly, to look square out the window. An airplane. It was heading toward his office, toward his window, it seemed. He could see the red and blue marking and the letter *U* as it approached. He dived under his desk, screaming to God, as his colleague in Chicago listened on the phone and watched the television screen in horror.

In the length of a drawn breath, the ceiling collapsed. The time was 9:02:59 A.M., and United Airlines Flight 175 now plunged through the south tower of the World Trade Center, including the room where Stanley Praimnath had jumped beneath his desk. The plane had banked slightly at the last second, its wingspan running diagonally across nine floors, from 77 through 85. The Mizuho/Fuji office was at the center of it. Praimnath's room was torn to bits. Wires and cubicles and drywall slumped into a tangle at once sinister and silent. The wing of the jet was jammed into a door, twenty feet from where Praimnath, still alive, huddled beneath his desk.

Down on the 44th floor, before Michael Otten could spit out the first word of reproach to the man with the backpack who had delayed his elevator, the car shook in a death rattle, a mouse swinging in the jaws of a cat. The woman next to him was hurled to the ground. A blanket of dust dropped over everyone. The cab swayed back and forth, left to right. Otten hopped out and ran down the hall. Now the building itself was pitching from side to side. He

South Tower: The Impact

United Flight 175 also tipped its wings just before crashing into the south tower, but it hit at one of only two places in the tower where the stairs were not bunched in the center of the building. The stairwells were spread at that point so they could detour around elevator machinery that took up much of the floor space. The combination of spread stairs and the girth of the machinery that the plane plowed into meant that stairway A was left largely intact.

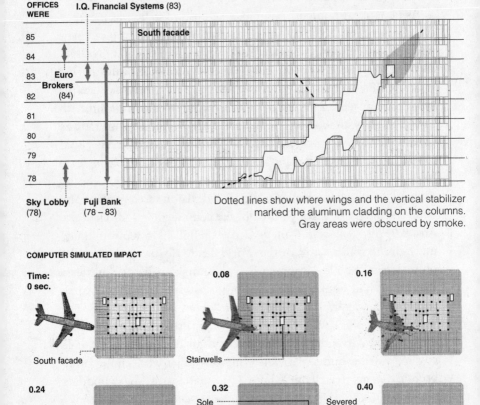

WHERE OFFICES WERE

Chuo Mitsui Trust and I.Q. Financial Systems (83)

85
84
83 — Euro Brokers
82 — (84)
81
80
79
78

South facade

Sky Lobby (78)

Fuji Bank (78 – 83)

Dotted lines show where wings and the vertical stabilizer marked the aluminum cladding on the columns. Gray areas were obscured by smoke.

COMPUTER SIMULATED IMPACT

Time: 0 sec.

South facade

0.08

Stairwells

0.16

0.24

Core columns

0.32

Sole surviving stairwell

0.40

Severed or significantly damaged columns

Damaged columns

Sources: National Institute of Standards and Technology; Weidlinger Associates

The New York Times

extended his arms for balance, like a surfer. Slowly, the building leaned back toward center. In the hallway were others from his office at Mizuho.

"I'm going to go," Otten said. "You guys want to come? Let's just go." In the gloom, they found a wall and followed the hallway to a door that opened onto the stairwell they had run down a few minutes earlier. It was filled with people. No one was going up.

Because the left wing of Flight 175 had tilted down, it had cut through the 77th, 78th, and 79th floors, grazing the 78th-floor sky lobby. The plane's speed was 545 miles per hour when it struck the building. Donovan Cowan, one finger poised at the button for his floor, was knocked from his feet. So was Doris Torres, his colleague from Fiduciary Trust. The heat burst across them in a ferocious, roasting wave that kept coming, ten or fifteen seconds of staggering intensity. The elevator car rocked so hard they could not get up. Finally, they got their balance. Doris said she couldn't feel her feet and couldn't walk, but she and Cowan stumbled into the sky lobby. Around them were the remains of people who had been breathing and thinking and chatting a few seconds earlier. Now they were flat on their back or torn apart, dead, or horrifically injured and alive. Inside one elevator, eighteen people were alive but sealed in.

Along the floor, at least another twenty people were alive. Of the Aon group, Judy Wein had several fractured ribs and a broken arm, but she could move. Howard Kestenbaum, who had just offered to pay her fare home, was motionless. Gigi Singer was battered but breathing, and able to move. Her colleague Richard Gabrielle was also alive, but had been partly buried by the ornamental marble torn from the walls.

The impact smacked Kelly Reyher in the back, shoving him into an elevator, and split the seams of the car. He could see fire roaring through the shaft. He considered just drawing deep breaths of the smoke, to kill himself before the flames got him, but then he saw through licks of fire in the car that the doors were still open an inch or so. He shoved a briefcase into the space, wedged it open, and climbed out. The ground was a foot deep in debris and bodies, some of them charred. Reyher crawled across them, shaking arms and legs to see if people were still alive.

The one living person he found was his colleague Donna Spera, burned and crawling along the ground, an arm broken, her face bleeding. She clutched Reyher. Another friend from Aon, Keating Crown, also found them. Crown had just happened to be walking from the south end of the building toward the north when the plane struck. The end of the building he had left was in tatters.

Ling Young, who worked in the state tax department, sat for what seemed like a long time in the rubble, then climbed to her feet. She and her coworker Sankara Velamuri pulled their colleagues Yeshavant Tembe and Dianne Gladstone out from the rubble; Tembe seemed to have badly hurt one of his kneecaps, and Gladstone had injured an ankle. Another person from the tax department, Diane Urban, was comforting a woman propped against a wall, her legs virtually amputated. A sixth colleague, Mary Jos, had been knocked cold. She then woke up with her back burning and rolled over to extinguish what felt like flames. When she did, she found herself moving over the remains of people who had been standing near her in the sky lobby.

After the impact, Christine Sasser of Mizuho, who had been trying to call home, thought her face was being burned by a wave of heat. The people who had been standing near her were now on the floor, dead. Her friend Silvion Ramsundar was behind her, banged around, but alive.

Ed Nicholls, thrown to the ground, saw a fire in the middle of the room; otherwise, the place was dark and afloat in dust and moans. His right arm from near his shoulder was nearly severed by some piece of the building or airplane that had turned into a missile. Bits of stone and cement had lodged in his abdomen. A window had broken open, and he stood there for a minute next to an older man, getting some air. Karen Hagerty, who had joked that she deserved a spot on the crowded elevator because her horse and two cats were waiting at home, was motionless on the ground. Nicholls saw his Aon colleague Gigi Singer, and they soon met up with Judy

Wein. Two other men pointed them toward a staircase. Wein, Nicholls, and Singer began their descent.

On Liberty Street, just outside the south tower, Michael Sheehan had been gazing at the airline itinerary that had drifted to earth when he heard the second plane roar directly overhead. He did not see it burst into the southern face of the south tower more than 900 feet above him, but he felt the rolling explosions. Sheehan clutched the woman he had just escorted down the bottom floors of the tower, and backed against the same wall the plane had just blown through. An overhang protected them from the river of catastrophe in the sky that now overran its banks. Shards of metal spilled toward the sidewalk, falling so far that they seemed to Sheehan to be floating, dropping at a speed far out of scale to the violence above. To go back inside the building now was unthinkable; to step away from it was to enter a space where the air itself was full of peril. Yet they could not remain where they were, pressed against the wall of the trade center. What would come next?

The first moment they sensed a lull in the debris storm, Sheehan and the woman ducked into a revolving door, back into the concourse. Then they made their way to the east and north.

On the 81st floor, where part of the wing was lodged in a doorway, Stanley Praimnath crawled the length of the floor, 131 feet, through the remains of the loan department, a lounge, the computer room, a telecommunications room. He pounded on walls. He called for help. Of the others who had come back upstairs with him from the lobby, the CEO and the president and the head of human resources, of all those who had dutifully evacuated and just as dutifully gone back upstairs, he neither saw nor heard another living soul. He called out onto a dark floor where no one else was alive to hear or help him.

"Help! Help!" screamed Praimnath. "I'm buried!"

In the 84th-floor office of Euro Brokers, Brian Clark had heard the bang. A moment later, a mighty thump, perhaps from an explosion or shock wave, perhaps fuel igniting somewhere. It was the thump, the second noise, that seemed to destroy the Euro Brokers space, blowing door frames out of walls, tearing lights and speakers from the ceiling, an explosion without fire. Parts of the raised floor buckled. At least fifty of the firm's traders, all in the southeast corner of the tower, most likely were killed at that moment: the plane had banked directly through their space.

Clark felt the building lean to the west, toward the Hudson River, the way it did in a high wind, but one that kept pushing, harder than any wind he had ever felt in the tower. He made a triangle of feet and hands to keep himself upright. The oscillations continued for four minutes, gradually ebbing. When the building first seemed to right itself, it went black. In his pocket, Clark had his fire warden flashlight, and he clicked it on. In its beam was trapped an infinity of dust, like a movie projector's lamp. With the small group nearby—Bobby Coll, Kevin York, Dave Vera, Ron DiFrancesco—he walked to a hallway that formed a crossroads. Clark turned left, toward stairway A.

They had gotten down about three flights when they ran into a heavyset woman and a slight man, on their way up. "Stop, stop," the woman said. "The floor below is all in flames and smoke. We've got to get above it."

An argument began. As each of the Euro Brokers workers chimed in, Clark shone the beam of his flashlight on that person. He did not take a position on which way they should go, but the vehemence of the woman retreating from the obstruction seemed to be holding sway. The group decided to help the woman go up, hands on her elbows and back, coaxing and soothing her. Both Bobby Coll and Kevin York had left the 84th floor when the first plane hit the other tower, but had come back upstairs when the announcement halted the spontaneous evacuation of the south tower. With them was Dave Vera, carrying a walkie-talkie.

At that moment, another sound came into the stairwell. A voice called out: "Help! Help! I'm buried! Is anybody there?"

Clark turned to DiFrancesco, put a hand on his shoulder. "Come on, Ron," Clark said. "We got to get this guy."

They struggled through the rubble of the Mizuho/Fuji office on 81. Against the pitch darkness, Clark played his flashlight, catching in wedges of light small clouds of suspended dust.

"Can you see my hand? Can you see my hand?" the voice called out. It was Stanley Praimnath. Clark and DiFrancesco were on one side of a wall of ruined doors, desks, and dropped ceilings. The dust was heavier than the smoke, it seemed to Clark. DiFrancesco held his backpack over his face and tried to breathe through it. Unable to get any decent air, DiFrancesco backed out of the floor, into the stairwell. He then decided to go up, to join the group escorting the heavyset woman.

Clark and Praimnath began to claw at the broken room that stood between them. Praimnath hit something and a nail went through his hand. He pounded it out by slamming his hand against a board. Then they ran out of things they could move, and Praimnath was still blockaded by rubble.

"You must jump," Clark said. "It's the only way. You've got to jump out of there."

On Praimnath's first effort, he did not reach Clark. He took another try. This time, Clark grabbed him and heaved him across the barrier, and they fell to the ground, hugging.

"I'm Brian," Clark said.

"I'm Stanley," Praimnath said.

They retreated to the stairs and began to head down.

Above them, Ron DiFrancesco had caught up with the group accompanying the heavyset woman. She was having more and more trouble breathing, so DiFrancesco gave his backpack to her. Maybe she could use the fabric to filter the air. Besides DiFrancesco, Coll, York, and the man who had come up the stairs with the woman, two other people from Euro Brokers, Michael Stabile and Brett Bailey, were also escorting her. Dave Vera, who had his walkie-talkie, was sending urgent requests for help to Jerry Banks, a colleague outside the building. They tried doors, hoping that the office floors would have air fresher than what they were breathing, but all the stairwell doors seemed to be locked. In the interests of security, the building code required only that every fourth floor be an unlocked reentry door. DiFrancesco could not open any of them. They met other people in the stairway, and the group swelled to about fifteen. DiFrancesco climbed ahead of them, getting as high as the 91st floor. Then he turned back.

A few floors down, he saw the people he had just left, sprawled on the landing. They had given all their strength over to the task of moving and were spent by it. DiFrancesco dropped down for a moment. The people around him seemed to be going to sleep. A bolt of panic shot through DiFrancesco. Would he see his wife and kids again? Confined to the stairs, unable to open a door, surrounded by people who were drifting away, he could not stay on that landing. He got up and decided to take his chances going down the stairs.

8

"You can't go this way."

Perhaps a minute or so ahead of Brian Clark in the stairs was Richard Fern, from Euro Brokers' computer room, who had just pushed a button inside an elevator on the 84th floor of the south tower at the instant of impact. Flung at the left wall, then the right, he landed on his hands and knees. Afraid that the doors would shut, he plunged out of the car, then scrambled to the door into the nearest stairway, a dark, smoky void. What drew his eye to the first step was the glowing line, a stripe of photo-luminescent paint that ran along the flight of stairs. He fixed his gaze on the lip of each step, defined by the glow-in-the-dark stripe, and started running. Now that he was in the stairs, nothing would slow him. Fern would navigate this line down the next 1,512 steps, give or take, that led from the 84th floor of the south tower to the lobby.

Steered by radiant paint, fueled by pure adrenaline, Fern had already survived a fistful of close calls. A few moments earlier, he had left his desk at Euro Brokers when the monitor screens flickered. He then went to the trading-desk area to look out the windows, where he saw the other building in flames, and men and women falling through the sky. Then he got onto the elevator, from which he had just escaped.

If there were lucky breaks to be had, Rich Fern caught every one of them. He had left the east side of the building shortly before the right wing of Flight 175 raked across Euro Brokers' trading desk, most likely killing everyone there instantly. He had gotten on an elevator a moment too late to be trapped in the shaft. And as he scrambled away from the elevator car, he turned to a door. It led to what turned out to be the only intact escape route in either of the two towers.

Just as Richard Fern was making his way down the south tower, James Gartenberg was talking on the phone in the north tower, explaining why he could not get off the 86th floor. Gartenberg worked for Julian Studley real estate, where he and a secretary for the company, Patricia Puma, were the only two people in suite 8617 that morning. They called friends and family, and those people began to dial 911, then news reporters, all to sound a broad alarm of their location. Gartenberg, thirty-five, was on his last day at work for the company. Puma, thirty-three, worked there just Mondays and Tuesdays, an arrangement that suited her life as a mother of three children. Puma spoke to a reporter for *The New York Times*, explaining that the elevators were gone and the stairs were lost to them as well. "It looked like the explosion came up through the elevator," she said. "It looks like the fire wall came down, and I believe the stairs are on the other side of it."

Gartenberg got on the phone. They had thought about climbing across the debris to reach the stairs, he said, but "more debris fell, so we backed off."

The door to another stairwell near them seemed to be blocked, and Gartenberg said that it must have been an automatic locking system activated during an emergency. Most likely, it was not—the exit doors could not be locked, even accidentally, because their cylinders had been turned to make that impossible, according to Michael Hurley, the fire-safety director for the trade center. What may have happened was that the door frame had been knocked out of alignment by the impact. "Tell the Fire Department I'm in 8617. I'm not the easiest guy to reach," Gartenberg said. "We need air."

As Richard Fern was beginning his escape from one burning building, James Gartenberg and Patricia Puma could do nothing but describe how they were trapped in another. The differences in their circumstances were not only a matter of luck, but also of design.

"The time and place to ensure life safety in high-rise buildings is during the period that the building is being designed," Chief John T. O'Hagan wrote in *High Rise/Fire & Life Safety*, his authoritative book on the dynamics of high-rise fire. As it happened, the World Trade Center was planned at a moment of radical transformation in the construction of tall buildings, and its owner, the Port Authority, availed itself of those changes in spectacular fashion. The new approaches made it possible for the Port Authority to build higher and cheaper, with the twin towers the first skyscrapers to use virtually no masonry in their construction. The changes of this era also allowed the Port Authority to turn far more of the towers over to rentable space—as opposed to safety and service functions, like stairways and elevators—than other skyscrapers. Some of those changes also made escape impossible for people on the upper floors after the attacks of September 11, 2001.

The trade center took its shape in the 1960s, first from the particular ambitions of the brothers David and Nelson Rockefeller, members of a family powerful in politics and finance, and then from the opportunities afforded by the historic shift in building construction practices. By the middle of the twentieth century, real estate values on the southern tip of Manhattan had dwindled, and the area had lost the vigor that carried it from New York's earliest days as a Dutch port. Chase Manhattan Bank opened a new downtown headquarters in 1960, a project led by David Rockefeller, the vice chairman of the bank. As part of his campaign to revive that part of the city, he gathered an alliance of businesses to plan a "world trade center" that, he hoped, would transform the area from a flagging, stagnant back-water to a vital mainstream. The job of building the trade center became the work of what was then known as the Port of New York Authority, an agency that had access to mighty rivers of cash—it operated many of the toll bridges and tunnels in the region—and was under the control of the governors of New York and New Jersey through a board of directors. Not coincidentally, the governor of New York then was Nelson Rockefeller, David's brother.

The first plans for the trade center did not call for construction of the world's tallest building, much less two of them. As originally conceived, the complex would have 5 million square feet of office space, spread across 13.5 acres on the east side of Manhattan near the Brooklyn Bridge. Then the Port Authority moved the site to 16 acres on the west side—closer to the Hudson and above a commuter rail terminal that served New Jersey, which, after all, controlled half the Port Authority. In the move, the project doubled in size, to 10 million square feet—an entire city's worth of office space. And not long after that, the Port Authority decided it would include the world's tallest building. No, make that two—the world's two tallest buildings.

During this dizzying, almost stupefying expansion of the plans, another drastic change was taking place, as vital to the Port Authority's building program as the political muscle of the governor and his banker brother. The New York City building code was being torn up. Ever since the city began writing codes for skyscrapers at the end of the nineteenth century, its requirements—typically, steel skeletons wrapped in masonry to resist fire—demanded the construction of dense, heavy buildings. Because the Port Authority was a public corporation, formed by a pact between New York and New Jersey, it did not have to comply with the local building laws. Even so, the Port Authority decided in May 1963 that the trade center would be built according to the city code that had been in effect since 1938. Had that code actually been used, it is likely that a very different world trade center would have been built. In fact, it is likely that no one at the Port Authority expected the old code to be law when the work actually began.

"You can't go this way."

In April 1962, a year before the Port Authority pledged itself to the 1938 code, Mayor Robert F. Wagner appointed the Brooklyn Polytechnic Institute to overhaul the code. The New York Building Congress, a trade organization of construction unions and real estate interests, paid $200,000 toward the costs of the revisions, for which it had long lobbied. The industry had argued for years that the 1938 code did not anticipate improvements in technology, particularly the availability of lightweight materials that, they believed, would serve just as well for many purposes as the much heavier masonry prescribed by the law. Another agenda, less spoken but just as important to the economics of building, was to reduce the amount of space demanded for escape-ways. If real estate in the tight confines of Manhattan Island had a soul, it certainly was vertical in shape; there simply was not enough land to spread out, only up. To turn over some of that precious floor space to outsize-seeming safety requirements surely was an imprudent and uneconomical regulation of business. The new code would quietly turn back some of that real estate lost to evacuation routes to the moneymaking side of the ledger.

The draft code was unveiled by city officials and the task force at a triumphant press conference in the summer of 1965. In an unabashed display of the power of the industry in writing the new document, the event was held in the offices of the Building Congress. Although that new code was still only in draft form, the executive director of the Port Authority, Austin J. Tobin, wasted no time. The World Trade Center design team would build to the standards demanded in the proposed code, he said. Indeed, articles and an editorial in *The New York Times* noted that the trade center was an example of precisely the innovative architecture and engineering envisioned by the new code. The reason the Port Authority turned to the new code for its big project was simple: it would make the trade center much cheaper to build.

"The projected world trade center is designed for use of materials and engineering principles which will be found in the proposed code," the city building commissioner, Harold Birns, explained in a speech to the New York Building Congress. "The fact that the Port

105

Authority of New York is not bound by the requirements of the present City Building Code makes possible the savings involved. Our existing building code does protect the public safety and welfare but it most certainly does not allow for all the efficiency and economy that industry and enterprise find necessary." As an example, he said the 1938 code specified wasteful amounts of fire-proofing, beyond what was needed for safety. "The proposed code more accurately evaluates the hazards and need for fire protection," he said. An article in the *Times* took note of the flexibility the new code would permit, citing the example of a fire-resistant wall. The old code demanded specific bricks and masonry; the new code would require only that the wall "must withstand flames for a stated number of hours. The wall can be made of brick, specially treated wood—or shredded wheat—so long as it can resist fire."

Although the article did not mention it, the new code significantly lowered the requirements for fire resistance in office buildings. The 1938 code had required that the columns of tall buildings be able to stand against fire for four hours; the new code reduced that to three hours. For the floors, the earlier code had demanded three hours of fire protection; the new code cut that to two hours. And while the old code had ordered concrete cladding or other masonry to provide fire resistance for the structural steel, the new code left that decision up to the owners. The cardinal sin of the old code, in the view of many in the real estate industry, was that it forced buildings to be far sturdier and heavier than needed. "Over-designing is the equivalent of cracking a walnut with a ten-pound weight rather than a nutcracker," said Frederick G. Frost, an architect who guided part of the code study. Office buildings, in particular, did not need so much fire resistance, he said; they had been stuck too long with the same burdens as far more hazardous places, like factories.

The outcome of the code revision was that tall structures were "softened," in the description of Vincent Dunn, an author and analyst of fire-safety practices, and a former chief in the New York Fire Department. In 1995, he wrote an article in *Fire Engineering* magazine that cataloged the hazards of high-rise fires, and the illusion of safety. "After fighting high-rise fires in midtown Manhattan, New York City, for the past ten years, it is my opinion that the fire service has been lucky," Dunn wrote. Chief Dunn and Chief O'Hagan noted that New York City abandoned the heavy, dense masonry that had defined the interiors of the old-style skyscrapers, epitomized by the Empire State Building, and had provided protection in fire. Now gypsum board and spray-on fireproofing would be used. Less weight meant that less steel would have to be used. The new code, which ultimately became law in 1968, made it cheaper to build taller buildings. These were changes that other cities across the country had already adopted. A new day was coming in New York, too. "The antiquated towers of commerce will fail," predicted Robert Low, chairman of the City Council's buildings committee and the council's official shepherd of the 1968 code. "And a new colossus, more pleasing to the eye, more pleasant to the ear, and more reflective of our dreams for the future will rise one day in their place."

Besides making high-rises cheaper to build, the new code also made them more profitable to own, because it increased the floor space available for rent. It did this by cutting back on the areas that had been devoted, under the earlier law, to evacuation and exit. Councilman Low pointed out that if the new code had been available for the design of one recent skyscraper, the Pan Am building in midtown, the owners would have had 2 percent more rentable space on each floor. That was worth about $1.8 million annually in 1968.

The previous generation of skyscrapers in New York was required to have at least one "fire tower"—a masonry-enclosed stairwell that was entered through a 107-square-foot vestibule. When people entered the vestibule, any smoke that trailed them would be captured and vented. Then to enter the stairway, they had to pass through a second doorway, so that they could flee down the stairs without bringing along trails of smoke. These reinforced stairwells were the residue of an age of mass catastrophes. In March 1911, about two miles from where the World Trade Center would be built, 146 people died in the Triangle Shirtwaist Factory fire. A locked exit door had trapped scores; a rickety fire escape collapsed, killing others. The image of young girls, leaping to their death from ninth-floor windows because they had no other way to escape the flame and smoke, was seared into the consciousness of that generation and the next. In January 1912, the Equitable Building—thought to be a "fireproof" structure—collapsed during a fire. Six people died. A few months later, the *Titanic* sank, with the lack of escape mechanisms once again the cause of mass death. The *Titanic* had space in its lifeboats for fewer than half the ship's passengers. (Despite what seemed in retrospect like a glaring shortcoming, the ship's owners had sailed with more lifeboats than were required under British law—as oceangoing ships grew larger and carried more passengers, no one had gotten around to increasing the number of lifeboats to keep up with the capacity.) In the first half of the century, when New York revised its building codes, the memories of the *Titanic* and the fires at the Equitable Building and the Triangle Factory remained strong. The heavy-duty stairwells demanded for high-rise towers by the 1938 code served as psychic life rafts. Thirty years later, these structures were seen as artifacts of an earlier, more plodding age, and the 1968 code eliminated the need for reinforced staircases and vestibules.

Not only the fire towers disappeared. So did half the staircases. The 1968 code reduced the number of stairways required for buildings the size of the towers from six to three. When those provisions were still a draft proposal, the Port Authority engineer in charge of construction, Malcolm P. Levy, ordered them incorporated into the plans. "The tower core should be redesigned," he wrote on September 29, 1965, "to eliminate the fire towers and to take advantage of the more lenient provisions regarding exit stairs." Moreover, those three stairwells would have less protection, as the new code lowered the minimum fire resistance for walls around the shafts from three hours to two, and permitted them to be built from much less sturdy material. All these changes offered significant financial opportunities. They would increase the space available for rent by getting rid of stairways and make the building lighter by eliminating the requirements for masonry. When New York City building officials

"You can't go this way."

Fewer Stairwells

A change in the New York City building code in 1968 reduced the number of stairwells required in tall buildings. The World Trade Center, completed in 1970, had fewer escape routes than the Empire State Building, completed in 1931.

Fire tower A stairwell running the height of the building, accessed through a vestibule that functions as an air lock to keep smoke out. A fire tower was no longer required when the World Trade Center was built.

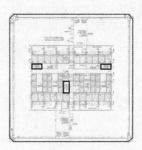

EMPIRE STATE BUILDING

102 floors

2.25 million square feet of office space

About **15,000** occupants

5 stairwells at the sixth floor, and the fire tower

9 stairwells at the base

WORLD TRADE CENTER

110 floors

About **4** million square feet of office space

About **20,000** occupants

3 stairwells throughout

Sources: Port Authority of New York and New Jersey; Empire State Building; Carol Willis, the Skyscraper Museum   *The New York Times*

pointed out in 1968 that the towers, as planned, did not meet the existing code, the Port Authority's representatives replied that they would satisfy the new code—the one that would become law in December. At the time, no city regulator noted a feature of the towers that would have required a fourth staircase, even under the less stringent requirements of the new code: atop each tower was a "place of assembly" for more than 1,000 people—the Windows on the World restaurant in the north tower, and an observatory in the south.

The signature building of New York in the first half of the twentieth century—the Empire State Building, which opened in 1931— had nine staircases at its broad base, six in its tapered middle, including the fire tower. The twin towers of the World Trade Center, which received their first tenants in 1970, had just three.

Another safety issue that would be of great consequence on September 11—the distance between the stairways—was all but ignored by the 1968 code. In 1959, a fire in a stairwell at Our Lady of Angels school in Chicago killed ninety-six children and three nuns. Around the country, building codes were quickly changed to require that exits be spread out, to create a second chance if one was somehow disabled. New York passed a law taking effect in 1961 that required exits in school buildings and other "places of assembly" to be on "opposite sides of the floor or space." Less than a decade later, the 1968 code did not press the standard for office buildings. The new code, and real-estate economics, encouraged the use of a single core in the center of the building. There, bunched as tightly as possible, would be shafts that housed essential services, including elevators, mechanical conduits, and, most important, stairs—all elements that did not directly produce rent revenue. The 1938 code generally required that exits on each floor be "remote" from each other, so that a single problem could not obstruct all the ways out. The new code amended that language in a small but significant way: each exit now had to be "as remote from the others as is practicable." New York would not explicitly demand remote stairways in office buildings until 1984, long after the trade center was open.

Finally, just as the *Titanic* was required by the British Board of Trade to have the same number of lifeboats as a ship one-quarter its size, the building code generally required the same number of exit stairways—three—for a building 75 feet tall as for one 1,350 feet high. So a 110-story skyscraper had to provide no more capacity for escape than a six-story building. The building code's limited stairway requirements not only embraced the implausibility of a total building evacuation for very tall buildings, but enshrined it.

The trade center was a marvel for the building trade in dozens of ways, but its singular triumph was in its use of space, the tight bundling of the building systems that made it possible for the Port Authority to offer for rent fully three-quarters of each floor. That was 21 percent higher than the best yield achieved in older skyscrapers, which were forced to commit that much more space to exit routes and so forth.

The Stairwells in the South Tower
Impact 9:02 A.M. Collapse 9:59 A.M.

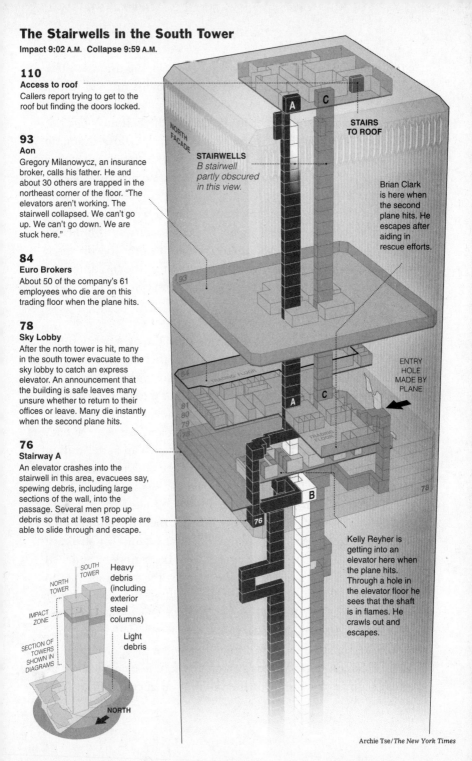

110
Access to roof
Callers report trying to get to the roof but finding the doors locked.

93
Aon
Gregory Milanowycz, an insurance broker, calls his father. He and about 30 others are trapped in the northeast corner of the floor. "The elevators aren't working. The stairwell collapsed. We can't go up. We can't go down. We are stuck here."

84
Euro Brokers
About 50 of the company's 61 employees who die are on this trading floor when the plane hits.

78
Sky Lobby
After the north tower is hit, many in the south tower evacuate to the sky lobby to catch an express elevator. An announcement that the building is safe leaves many unsure whether to return to their offices or leave. Many die instantly when the second plane hits.

76
Stairway A
An elevator crashes into the stairwell in this area, evacuees say, spewing debris, including large sections of the wall, into the passage. Several men prop up debris so that at least 18 people are able to slide through and escape.

NORTH FACADE

STAIRWELLS
B stairwell partly obscured in this view.

STAIRS TO ROOF

Brian Clark is here when the second plane hits. He escapes after aiding in rescue efforts.

ENTRY HOLE MADE BY PLANE

TRADING FLOOR

Kelly Reyher is getting into an elevator here when the plane hits. Through a hole in the elevator floor he sees that the shaft is in flames. He crawls out and escapes.

SOUTH TOWER
NORTH TOWER

Heavy debris (including exterior steel columns)

Light debris

IMPACT ZONE

SECTION OF TOWERS SHOWN IN DIAGRAMS

NORTH

Archie Tse/*The New York Times*

Building code reform hardly makes for gripping drama. A few feet chiseled here and there from stairwells by getting rid of fire towers. The elimination of masonry reinforcement around stairwells. Exits bunched together in the core of the building. And yet from the balcony of history, the new standards yield a dramatic view of contrasts. While the foundation of the trade center was being wrapped in a stupendous girdle of concrete, to stand against time and tide—it was three feet thick, more than half a mile long, and seventy feet deep—the stairways in the sky would be clad in a few inches of lightweight drywall. These stairways, bunched together, built for only a few hundred people at a time to walk three or four stories, would now have to carry out of the buildings the 12,000 people beneath the airplane impacts on September 11, 2001.

Richard Fern looked ahead to the stripes in stairway A of the south tower. They had been applied to the stairs after the fiasco of the 1993 evacuation, when thousands of angry, choking people emerged to describe pitch-black staircases, unlit because the emergency lights had failed when the power went out. Since then, the Port Authority had spent $2.1 million on emergency lighting and exit signs lit with light-emitting diodes. The emergency lights now had batteries that would stay on for at least ninety minutes if the building lost power. The stripes helped, too. Fern flew down the flights, nine steps a landing, then a turn, another nine steps. Coming from the 84th floor, he was going directly past the heart of the devastation in the south tower. Here again, he had the benefit of yet another stroke of luck. Only in two places in the towers were the stairs not bunched in the center of the building. At those spots, the stairwells had to detour away from the middle of the building because elevator machinery took up half the space on the floor. One of these detours ran from the 82nd to the 76th floors, just below where Fern had entered the stairs—and at the exact area where most of Flight 175 had hit. Because stairway A was about fifty-four feet northeast of its regular path in the center of the building, it survived in at least passable condition. The machine room may also have helped deflect damage from the plane.

Unlit and smoky, stairway A seemed possessed by gloom. Fern, however, was possessed by yet another chance. Beginning at 84, he ran through the smoke, finding it bad but bearable. A few floors down, most likely on the 82nd floor, he was shocked to discover that stairway A seemed to come to an end; this was in fact a corridor that led people coming down stairway A in the core of the building to the continuation of the staircase, along the periphery. He reached against the wall, found a door handle, and opened it. Some daylight fell on his eyes, and he felt a surge of relief.

"Do not go down that staircase," someone shouted. "Use this one." Fern walked quickly toward the voice, passing a bleeding woman who was being helped by a man. They seemed okay. He found the continuation of stairway A, and headed down. He hustled past the people ahead of him in the stairs. As soon as he made the next turn in the stairs, he saw another man and another woman, stopped dead. One of the wallboards had collapsed into the staircase, and they could not get by.

"Don't go this way," one of them said. They were ready to turn back.

Fern did not speak to them. He lifted the wall off the ground and rested it on the banister, creating a triangle that was just big enough for him to crawl under. At the next floor, a smaller piece of the wall had collapsed. This time, Fern simply jumped from the stairs onto it, rolled onto the landing, and kept going. A few flights down, he caught up with Peter, another man who worked at Euro Brokers. Fern was about to blow past when Peter stopped him.

"We should stay together," Peter said.

"Okay, but you will have to keep up with me," Fern said. He resumed his fast pace, but the initial surge of his flight had subsided. He noticed that few people seemed to be in the stairwell. He switched on his walkie-talkie radio and heard a member of Euro Brokers' security department, who was outside the building, speaking with Dave Vera, who was with the other group from Euro

Brokers, higher up in the building. By the time Fern got to the 30th floor, his legs were shaking. He thought he would collapse. At the bottom of the building, he met a phalanx of Port Authority police officers and security guards, who steered him and Peter out of the south tower, through the concourse and east to Church Street, where he came out near Borders.

A few people found the same staircase that Richard Fern had discovered, and they also met a man and a woman who were stymied by the fallen wall. But stairway A would prove to be a path out of the destruction for those in the south tower's 78th-floor sky lobby, where the ground was carpeted with the silent, fallen bodies of scores of people who had been standing there a few moments earlier. Perhaps two dozen people were alive. Keating Crown of Aon had gotten to stairway A with his colleagues Kelly Reyher and Donna Spera, who also had been waiting for the elevators. Reyher had used his briefcase to wedge apart the doors of a burning elevator car after the impact, and Spera and Crown had both been badly burned; Spera also had multiple broken bones. The three managed to stumble to stairway A at the northwest corner of the building. They hollered into the dusty, dying sky lobby that they had found a way out. A few others followed their voices to the door.

In the stairwell, Crown wanted to carry Spera on his back, but Reyher said, "That's not a very good idea," pointing out that they had a long way to go. Spera then slung her arms over Crown and Reyher, and they began to walk down. Very soon, they encountered a man and woman—quite possibly, the same people encountered by Fern—who reported that the stairwell was blocked. "You can't go this way," one of them said.

Fern's temporary solution to the collapsed wall near the 76th floor—propping up the drywall—apparently had not held. Crown had run ahead and seen that the wallboard had been knocked out by an elevator car, which ran in a shaft adjacent to the stairs. With Reyher, Crown could see the struts that had once held the wall, and they could see a conduit that had been running in the shaft, and it was all down in a heap. There was more discussion in the stairway about going back up, but Reyher and Crown, having just left the horrors of the 78th floor, were not turning back. They began to pick up junk from the floor and shove it aside, and they pushed the wall into place, but it quickly fell back onto the stairs. Then Crown realized that the wall could rest on the fallen conduit, which was relatively secure, and still leave space. A third man helped lift the board. Among them, they had cleared enough room to get by.

Crown traveled with a woman for a few flights, thinking it was Donna Spera, before suddenly realizing it was someone else. Another man stepped in to walk with that woman. Crown continued down on his own. His own left leg was broken. He was bleeding from the back of the head and from cuts on his arm. Another man took off a shirt, soaked it in water, and dabbed the back of Crown's head. Crown took off his own shirt to wrap around his wrist. As he caught up with people from the lower floors, the word was passed ahead that an injured person was coming, and the double line of evacuating people immediately folded into a single file. Some gasped or shrieked when they saw him, but Crown plodded on. A woman passed him the last ounce of a can of caffeine-free Diet Pepsi. It was mostly backwash, Crown figured, but it cleared his throat. He kept going. When he got to street level and an ambulance, a paramedic checked his bleeding head and pulled out a metal spring that somehow had gotten lodged in his scalp. Behind him a few flights, Reyher and Spera made steady progress. When she wanted to rest, Reyher gave no quarter. "Keep going," he insisted.

Brian Clark and Stanley Praimnath found light and fresh air around the 68th floor. They also met Jose Marrero, the administrative jack-of-all-trades for Euro Brokers who already had herded a group off the 84th floor, escorting them down into the 40s. Now he was walking back up.

"Jose," Clark called. "Where are you going?"

"I'm going to help Dave Vera," Marrero said. "I can hear him on the walkie-talkie." Vera was with the group that had gotten disoriented and dropped to the landing in exhaustion.

Clark tried to dissuade him. Next to him stood Praimnath, battered and bruised by his escape from the 81st floor. "I'm getting this man from Fuji Bank out," Clark said. "Dave's a big boy, he'll fend for himself. Come on down with us."

Marrero, whose insistence had helped sweep the floor at Euro Brokers, would not be turned back. Vera was in trouble. "I can help him," Marrero said. "I'll be along."

"All right," Clark said.

At the 44th floor, Clark and Praimnath left the stairs for a break. They had come onto the lower sky lobby, and all the lights were on. The place was deserted, except for a security guard in the blue blazer of the building staff. Before Clark could speak, the guard asked for help.

"Do you have phones?" the guard asked.

"No, why?" Clark asked.

"I am with this man who's injured," the guard said.

He gestured behind the guard's stand, where a man lay on the ground, moaning. He had a massive head wound. The phones on the 44th floor were not working.

"I'll stay with this guy, but you've got to promise that you'll get a stretcher and medical attention for him," the guard said.

"We'll do our best," Clark said.

At the 31st floor, Clark and Praimnath again stopped. This time, they found an open conference room in the offices of Oppenheimer Management Corporation. They each called home—Praimnath left a message, and Clark spoke briefly to his wife, telling her that he was okay. Then Clark called 911. He passed along the information about the injured man on the 44th floor, then was told he had to speak to someone. He waited a long time on hold, then related the story again. Just a moment, he was told. Yet another person had to hear his account. Someone picked up, and Clark spoke immediately.

"I am only telling you once. I am getting out of the building," Clark said. "Write it down." A 911 operator typed up a summary:

> Another call. Male caller states EMS badly need on the 44th
> floor, tower 2. EMS notified. Male caller states he will keep
> searching. Hung up.

Brian Clark and Stanley Praimnath departed for the lobby.

The trade center's three exit stairways satisfied the requirements of the 1968 code, but as was apparent in the 1993 bombing, three stairways were not sufficient to accommodate a rapid, full-building evacuation of each tower. Complicating matters, two of the three stairwells in each tower did not bring people out to the street, but actually deposited them in the mezzanine lobby, which was "a major building design flaw," Chief Donald Burns of the Fire Department had noted in a report about the 1993 bombing. These exits to the mezzanine required people to get on escalators to bring them to the street level, causing backups in the stairwells that stretched tens of floors up.

Perhaps as important, the three stairways in each tower were all in a triangle, with no exit more than forty-five feet away from another—except in those few circumstances where they took detours to accommodate elevator machinery, as with the south tower's stairway A. The folly of permitting buildings like the trade center to bunch their exits together became inarguable in the years following the adoption of the 1968 code. After a November 1980 fire at the MGM Grand Hotel in Las Vegas killed eighty-seven people, many of them trapped by poor exits, the Fire Department seized the moment to fix a law it had long opposed. The city set a new formula that doubled the required space between exits in tall buildings. The changes in the New York code did not take effect until 1984, more than a decade after the towers opened, and of course, the law was not retroactive; to put new exits in existing buildings would be very difficult. As Chief O'Hagan had said, the time for ensuring life safety was during the design. People would just have to live with the results.

If the survivors nearest the points of impact moved with cold determination, the people lower in the south tower knew nothing but the mysterious, terrifying shudder of the building when the plane hit. Nat Alcamo, a fifty-six-year-old former Marine who worked for Morgan Stanley, had gotten from the 60th floor to the 44th floor when Flight 175 struck. For the first time, he felt intense fear. People wept. Women threw high-heeled shoes into the corners of landings. Katherine Hachinski, a seventy-year-old architect, had left her office on the 91st floor after the first plane hit the north tower, despite the reassuring public-address announcement. *My foot, it's under control,* she recalled thinking. After the stairway rocked from the second impact, she prayed. A stranger handed her a paper breathing mask.

Steven Salovich had been herded off Euro Brokers' 84th floor by Jose Marrero before the second plane hit. As usual, the Wall Street guys were kidding in the stairs as they went down, comparing the event to 1993. His phone rang with his wife calling in a panic to tell him what she was seeing on television. They all kept going, but considered turning back when the announcement came that evacuation was unnecessary. As Salovich and his colleagues Andy Soloway and Dennis Coughlin discussed their choices, they felt the crash. The line moving along the stairs immediately resumed a fast, but not reckless pace, "as if a high-speed assembly line was thrust into motion from a flat start," Salovich recalled. Soloway took the arm of a woman having a panic attack; Salovich carried the bag of another woman, holding her arm, hearing about her two children. "Thirtieth floor," Salovich called out. "It's all downhill from here."

Richard Jacobs, a thirty-four-year-old loan administrator who worked on the 79th floor for Fuji, noticed that people started running when they felt the lurch. By then, the group he was with had made it to the 42nd floor; they reached the ground in less than fifteen minutes. Edgardo Villegas, thirty-one years old, who worked in the Oppenheimer mail room on the 32nd floor, saw the stairs filled with confused people, crying and clinging to each other even before Flight 175 hit. Robert Radomsky, a systems administrator for Aon who had come from the 101st floor, saw cracks in the stairwell wall. Traffic slowed as people entered from floors in the 60s. Everyone walked shoulder to shoulder. Sean Pierce, twenty-eight, who worked on the 73rd floor for Morgan Stanley, grabbed the hand of a colleague, Kristen Farrell. Around them, some people chatted casually and sipped their morning coffee, but others had difficulty making their way down. Louis A. Torres, a member of Morgan Stanley's administrative staff, came upon a woman from the firm who was being half carried down the stairs by a man struggling beneath her. The woman used crutches to walk. Torres picked her up at the 54th floor, put her over his shoulder, and carried her right down to the street. Around the 15th or 20th floor, someone from the building or one of the rescuers had urged Torres to put her down, saying that they were past the danger, but he carried her clear out of the trouble, and into a vehicle going to the hospital.

Terence McCormick, who worked for Kemper Insurance on the 36th floor of the south tower, had been in the trade center since 1978, and as he ran toward the stairs, he practically did not feel his feet touching the ground. He thought he was flying. He found the stairwell full, and slow; worried that the fire might be below them, he felt a sprinkler standpipe, fearful of finding that the heat was rising. No, it was cool to the touch. That was a trick he had learned from his father, who had been a top chief in the city's Fire Department. In fact, twenty-three years earlier, when McCormick was first starting work in the trade center, his dad had implored him to find a job elsewhere. Chief McCormick believed that the towers were among the most dangerous buildings in the city. The son regarded his warning as alarmist. Now the father was dead, and the son was trying to avoid looking at the floor numbers, averting his eyes as he moved at shuffle speed, praying that when he looked up he would discover progress. *God*, he whispered, *please let me get to the 25th floor*. Then: *God, please let me get to the 20th floor*.

In the north tower, after he was escorted from his 86th-floor office by Frank De Martini's crew, Louis Lesce wanted to move more deliberately than the people around him. He was sixty-four years old and had recently undergone a quadruple cardiac bypass. Someone carried his briefcase; another person took his coat. Norma Hessic, who worked on the 82nd floor for a state agency, was relieved that the stairway lights had stayed on, unlike in 1993, and that people kept good order. Richard Wright, a fifty-eight-year-old engineering inspector, moved from the 82nd floor to the 42nd, where he stopped for a break from the heat in the stairwell. A few people cracked open vending machines, and bottles of water and other drinks were passed along the lines. Michael Hingson, fifty-three, who worked on the 78th floor for a firm that specialized in disaster recovery of data, walked down with his guide dog, Roselle, a three-year-old yellow Labrador. Hingson had been blind since birth. He and Roselle brought David Frank, a guest from California, down with them. All three were offered water.

Sharon Premoli, an executive with Beast Financial Systems, prayed for much of the walk down the stairs from her office on the 80th floor. When she got to 44, she asked the security guard in the blue blazer whether they were going to be all right. He assured her they were. "I'm praying for you," he said. "Do you like to sing? Let's sing a hymn." He started and she heard his voice for several flights, supporting her, as she continued down the stairs.

Bill Hult, from a mortgage trading concern on the 51st floor, took note of the calmness in the stairs: people moving double file, instantly collapsing into single file to let injured people from the upper floors pass. Elaine Duch, who had been burned on the 88th floor and was one of the people led to freedom by the Frank De Martini–Pablo Ortiz team, was escorted down by her colleagues Dorene Smith and Gerry Gaeta. Around the 40th floor, a firefighter saw them and poured some of his extinguisher on the burnt woman,

The Stairwells in the North Tower

Impact 8:46 A.M. Collapse 10:28 A.M.

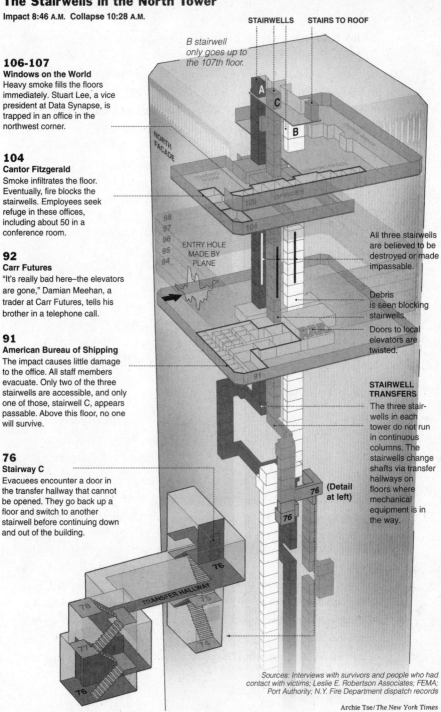

106-107
Windows on the World
Heavy smoke fills the floors immediately. Stuart Lee, a vice president at Data Synapse, is trapped in an office in the northwest corner.

104
Cantor Fitzgerald
Smoke infiltrates the floor. Eventually, fire blocks the stairwells. Employees seek refuge in these offices, including about 50 in a conference room.

92
Carr Futures
"It's really bad here–the elevators are gone," Damian Meehan, a trader at Carr Futures, tells his brother in a telephone call.

91
American Bureau of Shipping
The impact causes little damage to the office. All staff members evacuate. Only two of the three stairwells are accessible, and only one of those, stairwell C, appears passable. Above this floor, no one will survive.

76
Stairway C
Evacuees encounter a door in the transfer hallway that cannot be opened. They go back up a floor and switch to another stairwell before continuing down and out of the building.

STAIRWELLS   STAIRS TO ROOF

B stairwell only goes up to the 107th floor.

A
C
B

NORTH FACADE

ENTRY HOLE MADE BY PLANE

All three stairwells are believed to be destroyed or made impassable.

Debris is seen blocking stairwells.

Doors to local elevators are twisted.

STAIRWELL TRANSFERS
The three stair-wells in each tower do not run in continuous columns. The stairwells change shafts via transfer hallways on floors where mechanical equipment is in the way.

(Detail at left)

TRANSFER HALLWAY

Sources: Interviews with survivors and people who had contact with victims; Leslie E. Robertson Associates; FEMA; Port Authority; N.Y. Fire Department dispatch records

Archie Tse/*The New York Times*

which shocked Gaeta and appeared to hurt Duch. Another ailing person from the 88th floor, De Martini's secretary, Judith Reese, was having a terrible time breathing because of her asthma, and she and Jeff Gertler, who was with her, had to stop to rest every flight or so. After nearly a half hour, they had gotten to the 51st floor, and Gertler used his two-way radio.

> *Gertler:* Fire Command. This is Jeff Gertler.
> *Voice 1:* Copy.
> *Gertler:* I have a medical emergency in stairway B, we are on the [*audio cuts out*] floor. We have an individual who cannot walk down.
> *Voice 1:* Copy. We are working our way up B stairwell right now.
> *Voice 2:* What floor was that on the B stairwell?
> *Gertler:* Well, we're walking down from 51. We are going to do the best we can. But we do have a medical emergency. We have one individual who cannot walk down, has asthma.
> *Voice 1:* Copy. We are on the 11th floor, working our way up. [*alarms in background*]
> *Gertler:* Copy, we're heading down.

A moment later, Gertler realized that not only did Judith Reese need help, but so did Moe Lipson, the eighty-nine-year-old electrical inspector who was being helped down from the 88th floor by Mak Hanna.

> *Gertler:* We are in the B staircase, 51st floor heading down. We have *two* people with a medical emergency, elderly people, they cannot walk down.
> *Female Voice:* That's elderly people, what staircase . . . what tower is that? [*sirens in background*]

Gertler: That's Tower 1, staircase B.
Female: Tower 1, staircase B. That's a copy.

John Labriola came down from the 71st floor in the north tower, where he had a temporary contract job with the Port Authority. The steps had become slick with the sweat. Everyone, it seemed, had cell phones out, but no one was getting calls through. "We should buy stock in the first company whose service works," Labriola joked. An amateur photographer, he carried a Nikon camera, and when he got farther down the stairs, he snapped pictures, including several of firefighters coming up one side and the line of office workers on the other. Theresa Leone, who worked in a law firm on the 51st floor, was working the rosary beads she had gotten from the Church of St. Francis of Assisi. She had not eaten breakfast, and was perspiring heavily in the heat. A group of five or six firemen stood at one of the landings, fixing their gear, and one of them noticed how warm she seemed. He offered her a sip from a bottle of water. She was about to say no, thanks, then changed her mind. "God bless," she said. Michael Benfante and John Cerquiera, who worked for Network Plus, a communications firm on the 81st floor, saw Tina Hansen in a wheelchair, waiting at the 68th floor for a chance to go down. Hansen, a marketing analyst for the Port Authority, was in an evac-u-chair, a lightweight chair that the Port Authority had bought by the hundreds for the building after the 1993 bombing, and her motorized chair stood by. Cerquiera, twenty-two, recently graduated from college and in the full flush of life as a young man in New York, and Benfante, thirty-six, his boss, picked up Hansen. They went one flight. They had sixty-seven more to go.

Three flights below, as a parade of people moved down the stairs, a group inside offices on the 64th floor was not sure whether they really should be leaving. Not surprisingly, this uncertainty had settled on an office with many people who had been in the towers for the 1993 bombing, and who worked for the Port Authority. The senior manager was Patrick Hoey, the engineer in charge of bridges and tunnels who had told his colleague Pasquale Buzzelli that he had been nearly knocked out of his chair by the plane's impact. Hoey was one of those invisible and necessary citizens who keep the city moving. In his office, he could see video monitors that broadcast live pictures of all the spans that ringed New York. Ordinarily, they were the kinds of images that might capture Hoey's attention. He was a bridge buff. Now he wished he could refocus the cameras on the exterior of the building. How badly was it damaged? Did they need to leave immediately? Many people on his floor had left immediately. But some remained, including Buzzelli, one of his engineers. There wasn't much smoke on their floor. So at 9:11, twenty-five minutes after Flight 11 had hit the building, Hoey called the Port Authority police desk in Jersey City.

> *Patrick Hoey:* I'm on the 64th floor.
>
> *PAPD Sergeant John Mariano:* Okay.
>
> *Patrick Hoey:* In Tower 1.
>
> *PAPD Sergeant Mariano:* All right.
>
> *Patrick Hoey:* I've got about twenty people here with me.
>
> *PAPD Sergeant Mariano:* Okay.
>
> *Patrick Hoey:* What do you suggest? [*loud commotion*] Staying tight?
>
> *PAPD Sergeant Mariano:* Stand tight. Is there a fire right there where you are?
>
> *Patrick Hoey:* No, there is a little bit of smoke on the floor.
>
> *PAPD Sergeant Mariano:* It looks like there is also an explosion in 2.
>
> *Patrick Hoey:* Okay.
>
> *PAPD Sergeant Mariano:* So be careful. Stay near the stairwells, and wait for the police to come up.
>
> *Patrick Hoey:* They will come up, huh? Okay. They will check each floor? [*loud commotion*] If you would, just report that we're up here.
>
> *PAPD Sergeant Mariano:* I got you.

Patrick Hoey: And I'm on . . . if you need the number, it's 5397.

PAPD Sergeant Mariano: I got you.

Patrick Hoey: Thank you.

PAPD Sergeant Mariano: All right, 'bye.

As hundreds walked past their floor, the people on 64 closed the doors and began to seal them with tape.

9

"The doors are locked."

The safe spaces were disappearing as the smoke rose through seams in the buildings, as flames found fissures and created new ones. On some floors, things remained remarkably calm, even as people rifled through their dwindling lists of options. At 9:05 A.M., Peter Mardikian called his wife, Corine, using one of the few phones that still worked on the 106th floor of the north tower. An executive with Imagine Software, Mardikian had come to the trade center for the Risk Waters breakfast conference at Windows on the World.

He told his wife that the smoke was getting thicker and that he was worried about his breathing. He was going to head for the roof. There was much else to say, of course, but Mardikian told her he could not stay on the phone. Many others were waiting. Even in a time of confusion and coursing fear, small courtesies survived.

Across the high floors in each of the towers, dozens of people were reaching the same conclusion as Peter Mardikian: their next refuge would be the roof. In the south tower, Sean Rooney began climbing from the office of Aon on the 98th floor and Paul Rizza walked up from Fiduciary Trust on 90. In the north tower, Stephen

Cherry and Martin Wortley and Charles Heeran started up the stairs from the office of Cantor Fitzgerald, which occupied four floors near the top of the north tower. Heeran had called his father, Bernie Heeran, a retired firefighter, a few minutes after the first plane hit, when the smoke on the 104th floor had already become unforgiving. Bernie Heeran knew his son needed a buffer of fresh air to buy a bit of time so that rescuers might have a chance to reach him.

"Get everybody to the roof," Bernie Heeran told his son. "Go up. Don't try to go down."

Compared with the walk down, the climb up to the roof from a high floor seemed shorter and simpler. That was partly an illusion created by the scale of the trade center. To reach the roof required a trip that, for many, was the equivalent of climbing to the top of an ordinary office tower. In the south tower, the equity traders at Keefe, Bruyette & Woods faced a hike of more than twenty stories in smoke and dust from their offices on the 88th and 89th floors. The trading desk was heavily stocked with former college or high school athletes, and Stephen Mulderry, Rick Thorpe, and Frank Doyle, all very fit and ranging in age from their late twenties to early forties, decided it was worth a try.

Joining them at the top of the stairs in the south tower was an older man who was more familiar than most with the route. Roko Camaj had spent nearly half of his sixty years working in the towers, much of it on the roof of the south tower operating a custom-built contraption that automatically washed the windows. The rig crawled down the towers along tracks, washing a strip of windows as it descended before returning to the roof. As each strip was done, the machine rolled over to the next line of twenty-two-inch windows, pivoted, then descended 1,300 feet. It could clean seven floors of windows in a minute. But it could not do the windows on the 107th floor, which were thirty-three inches wide, one and a half times the width of the standard windows. The extra size had been demanded by a Port Authority planner to allow more expansive views for special spaces at the top of each tower. The north tower would have a grand restaurant; the south tower, an observation deck; in both places, ample windows would be vital to capturing the unmatched vistas. This order briefly touched off a snit by the height-fearing architect, who had designed the twenty-two-inch windows to comfort those similarly afflicted, but he eventually agreed to increase their width at the top of the building. That created work the automated machine could not do. So Camaj and a partner cleaned those wide windows by hand, sudsing them up as they hung from the side of the building, 1,300 feet in the air, in a basket with harnesses.

For this routine derring-do, Camaj had become part of the trade center's folklore, a poor man's Philippe Petit, the aerialist who had walked between the towers in 1974 on a tightrope. Camaj had been featured in a children's book, *Risky Business,* and had appeared in a documentary about the building. The book captured Camaj's fascination with the job, the sense of independence that came from working alone in an isolated setting. "It's just me and the sky," he said in the book. "I don't bother anybody and nobody bothers me." On September 11, however, as he tried to head for the roof, Camaj was traveling with a crowd.

In both towers, the people on the high floors were confronted with an unyielding reality: they had nowhere to go but up. All three staircases in the north tower had been wiped out; in the south tower, a single stairway remained open, but only a handful of people knew about it.

The Port Authority's plan for escaping fire in the towers did not have a page for roof rescues. Indeed, the roof was off-limits. This perspective was in line with mainstream thought in emergency-management circles. Los Angeles was one of the few American cities where aerial rescues were actively contemplated. The fire department there had secured its own fleet of helicopters and had made tall buildings install rooftop helipads. In Las Vegas, during the fire at the MGM Grand Hotel in November 1980, a bucket brigade of helicopters spontaneously formed, lifting hundreds of people from the roof. Even so, most experts did not view the roof as a viable escape route from a high-rise fire. For one thing, confusion about which way to walk on the stairs could cripple a large-scale evacuation. And the only way to rescue people from the roof was by helicopter, a method that could not be counted on to evacuate masses of people, certainly not anywhere near the number that a single intact staircase could accommodate. During a debate in New York in the 1970s on the use of helicopters, Fire Chief O'Hagan had argued that the central evacuation opportunities should be written on the blueprints and then permanently built into the structure, rather than shifting this responsibility to rescuers in helicopters that might not be available in a crisis.

Despite the aversion to aerial rescues, the Port Authority did not explicitly tell the occupants of its towers that the roof was not an option. At mandatory fire drills held in the tenant offices every six months, the building fire-safety directors focused solely on safe ways to descend the stairs. While that doctrine had sound reasoning behind it—flame and smoke rise—it overlooks human nature, which drives people to get outside of a building on fire. In the trade center, getting outside either meant the street, a quarter mile down, or it meant the roof, twenty or thirty flights up. Just as the fire drills made no mention that the roof was not an option, there were no signs in the stairwells saying that, either. Even if there had been, hundreds of people still might have headed up the stairs on September 11. They faced the brutal truth that all the planners and drills had evaded. They had nowhere else to go.

The roof offered fresh air. There was no ceiling to collapse, no furniture to burn, no floors to buckle. It seemed like a place removed from the hazard, a holding station that might buy time until rescuers arrived. A rooftop had often served as a refuge in terrible New York fires. During the Triangle Shirtwaist Factory blaze of 1911, many of the survivors—including an owner of the factory—had escaped by climbing to the roof. Although the real estate industry sought to restrict access to roofs whenever the building code came up for revision, the Fire Department had resisted.

The roof of the World Trade Center had also served as an embarkation point for rescues after the 1993 bombing, and on September 11 the prospect of an aerial rescue lived in the imagination of many of those trapped on the upper floors. Martin Wortley of Cantor Fitzgerald told his brother over the phone that he was hoping to leave by helicopter, and would head up the stairs in the north tower. Those who had been in the towers when the bomb had gone off in 1993 had heard countless times about how the helicopters had settled softly on the roofs and carried people to safety. Bob Mattson, a banker with Fiduciary Trust International and now trapped in the south tower, had been one of those lifted to safety that day. It had been the work of Police Department pilots, but for many, it had been an earthly approximation of heavenly intercession.

This was nothing like 1993, Detective Greg Semendinger thought as he and his copilot, Officer James Ciccone, circled the buildings in Aviation 6, one of the smaller police helicopters. He had landed a police helicopter on the north tower after the bombing eight years earlier and had lifted people off the roof who could not make it down the stairs. Today, he could barely see the upper floors of either tower. Semendinger and Ciccone had arrived about 8:54 A.M., eight minutes after the first plane's impact, scrambling from the Aviation Unit's base in Brooklyn. The first police helicopter to arrive, Aviation 14, piloted by Detectives Timothy Hayes and Patrick Walsh, had beaten them by two minutes, arriving at the building just six minutes after Flight 11 struck. Hayes and Walsh were flying a larger helicopter, a Bell 412, capable of carrying ten people, in addition to the crew. It was equipped with a 250-foot hoist that could be used to pluck people from a roof. No one had seen any opportunity for rescues yet.

"We're going to be unable to land on the roof due to the heavy smoke condition at this time," Hayes radioed in from just off the north tower at 8:58. They had barely stopped talking when Hayes spotted United Flight 175 roaring toward them through the sky.

"Jesus Christ, there's a second plane crashing," he yelled to Walsh. They pulled up quickly and the plane shot beneath them, bursting through the south tower, and sending a giant ball of flame coughing out the other side. Within minutes, the roof of that tower had also vanished behind the smoke.

Ciccone turned the controls and headed for another look at the north tower. The pilots approached from the uptown side to avoid the massive plumes of dark smoke blowing southeast, toward New York Harbor and Brooklyn. With the water and the blue sky as a backdrop, the buildings looked like the billowing smokestacks of an ocean liner—until they panned down to see the gaping holes, the leaping flames, the soot-darkened faces of people piled four and five high in broken windows, waving white cloths and gasping for breath. Semendinger could not abandon the idea of a landing, especially as he watched men and women plummet from the building. There were so many of them. They dropped in silence, fleeing horrors that were beyond speech. For a second, Semendinger felt helpless. The helicopter pulled in behind the smoke, and Semendinger noticed that a small patch of the north tower's roof was visible, near the northwest corner. He would need to get closer to measure his options, but they were far bleaker than they had been in 1993, the last time he had flown to this building.

Back then, the south tower roof had been filled with people when Semendinger flew over, about thirty minutes after the blast in the basement parking garage. They had huddled on the outdoor patio to the trade center's observation deck, a place where crowds typically gathered on warmer days. On February 26, 1993, it had felt like a portal to the Arctic. No one was on the roof of the north tower, with its forest of floodlights and antennas. Wisps of smoke drifted up from the higher floors. Most of the television stations in the city broadcast their signals from the roof of the north tower, and many had offices on the 110th floor just below it. Trapped inside one of the offices that February day was Deborah Matut-Perina, a thirty-four-year-old technician for WCBS-TV who was three months pregnant and asthmatic. She had been calling downstairs for help and had gotten only a busy signal while the black smoke built outside her door. The police had reports of people like her trapped on the upper floors. But as much as Semendinger wanted to help, he had a hard time finding a place to land on the north tower.

Inside the helicopter with Semendinger that afternoon eight years before had been two Emergency Service Unit cops, Sergeant Tim Farrell and Officer Bob Schierenbeck. They suggested taking down the antennas on the north tower to clear a landing zone. They dangled a thirty-foot rope out the door and just after 1 P.M. rappelled to the roof. Once they had made space for the helicopter, they cracked open the locked stairwell door, and headed down to the 110th floor. It was surprising how smoky the stairs were so far above the basement, but the explosion had set off car fires, and rubber tires burn slow, smelly, and dirty. Farrell found Matut-Perina in her office, where she and a colleague had wet clothes with bottled water and jammed them under the door. He helped her to the roof and Semendinger lifted off. She was the first of several dozen people who would be shuttled from the roof by police helicopters that day.

By nightfall, eight helicopters were ferrying ESU teams to the roofs of both towers. The cops descended through the buildings to escort the aged or infirm up the stairs. When the commander of the Aviation Unit later recorded the events of the day, he recalled the amazed faces of exhausted firefighters who had climbed for two hours and more, only to find fresh teams of police officers coming down the stairs.

About half the people who were airlifted to safety in 1993 came off the south tower. The helicopters started landing there only in the evening, after the smoke in the stairways had cleared and the crowds from the roof had descended. At one point in the day, as many as 200 people had gathered on the roof, led there by Mike Hurley, at the time an assistant fire-safety director for the building. He happened to be on the observation desk and saw the smoke in the stairs, but had no idea what had happened, or where. Communications systems were out of service, as were the elevators. All he knew was that the stairs seemed impassable. So he climbed atop a table and announced to the crowd of tourists and schoolchildren that they should head to the roof for fresh air. Tenants from the upper floors joined them. Three or four hours later, as darkness descended, Hurley led the shivering throng back down to the enclosed observation deck. He asked the concession stand to distribute free food and to give each person a few souvenir penlights, which they used to guide themselves down the pitch-dark stairways for 107 flights.

After that group headed for the stairwell, the first rescue helicopter landed on the south tower. By about 10 P.M., a dozen or so people were shuttled off the roof of that tower as well. Finally, when the building was clear, the pilot asked Hurley if he wanted a ride. He was the last civilian airlifted from the buildings.

From most perspectives, the 1993 bombing of the trade center, killing six people, had been a bleak moment, marking the arrival of terrorism in America. The rooftop rescues became one of the few bright spots in the early news coverage. The helicopter crews made the rounds on television. *Nightline. CBS This Morning.* While they were feted, fire officials seethed. In their view, the people atop the towers had never been in serious danger, not at least until the police helicopters scooped them off the roof in windy conditions. A month after the bombing, the New York City Fire Chiefs Association sent Mayor David N. Dinkins a letter. "This was nothing more than sheer grandstanding, a cheap publicity stunt done at the expense of public safety," the chiefs wrote. "The people removed via helicopter were in no danger until the Police Department arrived and gravely jeopardized their safety by this stupid act."

The tenants simply should have waited for the smoke to clear and then walked down the stairs. At least, that was how the chiefs saw it.

Ludicrous, police officials said. People were trapped. Time was of the essence. Who knew at the outset how the building would handle a major explosion at its base?

No doubt some emergency-management experts would have sided with the fire chiefs, but it was hard to see their position strictly as a matter of principle or public safety, devoid of pique over the acclaim the cops had received just for dropping onto the building tops in plain sight, while their firefighters invisibly trudged up and around 10 million square feet of office space. The Fire Department did not own or operate helicopters. On the issue of operating a sane, coordinated response, however, the fire chiefs had a strong point. Fire rescues were supposed to be their job. The police had never bothered to tell them what they planned to do, even though fire officials were supposed to have been in charge. The fire commissioner, Carlos Rivera, said, "Communications between the Police Department and the Fire Department were a problem at this incident." When reporters asked a police spokeswoman about communications difficulties, she replied, "I don't know what you're talking about."

The following year, in an effort to stop the squabbling, the city officially restated its position on the use of helicopters at fires: Rooftop rescues would be a last resort. If undertaken, they would be performed by firefighters, not the police. The firefighters would be carried to the roofs by police helicopters, which would be summoned to the scene by fire officers. There would be joint training runs so that the two agencies could work smoothly together when the time arose. Over the years, though, the commitment waned, and training became sporadic. Nevertheless, memories of that day remained vivid for veteran firefighters.

As Captain Fred Ill of Ladder Company 2 in midtown responded, he radioed the dispatcher. "I know you have your hands full with the trade center," he said, "but keep in mind about the helicopter units that have been trained for this. They didn't do it the last time, with the last explosion at the trade center. In case nobody prompts you on that. We do have these helicopter units that are available." Captain Ill himself had done the training. It was the first of several reminders he sent to the dispatchers.

Panes of glass from the upper floors, near where the plane had hit, kept shattering in the plaza outside the lobby of the north tower. Each time, the noise was startling, like a cymbal shot, and with each crash, several firefighters in the lobby looked up anxiously

Just minutes before American Airlines Flight 11 hit the north tower, Christopher Hanley *(left)* of Radianz and Bill Kelly of Bloomberg L.P. chat at a breakfast conference at Windows on the World on the 106th floor. Another Bloomberg salesman, Peter Alderman, stands near the window. The photographer left the building before the plane struck. (BLOOMBERG L.P.)

On the 89th floor of the north tower, Akane Ito, Raffaele Cava, Tirsa Moya, Walter Pilipiak, Dianne DeFontes, Harold Martin, and approximately twenty others were trapped when Flight 11 struck. (ANDREA MOHIN/*THE NEW YORK TIMES*)

Christine Olender *(left)*, one of the managers at Windows on the World, spoke to her mother in the morning before Flight 11 hit the north tower. After the plane's impact, she and her fellow manager Doris Eng *(right)* had several conversations with the Port Authority command desks, trying to find out what had happened and what she and the others in the restaurant should do. (COURTESY OF THE OLENDER AND ENG FAMILIES)

Stephen Miller, a computer systems administrator for Mizuho Capital on the 80th floor of the south tower, followed his firm's evacuation procedures and headed down the stairs immediately after the plane hit the north tower. (RICHARD PERRY/*THE NEW YORK TIMES*)

Ed Beyea; his aide, Irma Fuller; and his friend, Abe Zelmanowitz; pose in the office of Empire Blue Cross and Blue Shield on the 27th floor of the north tower, where they worked together each day. (BETH TIPPERMAN)

Battalion Chief Joseph Pfeifer, who was the first fire commander to respond after Flight 11 struck the north tower, helps direct rescue efforts from the lobby of that building. (AP/WIDE WORLD PHOTOS/GOLDFISH PICTURES)

Frank De Martini, the Port Authority construction manager, worked on the 88th floor of the north tower. He loved the World Trade Center and all its gadgetry ever since he started work as a consultant following the 1993 bombing. After a 1994 project to overhaul the window-washing and maintance rigs, he took an inspection ride along the side of the building, boarding at the roof, 1,350 feet above the street. On September 11, De Martini helped rescue people on his floor and then led a group that pried open doors on twelve floors along the boundary of the crash zone, rescuing dozens of others. (COURTESY OF ENRICO TITTARELLI)

Pablo Ortiz was one of the men in Frank De Martini's group who helped push back the boundary between surviving and perishing in the upper floors of the north tower. (COURTESY OF EDNA KANG ORTIZ)

Stanley Praimnath, an assistant vice president for Fuji Bank, made his way down to the lobby of the south tower less than ten minutes after the first plane's impact, but he was told to return to his office. He watched from a window on the 81st floor as United Airlines Flight 175 streaked across the harbor toward his building. (TYRONE JAIMANGAL)

A view of the Euro Brokers trading floor on the east side of the 84th floor of the south tower, showing the type of open floors used by many financial firms in the towers. The four people in the foreground were not on the 84th floor when Flight 175 hit. However, the fifth person at the left, Thomas Sparacio, in the white shirt and turned away from the camera, was among a group of about fifty still in or near the trading area at the moment of impact. (JANICE BROOK/EURO BROKERS INC.)

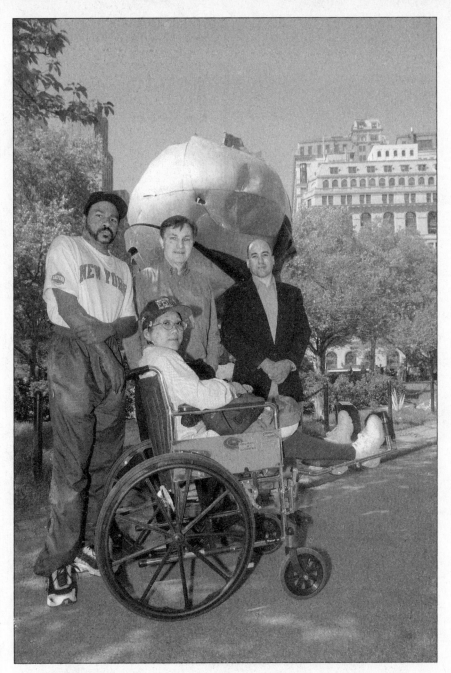

After Flight 175 hit the south tower, only eighteen people were able to get past the impact zone via the single stairway that remained open. Among them were Donovan Cowan, Brian Clark, Richard Fern, and Ling Young, seated. (FRED R. CONRAD/*THE NEW YORK TIMES*)

Dave Vera *(left)*, a telecommunications technician for Euro Brokers, cleared people from the 84th floor in the south tower, but would later send word by walkie-talkie that he needed help himself. His call was heard by his friend and colleague, Jose Marrero *(right)*, who had urged dozens of people to leave the 84th floor and had led them downstairs. He then headed back up to help Vera. (LEFT: JANICE BROOKS/EURO BROKERS INC.; RIGHT: JERROLD BANKS/EURO BROKERS INC.)

Roko Camaj, a window washer, had keys to the roof of the south tower, but he told colleagues that he could not get there from the 105th floor, perhaps because the electric doors did not work correctly after the plane's impact. (ANGEL FRANCO/*THE NEW YORK TIMES*)

Jan Demczur, another window washer, was trapped with five other men in an elevator that was stuck on the 50th floor of the north tower. They used his squeegee, the only tool available, to begin clawing out of the elevator. (JUSTIN LANE/*THE NEW YORK TIMES*)

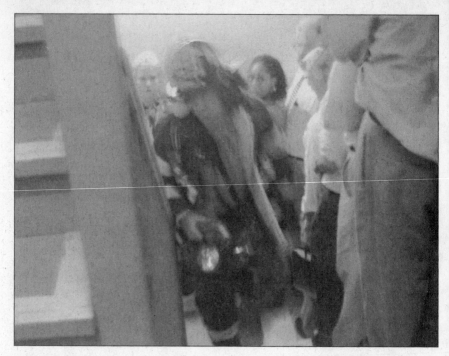

People fleeing down the stairs in the north tower make room for a firefighter climbing toward the impact zone. The mood in the stairwells of both towers remained calm throughout the morning. (AP/WIDE WORLD PHOTOS/JOHN LABRIOLA)

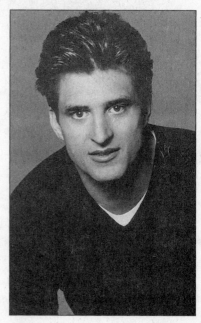

Greg Trapp, who had moved to New York to act and make films, worked as a security guard and was stationed on the 78th floor of the north tower. He led a group from the 84th floor to the stairway, then waited for instructions.
(MARTIN MEYERS PHOTOGRAPHY/COURTESY OF GREG TRAPP)

Many of the people who escaped from the north tower fled through the mezzanine, past windows that looked out onto smoldering debris that filled the plaza. (JOHN LABRIOLA)

NYPD Officer John Perry *(above left)* was turning in his retirement papers when the first plane struck. He asked for his badge back and ran to help. He joined up with his friend Capt. Tim Pearson *(right)*, directing people in the north tower mezzanine toward the escalators that would lead them to the concourse and safety. (NEW YORK POLICE DEPARTMENT)

Sgt. John McLoughlin *(right)* and Officer Will Jimeno were among a group of Port Authority police officers charged with transporting a cart filled with emergency equipment through the shopping concourse beneath the twin towers, to make sure their fellow officers had the proper gear. (PORT AUTHORITY OF NEW YORK AND NEW JERSEY)

From left, Sgt. Andrew Wender, Sgt. Al Moscola, and Capt. Joseph Baccellieri in the locker room at the Court Officers Academy several blocks from the World Trade Center. The court officers were in the locker room on the morning of September 11 and ran to the towers to help out. In the final minutes of the crisis, they would see firefighters sitting on the 19th floor of the north tower, apparently unaware that the other building had fallen. (ANDREA MOHIN/*THE NEW YORK TIMES*)

Battalion Chief Orio J. Palmer *(facing camera)* confers with Deputy Chief Peter Hayden in the north tower lobby before heading over to the south tower, where he would lead a company of firefighters up the stairs to the impact zone. (AP/WIDE WORLD PHOTOS/ GOLDFISH PICTURES)

Palmer's experience as a long distance runner (he is shown here finishing the *Newsday* Long Island Marathon in 1994) served him well as he climbed dozens of floors with over fifty pounds of equipment on his back and became the first firefighter to reach the impact zone in either building. (ISLAND PHOTOGRAPHY/COURTESY OF DEBORAH PALMER)

Firefighter Tom Kelly of Ladder Company 15 ran an elevator in the south tower that carried the injured to safety. As a young man thirty years earlier, Kelly had been a steamfitter working on the World Trade Center. On his first date with his future wife, he sneaked her into the construction site, and they looked over Manhattan from forty floors up. (FIRE DEPARTMENT OF NEW YORK)

Officer Moira Smith of the NYPD escorts Ed Nicholls, one of the eighteen people to escape from the impact zone in the south tower, toward medical help on Church Street. (COREY SIPKIN/*NEW YORK DAILY NEWS*)

at the ceiling. Many of the fire companies now arriving were from outside Manhattan and, to them, the trade center was an unfamiliar place, a maze of exits and entrances and buildings that looked alike. Some of the companies assigned to Tower 2, the south tower, were mistakenly reporting to Tower 1, so Chief Pfeifer told his aide to write the words *Tower 1* with a marker on the command desk in the north tower. Indeed, so many companies went to the wrong building that the commanders in the south tower ultimately ordered another whole set of companies to respond from their firehouses.

Inside the north tower lobby, around 9:15, about a half hour after the first plane struck, someone asked Pfeifer if he had put the helicopter plan into effect, and Pfeifer began looking for one of his radios. Although the city had bought radios that were supposed to make it possible for the Fire and Police Departments to communicate, the agencies could not agree on which one was in charge of the frequencies. So they remained unused. Instead, the fire commanders had to contact their own dispatchers, who would forward the request to the police. The police helicopter crew would then arrange to pick up the firefighters at a landing zone. But Pfeifer couldn't find the radio he needed to talk to the dispatcher, so he tried the phone. Some of the lines were dead. When he finally found a live line, he got a busy signal. Cell phones weren't working, either. With his options declining and other crises tugging at his sleeve, Pfeifer moved on to the next task. He figured that the commanders outside, the bosses who were running the department's overall operations, had probably ordered up the helicopter already. In fact, they had not.

The police aviation team had been anticipating a call from the firefighters, but when they did not hear from them, they just flew on. The Police Department's team of high-rise experts mustered to a landing zone near the building, preparing in case they were ordered to rappel down to the roof. But the chief of the department, Joseph Esposito, decided that the smoke and heat were too much. At 9:08 he had spoken over the police radio. "I don't want to see anybody landing on either one of these towers," he said.

It was a decision that would be revisited, but not revised, that morning. "Did we get anybody on the roof of either building?" an

ESU cop asked over the radio about twenty minutes later. "Negative," responded the dispatcher. "Nobody is landing on the roof up there."

"Well," the cop continued, "as soon as that clears up, we need people on that roof."

The need for intervention was horribly apparent to Semendinger, Hayes, and the other pilots watching the fires advance through the upper floors and seeing people on those floors hanging out of the windows. One pilot, Officer Yvonne Kelhetter, hovering off the north tower, got on the radio at about 9:30. "About five floors up from the top," she said, "you have about fifty people with their faces pressed against the window trying to breathe."

Ten minutes later, an officer in the field sent a radio message to one of the teams that were trained to drop from a helicopter: "You're on your way to rig the helicopter. We need you on the roof as soon as possible."

In the north tower, where the plane's wingspan had spread from the 93rd to the 99th floor, the heat and smoke were far more intense than in the south tower, where the impact zone was fifteen to twenty floors lower, from the 77th to the 85th floor. The people had hurled chairs and computer monitors and anything they could find to break the windows to get air, with the unfortunate effect of drawing fire closer to them and to others above them. On the 110th floor, Steve Jacobson, a broadcast engineer for WPIX-TV, had a breathing pack in his office, a piece of precautionary equipment distributed after the 1993 bombing. But in a telephone call to a colleague at the station, Victor J. Arnone, he said he could not make it to the roof.

"It's too hot in the hallway," he said. "I can't leave the room. Get me out of here. Send help."

The first people had been seen falling from the north tower at 8:48 or 8:49, two or three minutes after the crash of Flight 11, men and women at the seat of the inferno of jet fuel. The early plunges were less deliberate, more reflexive, like a person recoiling from a hot stove. To get away from the heat, they did not have to fight their way through fire and flame. The side of the building had been ripped open. Alone or holding hands, they climbed onto windowsills, the only refuge from heat and smoke.

A man. A woman. A man and a woman together.

Later, the people on the upper floors of the north tower retreated into rooms and sealed the doors, but the smoke was relentless, pushing them against the windows—windows that could not be opened. As the smoke and flames moved through the buildings, scores of people called 911 to ask permission to break the windows. No, the operators said, that would make matters worse. Then the people called again, to say that matters were getting worse. On the other side of the room, they said, people had already broken windows. And they were jumping.

When the smoke parted for a moment, Richard Smiouskas could see that not everyone was consciously jumping. Smiouskas, a fire lieutenant and departmental photographer, had climbed to the roof of a building across West Street from the trade center and was watching the developments through a long lens. He saw a man standing in a window frame on a high floor in the north tower. Around him were five or six other faces, crowded into the same narrow window frame. Then the man pitched forward, nudged, it seemed to Smiouskas, by others crowding for a mouthful of air. As the desperation rose, it was impossible not to remember that a drowning person will push a lifeguard under water if it means one more gulp of air.

So urgent was the need to breathe that people piled four and five high in window after window, their upper bodies hanging out, 1,300 feet above the ground. They were in an unforgiving place.

On one of the top floors—104 or 105—two men, one of them shirtless, stood on the windowsills, leaning their bodies so far outside that they could peer around a big intervening column and see each other. On the 103rd floor, a man stared straight out a broken window toward the northwest, bracing himself against a window frame with one hand. He wrapped his other arm around a woman, perhaps to keep her from tumbling to the ground.

That people were falling and jumping from the north tower was evident, not only to onlookers but also by the accounts of callers from within that building. Conversely, there is evidence that only a few people jumped or fell from the south tower. Why people would jump in greater numbers from one building than the other reflects the different paths that the crisis followed in each place. Both towers had similar volumes of smoke and heat, but because of where and when the planes hit, the impact zone in the south tower was not as crowded. Flight 175 had hit the south tower roughly seventeen floors lower than Flight 11 had hit the north tower. And because evacuation had started in the south tower before the plane hit there, fewer people remained in the impact area. In the north tower, about three times as many people were confined to roughly half the space.

From the 101st through the 107th floors of the north tower, nearly 900 people were trapped in the office of Cantor Fitzgerald, and just above it, in Windows on the World. In the restaurant, at least seventy people crowded near office windows at the northwest corner of the 106th floor, according to accounts they gave relatives and coworkers. "Everywhere else is smoked out," Stuart Lee, the Data Synapse vice president, quickly typed in an e-mail to his office in Greenwich Village. "Currently an argument going on as whether we should break a window," Lee continued a few moments later, "Consensus is no for the time being." Soon, though, a dozen people appeared through broken windows along the west face of the restaurant.

By now, fires were rampaging through the impact floors, darting across the north face of the tower. Since most of the space was open, the flames consumed the furnishings—about 20 minutes for each area—then moved on to the next reservoir of fuel. Coils of smoke lashed the people braced around the broken windows.

In Cantor Fitzgerald's northwest conference room on the 104th floor, Andrew Rosenblum and fifty other people temporarily managed to ward off the smoke and heat by plugging vents with jackets. "We smashed the computers into the windows to get some air," Rosenblum reported by cell phone to Barry Kornblum, a colleague who was not in the office.

Rosenblum called his wife, Jill, calmly discussing the situation. He did not mention that people were falling past the windows, but in the midst of speaking to her, he suddenly interjected, without elaboration, "Oh, my God."

Many of those who did not jump or fall from the windows were heaped in stacks along the frames, just as another generation had at the Triangle Shirtwaist fire ninety years earlier. This time, helicopter pilots broadcast descriptions of what they were seeing.

> *Kelhetter:* Aviation 3 has a couple of people hanging off the windows about five floors from the top. There's at least fifty people hanging on.

An officer on the ground radioed the helicopters. They could see a man poised on a high ledge.

> *Ground:* Definitely outside the building. Do you have an eyeball on him?
> [*inaudible*]
> *Ground:* He's the one with the white shirt. We've been watching him for about a good five minutes, he's . . . completely outside of the yellow line.
> *Kelhetter:* All right, let me go pass one more time.
> *Ground:* Right about the center of the building, looks like he's got on black pants and a white shirt.
> *Kelhetter:* Is he below the fire line?
> *Ground:* Affirmative. . . . You see where that white flag is. . . . He's directly below that white flag but several floors below it.
> *Kelhetter:* We're about 1,200 feet. Have him in view from 1,200 feet from the ground, whatever floor that would be.
> *Ground:* But you definitely see him, he's there by himself, correct?
> *Kelhetter:* He's standing there by himself.
> *Ground:* All right, 10-4. Thank you. I'm going to go over to . . . and try and let them know inside.

From his helicopter, Greg Semendinger saw just the highest order of desperation. Get to the roof, he wanted to yell, as he flew closer to the building. Another order came from the ground, this time from an ESU lieutenant, Steve Reardon:

> *Reardon:* Be advised that no one is to rappel onto the top of the building.

The dispatcher had a hard time repeating his words precisely.

> *Dispatcher:* Units . . . no one is to compel [*sic*] on top of the building, no one is to compel on top of the building.

But Semendinger held out some hope. From his vantage point, the northwest corner of the north tower roof was pretty clear of smoke. Unfortunately, the automatic window-washing machine had stopped on its rooftop track at that precise location, making a landing impossible. The ESU cops would not be able to climb down on ropes, as they had done in 1993. It was too dangerous, given the smoke and heat. The only remaining option, and it was a long shot, would be to lower the hoist and perhaps pull up a few people from the roof. It would take patience. Only two people at a time could be lifted because of the 600-pound weight limit. And the group would have to be orderly, to police itself. Even then it would be difficult. The cable might snag one of the rooftop antennas, tethering the ship to a burning building. Or the heat rising from the inferno might thin the air, weakening the updrafts that helicopters need to fly.

Semendinger knew that if anyone did make it to the roof, imploring him for help, he would face a torturous choice. His life. The lives of his crew. Those of the people on the roof. As it turned out, the decision was made for him.

Locked. The doors were locked. They had traveled all the way to the roof, in the smoke, up the stairs, and it was a blind alley. Sean Rooney from Aon; Roko Camaj the window washer; Frank Doyle,

Rick Thorpe, and Stephen Mulderry from Keefe, Bruyette & Woods. Dozens of people in the south tower had tried to get to the roof, only to find their way blocked.

The situation was identical in the north tower, where a man trapped in the stairwell at the 103rd floor exploded over the radio. "Open the goddamn doors," he yelled into his walkie-talkie.

In the south tower, Sean Rooney pounded on a door. It wouldn't move, he told his wife, Beverly, by phone. She told him to try it again while she waited on the line. They had been high school sweethearts and had just celebrated turning fifty together with special vacations to Vermont, to mark Sean's birthday, and Morocco, for Beverly's. When Sean returned to the phone, he told Beverly the door still wouldn't move. "Tell me what you see on TV," he said. He needed her to figure out how the flames were advancing in the building. He was on the 105th floor on the north side of the building, he told her calmly. That was seven flights above his office. He had already tried to go down without success. Now he couldn't fathom why the doors leading up would not open.

While she listened, Beverly dialed 911 on another line. The operators who fielded her calls and others' said that emergency crews were on their way. Hang in there. No one had told the operators that stairway A in the south tower—the one that Richard Fern and his Euro Brokers colleagues had gone down—was open, so they could not tell anyone inside the building to use it. Instead, while they spoke, the operators typed shorthand versions of what they were hearing onto a computer screen.

2 World Trade, 105th Floor. People trapped. Open Roof to Gain Access.

The Port Authority had been locking the roof doors for decades. Agency officials said that controlling access to the space allowed them to thwart vandals, daredevils, and suicides. True, Philippe Petit's tightrope walk between the two towers had cast a magical aura on what had been seen as dour architecture, but the Port

Authority did not want its roofs turned into permanent stages for people with grievances, exhibitionist impulses, or a desire to hurt themselves. Some managers for companies on the upper floors clearly understood the off-limits policy. Many people, inside the building and out, did not. The ex-firefighter Bernie Heeran had couseled his son, Charles, to go to the roof. After all, the city building code required that people be able to get onto roofs during an emergency. The roof access doors had to be left unlocked. If they were connected to a buzzer system, they were supposed to be fail-safe—meaning that they would automatically unlock if power failed or calamity struck.

The trade center, however, was exempt from the code. The Port Authority had decided to lock the doors and the Fire Department had chosen to go along with that decision, believing that such a policy would reinforce its message that down was the proper way to evacuate in a high-rise fire. As a result, three sets of doors blocked access to the roof in each tower. A person who climbed to the top of the stairs at the 110th floor needed an electronic swipe card to get through the first two. That put the person in a tiny vestibule facing a third door that opened to the stairs leading to the roof. To get through the final door, a person had to be buzzed in by security officers who watched on a closed-circuit camera from their offices on the 22nd floor of the north tower.

Marie Refuse, one of the security officers on duty in the 22nd-floor center, was still at her desk at 9:30. She spoke with Ed Calderon, a supervisor, whose radio code was S-5.

> *Marie Refuse:* Would you like me to release all doors and gates?
> *Ed Calderon:* That is affirmative. This is the S-5, that is affirmative.
> *Marie Refuse:* That's a copy, we're doing it now.

There was a problem: the computer that operated the doors was not working properly. ACCESS DENIED, the screen blared. The security agents on 22 could not open the doors to the roof, or to the floors just below it, which were mechanical rooms and also required electronic access. For that matter, they could not even open their own door, from the inside. A deputy security director, George Tabeek, led a team of firefighters up to the 22nd floor in hopes of getting them out.

>   **George Tabeek:** We're on 16 right now.
>   **Marie Refuse:** That's a copy. We can't use the software right
>   now to try to release the doors.

Roko Camaj, the window washer, had both the authorization and the swipe card, but he couldn't make it onto the roof, either. He told relatives by phone that he was stuck on the 105th floor with 200 other people. He never specified why he could not get to the roof. Perhaps Camaj and the others had gotten as far as the 110th floor, but the first floor they could call from was the 105th because that was the nearest stairwell door that would open. Camaj used his radio to call down to a colleague at the Port Authority operations desk. The colleague, John Mongello, told Camaj they needed his exact location. The 105th floor, Camaj told him.

"You coming up here?" Camaj asked.

"I don't think so, Roko," John said. "I'm going to talk to someone. They may have to find another way to get you."

"A lot of people up here, and big smoke," Camaj responded.

John told Camaj he should get down as far as the 98th floor. The stairwell was clear from there down. Somehow the operations desk knew about stairway A, which had not been severed by the plane, the one that a few others had been using to flee. The information had otherwise not circled back upstairs. Brian Clark and Stanley Praimnath and Rich Fern, among others, had escaped down stairway A of the south tower from above the crash zone. While some people in the command center at the trade center seemed to know about it, and spoke about it on their walkie-talkies, they could not communicate with the ordinary tenants on the upper floors. Those people did not know that there was a way out by going down—that there was, in fact, a passable staircase. Most of them were dialing not into the basement command center but into the city's 911 call center—and no one there was aware of the escape route.

"Roko, take your time," John said. "You are going to have to make your way down the stairwell." Camaj's response was inaudible.

Many others who had climbed to the roof of the south tower were also heading down, though not because they knew of a stairway that would carry them past the smoke and flames. They were simply trying to find a suitable place to make their last stand. Frank Doyle and the some of the other traders from Keefe, Bruyette & Woods struggled back to a conference room on the 88th floor. Doyle called his wife, Kimmy, from a working phone.

"Hi, sweetie," he said. "We need your help. We've tried getting out on the roof but the doors are locked."

More than a dozen people from the firm were with Doyle, including Rick Thorpe and Stephen Mulderry, who had been on the phone with his brother, Peter, just before the south tower was hit. Only one phone worked and each person used it to make his essential calls. Stephen called Peter again.

"Hey, brother," he said.

"Thank God, you're okay," Peter responded.

"I'm really not," Stephen said.

He recounted their failed attempts, both up and down, to escape. He asked for his mother's phone number because she had recently moved, and he had not committed the new number to memory. And he told Peter he loved him.

"Are you sure there's no way out of that room?" Peter asked.

"No, like I told you, we tried everything," Stephen said. "We're just going to wait for the firemen to come get us. But it's a long way for them to come, and the smoke's really bad. Some people are talking about throwing the fire extinguisher through the window, but I know that will be the end of us. But if someone panics and does it, there's nothing I can do."

A few minutes later, the phone was passed to Rick Thorpe, who called his wife, Linda, at a neighbor's house. Earlier in the day, after the second plane had hit, Rick and Linda had agreed that she would go there with their baby, Alexis. He would call when he knew more. But when the phone rang this time, for some reason, Rick could not speak.

"Hello—Rick—Rick," Linda called into the phone.

There was no response, but Linda and her neighbor could hear the ambient noise from the conference room. People were coughing as it filled with smoke. They were having trouble seeing across the room.

"Where is the fire extinguisher?" someone said.

"It already got thrown out the window," came the reply.

"Is anybody unconscious?" asked someone else.

Linda and the neighbor could not hear an answer.

The voices of some of the people sounded calm. Others trembled with strain. One man began screaming, the words lost to anguish. Another man tried to console him.

"It's okay," the man said, soothingly. "It'll be okay."

10

"I've got a second wind."

9:15 A.M.
NORTH TOWER

The street screamed. Fire trucks rolled in, and ambulances, and police cars, each with its siren spinning alarm into the sky. Another irregular wall of sound came from two-way radios, with hundreds of voices crashing through the aural pipelines. In the middle of the commotion, Gerry Drohan, a construction inspector from the Port Authority, stood on a sidewalk outside the trade center with an ear to his walkie-talkie, and immediately recognized one voice the moment he heard it: a slightly nasal tone, scented with the accents of a youth in south New Jersey, near Philadelphia, and adulthood on the streets of Brooklyn. In a riot of sound, Frank De Martini's voice was calm and collected. "Construction manager," he said, identifying himself. "The elevator . . . the express elevators could be in jeopardy of falling. Be prepared for that. Do you copy?"

The words were calibrated precisely to the task. De Martini was issuing a warning; then he continued what he, Pablo Ortiz, and a few others had been doing for the past half hour, methodically freeing scores of people trapped from the 90th floor down, in offices and elevators just below the impact zone in the north tower. They had been efficient, De Martini and Ortiz, working with a crowbar

146

and a long flashlight, as if rescuing people were the jobs that they had been hired for. The truth was that neither man had a role in the official evacuation or emergency plans for the buildings. Their regular job was to oversee tenant renovations, with De Martini supervising a team that made sure all changes met Port Authority standards. Both men knew the building, how it worked, and in some ways, they loved it. They were trying to leave, but kept stopping to clear floors. Now De Martini and his crew had reached the 78th floor and its sky lobby.

De Martini got no response to his warning about the express elevators, at least none that could be transcribed from the radio tapes. Around the same time, he issued another request. *"Any construction inspector at ground level,"* De Martini called out.

Drohan was at ground level, having left the 88th floor of the north tower before the first plane hit, thinking he had just enough time to run a simple errand. His daughter had given him a couple of rolls of film to get developed, and he hoped to drop them off, then make it back by 9:00 for an inspection in the south tower of renovations done in the offices of Aon Insurance. All his plans had come to a halt at 8:46, when the first plane struck.

From the street, with no access to television, Drohan assumed that something had exploded in a mechanical room. Then, for one of the few times in his life, he was paged by his wife, who told him that a plane had struck the tower. She was glad to find him already outside. A few minutes later, the second plane crashed into the south tower. Around 9:15, Drohan heard De Martini over the walkie-talkie.

"Any construction inspector at ground level."

Drohan acknowledged that he was on the street.

"Can you escort a couple of structural inspectors to the 78th floor?" De Martini asked.

De Martini had seen something in the steel—Drohan was not sure what—that he did not like. The drywall had been knocked off parts of the sky lobby, exposing the elevator shafts, and revealing the core of the building. That had prompted his first radio alert, warning that the elevators might collapse. Now De Martini wanted inspectors from a structural engineering firm to come up to the 78th-floor sky lobby and take a look. He thought Drohan could bring them into the building.

"I can't get back into the building," Drohan replied. "There's a police line."

De Martini did not settle easily. This, after all, was a man who had once stood on the roof of his restored brownstone in Brooklyn to make sure firefighters did not damage it when they were attacking a blaze next door; a man who had chased down litterbugs on the street to reproach them and point out the error of their ways. He had even faced down a burglar in his own house.

"Let me talk to a police officer," De Martini said. "Can you give the radio to one of them?"

For Frank De Martini to be worried about the structural integrity of even a small part of the World Trade Center was a giant leap. At his most expansive, De Martini could hold forth to young and old on the wonders of the place, the mighty machines that moved fresh air around the buildings, the giant pipes that carried water from the Hudson River for the cooling plant, the emergency generators that would keep computers running should all else fail. A group from his old high school in New Jersey had visited earlier in the year, and he gave them the tour of a proud insider. He also had been interviewed for a documentary about the trade center for the History Channel. Many of the old-timers at the trade center had not been interested in being filmed—perhaps they were tired of telling their stories—but De Martini relished the opportunity to show off the buildings. He had a fresh eye for the towers, and was himself a newcomer by Port Authority standards, having first worked at the trade center on a three-month assignment after the 1993 bombing. His job was to assess the damage and the progress of repairs, a task he performed for the Port Authority's consulting engineer, Leslie E. Robertson, who had been part of the team that did the original structural design for the towers during the 1960s. Given the conditions at the trade center after the bombing, De Martini had to make a standing start from chaos, a posture that he relished.

In those months after the 1993 bombing, De Martini, like many others, also absorbed some of the reassuring, even comforting lessons that were drawn from that first attack. The towers had proven their resilience. The bomb parked in the basement had done tremendous damage all through the confines of the garage, of course, but each tower had proved itself an unflinching colossus. Leslie Robertson was so taken with the strength of the buildings he had helped design in his youth, he arranged to ship a 14,000-pound steel brace that had been blown off the base of the building to his weekend home in Connecticut. There he mounted it on a pedestal in the yard. The point of this industrial sculpture was not the salvaged metal, but its evocation of the Olympian indifference of the structures to a blast that had been powerful enough to tear off a seventy-five-foot column. It was as if the *Titanic* had hit the iceberg and still steamed on to New York.

On the morning after the 1993 bombing, Robertson explained to a reporter that the bombers had parked the truck against the base of the north tower, on its south side—a spot that a layperson might have thought just right for knocking the north tower onto the south. The engineer had made a point that morning of reiterating one of the most striking claims about the strength of the towers, and it was one that Frank De Martini would recall nearly eight years later, when he was interviewed in January 2001 for the History Channel documentary about the towers. "The building was designed to have a fully loaded 707 crash into it," De Martini said. "That was the largest plane at the time."

Videotaped at his desk on the 88th floor of the north tower, where he was flanked by a series of framed photographs showing the towers as they rose during the 1970s, De Martini offered a simple but illuminating analogy to explain how that could be true. The answer, he said, was the pinstriped columns around the outside of the towers.

"I believe the building probably could sustain multiple impacts of jetliners because this structure is like the mosquito netting on your screen door, this intense grid," De Martini said. "And the jet plane is just a pencil puncturing the screen netting. It really does nothing to the screen netting."

That interview had been recorded in January. Now, eight months later, and thirty minutes into the crisis on September 11, De Martini wanted the structural inspectors up to the sky lobby, to look into the gaping holes. And if Gerry Drohan could not talk his way past a police officer, De Martini was ready to give it a try from the 78th floor. As it should happen, standing directly in front of Drohan was a senior police officer—an inspector, Drohan guessed, from the white uniform shirt.

Drohan approached the officer, told him about De Martini, and handed him the radio. The policeman talked to Frank, for a moment. Then he handed the walkie-talkie back to Drohan. No way was he getting across the line.

"We'll have the Fire Department take care of it," the officer said.

Rather than being rebuffed, De Martini appeared to have been reminded of something. He had to warn firefighters that the elevators looked extremely fragile. Fifteen minutes after his first warning, De Martini broadcast another.

> *De Martini:* Construction manager to base, be advised that
>   the express elevators are in danger of collapse. Do you
>   read?
> *Male:* [*inaudible*]
> *De Martini:* Relay that, Chris, to the firemen, that the ele—
> *Male:* Express elevators are gonna collapse? . . . Advise . . .
>   What elevators? . . . All express elevators? Which spe-
>   cific . . . specific ones? [*pause*]
> *Male:* [*inaudible*]

Far from the clamor on the street, De Martini faced another crisis on the 78th floor. Still trapped in an elevator was Tony Savas, a seventy-two-year-old inspector who worked on De Martini's construction team. Savas's predicament had been discovered early, since many of his colleagues from the 88th floor had passed through the 78th-floor sky lobby during their descent, and a number of them had made futile attempts to open his elevator doors. Savas had sent a message over his radio that was cool in syntax but urgent in content: there was smoke coming in. Word of his trouble had gotten back to De Martini and Ortiz while they were still prying open doors on the upper floors and leading people to safety. They made their way down to 78.

Among the other people on the 78th floor was a young security guard, Greg Trapp, who had moved to New York after serving in the army, to pursue a life in acting and to make his own movies. Earlier in the summer, he had started working as a guard at the trade center, catching any available shifts. That morning, he drew a post at the sky lobby, where he steered people transferring to an elevator for Windows on the World. (The elevator that ran directly from the ground to the restaurant was out of service, necessitating a transfer at 78 for the last leg of the journey.) Hundreds of people were expected for the Risk Waters conference at the restaurant, but only eighty-one had arrived when the first plane hit. In those early minutes, Trapp and a tenant had gone up to about the 84th floor, the first reentry floor from the stairway, and rousted some people from an office.

When he returned to 78, Trapp saw a group of three Port Authority employees at work on the doors to the elevator where Savas was trapped. Trapp peered into the small gap and saw Savas, a man with thinning white hair, seemingly serene. The Port Authority workers all knew him, Trapp noted. That was not surprising: Savas loved coming to work, rising at 5:45, and every couple of years, he promised his wife that he would retire—in a couple of years. Now the colleagues who knew him so well would try to get him out.

Unlike others who had passed through the floor and made a few fleeting efforts to pry open the doors, this group was consumed with the task of opening them. The project challenged their brains and brawn. They managed to move the doors an inch or two, but they knew that the safety locks would not yield easily. Tough as it was, this was work they could do. What could they use for tools? A few feet away was a sign, directing visitors to the elevators for the lobby. It stood on a metal easel. To hold the doors apart, one of the men grabbed the easel and wedged the legs into the little opening. That did not solve the problem: spreading the doors from the bottom, where they seemed to have the greatest leverage, had the opposite effect at the top of the doors, which seemed to pinch tighter. The doors also had an electronic lock at the top that kept them from opening if the car stopped more than a few inches from the landing.

John Griffin, who had started work during the summer as the trade center's director of operations for Silverstein Properties, the new leaseholder, came over to the elevator bank. At six feet eight inches tall, Griffin had no problem reaching the top of the elevator door to apply pressure as the others pushed from the bottom, and to manipulate the locking device. The doors popped apart.

Out came Savas, who was surprised to find Griffin, his new boss, involved in the rescue. Rubbing his hands together, Savas appeared exhilarated, possessed of a sudden burst of energy, or so he seemed to the security guard.

"Okay," Savas said. "What do you need me to do?"

One of the other Port Authority workers shook his head. "We just got you out—you need to leave the building."

No, Savas insisted. He wanted to help. "I've got a second wind."

The identities of the three Port Authority employees who freed Tony Savas are uncertain, but a number of circumstances—including subsequent photo identifications by Greg Trapp—suggest that Frank De Martini was definitely among the three. Trapp also remembered a man with an earring. Pablo Ortiz wore an earring. The third person may have been Pete Negron, a Port Authority employee who worked on the 88th floor but had not been there when the plane hit.

John Griffin, whose height had been so essential to opening the doors, moved to a bank of pay phones and tried to make calls. Over a walkie-talkie, Trapp thought he heard a transmission that firefighters had arrived on the 78th floor.

Griffin decided that he would go look for them.

"Do you want me to come with you?" asked Trapp.

No, Griffin said, he should stay.

Griffin disappeared down corridors, scouting around the one-acre floor, in search of the firefighters. He came back a few minutes later. Perhaps they had heard wrong.

Trapped in another elevator, on the 50th floor of the north tower, the six men in car 69A had been working steadily, urgently, for more than a half hour to get out. So far, they had torn and punched through nearly three inches of drywall. One more gouge, and surely they would be free.

Just as the towers were cut off from the outside world, even deeper levels of isolation were nested inside the buildings. About one-quarter of the space in each tower consisted of the core, which contained the shafts for the elevators. Deeper still were the elevator cars: cloistered boxes inside the shafts inside the towers.

The array of ninety-nine elevators in each of the towers had been the engines of wonder, making the impossible height of the trade center simply another few minutes tacked on to the workday commute. This morning, the flaming balls of fuel, in pursuit of oxygen, raced up and down the shafts in the two buildings, burning many people in the cars, killing some immediately. The concussions blew off elevator doors and shaft walls on the top thirty to fifty floors of each building. Even in the ground-floor lobbies, doors flew off. In the north tower, in the shaft for the express elevator dedicated to serving Windows on the World—and thus one of the few that ran uninterrupted from the bottom of the building to the top—the burning fuel seemed to hurtle through like a bullet in the barrel of a long rifle. The lobby doors shot off their frames. The elevator system that had made the trade center and buildings like it possible had become the carrier of devastation.

More than a century earlier, as New York City's population was exploding, the contours of Manhattan Island meant that the city could grow in only one direction—up, the same direction that many other cities, for one reason or another, would also take. Before tall buildings could become part of the landscape, New Yorkers had to be convinced that they could reach high floors without climbing;

conversely, they also had to believe that any machine that carried them to a high place would not simply plunge to the ground if it failed.

In 1854, Elisha Graves Otis, standing on a platform, was hoisted by a rope higher and higher above a crowd that had gathered at New York's Crystal Palace for an exhibition organized by P. T. Barnum. The platform rode along tracks at either side. At the top, Otis drew a knife and slashed the hoist rope, presumably all that kept him from falling back to earth. Instead, the car dropped, then came to a halt, thanks to the automatic safety braking system Otis had devised from a ratchet and the spring of a wagon wheel.

Over the decades, engineers developed multiple elaborations of the Otis principle: to make falling all but impossible, one system stopped the car if a cable was cut, and another returned it peacefully to its lowest floor and opened the doors. These features were naturally incorporated into the elevators at the trade center.

The most necessary innovation for the twin towers, however, was the creation of the express and local systems, with the sky lobbies at the 44th and 78th floors serving as transfer points. This cut down on the number of elevators. It also created one final depth of isolation, as the experience of the six men in car 69A showed.

At 8:46, just seconds before the first plane hit, the six men—Jan Demczur, George Phoenix, John Paczkowski, Shivam Iyer, Colin Richardson, and Al Smith—had boarded the car at the north tower's 44th-floor sky lobby, most of them having just stopped at a cafeteria on 43 for breakfast. Phoenix, a Port Authority engineer, was carrying coffee, milk, and a Danish pastry. Demczur, a window washer, had an old green bucket, its rectangular mouth perfect for his squeegee. Car 69A was a shuttle that picked up passengers at 44 and then made stops between 67 and 74.

The car rose, but before it reached the first landing, the men felt a muted thud. The elevator swung from side to side, like a pendulum. Then the car seemed to plunge. Someone punched an emergency stop button, and the car halted. They got a recorded response telling them that their message had been received, and that help was on the way. No one knew what was going on; the men in the elevator were as cut off 500 feet in the sky as if they had been trapped 500 feet underwater.

After ten minutes, a live voice delivered a blunt message over the intercom. There had been an explosion. Then the intercom went silent. Smoke began seeping into the cabin. One man cursed skyscrapers. Phoenix, the tallest, poked for a ceiling hatch. Others pried apart the car doors, propping them open with the long wooden handle of Demczur's squeegee. There was no exit. They faced a wall, blank other than a stenciled number 50. That particular elevator bank did not serve the 50th floor, so there was no need for an opening.

The six men were trapped by a feature of the trade center most cherished by its designers, and thoroughly despised by firefighters: the long elevator shafts devoted to express service. The firefighters' objection was not to quick travel or efficient use of space; the problem was that the towers had no provisions for getting into the shafts anywhere but on the floors where the cars made regular stops. So for hundreds of vertical feet, the shafts ran "blind," entirely closed by gypsum wallboard. To remove people from a car stalled in one of those shafts posed an enormous challenge: first, to find them—there were fifteen miles of elevator shafts in the towers—and second, to reach them. After the 1993 bombing, the United States Fire Administration collected reports from the supervising chiefs, and all expressed frustration with the design. "The blind shafts in the WTC extended 78 stories," Deputy Chief Steven C. DeRosa wrote. "Firefighters had to open the shaft every five floors to locate a car—it was impossible to see more than six floors into the blackness. Some local building codes require openings into blind elevator shafts at three-floor intervals; this feature was not provided in the case of the WTC."

Now, inside car 69A, Demczur felt the wall. His fingertips told him it was drywall. Having worked in construction after he first arrived in the United States from Poland, he knew that it could be cut with a sharp knife. A quick survey of the car found that no one had a knife. From his bucket, Demczur drew the only available sharp edge: his squeegee. He slid its metal edge against the wall, back and forth, over and over. He was spelled by the other men, and they scored deeper and deeper. Blinking and coughing in the smoke, they breathed through handkerchiefs moistened in the container of milk that Phoenix had just picked up in the cafeteria.

Sheetrock comes in panels about one inch thick, Demczur recalled. The men cut an inch, then two inches. Demczur's hand ached. As he carved into the third panel, his hand shook; he fumbled the squeegee and dropped it down the shaft. Now he had one tool left: a short metal squeegee handle. The men carried on, with fists, feet and handle, cutting a jagged rectangle about twelve by eighteen inches. Finally, they breached the last layer of Sheetrock, only to hit a layer of white tiles. A bathroom. They broke the tiles. Smith squeezed out first, then went into the hallways—where, remarkably, he immediately boarded another elevator that brought him down from 50 to the 44th floor sky lobby. There, catching his breath, was Mike McQuaid, the electrician who had been on the 91st floor installing fire alarms when the plane hit. McQuaid rode back up to 50 with Smith. In the bathroom the other men were still squirming, one by one, through the opening, headfirst, sideways, popping onto the floor near a sink. Demczur turned back. "Pass my bucket out," he said. By then, about 9:30, the 50th floor was already deserted. They hustled into the staircase.

On the single-file descent, someone teased Demczur about the battered old bucket he insisted on bringing. "The company might not order me another one," he replied.

Not all the elevators stopped in blind shafts. For that matter, not all the elevators stopped. An instant before Flight 175 hit the south tower, an express elevator left the 78th floor, bound for the lobby, packed with passengers including people from the research department of Keefe, Bruyette & Woods, and others from Aon. The plane's impact severed the cables to that car, and it began what felt like a free-fall, plunging toward the lobby. Here was a nightmare that long ago seemed to have been written out of the myth of tall build-ings. The people inside dropped to their knees. As the car fell through the shaft, screeching, it slowed, then rumbled to a halt, when one last emergency system kicked in: a brake that stopped them about ten feet above the lobby.

Inside, about twenty-five men and women lay in a tangle of twisted metal, in absolute darkness. Someone, they were sure, would realize they were stuck and get them out. They waited. One person pulled out a laptop, switched it on to provide some light. The box that had been the elevator car seemed crushed. Maybe five or ten minutes later, when flames began to lick into the bottom of the cab, a keening began.

"In the name of God," a voice wailed. "In the name of God. In the name of God."

Then, with a shift in smoke, or less dust, they could see some-thing: a little shaft of light. At the base of the car, the violence had peeled back the remnants of the door ever so slightly, revealing a glimpse of the lobby beneath them. Alan Mann, an executive with Aon, climbed to the front across people sprawled on the floor, and used his left hand to yank at a piece of metal. In some order, three people were able to get out of the car. Linda Rothemund of Keefe, Bruyette & Woods squeezed through, lowered by the people inside. She saw no one in the lobby, then ran into the concourse for help. Mann tried to go headfirst through the hole, and could not, but was able to wiggle through feetfirst, dropping into the lobby with his pants in shreds, his shoes gone, his left hand cut deeply on the metal. He saw few people in the lobby, then wandered into the con-course, spotting four firefighters, and led them back to the car. Then he stumbled out toward Church Street.

Finally, Lauren Smith, also of KBW, pushed through the same hole, but when she hit the ground in the lobby, pitched into an exposed elevator shaft. Her fall was broken by a beam in the shaft, fracturing five of her ribs and puncturing a lung. Her drop into the elevator shaft entered the annals of the catastrophe at 9:39, thirty-seven minutes after Flight 175 had hit the south tower, fifty-three minutes into the crisis.

PAPD Officer Thomas Grogan: Two World Trade Center, probably 3-10 level [the lobby], a female fell through the shaft. They need somebody to see if they can get her.

PAPD Officer Ray Murray: Two World Trade Center, fell through the shaft.

PAPD Officer Thomas Grogan: Two World Trade Center, I don't know what car, though.

PAPD Officer Ray Murray: Okay.

In a few minutes, Linda Rothemund returned. Help was gathering. Ron Hoerner, a supervisor for the private security guards, peered into the elevator shaft. Eight or ten feet down, Smith grabbed a cable and pulled herself up high enough so that the people in the lobby could reach her. She remembered being hoisted by a "human ladder."

Another message went out over the radio.

PAPD Officer Thomas Grogan: She's in the lobby, they . . . they actually have her, they need EMS. They [*inaudible*]

PAPD Officer Ray Murray: Okay, lobby, she's in the . . . all right, Tom, I'll tell them.

Smith moaned. Hoerner summoned James Flores, a Summit Security guard who usually served as quartermaster for the operation, distributing the blue blazers and clip-on ties to the 300 guards who worked at the trade center. After the plane hit the south tower, Flores had gone to the mezzanine, where two of the stairways terminated, and was among the volunteers and rescuers who had steered the evacuating people toward the escalators that would bring them to ground level.

Hoerner beckoned Flores to Smith's side.

"Hold her hand," he ordered. "Don't let go."

In search of help Hoerner hustled over to a silver door that led down a few flights to a basement communications center, and Flores glanced at him vanishing behind the door. A moment or two later, a paramedic appeared, but he had no gurney. Everyone agreed that Smith needed a backboard of some kind. A few Port Authority police officers appeared. Flores watched as one of them, a man with powerful arms, walked over to the concierge table. Covering the tabletop was a long, sturdy piece of glass. The officer picked up the glass and brought it to the elevator bank. The paramedic slipped it behind Smith, then had her roll onto it. Atop a piece of glass that rested at its four corners on the shoulders of three Port Authority officers and the paramedic, with James Flores lending a hand to keep it in balance, Lauren Smith left the World Trade Center for the last time, traveling through the concourse that took her east, to Church Street, where ambulances were waiting. Back at the elevator, firefighters were struggling to open the doors of the elevator she had managed to slip from.

Even cars whose cables were severed by the planes behaved normally, at least in part: they came to a stop, just as Otis and his successors had planned. Two other safety features—one that failed, and one that worked—cost lives. By law in New York City, elevators are equipped with sensors that are designed to return elevator cars to their lowest floor, and open the doors. Cars did return to their original floors, but in many cases, perhaps most, the doors did not open. Others simply stopped in blind shafts.

Perhaps the most lethal safety features were the resistors, which prevented doors from opening if the car stopped more than four inches from a landing. After gruesome elevator accidents in the 1970s and 1980s, the city codes required that resistors be installed on all doors, beginning in 1987. The requirement was updated in 1996. The elevator mechanics who worked at the trade center felt they were dangerous because they were so unforgiving, often requiring a mechanic to go to the roof of the cab to unlock the device if the elevator could not be moved back to level. Still, the Port Authority had promised after the 1993 catastrophe that it would strictly abide by building codes, and after internal debate, the resistors were installed, along with less controversial items like backup battery power for the lights and communications systems.

The two buildings were staffed by eighty elevator mechanics, but all of them left the trade center after the second plane hit. Initially, in the early moments of the attacks, they had started assembling in the lobby of the south tower, but when that building also was struck, they moved their meeting point to a spot across the street from the trade center, and then even further clear of the chaos, to the South Street Seaport, several blocks away. Many of the same mechanics had been part of the laborious 1993 evacuations, going to machine rooms, where they slowly moved the counterweights on cars stuck in blind shafts by the loss of electrical power. Now, however, that cadre of skills had moved outside the buildings—just as they had in 1993. The mechanics planned on reentering when the situation stabilized, as they had in the 1993 crisis, but events were moving too fast this time for any civilians to get back in.

Those who remained in the building improvised. On his way down from the 91st floor, shortly after Flight 11 had hit the north tower, Mike McQuaid, the electrician, heard the voices of two men in an elevator on the 82nd floor that had not stopped properly. The doors were shut tight by a resistor. McQuaid and his partner, Tony Segarra, managed to wedge it open a few inches. The men inside fretted that McQuaid and Segarra would dislodge the car and make it fall, so they slapped their hands away. They preferred, McQuaid would remember, to wait for rescuers to come up and get them.

To protect people in the long blind shafts, a city task force in the early 1970s required that consoles be set up in lobbies that would permit tracking of the location of the elevators. Francis Riccardelli, the chief elevator manager for the towers, was in the south tower lobby, answering a stream of intercom messages from people who were trapped in the cars and looking for help. As he worked, a fire alarm went off in the building, with a piercing, whooping noise. He sent a radio message to the command center in the basement.

> *Riccardelli:* Maybe we can turn off that alarm, people are in there crying for help, everybody is, like, stuck.
> *Male:* Copy, what alarm is that?
> *Riccardelli:* The fire alarm!

Male: Copy. [*pause*]
Riccardelli: Copy, they haven't been getting out at all!
[*echoes*] We've got people trapped above the 89th floor,
we're trying to [*inaudible*] right now.

Some people trapped in the cars managed to get calls to the 911
system, the staccato messages recorded by the operators not even
specifying which tower was involved.

Female caller states they are stuck in the elevator. States
they are dying. Between 84th and 87th floors. Fire Department notified. Need respirator.

On the 71st floor of the north tower, Bob Eisenstadt and Frank
Bucaretti, from the Port Authority's architecture team, were trapped
in an elevator car. A group gathered outside, including a man from
Bank of America and nine other Port Authority employees. Despite
all their efforts, the resistor would not allow the door to budge
more than a few inches. They jammed a paper puncher into that
tiny space to keep it open. Eisenstadt knew where tools could be
found—in the architectural model shop a few steps away.

"I can see a cable up here that's holding—if I can cut it, it will
open," Eisenstadt said. "Go to the model room, get me a wire cutter
or a cable cutter." Mark Jakubek and a few others went to the model
room. High and low, they hunted but could not find the toolbox
Eisenstadt had in mind. Instead, Jakubek found a post from an
office partition, and brought that over—maybe, he thought, that
would give them another lever. Even that turned out to be not much
use against the powerful resistors. Jakubek returned to the model
room but still could not find the toolbox. Back at the elevator he
stood on a couch to work on the upper part of the doors, which
seemed to be the spot where they were most tightly bound. Then
out of nowhere, it seemed, a stranger appeared and tapped Jakubek
on the shoulder. He held a wire cutter with red handles. Jakubek
passed it to the men inside the car.

Someone warned that the job had to be done carefully, because the cable might be under high tension and could snap. Eisenstadt made the cut, the door slid open, and he and Bucaretti emerged to great jubilation. It had taken a squad of strong men, with access to a toolbox, nearly half an hour of pushing, searching, and snipping to open just one stuck elevator. The complex had 197 others.

Farther up in the north tower, having freed Tony Savas from the 78th-floor elevator, Frank De Martini and his men kept finding tasks requiring their attention. Around 9:38, fifty-two minutes after Flight 11 hit, Pete Negron began hunting down a Port Authority colleague, Carlos DaCosta, who had stayed behind on the 88th floor. DaCosta had been reluctant to leave the Port Authority office, thinking the safer course was to await rescuers to bring everyone downstairs. To clear the smoke, he had smashed open an office window, cutting himself badly.

After most of the people had left the 88th floor, DaCosta apparently changed his mind about staying, because he made his way down to the 87th floor, where he was involved in this exchange:

> *Pete Negron–Environmental 96:* Environmental, 9-6, Carlos DaCosta.
> [*alarms, noise*]
> *Carlos DaCosta:* Go, please, Pete!
> *Pete Negron–Environmental 96:* Carlos, your location?
> *Carlos DaCosta:* I'm up by 87, with a couple people! Trapped in the, the elevator! In the 92 area!

While the transcript could be read to suggest that DaCosta himself was trapped in the elevator, that is highly unlikely, since he had been seen by at least a dozen people on the 88th floor, well after the plane had struck. Moreover, his reference to the "ninety-two area" appears to be elevator car 92, which did not stop on the 87th floor. At that point, car 92 ran in a blind shaft, and the shaft itself was within the walls of a bathroom. Because so many people had been trapped in blind shafts during the 1993 attack, the Port Authority had installed alarm bells, to provide some way of audibly signaling the location from inside those shafts. The people inside the 92 car may well have rung their bell, which would have permitted DaCosta to hear them.

His friend Pete Negron—somewhere downstairs, quite possibly with De Martini and Ortiz—decided to give DaCosta a hand.

> *Pete Negron:* What floor are you on?
> *Carlos DaCosta:* I'm on 87 right now, Pete.
> *Pete Negron:* All right, I'm on my way up.
> *Carlos DaCosta:* Roger, thank you!

By now, the 78th floor was quiet. The tenants from the upper floors were no longer passing through the sky lobby on 78 as they switched stairwells. One of the Port Authority workers turned to the security guard, Greg Trapp.

"Why are you up here?" he asked.

"I'm with Summit Security," Trapp said. "They told us to hold our posts. I figured I might as well do something."

"You get on your radio and find out if they need you up here," the Port Authority worker said.

"Okay with me," Trapp said.

> *Greg Trapp:* Hey, 63, this is security officer on 78 sky lobby.
>   [*alarms heard in background*]
> *Female:* Mr. [*inaudible*], where's your [*inaudible*]?
> *Greg Trapp:* Seventy-eight sky lobby. Seventy-eight sky lobby!
> *Female:* That's a copy. Are you okay, sir?
> *Greg Trapp:* Yes, I am. Yes, I am. What do you want me to do?
> *Female:* If it's possible, 10-6, try to keep your air clear, and
>   we'll send somebody up to you as soon as possible, you
>   copy?

After some consultations, the dispatcher came back to Trapp. They would not be sending someone up to get him.

"Mr. Trapp, can you go to a stairway and walk down?" she said. "If you have a stairway to walk down, please take the stairway down, do not take the elevator." As she spoke, the claxon alarm bellowed in the background of the 78th floor. Someone else chimed in with another piece of advice.

"A and B stairways," the dispatcher said. "You can take them, it's clear."

And one final instruction came: "Sky lobby, if he has someone with him, tell him to take those people with him."

With that, Greg Trapp turned for the stairs. It was now 9:49, sixty-three minutes since the first plane had struck the north tower.

For practically everyone still in the towers, including the men on the 78th floor with Trapp, who knew the buildings as well as anyone, the notion that they might collapse would have seemed far-fetched indeed. As the towers deteriorated, people who chose to stay—as opposed to those trapped in elevators or on the upper floors—did so for many reasons. Almost universally, it seemed, they did not think the buildings could fall.

Whatever worries Frank De Martini and his crew had about the building, they most likely concerned local problems they saw on the 78th floor, not its survival. De Martini had heard the founding dogma about the strength of the trade center: planes could hit them, and they would still stand. He, too, believed it.

As the security guard Greg Trapp walked into the stairs, he saw the Port Authority workers heading toward the other end of the hall, in the direction of another staircase. The evidence suggests that Tony Savas, having been rescued from the elevator, stayed some few minutes longer, as did John Griffin, before both men began to descend toward the lobby.

There was no further word or sightings of Pete Negron, thirty-four, father of two; or of Carlos DaCosta, forty-one, father of two; or of Pablo Ortiz, forty-nine, father of two; or of Frank De Martini, forty-nine, father of two—four men who worked anonymously for a faceless government bureaucracy. On the morning of September 11, 2001, they tore open walls with crowbars and shined flashlights and pried apart elevator doors on the 90th, 89th, 88th, 86th, and 78th floors, saving the lives of at least seventy people in the north tower. When last heard from, they were on their way to try to free more, no doubt believing that the building they were in would last long beyond their own old age.

11

"I'm staying with my friend."

9:20 A.M.
SOUTH TOWER

Eighty floors later, walking in the new shoes he had retrieved from under his desk in the Mizuho offices, Stephen Miller glimpsed the outside world again. Sunlight dulled by smoke filtered through the windows of the mezzanine, the spot where he and thousands of others emerged from the stairs of the south tower. Two of the building's three staircases ended at the mezzanine, and after spending more than half an hour in the stairwell, much of it waiting for the line to move, Miller hoped for a quick exit from the burning building. Instead, traffic slowed.

The mezzanine overlooked the lobby like a choir loft, running along the perimeter of the building. From the mezzanine, there were only two ways out. One set of doors opened in several places onto the plaza of the complex, the public square of the trade center where on sunny days people gathered for concerts and al fresco lunches. Now, however, it was filled with flaming debris and bodies, which were continuing to drop from the upper floors of the buildings. One Port Authority police officer thought he saw thirteen people jump in just a matter of seconds. Minutes before, a firefighter, Danny Suhr of Engine 216, had been struck and killed by a body falling from the upper floors.

A Critical Juncture in the Escape

Workers descending the stairwells on the ❶ east and ❷ west sides of the building arrived on the plaza level. ❸ As they passed by windows facing the plaza, many stopped to look out before going down the escalator and ❹ out through the underground concourse. But emergency workers prodded them to keep moving, preventing the stairwells from backing up.

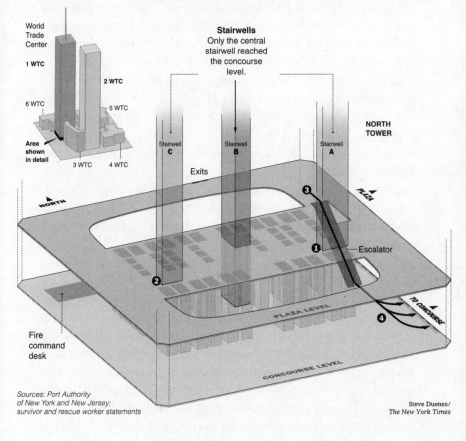

World Trade Center

1 WTC

2 WTC

6 WTC

5 WTC

Area shown in detail

3 WTC

4 WTC

NORTH

Stairwells
Only the central stairwell reached the concourse level.

Stairwell C

Stairwell B

Stairwell A

NORTH TOWER

Exits

PLAZA

❸

❶

Escalator

❷

PLAZA LEVEL

TO CONCOURSE

❹

Fire command desk

CONCOURSE LEVEL

Sources: Port Authority of New York and New Jersey; survivor and rescue worker statements

Steve Duenes/ The New York Times

The mezzanine doors led into that killing rain of people, fire, and debris. That left one other way out: an escalator that ran from the mezzanine to the lobby at street level. The motorized stairs quickly became the choke point of a funnel. The escalator was only wide enough for two, so the line of evacuees stretched back in an orderly but tense queue. No one this close to safety wanted to dillydally, including Miller, who felt quite satisfied with his intuitions at this point. He had almost gone back upstairs with the others when the public-address system in the south tower said that it was safe. But he had not felt completely right about it, so he turned around and left. As a result, he had been on the 55th floor when the second jet ripped through the offices of his company on 80. Now, with his feelings proving 100 percent reliable, Miller had another one. He felt like clapping his hands, and so he did, rhythmically. It was nervous energy. He wasn't trying to tell anyone to hurry up, at least not consciously. He was just having a hard time keeping himself occupied while he waited.

Someone yelled, "Shut the fuck up." A man glared at him and he stopped. In New York you could do a lot of unusual things in public places and people barely noticed. At a time of crisis you waited quietly in line.

This was the rapid, full-building evacuation that had never been written into the trade center's design or into the manual of its daily operations. Total evacuations were not part of life in tall buildings in the United States, so the plans did not envision thousands of people weaving down the three staircases in each tower. Yet it worked. Security guards and Port Authority workers and police officers rose to the moment to serve as human guideposts, to steer the evacuating tenants down what was not so obvious at all, the last few hundred yards toward safety. There had been no drills for this. No one had the duty of running such a full-scale evacuation because it was never supposed to take place. In a wave of improvisation, people had gone to these critical spots and saved lives by simply pointing their fingers.

Taking an Underground Route to Escape

The shopping concourse below the World Trade Center served as an essential escape route that allowed for the quick evacuation of both buildings. Two of the three stairwells in each tower ended at plaza level where the exit doors opened onto falling debris and carnage from the buildings. To avoid a logjam, rescuers directed people down and through the concourse, an underground route that offered protection from the dangers on the plaza above.

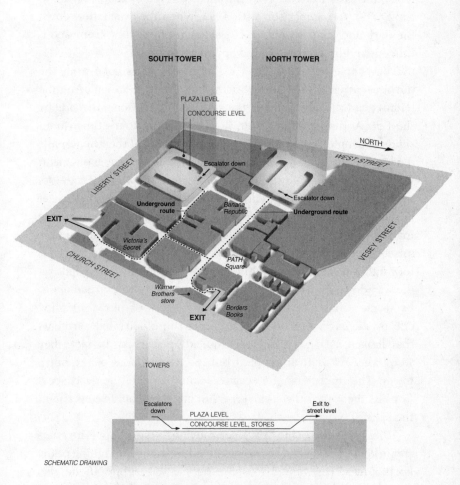

SOUTH TOWER

NORTH TOWER

PLAZA LEVEL
CONCOURSE LEVEL

NORTH →

WEST STREET

LIBERTY STREET

Escalator down

Underground route

Banana Republic

Escalator down

Underground route

EXIT ←

Victoria's Secret

CHURCH STREET

PATH Square

VESEY STREET

Warner Brothers store

EXIT ↓

Borders Books

TOWERS

Escalators down

Exit to street level

PLAZA LEVEL

CONCOURSE LEVEL, STORES

SCHEMATIC DRAWING

When people ascended from the concourse onto Church and Liberty streets, ambulances were waiting and the evacuees were a safe distance from the falling debris.

Sources: Port Authority of New York and New Jersey;
LZA Technology; survivor and rescue worker statements

Mika Gröndahl/*The New York Times*

That did not mean there were not lingering, frustrating delays. The injured could walk only gingerly or with the help of others. The stairwells had twists and turns that no one had anticipated because, as in most buildings, tenants had never actually been required to make a practice traipse down the stairs. And in each lobby, the exits were taxed by the sheer volume of people trying to leave. Still, in comparison with 1993, when the evacuation down the dark and smoky stairs had dragged on for hours, from noon-time into night, this one moved at lightning pace.

The people fleeing in 2001 did not face oily smoke from the burning garage on the lower floors, as those in 1993 had. And the tenants had the advantage of the stairwell improvements made by the Port Authority. As a result, in less than an hour's time, thousands of people, including many who had stared at their fingernails during fire drills, had successfully climbed down the stairs. That was the good news. Now they had to be routed down the escalators from the mezzanine to the lobby, and to do that, they had to get past the windows that looked out onto the plaza. The view froze many of them. The stairs had been windowless, the roaring fires unseen, the anxiety powerful but lacking shape. Now the evacuees found that however terrible the pictures playing in their heads on the way down may have been, the reality on the plaza turned out to be worse. Charred body parts. Shoes. Pieces of plane. Flaming debris. Luggage. A windowpane covered in blood. Red garments that looked as if they had been quickly discarded. In fact, they were what was left of people from the upper floors of the north tower. The impact on the evacuees was palpable. Some gasped. Cops at the top of the escalators thought they could see panic in their faces.

"Don't look. Keep moving. Keep moving," yelled Capt. Tim Pearson of the NYPD as the crowd streamed by in the mezzanine of the north tower. He wanted to spare people the sights but he also wanted them to keep going. If everyone started rubbernecking, they would never clear the building. Ordinarily, Pearson supervised cops who patrolled housing projects in Brooklyn. His unit had been among those called in to lower Manhattan when the Police

Department went on full alert. He had pulled up in a Ford Explorer at about 9:20, thirty-four minutes into the crisis, and had made his way into the north tower, where he found an eclectic collection of people helping with the evacuation. The group included police officers and firefighters, both off duty and on; people who knew the building well and people like him who did not really know it at all; civilians who felt compelled to get involved and ten-dollar-an-hour security guards who decided they could not just leave. Sue Keane, a Port Authority police officer, had been among the first to arrive at the mezzanine after running to the towers from her assignment at a Manhattan courthouse. Ken Greene, the Port Authority's assistant director of aviation, had stayed behind to help after escaping from the 65th floor. Nelson Chanfrau, a risk manager for the agency, had raced in from New Jersey.

Standing alongside Tim Pearson was another cop, his friend John Perry, whom Pearson had met by chance as he ran toward the buildings. Pearson and Perry had once worked alongside each other, pursuing cops with disciplinary problems. Within the Police Department, they were birds of a feather, independent types who stood out in a culture where conformity thrived. Pearson could be outspoken, a trait generally not viewed as a plus within the agency. Perry was an activist and an actor, a man who spoke five languages and had already earned his law degree. He was friendly with Norman Siegel, a former director of the New York Civil Liberties Union and one of the department's most vocal critics. Perry had only recently decided to leave the department to pursue a career in the law. Indeed, that morning he had been blocks away, literally handing in his retirement papers at Police Headquarters, when news spread that a plane had hit the trade center. Perry, in street clothes, asked the clerk for his badge back. He rushed downstairs to a police supply shop on the first floor, bought a thirty-five-dollar golf shirt with an NYPD logo and raced to the scene.

Now Perry and Pearson were directing people as they came off the stairs toward the escalator. Some needed more assistance than others. A middle-aged woman seemed to suffer an asthma attack as she left the stairs. Her breathing became labored and she clutched at her chest. Perry and a few others picked her up and began carrying her as Pearson collected her belongings. They headed toward the escalator. There were medics in the lobby just one flight down. Help was only 100 feet away.

When people reached the lobby of the north tower, they found their trip had one more leg that they had not counted on. The lobby doors that opened to West Street, to fresh air, indeed, to the very rest of their lives, beckoned. But just beyond those doors was a shower of debris, too much to make West Street a safe exit route. Instead, many people were directed south, through doors that led into the adjacent Marriott Hotel. There, hotel staff members steered people through the lobby and into the hotel's Tall Ships Bar and Grill. An exit from the bar opened south onto Liberty Street, where a police officer stood at the door, watching overhead for falling debris. "Okay," he'd say, and a few people would dash across the street. "Okay. Now," he'd shout, and a few more would follow.

While a thousand people moved through the hotel, most of the evacuees from the north tower were sent not into the hotel or onto West Street, but through a third set of doors. These led east, into the underground shopping concourse that stretched two blocks beneath the plaza of the trade center. Thousands of evacuees from the south tower were sent into the same concourse. Both groups were directed away from the buildings, through a maze of corridors and shops, by lines of cops and security guards stationed along the route, a human rope that people followed to the far side of the mall. Then they ascended on escalators into the bright sunlight of Church Street, the eastern edge of the trade center complex.

The trip brought people past the landmarks of their daily lives: the newsstands where they bought breath mints; PATH Square, where commuters from New Jersey descended each night to commuter trains; a Warner Brothers store, where plastic statues of Bugs Bunny and the Tasmanian Devil greeted passersby. Most of the seventy-five stores had closed soon after the planes hit, giving the windowless concourse an eerie, tomblike quality as people sprinted through the corridors and sloshed through water that was ankle deep at points. Nonetheless, the mall served as a sanctuary, a tunnel that allowed people to flee, safe from the flaming debris and hurtling bodies that were pelting the plaza, just above their heads. The evacuees were like prisoners of war who burrowed far enough under the guard towers and barbed-wire fences of their camp to emerge in the safety of the forest beyond. This route was their Great Escape.

That so many people were able to get out that way may have been due to revelations from the 1993 bombing. After the attack, a computer study showed that people had to travel too far to reach exits from the concourse, at least when measured against the requirements of the New York City fire code. To keep the promise of "meeting or exceeding" the code, the Port Authority's executive director, Charles Maikish, and its chief engineer, Frank Lombardi, took over space occupied by a record store, a five-and-dime, a restaurant, a bankrupt department store. These were demolished and turned into corridors, part of $34 million in improvements to the concourse. They had done underground what could not be done to the towers themselves: given more people better chances to get out.

Traveling against the flow of people in the concourse were five Port Authority police officers, wheeling a canvas laundry cart filled with Scott Airpaks, helmets, axes, and other tools. Sgt. John McLoughlin and four colleagues—Will Jimeno, Dominick Pezzulo, Christopher Amoroso, and Antonio Rodriguez—had collected the equipment in emergency-gear closets and were taking it to the north tower for officers waiting to go upstairs. Their supervisors were concerned about sending the officers in without the proper equipment. Some of them remembered how smoky the stairs had been in 1993 and did not think the rescuers would be much good without breathing apparatus. Four of the men walking with the cart were assigned to the Port Authority Bus Terminal in midtown and had just arrived by bus at the trade center. The fifth, Amoroso, had started his day at the trade center and had already helped shepherd people from the building. He ran into Jimeno, his friend from the academy, as they passed each other in the concourse. McLoughlin, their leader, was a veteran of the trade center, a rescue specialist who had won a medal of valor for his conduct during the bombing and its aftermath in 1993. Now, as he led his team through the concourse toward the north tower, they had to weave through the great tide of people rushing in the opposite direction, toward safety.

For all its activity, the scene in the concourse was still measurably calmer than it had been when the first plane hit. The corridors had been filled with people at 8:46—it was the middle of rush hour and thousands of people were arriving for work—and the noise and descending smoke when the fireball shot down the elevator shafts sent the crowd scurrying in all directions, as if a man waving a gun were walking the halls. A feeling of order, of composure, had settled in during the ensuing forty-five minutes. Some people were now so relaxed that police officer David Leclaire had to pull them off pay phones. There was no time for that. At PATH Square, an open space in the center of the shopping concourse, cops waved people past the escalators that descended to the PATH lines to New Jersey. Service on PATH and the city subway lines had already been shut down, the trains rerouted or canceled. The few PATH trains already en route at 8:46 had simply sped through the trade center station and headed back out without ever opening their doors, thanks to quick reflexes by the dispatcher.

When the evacuees reached the escalators back up to Church Street, they were now the equivalent of two blocks away from the burning buildings they had fled. As they ascended, they passed a Borders bookstore that filled the prime retail space at 5 World Trade Center, at the corner of Church and Vesey Streets. Several Shop the World banners hung overhead, to mark the entrance to the underground mall. As the evacuees crested at street level, rescuers led the injured and weak into ambulances. To the people coming up the escalators, these officers were as essential as the railings on stairs. Sgt. Robert Vargas of the Port Authority police had not expected to see singed hair and lacerations and peeling flesh.

For many, despair had set in. Now, as Vargas stood by the escalators watching the line pass, he lectured himself to stay strong. He represented order, security, even sanity, at this point. He could not show fear, he told himself, only calm and self-control.

Upstairs in each of the towers the evacuation was nearly complete, at least on the floors below where the planes had hit. Most of the middle floors were empty and the first cadres of firefighters were largely alone on the stairs as they made their way past the 30th floor. For many of the tenants, crossing paths with the firefighters was a moment of surging, sustaining emotional power. Of course, most people had gotten to the stairs and down on their own; they had relied on each other to claw colleagues out of elevators. They had, in large measure, rescued themselves. Yet the sight of the firefighters selflessly ascending to rescue those who could not leave, to save the building from whatever hell was now consuming it, was a mighty antidote to the dread so many had felt. The firefighters did not earn in a year what some baseball players got for a game, but here they were, charging into the teeth of the fire, driven by a collective sense of duty that tempered their individual fear. Firefighter Michael Otten of Ladder 35 climbed the stairs in the south tower toward an uncertain future while his brother-in-law, the stockbroker at Mizuho also known as Michael Otten, walked down, toward home and family. If the two men took the same stairs, they did not see each other as the two lines passed, firefighters to the right, evacuees to the left. People patted the firefighters on the back. God bless you. Thank you. Be careful. Some firefighters remained stoic. Others made jokes—sometimes, the same joke. Steve Charest, a broker from the May Davis Group, carried a golf club down the north tower stairs from his office on the 87th floor. A fireman noticed it as he passed.

"Hey!" he said. "I saw your ball, a few flights down."

A few floors down, more firefighters were coming up. One of them took a look at Charest's club. "I saw your ball," this fireman said. And, yes, it was a few flights down.

The firefighters felt fear, of course. They just didn't discuss it much. Worrying was counterproductive, and they generally buried their anxieties beneath a gruff jocularity that treated each job as just another hellhole. Firefighter Joseph Maffeo of Ladder 101 took the extra precaution of carrying a can of tuna with him as he reported for his assignment in the Marriott Hotel. Maffeo always carried tuna to a fire. It was his meal, he told people, if he ever got stuck in something weird, like a building collapse, and had to wait to be rescued. Capt. William Burke Jr. of Engine 21 also prepared for whatever the morning might hold. He called a friend, Jean Traina, twice from inside the north tower, assuring her that he was safe and asking her to call his sister in Syracuse and other family members to spread the word. His voice sounded calm, Jean thought, for a guy at one of the biggest building fires in history.

"Please stay safe," she told him.

"This is what I do," Burke replied.

As fit and focused as many firefighters were, many were over-matched by the lengthy climb with their dozens of pounds of gear. Sharon Premoli, the financial executive whose spirits had been buoyed by the security guard singing a hymn on the 44th floor, noticed the exertion on their faces as several firefighters passed her on the stairs in the north tower around the 35th floor. Many of the firefighters were flushed and sweating, and Premoli knew that they were not yet halfway to her office on 80, let alone to the fires raging above. In the steaming heat of the stairwells, the office workers had ditched their jackets and loosened their ties, but the firefighters still wore their bulky coats and leather-clad helmets. Inevitably, the radio channels rippled with reports of firemen having chest pains. Engine 9. Squad 18.

At the 19th floor, dozens of exhausted firefighters were taking a breather, a startling sight to Capt. Joseph Baccellieri of the Court Officers Academy and the two sergeants, Andrew Wender and Al Moscola, who had rushed into the building with him. On their way up, the three court officers had been hopscotching floors with firemen they met on the stairs. They'd search one floor. The fire-men would take the next. Most of the floors were empty, except for stragglers who seemed incapable of leaving their computers. When the court officers got to 19, they saw crowds of firefighters lying in the hallways, jackets and helmets off—a surprising gathering, but then Baccellieri felt hot, too, wearing only a light shirt and pants. The 19th floor, it seemed, must be the place where people hit the wall when they climb stairs and are clad in fifty-six and a half pounds of coat, helmet, and boots.

On the 31st floor, a dozen firefighters slumped in the hallway. Firefighter David Weiss, a member of Rescue 1, yelled down stairway B for help. A cop, Dave Norman, heard him and called back. He'd be right up. Norman was an ESU officer assigned to Truck One and trained as an emergency medical technician. ESU cops typically did not ticket cars or make arrests. They rescued people, which made them among the most popular cops in the city—popular with everyone but firefighters. ESU rescue efforts at emergencies such as explosions and auto accidents, where firefighter rescue units thought they were in charge, were the single greatest point of friction between the two agencies. Mayors over the years had tried to iron out the differences, with little success. The jurisdictional lines were left too fuzzy to ever settle the dispute.

On September 11, though, no one was jostling in the north tower stairwell. "Norman, is that you?" Weiss yelled down the stairs. Indeed, the two men knew each other. Norman's brother, John, was a fire chief who had once been assigned to Rescue 1. Norman pulled the medical gear from his pack. The ailing firefighters had their coats and helmets off, and their T-shirts were wet with perspiration. Some were dehydrated and were having trouble breathing. Others were having chest pains—so many, in fact, that a commander chastened them over the radio not to clog the airwaves with their complaints. Norman began administering oxygen and checking their vital signs. The setting was too somber for intramural rivalries.

Four floors below, in the 27th-floor offices of Empire Blue Cross and Blue Shield, Ed Beyea and Abe Zelmanowitz were still waiting to evacuate. Nearly all the people from 27 had already left, as had nearly all the people from Empire, which had 1,900 employees spread across ten floors. Indeed, most of the lower floors of the north tower were clear by 9:30. But with the elevators apparently out and Beyea confined to a heavy, motorized chair, it would take several sets of strong hands and backs to carry him down, and the firefighters were busy now, still pushing their way upstairs toward the fire.

The broken elevators had become traps not only for people who were stuck inside them, but also for those who could not get on them, like Ed Beyea. More modern, super-tall buildings had created special refuge elevators, with more durable construction, to serve rescuers and the disabled during emergencies. That had not been part of the practice during the late 1960s, when the final details of the trade center plans were being worked out.

As they waited for help, Beyea and Zelmanowitz moved about the 27th floor. They had been to the stairwell, to the elevator banks, and to a conference room where a firefighter told them to stuff wet rags underneath the doors. Several people did what they could to make those left on the floor comfortable. Anthony Giardina, an electrician who worked in the building, passed out Snapple and water from a hallway vending machine. Firefighters poured the drinks over their heads. One firefighter looked at Zelmanowitz as they stood together in the landing for stairway C. Zelmanowitz could have left much earlier, but the fire upstairs in the north tower seemed far away, the danger distant.

"Why don't you go?" the fireman asked.

"No, I'm staying with my friend," he replied.

Hundreds, perhaps thousands, of people fleeing the north tower had seen the pair as they walked past them on their way to the lobby and safety. Keith Meerholz took a long look at Beyea and Zelmanowitz when the line of evacuees paused as he approached the 27th-floor landing. Meerholz, who worked for Marsh & McLennan, had been in the 78th-floor sky lobby when the first plane hit. He had been scorched by flames that spit from an elevator door. He then raced down the stairs, unimpeded, until he hit pedestrian traffic around the 38th floor. Now, as he approached 27, he could see that the fellow in the wheelchair was younger than the man who stood with him. Maybe, Meerholz thought, he would help carry the paralyzed man down, get some help from one of the other young men in the stairway. But the firefighters seemed to have reached the 27th floor in great numbers now, peeling off to take a break and to replenish their wind. When Meerholz shuffled onto the landing, he ducked out of the stairs and onto the floor behind one of the firefighters. Perhaps the firefighters would have more solid information about what was going on—a bomb, a light plane, a helicopter— than Meerholz had picked up in the stairwell chatter.

"What happened?" Meerholz asked.

The fireman was bent over, panting.

"A plane hit each tower," the fireman said. "But don't tell anyone."

Meerholz understood. The news could start panic. He felt charged with the urgency of getting out, and he turned back into the stairway, joining the slow, downward shuffle. The firefighters were on the scene. No doubt, they would take charge of the man in the wheelchair.

Downstairs, in the north tower lobby, Chief Pfeifer took an occasional glance up at the mezzanine level, where people shuffled toward the escalators. The view served as a scorecard of progress. The early, longer lines meant the floors above were still far from empty. Later, thinner lines showed progress. It was good, he thought, to see the windows on the mezzanine, which earlier had been blocked by the fleeing crowds.

A few feet away, at the fire command desk, Port Authority officials spoke into the elevator intercom system, trying to reach anyone trapped in one of the ninety-nine elevators. "Is anyone in the car?" they said. "If you can't speak, hit the panel." One by one, they had been trying to contact each of the cabs, using a command board designed to show them where each one was stuck. Less than 100 feet away, though, stuck at lobby level in an elevator with six other people, Judith Martin, the woman who had lingered downstairs to have a cigarette, could not reach anyone who could help her.

Martin and her fellow passengers had tried pushing the alarm buttons, talking into the intercom, screaming at the top of their lungs. All they got was a recording that told them someone would be coming soon. At first, this did not seem like cause for too much concern. The elevator, an express to the 78th floor, had shaken for just a second after they had pushed the button to ascend. Some in the car thought they had gone up briefly before falling back down, perhaps as far as the basement. Certainly the elevator had bounced a bit, but then it just sat there. Inside, cut off from the turmoil that surrounded them, the seven passengers viewed it as just a particularly rotten start to an otherwise normal day.

When their initial efforts to pry open the door were unsuccessful, the seven of them, four men and three women—Dana Coulthurst from Judith's office at Marsh & McLennan, Mike Jacobs, Keith Ensler, Ian Robb, and a man and a woman whose names didn't stick with Martin—sat on the floor, trying to talk over the wailing alarm. One man read their horoscopes aloud from a newspaper. Another sat quietly and read his book. Martin eyed the coffee that one of the other women was carrying and joked that it was always nice to share. A trickle of water and white dust seeped into the car from the ceiling. Every once in a while, someone would get up and start yelling for help. No one seemed to hear them, though, except for Chris Young, a man who was alone in another express elevator that was also stuck, doors closed, in the north tower lobby. Through the walls Martin, Young, and the others exchanged what little information they had with each other. They promised that whoever got out first would make sure that rescuers knew someone else was trapped.

Young had been on his way down from 78 when his elevator suddenly shook and bounced to a halt, knocking him to the floor. His intercom system was working, however, and after fifteen minutes someone said that help was on the way. No one had come for the people in either elevator, though, and by 9:30, forty-four minutes after their ordeal had begun, their anxiety was deepening.

In Martin's elevator the mood had darkened considerably after the second plane hit the south tower. Martin and her colleagues in the elevators had no sense of what was actually happening outside. But they felt the second jolt, and it shattered the notion that this was some routine mechanical slipup. "Whatever it is, it's bad," said Keith Ensler, an ex-Marine who had been reading a book. From outside the cab, Martin heard sharp clanging sounds and small booms, as if they were at a construction site. Her fear rose with the noise. It was time, everyone decided, to get serious about opening those doors.

Ensler, who was wearing hiking boots, gave the doors a mighty kick. Mike Jacobs, an investment banker, saw a faint light in one of the cracks of the doors and began to pry them a bit. Working in tandem now, the men opened them wide enough to realize that they were in the lobby. Finally, the interior doors released. The second set was slightly easier then the first, and when they pushed them apart and walked out into the lobby, they found it humming with police and firefighters. Jacobs's first thought, when he saw so many emergency personnel within spitting distance of their elevator, was to raise a little hell. "What're you doing?" he asked an emergency worker in a blue T-shirt and green hard hat. Then the enormity of what had happened began to seep in. "Keep going. Keep going," the officials said. So the group started walking out of the building. But first a few of the people stopped to tell officials about Chris Young. He was still stuck behind them, in an elevator right near them, in the lobby. The rescuers nodded, okay, okay. But ten minutes later, Young was still alone in the car, trying to keep himself occupied and calm. It was disturbing, though, that no one answered when he called out to the other car.

Just before 9:30, a new note of alarm swept through the north tower lobby. Richard Sheirer, the director of New York City's Office of Emergency Management, came hustling across the floor, holding his radio and yelling in the direction of Thomas Von Essen, New York's fire commissioner.

"Tommy," he called out. "We got report of a third plane."

In the skies above the trade center, Greg Semendinger, the police pilot who was circling the buildings in his helicopter, told his dispatcher the same thing.

"Central," he radioed, "be advised there may be another aircraft inbound. There may be another aircraft inbound. La Guardia is tracking a fast-mover moving inbound."

More terror. Federal aviation officials had already closed the airspace around New York to civilian traffic, but thousands of planes were still in the air across the country. It was impossible to say which of them might also be turned into missiles. Moreover, air-traffic-control officials in New York knew no more about the attacks than anyone watching television—and sometimes, less. Controllers at La Guardia Airport, unaware of the hijackings, had continued to send out flights until 9:07, five minutes after the second plane had struck the south tower, and nearly an hour after the first plane had been hijacked. The air-traffic-control system was highly balkanized, with little interaction between one region and another, so as the airborne siege spread across the skies from New England to the Midwest, word of what was unfolding did not spread.

Communications were also poor between the Federal Aviation Administration, which controlled air traffic, and the military guardians of the North American Aerospace Defense Command, or NORAD.

Air controllers did not realize that at that moment military jets were racing down the Hudson, in pursuit of the first two hijacked planes; they knew only that streaks on their radar screens showed an aircraft moving at extraordinary speed. Thus, the warning that La Guardia was tracking a fast-mover, heading inbound. That the report was false was of no moment. To those at the foot of the gaping, roaring buildings, nothing was beyond belief.

A strike by a third plane would slaughter the rescuers who had gone up the stairs and the tenants coming down, Deputy Chief Hayden thought as he stood in the lobby. The buildings might even fall. Some police officers who had been preparing to go inside paused, as commanders sought a better read on just what was going on. Rescuers inside just looked at one another and kept working. Many cleared out of the lobby, some of them relocating to West Street, where the Fire Department had set up a command post that would oversee the response in both buildings.

"I need the military," Sheirer barked into his radio to a subordinate. He also wanted a message sent to the police helicopters circling overhead. Tell the pilots, he said, that under no circumstances could they allow another plane to hit the towers. Since the helicopters were not loaded with weaponry that could actually bring down a 767, what was Sheirer actually asking them to do? Fly into the path of a jumbo jet? Later, he would cite the order as a mark of the desperation that swept through the lobby in those moments. Just a few feet away, the stress was visible on the face of the Rev. Mychal Judge, a Fire Department chaplain. His clerical collar and white fire helmet made him stand out in the crowd as he paced the floor, his lips moving in prayer as if to gain additional potency by speaking the words aloud. In his face, a certain remoteness had taken hold, as if he were engaged in a dialogue that was taking place outside the burning building.

In the helicopters, the pilots now got word that the inbound aircraft was most likely a military jet, scrambling to protect the skies over New York. "Is that a U.S. military, Central?" Detective Semendinger asked, just to make sure. Yes, he was assured, it was. The fire chiefs downstairs, however, had already begun to order their people out of the buildings, at least until the situation cleared up.

"All units in Building 1," Assistant Chief Callan said into his radio as he stood in the lobby at 9:32 A.M. "All units in Building 1, come out, down to the lobby."

Radio communications with the upper floors remained feeble. More than 1,000 firefighters were now fighting for airtime on the same four or five channels, breeding considerable interference. Worse, the channels they were using in the north tower did not benefit from the amplification of the repeater, which had been abandoned because the chiefs had decided it was malfunctioning.

"Everybody down to the lobby," Chief Callan repeated again.

It did not matter how many times he said it. No one answered his call.

12

"Tell the chief what you just told me."

9:22 A.M.
SOUTH TOWER

All morning, Anthony Bramante had been dialing his brother, Jack, who worked in the south tower for Mizuho. Time and again, his call ended before it began, in fast busy signals or a taped announcement that the circuits were overloaded. Finally, he dialed just as a gap opened momentarily in the electronic pileup, and the signals pulsed from his office in Brooklyn to his brother's desk on the 80th floor. Bramante listened to the rings. He wanted the call to get through, but he did not want it to be answered. The phone rang on. Please, he thought, don't let him pick up. Six rings. Ten. Thirteen. Let him be out of there.

"Hello?"

The voice jolted Bramante, dashing the illusion that everyone had left. But the person answering was not his brother. No, the man said, Jack Bramante was not there. He was gone.

"The floor is on fire! Help us! The floor is on fire!"

After a few seconds, Bramante realized he was speaking to Jack Andreacchio, who normally changed lightbulbs and wired comput-

184

ers and ran the grab bag of errands essential to any corporate bureaucracy. Bramante had met Andreacchio on visits to his brother in the south tower.

Andreacchio reported that he was trapped with Manny Gomez, his boss. Both men had been part of the Fuji evacuation team that had herded people off the bank's floors. Andreacchio had even started downstairs and had gotten as far as the 70th floor, but turned back, apparently on hearing the announcement that the building was safe. In most circumstances, Andreacchio was famously amiable. An Italian American from Brooklyn, he had taken an extravagant liking to country music and became an energetic line dancer who wore a cowboy hat and vacationed in Nashville.

Now he was stuck with Manny Gomez and three other people in an office on the 80th floor. Bramante talked him through the options. What about the stairs? Destroyed, said Andreacchio, or blocked by rubble.

"Have you called 911?" Bramante asked.

"No," Andreacchio said. He was not getting a dial tone when he picked up the phone, so he could not make calls out. This did not make clear sense to Bramante, who had just dialed into the office, but he used a three-way-call function on his telephone and connected Andreacchio to 911. The call was logged in at 9:23 in the 911 center.

ROOF TOP ANOTHER CALL—TRAPPED ON 80 FLOOR— HOT AND SMOKY—FD 403 NTFD—STAIRWAYS BLOCKED—NW CORNER—CONF CALL—BRAMANTE ANTHONY 32 COURT ST

"I think we should break the window," Andreacchio said.

Bramante and the operator hollered at once that he should not do that. The oxygen would draw the fire into their refuge.

The operator explained that the Fire Department was mounting a big response, and speaking in the jargon of the dispatchers, rendered the department's abbreviation—FDNY—as a word.

"Fidnee is on their way," the operator said. "They have it. People are on their way to you, okay?"

"You've gotta help me," Andreacchio said.

"Fidnee is on the way," the operator assured him.

The impact zone of the south tower was closer to the ground than the ruined floors of the north; the nose of Flight 175 had entered at the 81st floor, sixteen floors lower than Flight 11 in the north tower. Moreover, a single escape route—stairway A—remained open, though this was known to only a few people, and the city's emergency-response program had no mechanism for communicating any live information, as opposed to canned scripts, through its 911 call centers.

The conditions in the south tower had become so bad, so quickly, that sixteen minutes after the plane had hit, at 9:02:59, people despaired of escape or rescue. Two of the young men at Keefe, Bruyette & Woods, Brad Vadas and Stephen Mulderry, made calls from the 88th floor of the south tower. At 9:19, Vadas left a message on the answering machine of his fiancée, Kris McFerren. "Kris, there's been an explosion. We're trapped in a room. There's smoke coming in. I don't know what's going to happen. I want you to know my life has been so much better and richer because you were in it." He added that he would do his best to get out. "I love you," he said. "Good-bye." Mulderry, the former college basketball star, called a friend, and on her tape said that whatever might happen, he would be okay. He had said all the prayers his mother had taught him. Five floors above them, Greg Milanowycz, an insurance broker for Aon, reached his father, Joseph, at work. "Can you call someone, can you tell them we are here in the northeast corner of the 93rd floor?" he asked. His father reached 911 on another line. The dispatcher sounded cool, calm, wise.

"Okay, this is what you have to tell them," the dispatcher said. "Get as close to the floor as possible, don't talk to conserve oxygen, and if they are in a room and have access to water or something, try to wet clothing or towels and wedge them under the doorways, to try to stop smoke from getting in there."

Joseph Milanowycz meticulously tracked the instructions. The words lifted his heart.

"We have set up a command post already down there," the dispatcher said. "We are on our way up. We will get him out of there." The father passed this message on to the son, who shouted to the room of people: "They are coming. My dad's on the phone with them. They are coming."

It was true, as the dispatcher said, that command posts had been set up at the trade center, but the more that fire commanders could see, the grimmer their outlook. At the main post, across West Street from the towers, Deputy Fire Commissioner Tom Fitzpatrick watched people falling or jumping from the high floors of the north tower and concluded that the firefighters simply could not get to the hundreds trapped above the fires. At the same post, Lt. Joseph Chiafari heard dispatcher reports—a blur of floor numbers and trapped workers, thirty people in a conference room somewhere, another group elsewhere—as a roll call of places that the firefighters would not get to anytime soon. His boss, Deputy Assistant Chief Al Turi, began to think about how long the buildings would stand up to the uncontrolled fires before they had partial collapses on the upper floors. Three hours of fire resistance, Turi figured. They were just a half hour into the fight.

The catastrophe could be seen for miles with the naked eye, across oceans and continents on television. To rescuers at the very base of the towers, the fires appeared to be in another world. They blazed so far beyond them, 1,000 vertical feet in the north tower, 800 in the south, they might have been looking at the light from distant, dying stars.

Yet in the lobby of the towers, the view was not as bleak—in large part because there was no view whatsoever of the raging fire overhead, but also because the impulse to try, to make an effort, had a momentum more powerful than the sense of futility. And at 9:18, a piece of electrifying news had come across the radio frequency used inside the towers. Just when Brad Vadas and Stephen Mulderry were making their farewells on the answering machines of loved ones, and as Deputy Commissioner Fitzpatrick was reluctantly concluding that people like Vadas and Mulderry were lost, and as Chief Turi was wondering if firefighters would get near the fires before the three hours of fire protection were up, the first group of firefighters climbing skyward had started to change the calculus of doom.

"This is Battalion 7 on floor 40 of Tower 2," Chief Orio J. Palmer reported. "We got one elevator working up to the 40th floor staffed by a member of Ladder 15, 'kay."

At that moment, the gap between the rescuers and the trapped people had narrowed from the implausible to the possible. One elevator—apparently car number 48, a freight car that served the lower zone of the south tower—had continued to function. Car 48 ran up to the 40th floor. By taking it, Palmer was already halfway to the border territory of the south tower, the area where Frank De Martini and his group had been so effective in the north tower.

Orio Palmer wore the traditional chief's helmet, a durable white shell that was part modern gear, part homage to tradition, with its Maltese cross. He often added a few custom alterations. Tucked into the band of his helmet were little chocks of different widths and angles, in case he needed to prop open a door; these were firefighter tools that he had kept on hand as he advanced through the ranks. Another item clipped to his helmet was a small, powerful light. Strapped to his back was a Scott Airpak, a portable supply of air; on one of his earliest days as a chief, he had been laid low by a dose of carbon monoxide poisoning, and a picture in the *Daily News* showed him as he was helped out of a fire in downtown Manhattan.

In one potentially critical area, the fire operations in the south tower differed from those in the north. Somehow, with enough fiddling, Palmer had been able to speak over his portable radio with his commander in the lobby of the south tower, using the specially amplified "repeater" channel. The chiefs in the other tower were having no similar success in communicating, although the same repeater served both buildings; in fact, the north tower commanders had stopped using the channel boosted by the repeater, believing that it was not working.

Like the chocks carried in his helmet, Palmer's ability with radios was no accident. While working full time as a firefighter, he had earned an associate degree in electrical engineering, and had written technical articles about the use of two-way radios inside high-rise buildings and subways. Still, none of the clever equipment or advanced study would mean a thing unless he could get higher in the building, another forty floors above the first forty.

Before they could fight fire, the firefighters would have to take on gravity, with each man wearing or carrying fifty-six and a half pounds of boots, coat, helmet, oxygen tank, and mask—plus tools. Here, too, Palmer was ready. As a young man, he had all but worn a path on the sidewalks around Woodlawn Cemetery in the Bronx, regularly running miles past the graves of Herman Melville and Joseph Pulitzer, Duke Ellington and George M. Cohan, Adm. David Farragut and Mayor Fiorello La Guardia. After he married, he and his wife, Debbie, moved out of the Bronx to a small Long Island suburb, into the only house they could afford. Palmer rebuilt the place, plank by plank. On breaks from the renovation project, he ran. About a half mile from home was Hendrickson Park, with a three-mile running track around Valley Stream Pond. Trees leaned over the path. Swans glided across the water. A white gazebo, utterly useless and perfectly lovely, was set back from the water's edge. He wore his Walkman—Van Morrison was a favorite, and he called his wife the Brown-Eyed Girl—and would knock off three or four circuits, depending on how much time he had. He had run the New York City Marathon in 1988, and every year after that, ran at least a half-marathon on Long Island. When the family watched TV in the basement he had rebuilt, he would do stomach crunches during the commercials. Not surprisingly, he had won the department's top fitness medal four or five times. With chocks in his hat, a good head on his shoulders, and the memory of hundreds of miles in the muscles of his legs, he now started up the stairs from the 40th floor, halfway to his destination.

At that moment, all the promises the dispatchers made to people trapped above and around the flames, the assurances from friends and family to the Brooklyn cowboy Jack Andreacchio, to Greg Milanowycz and his father, no longer were empty words, palliatives dosed out to the frantic and doomed. Help was not only on the way, it was getting there. At least some of it was. In the lobby, Deputy Chief Donald Burns heard Palmer's report that an elevator was running to the 40th floor.

"All right," said Burns, "but I got no units yet. There are no units here yet."

Many firefighters, coming from firehouses far outside lower Manhattan, simply could not find their way into the south tower, and had gone into the north tower instead.

Palmer, who had brought a company with him to the 40th floor, did not seem to hear what Burns was saying.

"Yeah, we're just starting them up," Palmer said. He led the way.

As Palmer was climbing stairs in the south tower, a wounded, struggling band was gathering at the building's 78th-floor sky lobby. Minutes before, the sky lobby had bustled with office workers unsure whether to leave the building or go back to work; now it was filled with motionless bodies, moans from people hidden in clouds of pulverized dust. The ceilings, the walls, the windows, the information kiosk, even the marble that graced the elevator banks—everything was smashed.

Mary Jos crawled across the ground, not sure how she had gotten to the 78th floor from her office in the New York State Department of Taxation and Finance on the 86th floor, or how she had ended up on the floor of the sky lobby, searing pain in her back, her clothes on fire, until she had rolled over and smothered the flames. About ten feet away in the smoldering darkness was her friend Ling Young. They had gone to college together, and now, at midlife, worked for the state tax department. At this grim moment, the two old friends had no idea they were only a few feet apart.

Not far away, Jos knew, was a door into a stairway. A colleague had the habit of getting exercise by walking up from 78 to 86, and Jos often saw her use a set of stairs in the northwest corner of the building. She headed in that direction. The door was still there. She stood and pushed it open. Her watch and left shoe had been blown off. She did not care: she was leaving.

"There's an exit here," she called out. A few paces into the stairs, she yelled. "Can somebody help me?" One flight down, a man named Eric Thompson heard her and came to escort her.

Young had not seen Jos on fire, nor had she noticed Jos crawling across the floor. Her glasses covered in blood, Young saw that the people nearest her had been injured, but were alive. The woman who appeared to have lost her legs had gone into shock, leaning against an elevator door. As Young looked around, she saw that her colleagues from the tax department also were hurt, though not so catastrophically as the woman by the elevator: Dianne Gladstone might have broken an ankle, and Yeshavant Tembe might have fractured his knee.

Young herself was badly burned, though she did not realize it until she tried to lift Gladstone. When Gladstone put her arms around Young's neck, pain shot through her. They all wanted water, but did not dare move, afraid that the floor would collapse beneath them. The lights were gone; fire banked and ebbed; a man walked past, pleading for help. "I'm on fire," he said, but Young recalled no one helping him. She was not sure why.

Perhaps twenty minutes or so after the plane hit, another young man appeared.

"I've found an exit," he said, and he led them to a door in the northwest corner, the same stairwell that Mary Jos had found right after the impact. Young walked to it, the pain shut down by the task of leaving. She saw a thin man behind her in the stairs. Gladstone, with her bad ankle, was helped by Diane Urban, the department's famously sharp-tongued boss. Another colleague, Sankara Velamuri, escorted Tembe with his bad knee toward the stairs. They were trailing her, though Young could not tell by how much.

In the stairwell, Young and her colleagues began to drift apart, with Young ahead of the others. She noticed that the young man who had found the door also was walking down the stairs.

"Don't get separated," he ordered.

About ten floors down, he stopped. Only then did Young realize that he had been carrying a woman on his back, apparently to get her past the drastic conditions in the area around the 78th floor. Once they reached the 60s, he put her down, then turned back up the stairs.

"Don't get separated," he called again.

Back on the 78th floor, more people struggled to orient themselves. Scattered around the bank of sky lobby elevators that served the floors of Aon, two women and three men had survived the plane's impact. Despite being battered, Judy Wein, Gigi Singer, Ed Nicholls, and Vijay Paramsothy were still able to walk. Rich Gabrielle, however, was pinned under marble, and Wein had been unable to move the stone from his legs. Wein had scouted part of the floor, looking for the guard's stand. She could not find it, and joined Paramsothy perched amid the rubble. Wein had a broken rib, a collapsed lung, and a broken arm. Singer was seriously burned. Paramsothy, apparently not drastically hurt, was able to walk. Nicholls was bleeding heavily: his right arm from near his shoulder was nearly severed by some piece of the building or airplane that had turned into a missile. Bits of stone and cement had lodged in his abdomen. A window had broken open, and he stood there for a minute next to an older man, getting some air.

From nowhere, a young man appeared. Judy Wein saw a red handkerchief or bandanna wrapped around his face. Was he the same person who had led Ling Young and the other people from the tax department to the stairs, the same man who had carried a woman down several flights of stairs on his back before putting her down and going back upstairs? It is one of many possibilities, but few certainties. Young, who had left a few minutes earlier and by now was a half dozen stories below the impact zone, would not remember the red handkerchief until Wein described it some months later.

"Do you have any idea where a fire extinguisher might be?" the man in the bandanna asked. Wein pointed out one she had seen earlier, but the man found that it was useless. He pointed the way to the stairs.

"Anyone who can walk should leave now," he said. "If you can help others to leave, help them." Wein and Singer moved to the stairs, followed closely by Nicholls. All three of them were hurt but able to move. Paramsothy, who was in similar shape, decided to stay. Of the five Aon employees still known to be alive, Paramsothy and Rich Gabrielle, pinned under the marble, remained on the 78th floor.

By 9:30, most of the 6,000 people who had passed through the south tower turnstiles on their way to work had reversed course and left the building, or were about to. The evacuation from the south tower had been under way since 8:46. The evidence suggests that by this moment, about 9:30, fewer than 1,000 of the trade center workers had not yet left the building; of these, 600 would never leave. Perhaps 200 were already dead, killed when the plane hit. A few people, well below the fires, were still making their descent. Eighteen men and women who had been at or above the impact zone were making progress down from the 78th floor and higher— everyone from Brian Clark from Euro Brokers on the 84th floor, and Stanley Praimnath, from Fuji on the 81st floor, to the people who had been waiting on the 78th floor, Mary Jos and Ling Young and Keating Crown and Kelly Reyher and Donna Spera. Considering the trauma and their injuries, those eighteen moved at a strong clip.

The floors above the impact zone teemed with urgency. Even on the floors where the plane hit, pockets of survivors were struggling to find a way out, or to comfort people around them. On the 78th floor, despite the wholesale carnage of those waiting for the sky lobby elevators, survivors were creeping into the stairwells. The witnesses account for about a dozen people, alive but injured or tending to the injured. Farther above them were Jack Andreacchio and Manny Gomez, stuck in the 80th floor, in the offices of Fuji with three others. From the 88th and 89th floors came calls to 911 and to family members, reporting that at least one hundred people were alive, with sixty-seven of them employees of Keefe, Bruyette & Woods, most of them traders. Some, like Linda Rothemund and Lauren Smith and their colleagues in the elevator that had nearly plunged to the ground, were trapped in the lobby.

Of the eighty-seven people who had come to work at the trading firm of Sandler O'Neill on the 104th floor that morning, only twenty had left the building, or had gotten far enough down to have a clear path out. At Aon, 176 were still inside.

Around this time, Alayne Gentul of Fiduciary Trust, whose father had helped to build the trade center's elevators, phoned her husband, Jack, who worked at the New Jersey Institute of Technology.

"Thank God, you're okay," Jack said.

"Well," she said, "we came up to 97 to get tech support out. There's smoke coming in, and it's really hot out there."

Before the second plane hit, Gentul and her colleague Ed Emery had ordered everyone off the Fiduciary floors. Emery had escorted crowds of them to the 78th-floor sky lobby. Then Emery climbed back up to the 90th floor, meeting Gentul. That very morning, a group from Fiduciary's parent corporation, Templeton Strong, had come to the 97th floor for disaster backup planning. Before the second plane hit, Gentul and Emery had gone up there to lead that group out. Then they became trapped.

Emery climbed onto a table, trying to block smoke by stuffing the vents with a new jacket he had bought just that weekend. From his office in Newark, Jack Gentul called to members of the school's security and engineering staff. They advised hitting the sprinklers, with a shoe or anything at hand. Nothing seemed to work. Jack Gentul also called the minister of their church, and they began a prayer chain.

Another Fiduciary employee on the 97th floor, Shimmy Biegeleisen, phoned his wife, Marion, at their home in Brooklyn. He was desperate. He told her that a group had tried to go upstairs, but found the way unpassable. Marion passed the phone to David

Langer, one of a group of friends who worked in the neighborhood and had gathered at the Biegeleisen house. He patched in a local doctor, who advised wetting his clothes and using the dampness to filter the smoke. Biegeleisen was due to travel to Israel four nights later with his oldest son, to observe Rosh Hashanah. In the first several phone calls, he had been calm, but as the smoke advanced, his messages sharpened in focus, and rose in intensity: there was a clock running. He asked a friend, Jack Edelstein, to attend to some of his personal business. With every breath becoming a struggle, he asked Edelstein to pray with him.

"Why don't you say it and I'll listen and say it along with you?" Edelstein said.

"*Of David. A psalm,*" Biegeleisen began, speaking in Hebrew. "*The earth is the Lord's, and all that is in it, the world and those that live in it. . . .*"

Biegeleisen was using a phone plugged into back of a computer, bypassing the central phone systems that relied on the building's electrical power, and he had to share it with others in the room. Ed McNally, the director of technology for Fiduciary, called his wife, Liz. He wanted to tell her some things. She and the children had meant the world to him. The papers for his insurance were in this file; other important documents could be found in another file. He had to go. He hung up, then called back a few minutes later. Liz's fortieth birthday was coming up, and he had made plans to surprise her.

"I feel silly," he said. "I booked a trip to Rome. Liz, you have to cancel that."

His wife tried to shake that entire line of thinking.

"Ed," Liz said, "you're getting out of there. The firemen are coming up to get you. You are a problem solver. You're going to get out of there."

Over the radio, the fire dispatcher sprayed buckshot of information about the south tower onto the airwaves.

"Okay," he announced. "The 82nd floor, west side; the 88th floor;

73rd floor, west side; 10th floor, east side; 104th floor, east side; 47th floor; 73rd floor, west office; 83rd floor, room 8-3-0-0; and 80th floor, northwest. That's what we have at this time."

These were not just numbers in a big skyscraper with metal pinstripes down the sides: these were pulse beats of people who had called 911 to report that they were present, alive, in trouble. To Orio Palmer climbing the stairs, the particular floor numbers did not tell him what he needed to know. As the chief leading the way up, he had a single task: to find out where the fire was, then to set up a command post two floors below it. From there, he would send firefighters to put water on any fires they could reach, and to clear a way for the trapped people. This was the Fire Department textbook on fighting high-rise fires, and Palmer knew it backward and forward. (As a sideline, he ran a small business tutoring other fire officers who were going to take the test for chief.) Some months earlier, a number of battalion chiefs had been reassigned, and Palmer was sent to the Bronx. He quietly lobbied to go back to Manhattan. After all, he had researched and practiced high-rise firefighting. He had made a study of the radio system inside Pennsylvania Station, the railroad depot where trains set off from New York for the whole nation. He got his wish, and was sent to Battalion 7, based in the Chelsea section of Manhattan.

Coming up the stairs was Ladder 15, a company based on Water Street, in the South Street Seaport district, and led by another officer devoted to skyscrapers, Lt. Joseph Leavey.

"Fifteen Irons to 15."

The "irons" firefighter carries tools for prying open doors, and is always among the first up the stairs. That morning, the irons man for Ladder 15 was Scott Larsen.

"Go ahead, Irons," Leavey said.

"Just got a report from the director of Morgan Stanley," Larsen said. "Seventy-eight seems to have taken the brunt of this stuff, there's a lot of bodies, they say the stairway is clear all the way up, though."

"All right, 10-4, Scott," Leavey said. "What, what floor are you on?"

"Forty-eight right now," Larsen replied.

"All right, we're coming up behind you," Leavey said.

The director of Morgan Stanley mentioned by Larsen was most likely Rick Rescorla, the firm's director of security, who was instrumental in planning and then leading the firm's mass evacuation from the south tower. Morgan Stanley had some 2,700 people based in the south tower, between the 44th and 74th floors, and Rescorla, who had served in Vietnam and was featured in the book and feature film *We Were Soldiers Once . . . and Young,* had been fixed on the trade center as a possible terrorist target. During the early part of the evacuation, someone took a photograph that showed him standing in the stairway at the 10th floor, with a bull-horn shouting encouragement. By the time firefighter Larsen crossed paths with Rescorla, all but a handful of the Morgan Stanley workers had left the building. Orio Palmer, moving up quickly, was not part of that exchange, but no doubt had tracked it on his radio. A moment later, he heard from Tom Kelly, the firefighter assigned to run the elevator that was shuttling fire companies from the lobby to the 40th floor.

"I got an engine company on 40, do you want them up there?" Kelly asked.

"Tell them we're going to have to try to get the high-rise bank of elevators into operation," Palmer said. "Until we verify the fire floor, we can't do that."

The process was logical. Before he could send up elevators, Palmer needed to find out where the fire was. Once he had confirmed the location, someone could tinker with whatever cars were still in running condition, and perhaps bring the teams up to the floors just below the fire. Palmer himself had been an elevator mechanic before he joined the Fire Department, but it was the kind of job that could be done by any number of firemen who were well versed in how things worked.

A few seconds later, Palmer called Kelly back. The chief apparently had gotten information from people in the stairways. He wanted to set up his command post on the 76th floor.

"Try to get down to the lobby and find out what bank of elevators terminates below the 76th floor," Palmer said. "That's the bank we're going to want to use."

"Ten-four," Kelly said.

By 9:32, almost precisely thirty minutes after Flight 175 had struck the south tower, Ed Geraghty, the chief of Battalion 9, also had taken the elevator to the 40th floor, and was preparing to deploy his firefighters. He checked in with Palmer.

"What floor should we try to get up to, Orio?" Geraghty asked.

Palmer told him what he had just told Kelly: they needed to find elevators that would get them to the 76th floor. Otherwise, it was thirty floors or so of walking.

"I'm up to 55," Palmer reported. He had covered twelve floors in his first ten minutes of climbing after riding the freight car as far as 40. At home, his favorite time to run in Hendrickson Park was the hottest part of the hottest days of the year; now he was climbing in turnout coat, boots, and helmet, with oxygen tanks strapped to his back. Even so, as he rose, Palmer seemed to find a new burst of speed in his legs, and after he reached the 55th floor, his radio transmissions mapped an ever-faster ascent. People were starting to come down the stairs, with word of a hellish sprawl of destruction on 78.

By about 9:35, Ling Young had gotten down to the 51st floor, then stood at the landing, her burned arms extended from her burned body. Her eyes were closed. Coming up the stairs were two fire marshals—Ron Bucca, trailed a few floors behind by Jim Devery, who had gotten into the building within minutes of the plane hitting, and had not used the elevator, but had walked up the steps. Devery noticed Young on the 51st-floor landing. She seemed ready to faint, but then launched herself toward the stairs. Devery, exhausted by the climb, decided to go down the stairs with her, to make sure she got out.

Not far behind them were Judy Wein, Gigi Singer, and Ed Nicholls from Aon. Around the 50th floor, they saw the first firefighters.

"What floor did you come from?" one of the firefighters asked.

"Seventy-eight, and there's a lot of people badly hurt up there," Wein answered.

Just those three people had enough injuries among them to keep a trauma ward busy: Ed Nicholls, with his nearly severed arm; Wein, with her collapsed lung, broken ribs, and torn arm; Singer, with serious burns.

The firemen looked at them. "Go to the 41st floor, there's firemen there," one of them said. "There's an elevator to take you to the ground." In fact, the elevator was on the 40th floor, but they would find it.

Even more people were coming down behind the Wein group. Lieutenant Leavey got on his radio. He wanted to make sure that Tom Kelly had the elevator ready.

"Tommy, listen carefully," Leavey said. "I'm sending all the injured down to you on 40. You're going to have to get them down to the elevator, there's about ten to fifteen people coming down to you."

"Okay," Kelly replied.

"Ten civilians coming down," Leavey said.

"Got that, I'm on 40 right now, Lieu," Kelly said.

"All right, Tommy," Leavey said. "When you take people down to the lobby, try to get an EMS crew back."

"Definitely," Kelly said.

The radios crackled with messages, the humming of a crisp high-rise rescue operation, all business from the mouths of Palmer, Geraghty, Leavey, Kelly, Larsen. Scott Kopytko was designated "roof man," a title that at the trade center meant he would be trying to get up as high as possible, as quickly as possible. Douglas Oelschlager was the can man, bringing up extinguishers. They kept pace with the hard-driving Palmer.

They soon got bad news about the elevators: the people on the ground could not find working cars that would bring them above the 40th floor. "We're going to have to hoof it," Palmer said. "I'm on 69 now, but we need a higher bank." It was 9:42. It had been ten minutes since the last report of his location, and he had moved even faster. He had covered fourteen floors in those ten minutes. They were going to get to the fire.

The elevator ride from the 40th floor to the lobby lasted no more than thirty seconds, so for Ling Young, Judy Wein, Ed Nicholls, and Gigi Singer, it was just another leg in their flight from the devastation of the 78th floor. They would remember little of the ride, or of the man who brought them down. Firefighter Tom Kelly struck people as the classic, ordinary working stiff. No one mistook him for a mythic fireman of steel. He did not run marathons in his spare time, but played outfield for a bar's softball team. During television commercials, he did not do sit-ups, but often enjoyed working on a beer or two. After eighteen years as a firefighter, he had not climbed the promotional ranks, but put spare time and energy into a second job, as a construction worker. He had worked his entire career at the firehouse in the South Street Seaport, and knew the drill on high-rise fires. Now, a week before he was to turn fifty-one, he was among the oldest firefighters to go up in the south tower. As it happened, his knowledge of the trade center stretched back decades, to its beginnings.

On a late September night in 1971, he had taken a young woman from his Brooklyn neighborhood out for their first big date. Her name was Kathleen, known to everyone as Kitty. He brought her to the Copacabana, the storied nightclub in midtown Manhattan. To make the night even more special, they caught a cab and rode downtown to West Street, to the construction site where Kelly worked as an apprentice steamfitter, welding pipes and joints. It was long after regular work hours, of course, but he wanted to give Kitty a private tour of the colossus he was helping build. It was called the World Trade Center. He slipped a twenty-dollar bill to the security guard, who waved them inside. Then the guard thought of something.

"Hey!" he called. "Put a hard hat on your young lady."

They took a construction elevator to the 40th floor of the south tower, and stepped into the steel skeleton. To leave a swanky nightclub for a raw, unfinished building hardly seemed like the classic gondola ride to romance. Yet from there, on the 40th floor, the world and all in it were spread before them. To the north, the sky was stenciled by the night-lit forms of office towers; to the west, the low plains of New Jersey glowed against the horizon; to the east and south, bridges twinkled. They were one hundred feet higher than the torch of the Statue of Liberty, just below them in New York Harbor. Kitty was nineteen. Tom had just turned twenty-one. They had become part of the city's candlelight, in a building that was still being born. Six months later, they married. When construction slumped, and jobs for junior steamfitters were scarce, Kelly took a test to join the Fire Department, the better to support his family and two growing children. The firefighting schedule allowed ample time for a second job, so he continued to work steamfitting shifts whenever they were available.

Now, three decades after his big night out with Kitty, he was back in the trade center, once again on the 40th floor, collecting an elevator full of people—bleeding, broken, battered. The building he had come to in muscular youth was dying. Kelly's lieutenant had sent word that ten injured people were coming down. He brought the first four to arrive, Ling Young (accompanied by Marshal Devery), Ed Nicholls, Gigi Singer, and Judy Wein, to the ground. Then he went back up.

The four people in the elevator were among eighteen people making their way down from the 78th floor and above; the fourteen others were moving at a remarkably strong pace that would bring them out of the building. Still others were trailing, but at a slower pace. Those first eighteen people, as they reached the lower floors and the lobby, brought hard-won intelligence on the state of the stairways. They had found a way past, a seam in the destruction. Above the fire were hundreds of people who were not on their way, who believed they were stranded—some had gone to the roof, others believed the stairs down were fraught with danger.

Richard Fern, one of the first to escape from the upper floors, had raced down stairway A from the 84th floor, through the concourse and out of the east side of the trade center. He continued east to Park

Row, and by 9:45 had wound up outside his regular barbershop. He all but collapsed into a chair, and one of the barbers brought him cold wet towels. As he sat there, his Euro Brokers walkie-talkie was capturing transmissions from inside the south tower. Dave Vera was sending word for help. The last place Vera had been seen was in stairway A, just below the 84th floor, in the company of a half dozen other people. The group had been going down the stairs, but were turned back by the heavyset woman and skinny man coming up, insisting that the smoke below them was too intense. That, as it turned out, was the same stairway used by Fern and the seventeen other people. Inside the building, one of Vera's colleagues, Jose Marrero, who already had gone well below the fire, had turned back and had started climbing the stairs to help him, crossing paths with Brian Clark and Stanley Praimnath along the way.

News of the open stair did not reach Vera, or the people in Keefe, Bruyette & Woods or Fiduciary Trust, or Jack Andreacchio, the Brooklyn cowboy, or the scores of workers in the offices of Aon, Sandler O'Neill, the state tax department. Those who took that open stairway did not realize that it was the only way out. Collecting this information did not seem to be anyone's job. And even if the intelligence had been gathered, the building's public-address system apparently had been knocked out by the impact of the plane. The people on the upper floors had adapted quickly, fashioning their own communication network with cell phones and with phones plugged into the backs of computers. They dialed the city's 911 operators, many of whom tried, but could not dispel, their anguish. The operators did not know about the open stairway and advised people to stay put. The city's 911 operation had been in turmoil since the early 1990s, when the city began plans to overhaul it; in its daily operations, the 911 system was run by the Police Department. The people who answered the phones were civilians, among the lowest-paid workers in city government, relegated to the bottom caste in a world of uniforms. So poor was the coordination with other emergency agencies that fire dispatchers actually had to dial back into 911 themselves in order to reach police dispatchers.

And so the people inside the south tower remained unaware of the open staircase. They spoke to their families, who watched the towers burn on television, but also did not know about the stairway. The word had not gotten back to the fire commanders, to the 911 call center, or to broadcasters, so the information that stairway A was available did not circle back to the places where it might have done some good. Like the lifeboats that left the *Titanic* half-empty, stairway A remained little used.

Not only were the rescuers unable to communicate with the people they were trying to help, they often could not communicate among themselves. A number of city agencies sent representatives to 7 World Trade Center, the headquarters of the Mayor's Office of Emergency Management, about 300 yards from the main fire command post on West Street.

By the time John Peruggia, the Fire Department's delegate, reached 7 World Trade Center, that building was being evacuated because of worries that a third plane was bound for New York. So instead of using the mayor's bunker, the emergency-response officials huddled in the lobby. Over the next few minutes, Peruggia heard a warning that he could scarcely believe, but did not dare to dismiss.

An engineer from the Department of Buildings reported that the structural damage appeared to be immense. The stability of both buildings was compromised. In particular, the engineer was worried about how long the north tower would stand.

This was an astounding possibility. Like many others, Peruggia was a veteran of the 1993 bombing, and after that attack, he had heard the presentations about the strength of the two towers. No one could forget the claim by Leslie Robertson, the structural engineer, that the towers were designed to stand up to the impact of a Boeing 707.

The Buildings Department engineer did not care what had been promised a decade earlier, or three decades earlier. In glimpses when the flow of smoke parted, he could see the damage.

Peruggia summoned an emergency medical technician, Rich

Zarillo, who was working for him as an aide. He was to go immediately from 7 World Trade Center to the command post where the senior fire commander, Chief of Department Peter Ganci, was located, on West Street, across from the north tower.

"You see Chief Ganci, and Chief Ganci only," Peruggia said. "Provide him with the information that the building integrity is severely compromised and they believe the building is in danger of imminent collapse."

Peruggia could not communicate with the chief by radio. He simply did not have the means. The emergency operations center had been shut because of fears that terrorists would fly a third plane into it. The expensive 800-megahertz interagency radios were all in the trunks of cars, unused, because no one with clout in the city government ever got around to pressing the issue. Peruggia himself was not carrying a fire ground radio that morning, because his ordinary assignment did not call for it. In the world capital of communications, he had only one way to get the engineer's assessment to the chief of the Fire Department: to send a messenger dodging across acres of flaming debris and falling bodies. He would have to deliver this warning in person.

As he reached higher ground, Orio Palmer's voice rang with the exertion of the moment, and the conviction that he was getting close to the mouth of the fire. After climbing thirty floors, he accelerated, moving at a pace of thirty-six seconds per floor.

"Where are you, Chief?" Lieutenant Leavey asked.

"Seventy-four," Palmer responded at 9:45.

"We're making our way up behind you," Leavey said. "We took our coats off."

Palmer covered the next flight in twenty-one seconds. He reported that he saw no smoke or fire problems in stairway B, but some walls had been damaged at the 73rd and 74th floors. "Be careful," he said. And he had run into fire marshal Ron Bucca, who had rushed into the building with his partner, Jim Devery. At the point where Devery turned back to escort Ling Young out of the building, Bucca kept climbing. Bucca was a registered nurse, a reservist in the United States Army Special Forces. He kept a set of blueprints of the trade center in his locker, concerned that terrorists would return to attack the building.

"I found a marshal on 75," Palmer reported, a few seconds later, no doubt pleased to have some company as he neared the fire. They were leaving stairway B, he reported. As many others had found, it was hard to pass. After some scouting, he discovered that stairway A was open, the proven portal out of the calamity. From the 75th floor, Palmer radioed back to the trailing firefighters, telling them they should head for stairway A.

Behind him, Joe Leavey had made it to the 70th floor by 9:50. He found some of the people hurt by the plane, who had crept down a few floors, but apparently were unable to move much lower. The elevators were essential. He knew that Tom Kelly had shuttled one group of the injured to the lobby, and had come back to the 40th floor to collect more of the walking wounded.

"Tommy, have you made it back down to the lobby yet?" Leavey asked Kelly.

"The elevator's screwed up," Kelly replied.

"You can't move it?" Leavey asked.

"I don't want to get stuck in the shaft," Kelly said.

Kelly's caution was hardly excessive. Yet to Leavey, thirty floors above Kelly, the situation was too dire for hesitation. Injured people had reached the 70th floor, and no doubt those people were telling him about the devastation on the 78th floor and above.

"All right, Tommy," Leavey said. "It's imperative that you try to get down to the lobby command post and get some people up to 40. We got injured people up here on 70. If you make it to the lobby command post, see if they can somehow get elevators past the 40th floor. We got people injured all the way up here."

One minute later, at 9:51, Palmer's voice came across the radio in a short, urgent burst. He had last been heard from two minutes earlier, on the 75th floor, where he had met Marshal Bucca.

Now, Palmer did not say where he was, but he was trying to reach Donald Burns, the chief in charge of the south tower. His words conveyed less than his tone. His voice sounded a higher pitch. Most likely, Palmer had reached the 78th floor, the first uniformed rescuer to reach the impact zone. Because of radio traffic, it would take another minute before he was able to contact other firefighters on the radio. At 9:52, he spoke with Joe Leavey, who was to relay the message down.

"We've got two isolated pockets of fire," Palmer said. "We should be able to knock it down with two lines."

The next part of his message was a report not about fire or broken walls, but about the condition of the people. In radio transmissions, the Fire Department avoids the term "civilians," referring to them as "10-45s," and does not describe anyone as "dead," but as "Code One." He stammered, just slightly, perhaps from exertion, perhaps from what he, the first person from the outside, was seeing.

"Radio, radio, radio that—78th floor, numerous 10-45 Code Ones," Palmer said.

On the 78th floor, he was saying, there were many dead civilians.

"Floor 78?" asked Leavey.

"Ten-four," Palmer replied. "Numerous civilians. We're gonna need two engines up here."

"We're on our way," Leavey said.

In the lobby, Ed Nicholls had emerged from Tom Kelly's elevator, bleeding from the head, the arm, the abdomen, uncertain of where to go next. He would have little recollection of how he got out, but a photographer snapped a picture as he emerged from the concourse onto Church Street. In the photo, a young policewoman, Moira Smith, puts one hand under Nicholls's elbow, another on his shoulder. She is wearing blue disposable gloves. Her blond hair is pulled back from her face; she had left her police hat on the seat of the van in which she and her partner drove down to the trade center from Greenwich Village. Smith had not been dispatched to the trade center; she had been filling out forms when she saw the van loaded and ready to go. She jumped on. No ordinary city patrol officers were sent inside the buildings, an assignment left to the ESU teams, and to the Port Authority police, trained in firefighting. In this division of labor, no one had the quotidian task of shepherding people from the buildings to the ambulances. Moira Smith, policewoman, joined the security guards, firefighters, and Port Authority bureaucrats who had taken that job upon themselves. Smith escorted Ed Nicholls through the concourse of the trade center, leading him out to Church Street on the east side of the complex, where ambulances were staged. Then she returned to the lobby of the south tower.

By now, about ten minutes to ten, nearly fifty minutes after the south tower had been hit, a line of molten aluminum was pouring from a window on the corner of the 80th floor: the airplane was melting. The 83rd floor appeared to be draped across windows on the 82nd floor, and was gradually drooping even lower. These were details on photographs, analyzed in depth months later. From the inside, though, the people on the high floors narrated the rapid undoing of the building. On the 80th floor, where the Brooklyn cowboy Jack Andreacchio and his boss, Manny Gomez, were trapped, the smoke and heat had all but engulfed the men and those with them. A colleague who had made it outside, Bobby McMurray, reached Gomez by radio. "It don't look too good, Bobby Mac," Gomez said. Kevin Cosgrove from Aon had walked down twenty flights from the 99th floor, only to be turned back by smoke at 79. He walked back up to the 105th floor, where so many people had gone in hopes of escape to the roof. He called his brother, Joe. "I'm not getting out of this, I need you to take care of my kids, tell my wife I love her," Cosgrove said. "I'll call you back." He hung up.

The voices from the 105th floor, twenty stories above the top of the impact zone, grew more urgent. One woman called 911 and said the floor was collapsing. A moment later, a man called from 106 and said a floor below was collapsing. From the 88th floor, Rick Thorpe of Keefe, Bruyette & Woods told 911 that people were passing out, and that he would break the windows.

Calling from the 93rd floor, Greg Milanowycz spoke to his father and then to a colleague of his father's, Marcia De Leon.

"The ceiling is caving," Milanowycz said. "The ceiling is caving."

On the street, Rich Zarillo had arrived at the West Street command post with the message from the Buildings Department engineer that the towers were near collapse, and told Chief Ganci's aide, Fire Marshal Steve Mosiello.

The aide turned to his boss, a few steps away, involved in other business.

"Chief, these buildings are in imminent danger of collapse," Mosiello reported.

Ganci looked stunned. "Who would tell you something like that?" he asked. After thirty-three years in the Fire Department, Pete Ganci had risen to chief of department, and he knew full well that skyscrapers do not collapse from less than an hour of fire.

Mosiello turned to the messenger.

"Richie, come over here and tell the chief what you just told me," Mosiello said.

In the south tower elevator, Tom Kelly, sent back down to the lobby, had not gotten very far: his worries about the balky car turned out to be justified.

"Stuck in the elevator, in the elevator shaft," Kelly reported on the radio. "You're going to have to get a different elevator. We're chopping through the wall to get out."

Palmer, on the 78th floor, heard Kelly. "Radio lobby command with that," he said.

Strangely, the 78th floor was quiet. On all the radio transmissions from firefighters lower in the building, the whooping of the building's alarm could be heard in the background. Behind Palmer's voice from the 78th floor, there was no alarm, no clamor. By now, Palmer had caught his breath, and his voice was fully composed.

He sent one group of firefighters up to the 79th floor: the 78th and 79th floors were connected by an escalator, and the fire on 79 was visible from 78. The firefighters had made it to the border territory between life and death, just as Frank De Martini and his men had in the north tower an hour earlier. The sky lobby floor was carpeted with the dead, but also the immobilized living, perhaps in despair of ever getting any help. Yet here was Palmer, organizing the troops, alongside Bucca, a registered nurse, a soldier, a firefighter, all in one.

They discovered, when they reached the floor, that the people had not been entirely alone: a security guard was on the scene. A few months earlier, twenty-four-year-old Robert Gabriel Martinez had left his job at McDonald's and gone to work as a security guard at the trade center, finding a pay hike in the $11.61-an-hour salary. Normally, Martinez did not work on the 78th floor. But he had stayed up late the night before, watching the New York Giants on *Monday Night Football*, and he had overslept that morning. When he got to the trade center, he learned that his regular assignment—in a loading dock on the north end of the complex—had been given to someone else. So he was headed for the south tower's upper sky lobby. "They sent me to the 78th floor," he told James Flores, the quartermaster for the security guards. Flores issued him the blue-and-gray striped clip-on tie that all the security guards were issued, and the heavy-duty portable radio that allowed them to communicate throughout the complex.

When Palmer and Bucca arrived on the 78th floor, the evidence suggests that they found Martinez, a big, burly man. Somehow, he had survived the impact of Flight 175. He had not left his $11.61-an-hour post. He had stayed in the slaughterhouse. At 9:57, the voice of the 78th-floor security guard burst onto the airwaves. His messages rang with desperation, but also, it seemed, a gust of exhilaration and hope.

An entire elevator car full of people had been trapped on the 78th floor, stuck for nearly fifty-five minutes, ever since the second plane had hit.

Central, please be advised, I need EMS at 78 sky lobby, 2 World Trade Center. I've got people coming out of the elevator banks. Listen, please be advised, I've got, like, eighteen passengers stuck on the 78th sky lobby elevator. They're trying to get them out, we need EMS over here! ON THE DOUBLE! TWO WORLD TRADE CENTER!

The dispatcher tried to calm him down.

"Is that an elevator entrapment, sir?" she asked.

"That's a ten-four," the guard said. "The firefighters have eighteen passengers stuck, and they're going to try to get them out!

"They're trying!"

Fourteen floors up, a man on the 102nd floor was speaking to a 911 operator. He was a young man, he said. He had children. He did not want to die. He pleaded his case over and over: He did not want to die. He did not want to die. Suddenly, his words were drowned out by crashing noises, a terrible scream, an even worse silence.

At that moment, at the command center on West Street, Chief Ganci had just finished hearing the message delivered by Rich Zarillo about the threat of an imminent collapse. A gathering rumble filled the air.

"What the fuck is that?" Ganci asked.

A glance at the south tower, its top dissolving into smoke, answered his question.

13

"We'll come down in a few minutes."

9:59 A.M.
NORTH TOWER

Mom," asked Jeffrey Nussbaum. "What was that explosion?"

Twenty miles away, in Oceanside, New York, Arlene Nussbaum could see on television what her son could not from the office at Carr Futures on the 92nd floor of the north tower.

"The other tower just went down," Mrs. Nussbaum told her son.

"Oh, my God," Jeffrey said.

Decades earlier, before the towers rose to altitudes nearly out of sight, each one had been bolted to bedrock seven stories below the street, a depth virtually out of sight. At their nearest point, the buildings were separated by 131 feet. For twenty-eight years, in weather fair and foul, they kept their distance, parallel lines that could not cross, no matter how high the towers rose into the sky or how deep they sank into the earth. In a span of ten seconds, the south tower pulverized itself and became a mammoth cloud of dust that blasted into the base of the north tower, curling up the shafts and stairways of its twin. Geometry dissolved, the two buildings had met.

More than a gigantic tower had fallen. The construction of the trade center had absorbed the labor of men, women, and machines.

As the order and shape of a mighty work came undone, the efforts of thousands of people dissolved. Still, the laws of physics hold that energy is not destroyed. All the power used by the construction workers to lift steel, pour concrete, hammer nails had been banked in the buildings as potential energy for three decades, just as a sled at the top of a hill stores the verve of the child who tugged it up there, or a bicycle at the crest of a mountain road holds all the pumping and pedaling that got it to the high place. Stockpiled in the south tower was a tremendous reserve of energy, 278 megawatt hours. All of it was released at the moment of the building's demise, floors picking up speed as they slammed downward. Scientists would struggle later to describe the burst of power in terms that ordinary people could grasp. It was equal to 1 percent of a nuclear bomb. It was enough power to supply all the homes in Atlanta or Oakland or Miami for one hour. It was so strong, the earth shuddered in waves that were captured on a seismograph in Lisbon, New Hampshire, 265 miles distant. Yet it made no sense in the building next door.

The blast of air from the south tower traveled 131 feet into the lobby of the north tower and then burst through the passageways across the complex. It found Sharon Premoli just as she ascended from the concourse northeast of the tower that was still standing. An hour earlier, she had begun her descent from Beast Financial, on the 80th floor of the north tower, dressed for a business meeting in a navy blouse and a beige skirt. In an instant, she was in the air, her navy blue shoes flashing before her eyes just before she slammed into the window of Borders Books. Her mouth, nose, and ears were clogged with gunk, her eyes covered with fiberglass splinters. With every breath she drew grit into her chest. She felt intense pain in her chest; shards of glass pierced her hands; she could not hear out of her left ear. The air was black. She could not see, hear, speak, or breathe. I'm dead, she thought.

The death tremors of the south tower rattled along the bones of the north tower. On the 51st floor, the court officers Joseph Baccellieri, Al Moscola, and Andrew Wender were nearly knocked to the ground. They had heard the radio chatter that a third plane was en route: this must have been it. Their walkie-talkies spat out sounds, but none of it amounted to a message they could grasp.

Standing at a window on the 27th floor, where she was taking a break on her descent from 88, Patricia Cullen watched a massive cloud explode into her line of sight, a galloping darkness coming straight toward her building. The floor trembled, the rumble passing from her feet to head. She fled toward the elevator lobby in the core of the building. There, she saw the big man in the wheelchair, Ed Beyea, and his friend, Abe Zelmanowitz.

The physics of the moment had registered in the eyes, the ears, and the muscles of people in the north tower. These sensations did not form a coherent shape. Hardly anyone in the north tower, whether civilians or rescuers, realized that the other building had fallen. Moving in the stairwells, they had little reliable information from the outside. Early in the crisis, the office workers could smell the odor of splattered jet fuel, but that did not linger. True, there were ponds of water to ankle through. That was part of the ordeal of departure. So, too, were the aches in the feet and the calves, the heat shimmering from all those thousands of people, the dizzying reversals of direction at each landing of stairs. These were the present-tense realities of the departing people. The inferno, though, was out of sight. Mercifully so, too, were the bodies dropping from the high floors. Indeed, the very fact that the building—both buildings—had been struck by commercial aircraft was not widely known inside the towers. Millions around the world watched the south tower fall, but the true peril of the moment had not revealed itself widely inside the surviving building. That the buildings were collapsing not only was beyond expectation; it was beyond conception.

Mak Hanna, from Frank De Martini's crew, was making his way down from the 88th floor with his eighty-nine-year-old colleague, Moe Lipson. After the rumble of the south tower's collapse, Patricia Cullen, who also worked for the Port Authority on 88, saw them in the hallway at the 27th floor. Hanna carried a pager that sent not only phone messages, but also news headlines. For some reason, it had kept working through the descent. Hanna knew that terrorists had taken over airliners and were crashing them into buildings. He knew, as he neared the 27th floor, that the south tower had collapsed. Hanna did some calculations in his head. Everyone was leaving as quickly as possible. They were reasonably calm. If he spread word of the collapse, what would be gained? Nothing, he decided. And panic might set in. He held his tongue.

"You're doing okay, Moe?" he asked.

Lipson said he was. They plodded down. Patricia Cullen, after her break on the 27th floor, also resumed her departure.

By 10:01, two minutes after the south tower collapsed, seventy-five minutes from the beginning of the calamity, a police dispatcher went on the air to contact the ESU officers who had gone inside the north tower.

"Citywide central to unit, 'kay, with emergency message."

The dispatcher was interrupted by other transmissions, then continued.

"Emergency services out of 1. Emergency services out of 1, 'kay?"

Four more times, he gave the order: All of the NYPD emergency service officers were to get out of Building 1. Over a special channel for the ESU, Det. Ken Winkler, who was just across from the buildings and had taken shelter from the torrent of dust beneath a car, ordered everyone to leave, saying that the other tower had fallen. The news astounded cops inside the north tower, who asked him to repeat it.

At just about the same moment, Chief Joe Pfeifer wiped the dust from his eyes. The avalanche of soot from the south tower had driven him and the other fire commanders out of their command post in the lobby of the north tower. They raced into a passageway that led to 6 World Trade Center, a low-rise structure just north of the north tower. The cloud pursued them, but they outran and outturned the worst of it. Pfeifer assumed there had been a local collapse; he had no idea that the other building had fallen to the ground. All morning, institutional prerogatives and customs and obstinacy had blanketed him and his colleagues in a thick fog of ignorance. The people fighting the two worst building fires in the nation's history had no video monitors. No radio communications with other agencies. No way to get reports from police helicopters and only a limited ability to communicate among themselves. Moments after the south tower collapsed, a fireboat in the harbor reported the disaster over the radio channel used to give fire companies their assignments. The radio that captured that channel and those messages had been left behind, however, in the north tower lobby when the fire chiefs made their desperate flight from the debris. Now, from inside a heavy, choking, blinding cloud, Pfeifer spoke on his radio, betraying no sign of agitation, no hint that one of the world's largest buildings had just collapsed a few yards away. He did not know.

"Command post in Tower 1 to all units," he said. "Evacuate the building. Command post to all units." At their feet, Pfeifer and his group found Father Mychal Judge, the Fire Department chaplain who had been alongside them all morning, murmuring prayers. They opened his collar, felt no pulse.

On the 30th floor of the north tower, Steve Modica, a fire lieutenant, had stopped to rest, stripping off his bunker coat, helmet, oxygen tank. Modica served as the aide to John Paolillo, the chief of the special operations battalion. Paolillo, a marathon runner, had outpaced Modica once they got into the 20s. Now Modica sat with two other firefighters, similarly worn by the climb. They had just about caught their breath when the south tower collapsed. To Modica, the shudder suggested that a bomb had gone off somewhere below them. Or maybe a third plane had hit. He listened for radio transmissions, but did not catch a whisper of any explanation or instructions. The order made by Chief Pfeifer to evacuate the buildings did not reach his radio. He could hear fragments of chatter from people inside the building—firefighters with chest pains, oxygen needed on one corridor, a particular floor that a company had stopped on. Nothing about getting out.

A moment or two after the shudder, though, Modica heard banging in the stairwell. He saw four ESU police officers charging down, moving so fast, he thought their feet were not touching the treads of the stairs. Modica tried to absorb all that had happened in the last few minutes: The building had been shaken. For some reason, the cops were flying out of there. His chief was somewhere upstairs. For a long moment, he was frozen in place.

Modica's place was the lowest zone in the building. In essence, the tower was three buildings, stacked atop one another: the first ran from the lobby to the 44th-floor sky lobby; the middle section rose from 44 to the 78th-floor sky lobby; the highest zone stretched from 78 to the top of the building. Most of the people who remained in the north tower were in either the top zone—trapped on the high floors where the fire was roaring—or in the bottom zone, office workers making their way out and the rescuers on a slow climb.

In the middle zone, the building was quiet. A group of six rescuers, traveling lighter than the firefighters, had made it to the 51st floor. The three court officers who had rushed into the building, Baccellieri, Moscola, and Wender, were moving up with three Port Authority officers. They found no one in the offices. The stairways also were empty. They did not even meet any firefighters. All the noise that they heard was from the staircases far below them, until the south tower collapsed. Then the lights shut down and the stairs fell dark. A moment later, the emergency lights kicked on. From the court officers' radios, reports blared of other trapped court officers, their colleagues. Al Moscola assumed that the voices were calling for help from their usual place, in the Court Officers Academy, a few blocks away from the trade center.

"Those bastards! They attacked William Street!" Moscola screamed.

"Al," Baccellieri said. "They're downstairs. They're not at William Street."

Wherever and whatever the trouble was, the dynamic had changed. The court officers felt they had gone as far as was prudent, nearly 600 feet up, every step on their own initiative. They decided to head downstairs and reconnect with the three Port Authority officers. Together, the group began to go down from the 51st floor. Just then, the Port Authority officers' radios crackled with orders to evacuate.

"We'll come down in a few minutes."

Sixteen floors below the court officers, on the 35th floor, a battalion chief stood with parts of five fire companies: Ladders 5, 9, and 20, and Engines 33 and 24. The streams of people leaving had slowed their progress up the stairs, keeping them near the ground, and closer to safety. So had the ballast: the gear they were carrying, much of it useless. The senior fire commanders all felt there was no hope of extinguishing a blaze that was burning so high in the tower, over so many floors, but the orders they thought they had given the ascending companies—to leave half their gear behind— were largely ignored or unheard. As they had started their trek to the fire ninety-two stories above them, many companies carried hundreds of pounds of equipment that no one expected them to use. That surely slowed the climb—and kept them from penetrating so far in the tower that they had no prospect of quickly backing out. On the landings in the 20s were traces of the struggle of those climbing up: coils of hose, fire extinguishers, even pry tools, abandoned.

Now, on the 35th floor, these five companies, who had been among the earliest to arrive, were taking a break and trying to gather the firefighters who had fallen behind. Someone had found a kitchen, so they were drinking to replenish the fluids they had sweated out. The staircases were virtually empty of civilians now. One of the lieutenants on the 35th floor, Warren Smith, had fought fires in Manhattan for most of his twenty years in the department, and knew that they could not put out eight floors of raging fire, or whatever the scope of that ghastly hell was. Dropping gear made sense. Maybe they would settle for finding people who needed a hand and get them out. Mike Warchola, the lieutenant from Ladder 5, was on his last day of work, and earlier in the morning, had been congratulated by other firefighters. Now, as he stood on the 35th floor, sweat poured off him. Gregg Hansson, the lieutenant from Engine 24, spotted him.

"How are you doing, Mike?" Hansson asked.

It was more than a casual question. Warchola looked Hansson in the eye.

"I'm doing fine," he replied.

Another lieutenant taking a break on the 35th floor, Kevin Pfeifer of Engine 33—brother of the battalion chief—recognized Hansson from other fires. As Hansson sipped iced tea, he and Pfeifer discussed pairing up so they could scuttle half their load and make the climb a bit easier. Just as they were bringing the idea to Richard Picciotto, the battalion chief taking a break on 35, the building began to shake.

"What's going on?" Smith asked Picciotto.

The chief was not sure. A moment later, Hansson—and probably Pfeifer, as well—heard a cry of "Mayday! Evacuate the building" from Picciotto's radio. It is possible that this was the message sent from 6 World Trade Center by Lieutenant Pfeifer's brother, although Chief Pfeifer had not used the term "mayday," not realizing the other tower had collapsed. While some firefighters in trouble gave mayday calls, there is no clear evidence that any chief specifically issued that most urgent of distress warnings.

In any event, Chief Picciotto told them all to leave. Then he hollered the order to other fire companies on the 35th floor. No one among that group knew the other building had fallen, but the urgency of the situation seemed apparent to Warren Smith, the lieutenant who had been thinking about dropping gear. When firefighters pull back from a high-rise, it usually involves dropping down a few floors, not leaving the building entirely. *Something's fucked up beyond what we can handle,* Smith would remember thinking. He and the other officers shouted out the orders to leave. Kevin Pfeifer rounded up his troops. Gregg Hansson turned to his men, and said, "Drop your gear and get out." Robert Byrne, a probationary firefighter on his first job, followed to the letter what he thought Hansson intended: Byrne put down not only his tools and rope, but also his face mask—a piece of equipment used for breathing when the air is fouled by smoke or dust.

Hansson and his men went to stairway A, where they spotted Lt. John Fischer and a few firefighters from Ladder 20.

"Not all my guys are here," Fischer said. "Where is everybody?"

One of the firefighters replied, "I think a couple of them went upstairs."

Fischer was annoyed. "We've got to stick together," he said. He got on his radio and tried to contact them, but got no answer. He had to go up and get them.

"I'm going down," Hansson said. "I'm taking my men down."

He saw Fischer start up the stairs.

Eight floors below, on the 27th floor, another congregation of firefighters and police officers had gathered. After the collapse, two fire captains, Jay Jonas and William Burke, split up to check the windows, Jonas to the north and Burke to the south. Jonas could see nothing through the windows on the north, and circled back to the vestibule. Burke returned with his report.

"Is that what I thought it was?" Jonas asked.

"Yeah," Burke said, "the south tower's just collapsed."

"We're going home," Jonas said, giving the order to leave.

The firefighters began to clear off the floor, though many did not realize why they were being sent back downstairs. Still waiting on that floor were Ed Beyea and Abe Zelmanowitz, who had already turned aside many suggestions that he leave Beyea behind to the care of firefighters. Now the firefighters themselves were packing up to go. Firefighter Rich Billy, in need of a break, had been left on the 27th floor by Lieutenant Hansson. Billy continued the ritual of clearing each floor—he counted eight people still on 27, including Beyea in his wheelchair and Zelmanowitz—and the firefighter felt he had taken over responsibility for Beyea.

Billy recognized Captain Burke, an officer he had once worked with, and told him that he had taken charge of Beyea. It was evident that Rich Billy, on his own, could do little to evacuate Beyea.

"We've got to get them out," Burke said. At that moment, Lieutenant Hansson arrived from the 35th floor. He was there to pick up Billy, whom he had left behind. Hansson heard some talk about using an elevator—in fact, Captain Burke had come up to the 20th floor on an elevator that few firefighters realized was working—but he wanted no part of anything but a staircase leading directly to the ground. In any case, Burke was taking control of the situation. That was fine with Hansson. He told Billy to come along, and they left the floor.

Burke had his own company of firefighters, from Engine 21. In their recollections, Burke told them to head downstairs, and they did not notice for a couple of floors that he was not with them. When they radioed back, Burke told them he would meet them at the rig. If William Burke was indeed still with Beyea and Zelmanowitz, that would have surprised few who knew him. Burke, like the two friends from Empire Blue Cross and Blue Shield, was another variation on the theme of bachelor life. Forty-six years old, he had worked for twenty-five years as a lifeguard on Long Island, at Robert Moses State Park. One day, the oldest living former lifeguard came to the beach, and his fondest wish was to swim in the ocean one more time. The man was frail, and in a wheelchair. Burke lifted the man into the waves and swam with him. Then they shared a beer.

The elevator door was moving as he pushed it. Chris Young almost didn't believe it was happening. The other times he had tried, the door would not budge. Now, with no more effort, it was sliding out of the way, toward the corner of the car.

Young was elated. Being stuck in the huge north tower elevator alone had gotten very old—and very scary. The thirty-three-year-old temp from Marsh & McLennan had been waiting nearly ninety minutes to be rescued. It had been more than half an hour since the people trapped in the other elevator nearby—Judith Martin and the rest—had last answered his calls. It had been twenty minutes since the elevator had shaken so violently again that he dropped to the floor in a ball.

When he first got stuck, Young had not been too worried. In fact, he initially blamed himself for his predicament. He'd been coming down in one of the express elevators when he decided to test out a precept from adolescent physics—the one that says if you jump up in a speeding elevator, you will somehow create a state of floating weightlessness worthy of NASA. A few jumps later, though, his spirit for adventure drained when the elevator suddenly bounced to a stop.

Over the ensuing hour, the dust, the screams, the alarms and the other people who were stuck near him in the lobby had persuaded him that something much larger and more serious than his own antics was involved. He had no idea what that was, though, and the building staff he reached over the elevator intercom would only say there was "an emergency situation."

Young was similarly mystified about why the doors were suddenly so easy to open. He would find out later that the collapse of the south tower had knocked out the power in its twin, and disabled the motor that normally kept the doors from opening between floors.

When Young looked out into the lobby, the exhilaration of escape quickly lost steam.

There was no one there.

No one.

The bright, modern lobby of tan marble and polished chrome had been replaced by ruin. Debris was everywhere. As Young stepped from the elevator, his feet sank into several inches of pulverized concrete dust. It muffled his footsteps as he hustled toward the windows facing West Street, stepping out through one that was broken. Outside, he looked up, toward the offices on the 99th floor where he had been earlier that morning. Smoke and fire were shooting from the upper floors. "Oh, my God," Young said. A firefighter grabbed him and told him to keep moving.

Among the parties searching floors in the bottom zone of the building was a team led by Inspector James Romito of the Port Authority police. At the collapse of the south tower, Romito listened to his radio, then turned to the half dozen people accompanying him. The searches were over, he said. They were getting out of the building. Frank DiMola, a civilian Port Authority worker, had been helping Romito as he worked his way toward the command center on the 64th floor.

"Two is down," Romito said.

"Building 2?" DiMola asked.

"Building 2 is down," Romito said.

Romito's search crew was at least the fourth agency to cover the same ground, for the same task: checking the floors for office workers. All those searches of floors represented another fortunate inefficiency, like the extra loads of gear that slowed the firefighters from getting higher into the building. During the evacuation from the 1993 bombing, firefighters ended up searching the millions of square feet of office space multiple times, a point of frustration noted stingingly in the reports prepared by the fire chiefs after that attack. Even so, little had changed in the eight years since then. Once again, duplicative searches were under way. Firefighters searched floors. The Police Department's Emergency Service Unit also reported that it was searching floors. Joseph Baccellieri's team of court officers and Port Authority police had searched all the way up to 51. And the group led by Inspector Romito also was searching floors. This time, the multiple searches had the beneficial effect of keeping many rescuers closer to the ground. Yet the lack of coordination among the agencies, particularly between the Police and Fire Departments, would have other costs.

The word to leave finally got to Steve Modica, the aide to fire chief Paolillo, who had watched, uncomprehending, as police officers pounded down the stairs at the 30th floor. A fire captain, coming down after the police officers, shouted at him.

"Evacuate! Evacuate! I want everyone to evacuate the building." Then the captain continued down. Modica tried to reach Chief Paolillo, but couldn't raise him. He switched to all three channels used by the department. He still could not get anything. He considered the circumstances, and would recall thinking: "We were doing nothing. Nothing. What's the plan? Nobody had a plan." He started down the stairs.

On the street outside, the ESU police wanted more intelligence, quickly, on the status of the remaining tower. In the frenzy of radio transmissions, the dispatcher demanded attention, and with some effort, got through to the police helicopters hovering over lower Manhattan.

"Aviation base, ESU One needs someone to, one of the aviations, to check Tower 2 and give them an update," the dispatcher said, giving the address of the destroyed building, but with no one in doubt about the question.

The answer came at 10:07, eight minutes after the collapse of the south tower. The pilot of Aviation 14, Tim Hayes, replied with a grim forecast.

"Advise everybody to evacuate the area in the vicinity of Battery Park City," said Hayes. "About fifteen floors down from the top, it looks like it's glowing red. It's inevitable."

To be certain that the message was delivered, the dispatcher repeated it, practically word for word, so that all the police officers on the air heard the warning. "All right, he said from the fifteenth floor down, it looked like the building was going to collapse and we need to evacuate everybody from the vicinity of Battery City," the dispatcher said.

A moment later, Greg Semendinger, the pilot of the other police helicopter, Aviation 6, also reported in.

"I don't think this has too much longer to go," he said. "I would evacuate all the people within the area of that second building."

No matter how many times the police dispatcher repeated that message, none of the firefighters in the north tower—by a factor of ten, the largest group of rescuers in the building—had radios that could hear those reports. Indeed, many of them could not hear reports from their own commanders. The ESU police officers did spread the word as they evacuated, urging everyone they saw, firefighters and civilians and other rescuers, to leave at once.

The tide that had drawn them all up the stairs was now slowly turning, even though the demise of the south tower, and the grave peril in the north, remained broadly unknown to the firefighters.

For more than eighty minutes, the bridge and tunnel engineer Patrick Hoey and his Port Authority colleagues on the 64th floor had waited dutifully, as instructed, for the firefighters or the police to arrive. No one showed up. Nothing was stopping them from leaving, except the direct instructions they had gotten at 9:11 to "stand tight" and wait for the rescuers. They would get other messages, of course, from family, friends, even from Port Authority colleagues outside the building, who urged them to get out, who reported that the police were now saying people should leave. The police sergeant who first told them to stay was among those who later tried to send word to get out. As hundreds of workers from higher floors had walked past, the people on 64 wet their coats and put them under the doors to bar the smoke. They taped crevices. Many in the room had been through the exasperating 1993 evacuation, the arduous walk through biting, choking smoke. Perhaps that could be avoided this time. Staying put was official policy in a crisis—evacuate only those floors in the direct vicinity of the fire. Although the fire and Port Authority police commanders had abandoned that approach by 9:00 and ordered a full evacuation, the message did not seem to reach Hoey and his colleagues. The public-address system in the north tower had been severed by the attack. Hoey and the other Port Authority employees had lights and working phones. At one point, Hoey and his colleague Pasquale Buzzelli had traveled across the floor, looking for places where the smoke was seeping in. They found a door that was open, closed it, and then taped it shut. That had worked, for a while. Then the south tower collapsed—although they did not realize it—and in the shuddering that followed, more smoke appeared. People who had been debating for an hour whether to leave, against what they thought was the official advice, decided to make a go of it. By then, sixteen people were left on the floor.

Hoey called the police desk first. "I'm in the trade center, tower one. I'm with the Port Authority and we are on the 64th floor. The smoke is getting kind of bad, so we are going to . . . we are contemplating going down the stairway. Does that make sense?"

"Yes," the police officer replied. "Try to get out."

"All right," Hoey said. "Bye."

It was 10:12 A.M., eighty-seven minutes after the north tower was struck.

The message to leave spread fitfully. Warren Smith, the lieutenant who had gotten the word because he was standing near a chief on the 35th floor, found that the civilians had departed—even the people who looked most responsible and diligent, those who Smith supposed might be company fire wardens. They were the ones who had cleared their colleagues and then stayed around to hand out bottled water to the rescue teams. Yet as Smith went down, he kept coming across firefighters still carrying their heavy coils of hose, still forcing open doors. It was as if nothing had changed. Another cycle of firefighters would search the floors. They had no idea that the order had been given to get out. When Smith told them that everyone was leaving, he felt they did not believe him.

"Listen," Smith said. "Forget about that. Drop your roll-ups. You can get them later if you want. Just get out."

Those firefighters did not have any sense of urgency about complying with a secondhand order, Smith felt. He noticed them stopping to look out windows, to see what was happening in the street. Because the fire was so distant, many of them had gone up without a specific order—basically, to see what they could do—and Smith felt they were very confident about the building. He couldn't blame them. The 1993 bombing had shown them it could stand up. It was, he thought, the *Titanic* mentality.

Another lieutenant who had left the 35th floor, Gregg Hansson, was moving fast with his company. They had stopped at 27 to pick up Rich Billy, who had been with Ed Beyea and Abe Zelmanowitz. As they reached the 19th floor, a firefighter popped out into the stairway. Hansson did not recognize him.

"I need some help," the firefighter said. "We've got a lot of people on the other part of the floor who aren't leaving."

Hansson had to stop, but before he went onto the 19th floor, one of his own men, the probationary firefighter Robert Byrne, told him that he had left his respirator mask back on the 35th floor. Not having the mask could slow them down if they needed to share air. Hansson, however, did not want Byrne to turn back. The trouble, vague as it was, held enormous menace. "I want you to go," Hansson told Byrne. "Just get out of the building."

Then Hansson walked onto the 19th floor, and in the gloom, saw a crowd of firefighters and some civilians. In the group was Kevin Pfeifer, who had been on the 35th floor with Hansson.

"What's going on?" Hansson asked. "We gotta get out of here."

A firefighter from Rescue 3 approached Hansson and addressed him with the universal nickname for lieutenants.

"Lieu, can I talk to you?" he said. The firefighter walked Hansson over to a window that overlooked West Street. It was Hansson's first glimpse of the outside world. He could not see the Marriott Hotel, which stood between the two towers, but West Street seemed jumbled and strange to him. He did not even know that the other tower had also been hit with a plane, much less that it had collapsed.

The firefighter who brought him to the window said, "I don't think we can get out."

"We gotta try to get out of here," Hansson said. "We gotta go."

He headed back for the stairs, calling out that people had to leave. They were moving far too slowly, he thought. They could not have heard the same urgent orders.

Around that same time, another group had also reached the 19th floor—the court officers, Baccellieri, Moscola, and Wender, coming down from 51. They had stopped there on the way up and noted the mass assembly of firefighters. Now, on their way down, they again stepped out of the staircase and into the corridors. They could scarcely believe their eyes. The 19th floor was just as full as it had been when they came up, still packed with firefighters. From end to end of the hallway, and down other corridors, so tight it would be tough to find a place to squeeze in alongside the wall with them, the place was carpeted with firefighters. Most were sitting, and had stripped off their turnout coats. Helmets off. Some were down to their blue T-shirts, maps of sweat blotting through the fabric emblazoned with the Fire Department shield. Wender saw that some were lying down. Axes leaned against the wall. Legs stretched out. Arm resting against oxygen tanks. They could not be hearing, Wender thought, what we are hearing.

Baccellieri and Moscola took in the scene. They guessed there were at least 100 firefighters on the floor.

"We're getting out of here," Baccellieri yelled. "We've been told we've got to get out of the building."

No one moved.

"We'll come down in a few minutes," someone said.

But all the rescue workers are bailing out, the court officers said.

"Yeah, all right, we'll be right there," another firefighter replied.

"We'll come down in a few minutes."

As the court officers tramped downstairs, the alarm outside the tower grew more urgent. Hayes, in police helicopter Aviation 14, broke through the jumble of radio traffic to reach the dispatcher at 10:19, ninety-three minutes into the crisis.

"Be advised, just not one hundred percent sure—but it does appear that the top of the tower might possibly be leaning at this time," Hayes said.

"Tower's leaning?" the dispatcher said. With that, he began to alert the other cars in the field that they had to "read direct," meaning they needed to pay attention to the message, rather than waiting for it to be relayed from the central dispatch office. "Car 3, car 1, ESU 1—read direct on that."

Hayes came back on the air.

"It is confirmed," he said. "It is buckling and it is leaning to the south."

"Which tower is that?" asked the dispatcher. "One or two?"

"The remaining tower, the north tower is leaning to the southwest at this time," Hayes said. "It appears to be buckling in the southwest corner."

To be sure that all the officers on the air got the word, the dispatcher repeated the message.

"The northwest tower is leaning," he said. "And it appears to be buckling at this time at the southwest corner."

That was at least the fourth time police officers in helicopters had broadcast warnings of ominous conditions at the top of the towers, yet another dire message carried solely on police channels. The rescue workers of New York City did not have a system for sharing that information: no common frequencies, no practice of working together at command posts, nothing they could count on beyond the serendipity of an encounter with someone carrying the right radio.

Fred Ill, the captain of Ladder Company 2, who had radioed dispatchers early in the crisis to remind them about getting firefighters on the helicopters, was in the north tower, rounding up his men. They could not hear the warnings from the sky.

227

14

"You don't understand."

10:20 A.M.
NORTH TOWER

Ten minutes. Maybe longer, but nothing in the quiet, deserted stairwell around the 10th or 12th floor marked the passing time. A woman drew short, quick breaths, as if she had run a race and could not catch her breath. A man who sat near her carried a two-way Port Authority radio, but even that had fallen silent. No one else stirred. The north tower seemed more than empty. The place itself felt exhausted and depleted. The woman sat on a step, unable to face another flight.

"We're gonna die," Judith Reese said between gasps.

No, no, insisted Jeff Gertler. "Look—wet your finger, feel the fresh air coming up from the street," he said.

Reese had severe asthma. Everything about the long descent—the exertion, the heat, the anxiety—tightened the clamp around her tormented airways. Gertler, her colleague, tried soothing assurance, pep talks, pleading. Anything to keep her going. Another ten flights or so and they would be out of the building, and she would get help from an ambulance. She had to sit.

It had been about twenty minutes since they had felt the quivering

228

from the collapse of the south tower. They had no idea what had happened, to their building or the other one.

They had been on the move for close to an hour and a half, ever since they left their offices on the 88th floor, where Gertler worked as a project manager for the Port Authority, and where Reese worked as the administrative assistant to Frank De Martini. In the early clamor, when the people on the 88th floor debated waiting for help or leaving, it was the labored breathing of Judith Reese that helped settle the issue. No one with her chronic breathing problems could stay in a space even with small fires. She had been among the first to go, but every step taxed her, and she could move down only one or two flights before stopping. Soon, she had fallen to the distant rear of the procession. Gertler, a colleague but not a close friend, had stayed with her. As with everyone who worked in the towers, the morning's alarm had instantly revived the memory and stories of the 1993 attack and the brutal evacuation. Gertler realized that for Reese, going down the stairs was also to walk into the dread of the evacuation eight years earlier. He had prodded her forward.

"It's not like '93," he said. "Look down the center of the stairs." This was not empty cheerleading. The stairways were lit, the steps marked in glow-tape. They were crowded, but people moved. Prodded by Gertler, she continued. Along the way, she had gotten oxygen from rescuers, permitting her to continue, but now she had to stop.

Spent, Reese sat on the stairs. In the silent stairway, Gertler waited for her to catch enough breath for the final leg of their trip. The time was approaching 10:20, ninety-four minutes since Flight 11 had struck.

If the twin towers could be thought of as two shoeboxes stood on end, then the Marriott Hotel was like a child's shoebox that lay flat between the two big ones. For much of the morning, the hotel lobby had served as an exit ramp from the north tower, which it abutted. By using the hotel, people were able to leave the north tower without walking outside, emerging on Liberty Street, at the south end of the trade center complex. Close to a thousand people had done just that, steered by a team of hotel employees who had gathered in the lobby in the early moments of the crisis. A few of the hotel workers, like Abdu A. Malahi, an audiovisual engineer, had gone upstairs, to make sure the rooms were empty; others, like Joe Keller, the thirty-two-year-old executive housekeeper, had formed a cordon in the lobby. This kept people from using the doors onto West Street, where a lethal rain of glass and building parts and people were falling from the high floors.

The hotel lobby also became a launchpad for the arriving fire-fighters, many of whom had never worked in that part of Manhat-tan and knew little of the layout of the trade center. The hotel had a sweeping entrance on West Street, the approach taken by many of the companies. It was the most obvious way into the trade center, even if it required dodging the plummeting debris and bodies. A chief sent a few companies upstairs to check the rooms; others milled around in the lobby, trying to find a route to their assigned building.

By 9:59, the evacuation had slowed to a trickle, and the lobby, no longer taken over with the urgent task of evacuation, now was occupied mostly by hotel workers who lingered at their stations, and firefighters and police officers who were mustering to go upstairs. Then it came: a rumble, the crashes, the blotting out of light, as if a cosmic drain had suddenly been opened, sucking away the ordinary, familiar shapes of everyday life.

Joe Keller, the executive housekeeper, vanished. He had been less than ten feet from Rich Fetter, the hotel's resident manager. In an instant, he was gone. Fetter pressed himself under and against a column as dust whipped through the lobby. He put his hand out for a second and was smacked with a piece of flying debris. The place went pitch black. Fetter's glasses disappeared. His eyes and nose clogged. Then, suddenly, it seemed to him impossibly quiet. Through the haze, he could make out a group of hotel workers huddled near the Tall Ships bar, along with some firefighters. They began to climb out onto the street.

Fetter knew if he could get near the concierge desk, he could find a walkie-talkie. He felt around, then put his hands on it. Coughing out dust, Fetter called for Keller over the walkie-talkie, knowing that Keller usually carried one. He had been standing in chatting range. How could he have disappeared?

Suddenly, Keller's voice came back.

"Rich, I'm fine—I'm in a void by the bell-stand area," Keller said. "I'm on a ledge, there's a big hole and I can see down to the lower levels of the hotel. There's two firemen in here with me and they seem to be hurt bad." The collapse of the south tower had cleaved the hotel from top to bottom, as if a giant scissors had snipped the building in two.

The two men were separated by a wall of debris. Fetter assured Keller they would get him out. Part of the lobby turned out to be a safe zone shielded during the collapse by reinforced beams that had been installed after the 1993 bombing. Fetter was in the safe area of the lobby, while Keller was caught in the area that collapsed, but in a space that had been sheltered from direct impacts. Also with Fetter on the safe side were seven or eight firefighters, looking for openings in the debris wall because they, too, were missing colleagues. Whole companies had disappeared—at least forty firefighters were either in the part of the lobby that was crushed, or on the severed floors upstairs. Fetter told the ones who had escaped serious injury about the two firefighters trapped with Keller, and they tied a rope to mark the spot, then climbed out through holes and intact passages to get more help. When Deputy Chief Tom Galvin made it onto West Street, he saw a fresh crew from Ladder 113 and told them about two companies that were trapped inside, Engines 58 and 65. Ladder 113—Lt. Raymond Brown and Firefighters Dennis Dowdican, Willie Roberts, Rich Nogan, Bob Pino, Tom Feaser, and Bill Morris—had pulled up just a few minutes before the south tower collapsed. Now, the ladder company headed into the husk of the Marriott, following the rope line. They met two of the firefighters from 58, Mike Fitzpatrick and John Wilson, who happened to be standing in the safe area of the hotel and now wanted to get the rest of their team out, including their lieutenant, Bob Nagel.

Brown and Fitzpatrick crawled through a void and began to cut at the debris. They were able to speak through the debris to Lieutenant Nagel, caught on the wrong side of the debris wall. "I'm okay," Nagel said. "There are two chiefs and another company behind us."

The rescue group began working with power saws. Someone passed a flashlight through to Nagel.

Trapped behind the same wall, Joe Keller of the hotel housekeeping department watched the activity to free Nagel. He spoke to Fetter. "I can see the sparks, I can see where you're working," Keller said. "You're twenty or thirty feet away from me."

About 100 yards east of the hotel, in a collapsed hole at the center of the trade center, other voices called across dark crevices to one another.

"Sound off!" the sergeant, John McLoughlin, hollered.

"Jimeno," said Will Jimeno.

"Pezzulo," said Dominick Pezzulo.

They waited for an answer from Officers Antonio Rodriguez and Chris Amoroso, but heard none.

The five Port Authority police officers had been fifteen or twenty feet underground, not far from a globe sculpture that rested on the plaza. The officers had been running through the concourse, a small arsenal of tools clanking around each man's waist: Guns. Ammunition. Flashlight. Handcuffs. Their task was to collect safety and rescue gear for the climb into the buildings, and they had stopped at security closets to gather Scott Airpaks, helmets, axes, piling it all into a canvas laundry cart. Then they ran the cart toward a meeting point with other officers. With the fall of the south tower, part of the plaza had caved in, trapping them.

Jimeno called for Rodriguez, a friend: "A-Rod. A-Rod." McLoughlin yelled for Amoroso. They got no answer. Pezzulo, a powerful man who lifted weights, began to plow his way out of the rubble, lifting concrete. He had joined the Port Authority police about a year earlier, just making the age-thirty-five cutoff; before that, he had taught shop at a high school in the Bronx, and had spoken about going back to that. He could handle tools, he could fashion his own, and he certainly could handle heavy weights. He struggled to his feet, and turned to the rubble that pinned Jimeno. Sergeant McLoughlin was buried beyond Jimeno, deeper in the rubble.

On the mezzanine of the north tower, where the two police officers Tim Pearson and John Perry had been helping to carry an ailing woman, the debris storm from the south tower separated Pearson from the woman and Perry. Pearson crawled along the floor, shouting out for Perry, for Port Authority people, for anyone who might know the way out. No one answered. The woman and Perry did not seem to be there anymore. The mezzanine was intact, but was no longer a promenade around a proud marble-lined lobby. Instead, it was now a ledge on a cavern, dark and silent. A light appeared—someone must have had a flashlight—and with the emergence of that single beam came sounds: groans and coughs and people saying, I'm over here. One voice found another, then more, aural links that became a hand on a shoulder that led to a hand on yet another shoulder: a sputtering human chain that shuffled toward where the escalator had been. They found it by groping, the smooth skin of the handrail familiar and steadying. Still unable to see one another's faces, they started walking down from the mezzanine to what had been the lobby. As they got lower, the way became clearer. The lobby was lit by fires.

All morning, making the last few hundred yards out of the trade center, drawing clear of the falling bodies and the shredding structure, had been the most arduous and delicate portion of the escape. With the collapse of the south tower, the lowest floors of the north tower now had a new web of obstacles. Rubble blocked the last few feet of stairways. The air had been fouled with smoke and dust. The pace of departure drastically slowed.

Leaning against those snags, pushing everyone toward the exits, however, was the momentum built up over the previous hour and a half. Michael Benfante and John Cerquiera from the communications company Network Plus had carried the Port Authority marketing analyst Tina Hansen from the 68th floor in an evacuation chair, a rolling buggy that can slide down stairs for adults who normally use wheelchairs to get around. Along the way they received help from a shifting cast of strangers. At the 21st floor, firefighters suggested leaving Hansen with them. She insisted that they go on. Around the 5th floor, the stairway had become clogged with traffic backing up from the broken lobby. A pair of firefighters led the Hansen entourage out of the stairway, into the dark corridors. They sloshed through the puddles of water from sprinklers or broken pipes, and then found another stairway. It was blocked, too.

"What are we going to do?" one firefighter asked the other.

"I have no idea," his partner replied.

A bolt of fear ran through Cerquiera. They kept searching and found an intact exit. Benfante, Cerquiera, and Hansen continued, making their way to the bottom. Long ago—when they had started the journey—they had hoped to find a working elevator along the route so that Hansen could ride down. Now, in the lobby, they saw elevator doors blown out of their tracks, security turnstiles torn from their moorings, the frames of the great soaring windows twisted. Any glass that was not in bits on the ground stood in shards. On the street seemed to be a fresh fall of snow. Over this terrain of ruin, Benfante and Cerquiera lifted Hansen out of the building. They spotted an ambulance and delivered her to its doors. She was unhurt, Benfante explained, but she could not walk. The two men turned north, uptown, toward safety.

John Abruzzo, a quadriplegic from a diving accident, had come down from the 69th floor in an evacuation chair flanked by ten of his colleagues from the Port Authority—Michael Ambrosio, Peter Bitwinski, Phillip Caffrey, Richard Capriotti, Michael Curci, Michael Fabiano, Wilson Pacheco, Tony Pecora, Gerald Simpkins, and Peggy Zoch. They had taken turns at the head and foot of the chair, or holding jackets and briefcases. They teased Abruzzo, telling him that he would have to lose a few of his 250 pounds before they would carry him out of another skyscraper.

Like Tina Hansen before him, John Abruzzo caught the attention of the firefighters on the 21st floor, who offered his coworkers the opportunity to leave him with them. Like Michael Benfante and

John Cerquiera, Abruzzo's colleagues declined. They thought they could handle the rest of the trip. They did.

In the dim, soundless landing, the approaching footfall grabbed the attention of Jeff Gertler and Judith Reese, whose breathing problems had not eased. Moving quickly down the stairs, but not galloping, was a group of people in uniforms—Gertler thought he saw a Port Authority police officer, a firefighter or two, maybe a city officer.

"What's going on?" the Port Authority policeman asked.

Gertler explained Reese's condition—her asthma, the descent from the 88th floor, the exhaustion that had marooned them on the landing. The officer turned to one of the others.

"Get a chair," he said, and a moment or two later, one of the men came back with a desk chair from the 10th floor.

"Go ahead," the cop said to Gertler. "We're going to carry her down."

"I'll walk down with you," Gertler said.

"This is police business," the cop replied. "We will carry her down. You need to leave now."

"You carry her, I'll just walk with you," Gertler said.

The policeman stepped closer to Gertler, and whispered into his face.

"You don't understand," he said. "The building is going to collapse."

That sounded like madness to Gertler, but having been told twice to get out, he turned and headed down the stairs.

Susan Fredericks had gotten as far as the 2nd floor, a long way from the offices of Beast Financial on 80, then found traffic on the stairway at a standstill. Behind her, twenty or thirty people were packed in two lines, backing up the stairs a few floors. As word spread that the stairway was impassable, the lines began a slow retreat, turning back. In the throng was a firefighter, Bill Spade, who eventually found two police officers from the Emergency Service Unit, Sgt. Michael Curtin and Officer John D'Allara. Shoving mightily, the three of them forced open the door at the bottom of the stairs. Minutes later, word was passed up the line: "Come back down. We found a way out."

A faint hint of daylight drifted into the staircase, revealing the mezzanine and the plaza beyond it.

"Come this way—move quickly!" Spade yelled. "Hold hands. Don't let go. We're almost out."

He lit the path with his flashlight. Back up the stairs, ESU officers and firefighters were standing in pitch-black corridors with flashlights, their beams pointing the way from blocked stairs toward ones that were open. As Fredericks and the others moved out of the building and onto the plaza, near the Custom House at 6 World Trade Center, she glanced at her watch. It was 10:24, ninety-eight minutes since the first plane struck. Spade did not exit with her. He turned to the two police officers, and they began to steer the line of people behind her to the concourse. Those who navigated the shattered mezzanine and lobby included Michael Hingson, the blind man who had left the 78th floor with Roselle, his Labrador guide dog, and his visitor from California, David Frank. Moe Lipson, the eighty-nine-year-old man from the 88th floor, had gotten out, escorted down by Mak Hanna. Dianne DeFontes, who had started the day in the law office on the 89th floor, had been separated from her friends on the last leg of the trip, but she made it to the street. So had Raffaele Cava, the elderly man with the hat who came and sat in DeFontes's office when the plane first struck, helped to the street by Tirsa Moya, the young woman who worked on his floor at the insurance company. Cava had been one of the very first tenants to move into the building, before it was even completed. Now he was one of the last to leave. Some of the oldest people in the building, from the highest open floors, were getting out.

As the two cops, Curtin and D'Allara, stood with Spade, they joked mildly about the circumstances. Is this what it takes, Spade joshed, to get cops and firemen to work together?

A moment or so later, Jeff Gertler got to the lobby, bypassing the mezzanine because he had taken stairway B, the only one of the three that went all the way to the bottom. He had thought about waiting for Judith Reese and the people carrying her in the chair, but the sight of the shattered lobby left him bewildered. He looked around, trying to figure out what had happened. A voice yelled to him.

"Run this way." It was a fireman. He pointed to a cavity that once held a floor-to-ceiling window. "We're going that way," the fire-fighter said. They climbed onto West Street, and someone turned them to the right, going north. Gertler looked to the south, toward the Marriott Hotel, which seemed to have been split open. He could see inside the rooms. How could that be? The south tower he could not see. But it had to be there.

Iliana McGinnis finally heard from her husband, Tom. She had been dialing his number all morning, but each time the call had gone into his voice mail. She knew there had been a catastrophe at the towers, but he worked across the trade center plaza, in the Mercantile Exchange. This morning, though, he had been summoned to the special early meeting at the Carr Futures office on the 92nd floor in the north tower. The firm was cutting commissions for McGinnis and his group of traders, and they were getting the news at the meeting. It was to have broken up at 8:30 so that the boss could get on a conference call, and the traders could get to the exchange in time for the opening of the markets.

Iliana had not been able to get through to him at his desk, but she expected that he had long since left the trade center. Still, she waited by her desk for him to call as her colleagues huddled around a television set. Finally, the phone rang, at 10:20.

"This looks really, really bad," he said.

"I know," said Iliana. "This is bad for the country; it looks like World War Three." Then something in the tone of Tom's answer alarmed her.

"Are you okay, yes or no?" she demanded.

"We're on the 92nd floor, in a room we can't get out of," he said.

"Who's with you?" she asked.

Three old friends—Joey Holland, Brendan Dolan, and Elkin Yuen, people he had known for years.

"I love you," Tom said. Then he mentioned their daughter. "Take care of Caitlin."

Iliana was not ready to hear a farewell.

"Don't lose your cool," she urged. "You guys are so tough, you're resourceful. You guys are going to get out of there."

She was right: these were men who had grown up in the city, gone right from high school to Wall Street, and made their livings not on credentials from fancy colleges, but on nerve and guile.

"You don't understand," Tom said. "There are people jumping from the floors above us."

It was now 10:25. The 92nd floor seemed to be safely below the plane crash. In the ninety-nine minutes since Flight 11 had struck, the 92nd floor had not been afflicted with unbearable smoke or flame—the worst of that had been six or seven floors above them for much of the time. The sprinkler system had gone off or the pipes had burst; water had risen to the ankles. The big problem was getting out: seventy people were on 92, sixty-nine of them with Carr, and none of them could open the doors. McGinnis and his group were stuck in a conference room where the door had jammed. Over time, the flames had spread along the 93rd and 94th floors, even down to the 92nd floor, and were now bearing down on the pockets of refuge. The people who had survived for the terrible hour and a half, unable to find an escape route, found themselves forced to the windows for air. More and more people began to fall. As the fire raged along the west side of the 92nd floor, forty-one-year-old Tom McGinnis, who had met Iliana when they were kids in Washington Heights, again told her he loved her and Caitlin.

"Don't hang up," she pleaded.

"I gotta get down on the floor," he said.

With that, the phone connection faded out.

It was 10:26, 100 minutes from the time the plane hit.

For most of the evacuation, the tenants of the north tower had largely taken themselves as far as the lobby or the concourse, and then been steered to safety. Most of those left in the building now were the people who could not move without help. It was around the 7th floor of stairway B that the cause of John Rappa, a heavy man, exhausted, unable to walk, first intersected with the rescue workers scrambling to leave the building. "Help me," he said, and two Port Authority police officers, Patrick Lucas and Barry Pikaard, gave him oxygen, then carried him down a few flights. They could not bring him any farther. Lucas would remember that firefighters ran past, screaming at him to just drop the man and go, but the next documented hand on Rappa belonged to Pat Kelly, a firefighter from Squad 18. At the fifth floor, Lt. Greg Hansson of Engine 24 came on the scene, on his way down from the 35th floor. Already he had stopped twice, at the 27th floor to round up Rich Billy and then at the 19th floor, where he had tried to prod the congregation of resting firefighters into leaving. And now, on the 5th floor, he was waylaid for a third time by Pat Kelly, who was unable to move John Rappa.

"You can't get out that way," Kelly said. "I need help with this guy."

Upon meeting this latest crisis, Hansson sent his men down ahead: they had been lugging gear up the stairs, while he had been traveling with the lighter load of an officer. Now that they all were going down, he felt he had more strength in reserve to grapple with the job of moving the disabled man sprawled on the floor. Someone found a chair, and they tied him into it with a belt and managed to wheel him back into the corridor and toward stairway A. The chair barely squeezed through a hallway. Just keeping Rappa perched on it was exhausting. Then the belting arrangement broke down. Around that moment, a group of Port Authority police officers arrived. The chair no longer made any sense. Rappa was again on the floor. They would drag him down the stairs. Hansson and James Hall, one of the police officers, grabbed him by the legs and pulled him. Those steps ended at a door that was propped open, onto the mezzanine.

There, they met the trio that had opened the door a few minutes earlier—Bill Spade, the firefighter, and Mike Curtin and John D'Allara, the two ESU officers. Together, they would make a run for the plaza, propelling John Rappa and themselves.

The building was unstable, the ESU officers told Hall.

"We better get out of here," Curtin said. "Hurry."

But how? All morning, a committee of the willing—self-selected civilians and self-assigned uniformed rescuers—had stationed themselves on the mezzanine, to make sure that people coming down stairways A and C did not try to use the doors that led directly from the mezzanine to the plaza. Not only that, they urged the people not to even look at the plaza, for death was raining there. They sent them down the escalators to the lobby, and through the concourse to the east.

Now most of that group of steerers was gone. And going down the escalator, to the broken lobby, did not seem much of an alternative. For the group carrying John Rappa, the best way seemed to be a dash onto the plaza, directly from the mezzanine—to take their chances on the plummeting bodies and the peels of aluminum skin of the building that seemed to float and wobble toward the ground, giving the illusion of delicacy. And they would be carrying a large man unable to move.

Spade, the firefighter, took a count. They were seven. No, they were eight. Nine, counting Rappa.

"We go together, we stay together," Spade said.

At the north end of the mezzanine was a door. Across a few open feet of the plaza was an overhang jutting from 6 World Trade Center, the Custom House.

D'Allara dashed first, reaching the overhang. He gazed up at the top of the tower, smoke and flame ripping from its crown, nothing and no one coming down just that second. A body could emerge from the billowing cloud of blackness at any instant.

"It's clear," D'Allara yelled.

It was now 10:27, 101 minutes since the first plane struck. Hall and Hansson and the others grabbed Rappa. In as close to a sprint as they could manage, they broke for the overhang of the Custom House.

Fourth floor. Almost there. If only she could move.

Jay Jonas, the captain of Ladder 6, knew the south tower had fallen—he was with Capt. William Burke on the 27th floor of the north tower when Burke saw it from the window. This one would fall, too, Jonas suspected, so he was driving his people out. Around the 12th floor, they had spotted Josephine Harris, age sixty, in agony from fallen arches and from a sixty-story walk. She was now hanging onto Billy Butler and Tommy Falco, firefighters from Ladder 6. Even with their help, she moved slowly: In the time she would take two steps, someone else could travel an entire flight. Her bad feet were now setting the pace of escape for eight people who were helping in some way, the Ladder 6 crew of six firefighters—Jonas, Butler, Falco, Michael Meldrum, Matt Komorowski, and Sal D'Agostino, along with a lieutenant from another company, Mickey Kross of Engine 16, and a Port Authority police officer, David Lim.

Keep moving, Jonas whispered. They were clogging the stairway, so they pulled aside at the landings to let other exiting fire companies speed past. Hurry, said Jonas. Harris groaned, not from a shortage of willpower, but from the agony that knifed from her feet through her body. You will see your family, Butler said. Come on, Josephine, said Jonas. Another company went by, dashing toward the lobby. Go, said Jonas. At the 4th floor, though, Josephine Harris could not. Her fallen arches had collapsed. They were so close to getting out.

"Stop," she cried. "Leave me alone. I can't go any farther."

Jonas peeled off from the stairwell to find an office chair, a solution: They would put her in it and run down the stairs. He saw a couch and a stenographer chair with no arms. Surely, there was a regular desk chair somewhere on the 4th floor. For crying out loud.

It was a mechanical floor, with nothing obvious that would serve. Jonas headed for the other side of the floor, then decided that, no, they would leave now and just drag her down the stairs. Maybe there was time to find a better way, but maybe there wasn't. He turned, and fast-stepped toward the door to stairway B, but the floor beneath him shuddered in waves.

It is now 10:28, 102 minutes since the nose of American Airlines Flight 11 shot into the 98th floor of the north tower. The bangs are distant, then grow nearer and louder, and in stairway B, Josephine Harris and the men hear the approaching collapse: a bowling ball rolling down the steps. They curl in corners, or grab doors to use the frame as shelter, but the doors are hard to budge. The building is twisting. So are the door frames. Jonas pulls at the door from inside the 4th floor. It will not open.

He yanks again, and it springs open, and the wind blasts ahead of the collapse—not a gust, but a raging storm of a wind. As each floor drops, one upon the other, it is as if a giant accordion is being squeezed, pushing 55 million cubic feet of air. Behind the rush of air comes the screech of the failing trusses, the slap of tons of metal columns against other tons of metal, percussive bangs, end sounds.

From the street, the building seems to spill out of itself, the dust boiling up, then pouring down the four facades toward the ground. Those who had escaped the collapse of the south tower know the impossible is happening yet again, twenty-nine minutes later. A team of men hurry north, carrying a chair that holds the slumped form of Mychal Judge, the Fire Department chaplain, who died during the flight from the lobby of the north tower as the south tower fell.

Now, as the north tower crumbles, another fire chaplain, John Delendick, runs toward the Hudson River. Next to him is a police officer.

"Father, can I go to confession?" the cop yells.

The priest thinks for a moment. "This is an act of war, isn't it?" Delendick replies.

"Yeah, I believe so," the policeman says.

"Then I'm giving general absolution," Delendick declares, never slowing down.

He speaks at the moment of death, particularly for those at the top of the north tower, the 1,000 or so people who survived the crash of Flight 11 at 8:46 but have not been able to find an open staircase. Their fate was sealed nearly four decades earlier, when the stairways were clustered in the core of the building, and fire stairs were eliminated as a wasteful use of valuable space. The top floors of the north tower, weakened by the unabated, uncontained fire, now crater in a tremendous rush.

As the floors fall, they pick up speed: ten stories in a single second. They sweep through a tower that seems empty, because 99 percent of the people who worked below the fire floors are now out of the tower. But this building is not empty. Still inside are Pablo Ortiz and Frank De Martini, who freed scores from the upper floors. Perhaps a dozen or so firefighters have climbed into the 40s, some a bit higher; other officers are wandering the halls and stairs to round up members of their companies who got separated during the ascent.

Lower in the building, probably still on the 27th floor, is Capt. William Burke, who saw the collapse of the south tower, ordered his company out, but stayed with Ed Beyea in his wheelchair. No doubt, so is Abe Zelmanowitz, who stood by Beyea through the long morning, as thousands of people marched down the stairs, as rescuers came and went from the 27th floor, until only Captain Burke remained with them.

Of uncertain status are the firefighters—perhaps as many as 100—last seen resting on the 19th floor by the three court officers, apparently unaware of the dire situation. Few could have made much progress to safety.

Mike Warchola, the lieutenant from Ladder 5, on his last day of work, is on the 12th floor, helping a woman who cannot breathe. Possibly, it is Judith Reese, who was resting in that area when Jeff Gertler turned her over to a group of firefighters and Port Authority police officers. She remains under their care. They are trying to get her the last few steps to safety, but the building is coming at them faster than she can move.

And most of the firefighters and police officers who carried John Rappa, the heavy man, to safety across the plaza have now ducked under the overhang of 6 World Trade Center, the building to the north, and they are starting to make their way inside. The two ESU officers, Michael Curtin and John D'Allara, however, wait outside, by the door of the building. The tower is falling at them.

In the Marriott Hotel, where people on one side of a debris wall have been speaking to those trapped on the other side, even passing a flashlight across, this second collapse again spares the lobby area protected by the reinforced beam. It decimates the area where the people were trapped.

Under the center of the plaza, Port Authority police officer Dominick Pezzulo has been trying to free two other officers, Will Jimeno and John McLoughlin, trapped by the first collapse. As Pezzulo lifts the rubble, he is struck and crushed by debris falling from the collapse of the north tower.

In stairway B, among the firefighters who have taken on the cause of Josephine Harris and her fallen arches, there is a prayer or two for a swift end. The impossible collisions of floor, steel, glass are belting toward them. Even stronger than the noise is the wind. Sal D'Agostino tries to open a door to leave the stairwell, but it flies out and throws him against the wall. The wind lifts the engine's chauffeur, Mike Meldrum, off his feet and heaves him one floor down; it carries Matt Komorowski down three floors.

As the floors drop, the air has nowhere to go. So much of a skyscraper is nothing but air, empty spaces filled by people in buildings like 1 and 2 World Trade Center, putting little pieces of their daily lives onto these platforms.

Here is a desk drawer where Dianne DeFontes keeps her sensible shoes. The rack where Raffaele Cava first hung his hat, thirty years earlier. The couch in Frank De Martini's office where his aides' children nap on their afternoon at Daddy's job. The big table up in Keefe, Bruyette & Woods, where the wealthy young men and women dine out of paper bags on Junk Food Fridays. The flower vases in Windows on the World that Christine Olender checks, so that the well-set tables of crystal and linen are as pleasing to the eye as the forty-mile vista of city and harbor, river and road.

"You don't understand."

Now the lights have gone out. The giant platters of air plunge past the people in the north tower and hit bottom. The wind seems to be bouncing back up stairway B, whipping tons of crushed building particles along the shaft. The people stretched up and down the lower floors of that stairway—the ones with Josephine Harris, a couple of the stragglers who had stayed in Pat Hoey's office on the 64th floor all morning—can see nothing. They pry open a door, but it goes nowhere: they huddle, alive, in the last intact stub of the World Trade Center. Above them is only sky.

Epilogue

Some time later, Will Jimeno found himself buried but alive, pinned below the burning ground at the center of the trade center plaza. A load of concrete had fallen onto his lap, and a cinder-block wall rested on one of his feet. The oxygen tank strapped to his back also was wedged into rubble, fixing him in a semblance of a seated position, bent at a forty-five-degree angle. Of the four other Port Authority police officers who had been running with him through the concourse, pushing a cart full of rescue gear, only one, Sgt. John McLoughlin, was still alive. Two members of their group had been killed immediately by the collapse of the south tower. A third officer, Dominick Pezzulo, had managed to free himself and was picking at the rubble around Jimeno when the collapse of the north tower killed him.

Now Jimeno was slumped in the hole, talking occasionally with McLoughlin, who was even deeper in the heap than Jimeno. The two men had no view of each other.

"Can you see sky?" McLoughlin asked.

"No sky, but light," Jimeno replied.

The sergeant worked his radio. No one answered. McLoughlin, who over the years had led elevator rescues at the trade center and rappelled into the blind shafts, told Jimeno that the rescue operations would have to pull back for a day, until the scene was stable. They were on their own.

All across the northeastern United States, people were essentially on their own, stepping into the first minutes of a new epoch without the protections of an old world order whose institutions and functions seemed to have turned instantly decrepit. So a consideration of the events of September 11, 2001, could begin at any one of numerous spots across the globe, at almost any moment over the preceding four decades: the end of the Cold War; the collapse of the Soviet Union; any hour of any year in the unfinished history of the Middle East; in the often empty and petty exercise of authority in the capital of the world's only superpower; at the boiling, nihilistic springs of religious fundamentalism that not only have endured but have thrived as forces in opposition to globalism, capitalism, modernism.

Those historic currents, and others, merged and crashed on the morning of September 11 at the two towers of the World Trade Center, and at the Pentagon, and in a field in Pennsylvania. The particulars of the era that had just passed—the expectations of protection, the habits of defense, the sense of safety—seemed to have fossilized from one breath to the next. What happened in New York City that morning was replicated through all the arms of government, differing only in details, duration, and cost.

For nearly the entire period of the Cold War, in the second half of the twentieth century, the air defense system, while rarely seen, existed in public consciousness as an invisible web to block nuclear attacks. During the September 11 crisis, Vice President Dick Cheney instructed that rogue planes be shot down. The order, it turned out, was never transmitted to the fighter pilots, a failure that, in any event, proved to be of little relevance: the national air defense and civil aviation authorities had been unable to pool their resources to track even one of the hijacked planes during the two-hour siege. So the order to shoot was not heard, and the planes to shoot at were not seen. The suicidal zealots on three of the four hijacked planes hit their targets—the twin towers and the Pentagon. They were stopped from diving the fourth plane, United Airlines Flight 93, into the Capitol or the White House only because the passengers learned of the events in Washington and New York from cell phone calls. They stormed the cockpit. The pilot of a passing airliner saw the wings of the United plane wiggling, apparently an attempt by the hijackers to defeat the onrushing passengers. The plane went down in rural Pennsylvania, 125 miles from Washington.

As with events in Washington, in the air-traffic-control towers of the Northeast, and inside the twin towers, large institutions could scarcely begin to cope with one attack, much less four of them simultaneously. Little of that reality emerged in the early days following September 11. In the haze of grief, the nation simply was staggering from the loss of life and the shock of realizing that it was now the single most desirable target for terrorists. In a world where zealots could see only icons to smash, the attacks made sense; in a world where people like Dianne DeFontes sat alone in an empty law office, eating yogurt and answering phones, the idea that the attack had fallen on the representatives of a superpower seemed hallucinatory.

At scores of funerals for firefighters and police officers, Mayor Giuliani declared that the police officers and firefighters had saved the lives of 25,000 people, "the greatest rescue ever recorded." On occasion, the estimate of those "rescued" rose to 50,000. The mayor created a special charitable fund for the families of the city's uniformed rescuers, and later expanded it to include Port Authority police officers; a grateful nation poured $216 million into it. In the first telling of the story of the trade center rescue, civilians played little role, except as helpless victims who were saved by the police and firefighters. That civilians had collaborated in the rescue—and indeed had been instrumental in saving many people on the high floors—simply did not make the early chronicles.

It was an incomplete history, though not uncommonly so. Every calamity casts its own long shadows of confusion. Myth is always embedded in the early drafts. A few months after the *Titanic* went down, George Bernard Shaw commented that the disaster had led to an "explosion of outrageous romantic lying."

More than a year after the attacks, Congress created an independent national investigative commission under pressure from families who lost husbands, wives, and children, and against the wishes of President George W. Bush and Giuliani, who was no longer the mayor of New York but had become an iconic figure in politics and in business, thanks to his graceful deportment in the hours after the attacks.

The commission documented years of difficulties in intelligence gathering and coordination, in border control, in airline security, and in emergency response. These were painful revelations. The attacks were hardly the bolt from the blue that they seemed in the early days: the hijackings were only the latest and most lethal link in a chain of events that stretched back years and had been foretold, in one fashion or another, during the months before them. In fact, the commission found that the threat reports were more clear, more urgent, and more persistent than the government had acknowledged. Some intelligence reports had focused on Al Qaeda's plans to use commercial aircraft as weapons. Others stated that Osama bin Laden was intent on striking on United States soil. While some pieces of the intelligence had been gathered in the mid-1990s, warnings that Al Qaeda soldiers had infiltrated the United States, and seemed interested in hijacking a plane, were delivered to the president on August 6, 2001, just a month before the attacks, under the headline, "Bin Laden Determined to Strike in the U.S."

The diagnostic postmortems by the press and by the commission threw light into the long shadow of secrecy, dissembling, and myth that had surrounded the events of September 11, 2001. That said, no level of American government had practice for such ferocious attacks on civilians. Neither New York nor the United States had any muscle memory of sustained attacks on the homeland, and given the speed of events that morning, there was no time to invent new moves. In New York, the two towers stood for 102 minutes—less than two hours—before they collapsed. That gives no hint of the morning's velocity. One plane crash. Sixteen minutes later, another plane crash. Twenty-five minutes later, word of a third plane approaching—untrue, but certainly not outside the freshly staked borders of the plausible. Then, about thirty minutes after that, the first building falls. Twenty-nine minutes later, it was over. It was as if a car going ninety miles per hour were making a ninety-degree turn every few minutes. Each moment brought fresh demands, fresh hell.

Speed does not, however, explain everything. A cascade of lapsed communications—much like the undelivered Cheney shoot-down order—cost lives. The police helicopters reported the deterioration of the two towers and specifically predicted the collapse of the north tower. The fire commanders had no link to those helicopters or reports, but for that matter, they had few or no links to their own troops. The interagency radios were sitting on shelves and in the trunks of cars, unused. It is likely that as many as 200 firefighters were inside the north tower when it collapsed. Most of them had been in striking distance of safety when the south building fell. This gave them twenty-nine minutes to go down no more than thirty or forty flights of stairs, and many people did, including eighty-nine-year-old Moe Lipson, who was walking down from his office on 88 and had reached the 27th floor when the south tower fell. Few of the people inside the north tower, even those who had heard the evacuation orders, knew that the other building had collapsed. Virtually none of them—apart from some police officers and those they encountered—realized that helicopter pilots were predicting the imminent failure of the one they were in. For no good reason, firefighters were cut off from critical information. This was as much a matter of long and bad habit as it was of the extreme circumstances.

At a hearing in the spring of 2004 on the emergency response, Giuliani spoke with great passion about the firefighters who did not leave the north tower. "The reality is that they saved more lives than I think anyone had any right to expect that any human beings would be able to do. Done differently with different people and people maybe unwilling to be as bold as they were, you would have had much more serious loss of life."

Moreover, Giuliani said that the firefighters had indeed heard the warning that it was time to leave, but asserted that they had "interpreted the evacuation order" to mean that they should make sure the civilians got out. "Rather than giving us a story of men, uniformed men fleeing while civilians were left behind, which would have been devastating to the morale of this country; rather than an *Andrea Doria*, if you might remember that, they gave us an example of very, very brave men and women in uniform who stand their ground to protect civilians," Giuliani said. "Instead of that we got a story of heroism and we got a story of pride and we got a story of support that helped get us through."

If history is to be a tool for the living, it must be unflinchingly candid. The full chronicles of D-Day in World War II note that a number of landing boats opened in deep water, sending troops to drown, a fact of vital importance to those who would someday follow the D-Day soldiers onto another beach. The evidence shows conclusively that in the critical final minutes of the north tower, firefighters were indeed helping civilians, but that involved no more than a fraction of the rescuers. There can be no doubt that the firefighters' purpose in going into the building was to help, and that a number, like Captain Burke, stayed behind even when the future took its fearsome shape. Even so, there is substantial reason to discount Giuliani's assertion that specific duties—rather than widespread ignorance of the peril—kept the bulk of those 200 firefighters inside during the time they might have escaped.

Nearly all of the 6,000 civilians below the impact zone had left the north tower by the time of its collapse, a fact hard to square with the notion that most of the approximately 200 firefighters who died in the north tower could not get out because they were busy helping civilians. In the oral histories collected by the Fire Department, numerous firefighters recalled that they were unaware of how serious the situation had become in those final minutes. This does not mean that the firefighters were not a welcome and uplifting presence; indeed, teams were helping people like Josephine Harris, and had stopped to offer aid to Judith Reese, and had opened stairways after the collapse of the south tower. Yet those efforts do not explain why so many firefighters died in a building they could have escaped and where there was scarcely anyone left who could be helped.

On the 19th floor of the north tower, scores of doomed firefighters were seen—by, among others, the court officers Joseph Baccellieri, Al Moscola, and Andrew Wender—taking a rest break in the final minutes, coats off, axes against the wall, soaked in sweat. As an explanation for why that group did not escape, a lack of "situational awareness," to use the military term, seems far more likely than the mayor's position that firefighters were tied up helping civilians. That shortcoming was not simply a consequence of being overwhelmed by the new epoch in terror that had arrived. The Fire Department's reports after the 1993 trade center bombing had highlighted the poor coordination and communication among the emergency agencies. Even so, when questions were raised in 2004 by the 9/11 Commission about the Fire Department's tactics, planning, and management, past and present city officials responded with outrage, demanding to know how anyone could challenge the bravery or sacrifices of the firefighters. No one had.

At first glance, the collapse of both towers hardly seems startling or complicated, given the nature of the attacks on them. Important columns were destroyed. The structural elements that initially survived—most importantly, the floors and ceilings—were then subjected to intense fires, unlike anything considered in the design of ordinary buildings. Indeed, federal investigators concluded that it had been primarily the impact of the planes and, more specifically, the extreme fires that spread in their wake, that had caused the buildings to fall, and nothing that they termed a "design" flaw. After the planes hit, the towers shuddered for four minutes. Much of the spray-on fireproofing in the impact zone was dislodged, leaving the structural steel exposed and mortally vulnerable to the intense heat.

No one, it turned out, had fully considered the effects of a plane crash, particularly the loss of fireproofing followed by intense fires, when the buildings were being designed in the 1960s, even though the Port Authority and its engineers had announced the towers would be built to withstand a direct hit from a Boeing 707. These assurances were reaffirmed after the 1993 bombing and again only a week before September 11. In a matter of minutes, the unthinkable had become inevitable.

As investigators reviewed how the towers were conceived and built, it also turned out that no one had relied on any technical standards or done any tests to determine how long the spray-on fireproofing could protect the floor system that connected the building's core to the exterior. The thickness of the fireproofing applied to the floors in two of the world's tallest buildings seemed to have been based on little more than a hunch.

Those floors were held up by long, unsupported trusses, familiar to anyone who has glanced at the ceilings in warehouse-type supermarkets. In buildings with a high premium on open space, uninterrupted by columns, trusses are often used to hold up floors and ceilings. To turn such a structure into a 110-story building—much less two of them—involved considerable daring and ingenuity, and towers of this type remain a rarity in New York City. Given the inherent difficulty of evacuating the high floors of skyscrapers, the construction of two monumentally tall buildings of novel structure without testing the adequacy of the fireproofing put thousands of people at risk.

Not until the summer of 2004 was the fireproofing tested, in the course of a lengthy postmortem by the National Institute of Standards and Technology. The results showed, on the one hand, that the fireproofing was sufficient to protect a seventeen-foot length of steel for two hours, which met the requirement of the code at the time. But the towers had not been built using seventeen-foot lengths of steel; the actual pieces in the floors were at least twice that length. When a thirty-five-foot length of steel, the true size used in constructing the floors, was tested in 2004, the federal investigators found that the fireproofing could not provide two hours of protection.

Long before September 11, the floors in two of the world's landmark skyscrapers had been more vulnerable to fire than was thought.

This was an alarming finding even if investigators believed that the shortcomings of the original fireproofing—however disturbing—were probably not the direct cause of the collapses. For decades, the generations that rode higher and higher into the upper floors of skyscrapers had taken it on faith that the evolution of such buildings had been solely a story of progress, of innovations and enhancements that made new buildings safer than the old. The World Trade Center towers were presented as marvels, as buildings so robust they could withstand the impact of an airliner. By code, the floors were supposed to be able to withstand fire for two hours. When Chief Orio Palmer and the other firefighters reached people in the crash zone of the south tower, fifty minutes after the plane hit the building, they had every reason to believe there was another hour available for their rescue work. Instead, the tower collapsed seven minutes after they got there.

Not only the Port Authority had a hand in shaping safety for people inside the trade center. To make skyscrapers more profitable to own and less costly to build, New York City had overhauled its building code in the 1960s, part of a national trend that permitted developers more flexibility in their choice of materials. The revisions in New York had another dimension, one that was little remarked on by the new code's champions in politics and the news media. In 1968, the city reduced the number of stairways required for tall buildings by half, and eliminated fire towers—reinforced stairs that would provide a smoke-free way to escape during an emergency. All these stairways were, in the view of the real estate industry, the wasteful legacies of a bygone era that lacked modern fireproofing techniques. In fact, the stair requirements were the residue of reforms that followed dreadful high-rise fires in the early years of the twentieth century. By the time the codes were changed in 1968, though, more than fifty years had passed since young women, with no other way out, had gone to the windows of a building two miles from the trade center site to escape the Triangle Shirtwaist fire. At the start of the twenty-first century, young men and women in the prime of their days were, once again, leaping from windows to escape the heat of a tall building. The hijackers—and history—had left them no other way out.

The indifference to the lessons of history, or the inability to integrate them, were hardly limited to the municipal government of New York, of course. Ultimately, all of the people in the trade center that morning were at the head of a pin on which history had come to rest. "On the morning of September 11, 2001, the last, best hope for the community of people working in or visiting the World Trade Center rested not with national policymakers but with private firms and local public servants," a staff report from the 9/11 Commission stated.

Virtually no one was able to escape from the collapse of the south tower—not the firefighters Orio Palmer and Tom Kelly, not the building's fire-safety director, Phil Hayes, not the supervisor of elevators at the tower, Francis Riccardelli. The people upstairs perished as well—those trapped on the 78th-floor sky lobby, those in the offices of Keefe, Bruyette & Woods, Aon, and Fiduciary Trust. Even Roko Camaj, the window washer with the keys to the roof and an inside knowledge of the building, had not been able to get out. Indeed, above the 78th floor, only four people survived: Richard Fern and Ronald DiFrancesco found a staircase that was, relatively speaking, intact. Stanley Praimnath survived because Brian Clark heard his cries for help; Clark says that had he not heard Praimnath, he might have wound up in the staircases with his colleagues who were persuaded by an ailing stranger to go up, not down. Fourteen other men and women were able to get out of the building from the 78th floor, the lower part of the south tower crash zone. Hours after the collapse, one building worker, Lenny Ardizzone, who had been in the lobby of the south tower, was discovered alive. He was not sure how.

In the north tower, the high floors became a tomb: Cantor Fitzgerald lost 658 people. Marsh & McLennan lost 292. Everyone at Windows on the World, 170. Fred Alger Management, 35. Carr Futures, 69. James Gartenberg's calls for help from the 86th floor had been heard by many but could be answered by none. The collapse caught him and Patricia Puma trapped in their office. It overtook others as they made their way down. Lt. Kevin Pfeifer, the chief's brother, was found near the pry tool he had carried upstairs. Tony Savas, the construction inspector who had been freed from an elevator on the 78th floor, was found in a stairwell near the bottom of the building, along with John Griffin, who had helped to get him out.

The stub of stairway B proved to be a refuge for Capt. Jay Jonas of the Fire Department and the men accompanying Josephine Harris out of the building, who were among sixteen people who survived the building's collapse there. They included Port Authority Police Officer David Lim, a dozen firefighters, and two other civilians—Pasquale Buzzelli and Genelle Guzman—who were themselves the only survivors of a group of sixteen workers from the Port Authority office on the 64th floor. That group had left their offices at 10:12, after the boss, Patrick Hoey, made a phone call and got word that they should go.

Others in that staircase survived the collapse, but could not escape. Mike Warchola, the fire captain on his last day of work, radioed from the rubble that he was around the 12th floor, although the staircase no longer went that high. It is likely that he was among the group that had stopped to help Judith Reese, the woman with asthma from Frank De Martini's office. None of them made it out. In all, 2,753 people were killed at the trade center.

An hour or so after the collapse, Will Jimeno, buried beneath the plaza, heard a voice coming through the same hole where the light was entering. The voice wanted to know if a particular person was down in the hole. Jimeno could not quite make out the name, but he was delighted by the sound of another human voice.

"No, but Jimeno and McLoughlin, PAPD, are down here," he yelled.

The voice did not answer, but moved off, and they heard no more from him.

Balls of fire tumbled into their tiny space, a gust of wind or a draft steering them away, the fire spending itself before it could find another morsel of fuel. Jimeno, thirty-three years old, felt that death was near. His wife, Allison, and their four-year-old daughter, Bianca, would be sad, but proud, he thought. The Jimenos' second child was due at the end of November. So he prayed.

Please, God, let me see my little unborn child.

Jimeno tried to make a bargain. He might die, but surely there was a way he could do something for this child.

Somehow in the future, he prayed, let me touch this baby.

Then shots rang out.

The fireballs had apparently heated up the gun of the late Dominick Pezzulo. The rounds pinged off pipes and concrete, erratic and unpredictable, until the last of the ammunition was gone.

With his one free arm, Jimeno reached his gun belt for something to dig with. He had graduated from the Port Authority Police Academy in January and was issued the standard police tools, but he already owned his own handcuffs—a pair made by Smith & Wesson, bought when he was a security guard in a store, arresting shoplifters. He scraped at the rubble with them, but the cuffs slipped out of his hands, and he could not find them again.

No one had heard from Chuck Sereika, and by midmorning, the messages had piled up on his telephone answering machine and in his e-mail. Can't believe it. Hope you're okay. Our hearts are with you.

Sereika woke up. He had slept through everything, not a whisper of trouble in his apartment in midtown Manhattan. The e-mails told him something awful had happened, then news on his computer spelled it out, and as he blinked into the new world, he heard the messages on his answering machine. His sister had called.

"I love you," she said. "I know you're down there helping."

Actually, he had been moping. In his closet, he found a paramedic sweatshirt and a badge he had not used for years. He had lost his paramedic license, let it lapse after he squandered too many days and nights carousing. He had gone into rehab programs, slipped, then climbed back on the wagon. He had fought his way back to sobriety, but the paramedic work was behind him. He still had the sweatshirt, though, and no one had taken the badge away. Maybe he could do some splints and bandages. He walked outside. Midtown Manhattan was teeming with people, a stream of humanity trooping in the middle of avenues, the subways shut down and scarcely a bus to be seen. The only way to move was on foot, and by the tens of thousands, people were walking north, or over to the river for ferries, or into Penn Station for a commuter train that would take them east to Long Island or west to New Jersey.

Sereika walked a few blocks from his apartment to St. Luke's–Roosevelt Hospital Center. Then he hitched rides on ambulances going downtown.

Seven World Trade Center—a forty-seven-story building—collapsed at 5:20 that afternoon. The firefighters had decided to let the fire there burn itself out. There was no one inside. Against all that had happened, the loss of even such an enormous building seemed like a footnote.

David Karnes had arrived downtown not long after its collapse, and as far as he could see, the searches were confined entirely to the periphery of the complex, picking through the rubble at the edges for signs of life. Other structures were now burning—the low-rise building at 4 World Trade Center was shooting flames—and all hands were staying clear of the ruins of the two towers and the plaza between them.

Karnes had started the morning in a business suit, working as an accountant for Deloitte and Touche in Wilton, Connecticut. After the attacks, he drove from Connecticut to Long Island and went to a storage facility where he kept his Marine kit. His utility trousers and jacket were freshly pressed, though his commitment had ended months earlier. Trim as a whip, he slipped into them, drove to a barber, and ordered a high and tight haircut. He stopped at his church and asked for prayers with the pastor, then with the top down on his new convertible, drove straight for lower Manhattan.

He found the rescue workers in shock, depressed, doing little by way of organized searches. Karnes spotted another Marine, a man named Sergeant Thomas, no first name.

"Come on, Sergeant," Karnes said. "Let's take a walk."

Not another soul was around them. They swept across the broken ground, yelling, "United States Marines. If you can hear us, yell or tap."

No one answered. They moved forward, deeper into the rubble. The fires roared at 4 World Trade Center. They plowed across the jagged, fierce ground.

Lost in thought, waiting for release, Will Jimeno listened to the trade center complex ripping itself apart. He had gotten tired of shouting at phantoms. He asked McLoughlin to put out a radio message that Officer Jimeno wanted his newborn baby to be named Olivia. The sergeant was in excruciating pain, his legs crushed. There was nothing to do, Jimeno thought, except wait until they sent out rescue parties in the morning. If they lived that long.

Then came the voice.

"United States Marines. If you can hear us, yell or tap."

What? That was a person.

Jimeno shouted with every bit of strength he had.

"Right here! Jimeno and McLoughlin, PAPD! Here!"

"Keep yelling," Karnes said.

It took a few minutes, but Karnes found the hole.

"Don't leave," Jimeno pleaded.

"I'm not going anywhere," Karnes said.

Karnes pulled out his cell phone and dialed 911, but the call did not go through. He tried again, without success. How could he get help, without leaving Jimeno and McLoughlin? Maybe the problem was with phone lines downtown, and he could find an electronic bridge via someone outside the city. He dialed his sister in a suburb of Pittsburgh and got through. She called the local police. They were able to reach the New York police. The message had traveled 300 miles from the pile to Pennsylvania, then 300 miles back to police headquarters, but the NYPD finally learned that a few blocks away, two cops were buried in the middle of the pile, and a United States Marine was standing by to direct the rescuers.

Chuck Sereika had been wandering the edge of that pile as evening approached, when he heard people yelling that someone had been found in the center of the place. Sereika set out, walking part of the way with a firefighter. They could see the flames roaring from the remains of 4 World Trade Center, an eight-story building. The firefighter peeled away. By himself, Sereika stumbled and climbed, until he found Dave Karnes standing alone. From the surface, he could see nothing of Will Jimeno, but he could hear him. Sereika squeezed his way into a crevice, inching his way down the rubble, finally spotting Jimeno's hand.

"Hey," Sereika said.

"Don't leave me," Jimeno said.

Sereika felt for a pulse. A good, strong distal pulse, a basic in emergency care.

"Don't leave me," Jimeno said.

"We're not going to leave you," Sereika said. He pawed at the rubble and found Jimeno's gun, which he passed up to Karnes. Then he sent word for oxygen and an intravenous setup. Two emergency service police officers, Scott Strauss and Paddy McGee, soon arrived, and Sereika handed rocks and rubble back to them. A fireman, Tom Ascher, arrived with a hose to fight off the flames. They could hear McLoughlin calling out for help.

We will get there, they promised.

The basics of trauma care are simple: provide fluids and oxygen. Simple—except that in the hole at the trade center, they could not take the next step in the classic formula: "load and go." First they had to extricate Jimeno, a highly delicate proposition.

Sereika could hear 4 World Trade Center groaning to its bones. To shift large pieces off Jimeno risked starting a new slide. There was room in the hole only for one person at a time, and Sereika was basically on top of him. It was not unlike working under the dash-board of a car, except the engine was on fire and the car was speeding and about to crash. The space was filled with smoke. Strauss and McGee were carefully moving the rubble, engineering on the fly, so that they could shift loads without bringing more debris down on themselves or on Jimeno and McLoughlin. Tools were passed from the street along a line of helpers. A handheld air chisel. Shears. When the Hurst jaws of life tool arrived, the officers wanted to use it to lift one particularly heavy section, but they could not quite get solid footing on the rubble. Sereika, the lapsed paramedic, immediately sized up the problem and shimmed rubble into place for the machine to rest on.

The work inched forward, treacherous and hot and slow.

After four hours, at 11 P.M., Will Jimeno was freed. They loaded him into a basket, slid him up the path to the surface. That left only John McLoughlin, deeper still, but none of the group in and around the hole could go on. They called down a fresh team that would work until the morning before they finally pulled him out, not long before the last survivor from stairway B, Genelle Guzman, would also be reached.

Aboveground, the men who had gone into the hole with Will Jimeno found they could barely walk. Smoke reeked from the hair on their heads, soot packed every pore on their skin. Sereika stumbled up from the crevice in time to see Jimeno in his basket being passed along police officers and firefighters who had set up a line, scores of people deep, across the jagged, broken ground.

He could not keep up with his patient. He could just about get himself to the sidewalk. He had worked for hours alongside the other men, first names only, and Sereika was employed by no official agency, no government body. Once they left the hole, the men lost track of each other. Just as people had come to work by themselves hours earlier, at the start of the day—an entire age ago—now Chuck Sereika was starting for home on his own. His old paramedic shirt torn, he plodded north in the late-summer night, alone, scuffling down streets blanketed by the dust that had been the World Trade Center.

Afterword

The stock market reopened within a week. After a year, the subway lines that ran beneath the towers resumed full service. In December 2002, Deborah Mardenfeld, who had been among the first people injured, left New York University's Rusk Institute, where she had relearned how to use her shattered legs. She had been at the corner of Church and Vesey streets on her way to work at American Express when she was hit by cascading debris as the second plane hit the south tower. That morning, she arrived, unidentified and barely alive, at NYU Downtown Hospital as Jane Doe No. 1. Fifteen months later, she was the last of the 4,400 injured to go home.

For months after the attacks, the people who had escaped from the 89th floor of the north tower wondered about the men who had come to save them. That group, including Diane DeFontes from the law firm, her friend Tirsa Moya from the insurance company, and Raffaele Cava, the older man with the hat, had crept from their offices to discover that they were trapped. Their elevator bank had become a gaping, burning hole. Their staircase doors were jammed and impassable. The floor itself was heating and melting beneath their feet. Suddenly, someone in the staircase pried open an exit door, unsealing their fate.

The survivors sent word to the Port Authority that they recalled one of their saviors as a man with an earring and salt-and-pepper hair. Alan Reiss, who had been in charge of the building and worked on the 88th floor, recognized the description at once. To be sure, he assembled a lineup of mug shots, using ID card photos, and passed that along to the tenants of the 89th floor. They immediately picked out the man Reiss had in mind, Pablo Ortiz. And Mak Hanna, who had accompanied Ortiz and Frank De Martini to the 89th floor but left ahead of them to escort out an older colleague, confirmed the names of the men who had gone up the stairs. For the first time, the people on the 89th floor learned that two of the three men who had saved their lives—Ortiz and De Martini—never made it home. More of the De Martini–Ortiz pilgrimage through the north tower was pieced together by Roberta Gordon, an attorney who represented Nicole De Martini in her application to the compensation board set up by Congress for the families of people killed or hurt in the attacks.

The 89th floor tenants posted their condolences and thanks to an online memorial site. The remains of Frank De Martini and Pablo Ortiz were not recovered, but when the Ortiz children held a memorial service for their father in upstate New York, Tirsa Moya and other survivors attended.

The accounts of Frank De Martini's valor reached Italy through his cousin, Enrico Tittarelli, who had visited the trade center in 1994 and snapped a picture of him riding an inspection bucket along the side of the building, smiling, perhaps at the audacity of an open-to-the-air journey a quarter mile in the sky. Cousin Enrico brought word of Frank's deeds to their aunt in Italy.

"In the house where I spent unforgettable days with Frank, when he was in Italy as a student, I sat in front of the fireplace with my old aunt who really loved him," Tittarelli recalled. "Some young cousins were with us. There was silence, unusual in that room, while I was reading . . . what his fearless personality made him do and say in a 'calm and collected' way. My voice was not so much calm and collected as his.

"For some moments Frank was again among us. Alive, courageous, generous, and fatally imprudent. As we had known him."

Brian Clark and Stanley Praimnath, who had escaped from the south tower, made it to the southeast corner of the trade center, stopped in a delicatessen for water, and were given a breakfast tray that had not been picked up. They walked a block to the west side of Trinity Church. They met a clergyman who invited them to come into the church, but as they walked in, Praimnath said, "You know, I think those buildings could go down." Clark scoffed at the notion. The interior furnishings might burn, he said, but the structure was steel. "There is no way."

At that instant, the south tower boiled into dust. They retreated into an office building, with Clark still carrying the tray of fruit and rolls and offering them to the people in the lobby. The refugees devoured them. After a half hour or so, the two headed down New Street. Praimnath slipped Clark a business card, and told him to stay in touch. In the throngs moving to the East River, they were separated and quickly lost track of each other.

Clark wandered over to Pier 11, and heard someone calling out on a bullhorn that a ferry was going to Jersey City, so he jumped on. As the boat came around the foot of Manhattan island, he saw that the south tower had not just lost the burning floors at the top, but had completely vanished. He had worked there for twenty-seven years.

On board the ferry, the unlikely steps of his flight came back to him: the people in the staircase, arguing about whether to go up or down; the calls for help that he heard from the 81st floor, diverting him from that debate. As he pulled Praimnath out of his ruined office, the people he had been with on the stairs were going up. It was Praimnath's voice that had saved him from that fatal diversion.

But what had happened to this Stanley, this stranger whom he had pulled over the rubble and fell to the ground with in an embrace? Where had he gone? Perhaps, Clark mused, he had dreamed the whole thing. Or maybe that stranger had been an angel, some sort of spectre, a metaphysical presence. Then, in his breast pocket, he felt a small business card. On it was the name of Stanley Praimnath.

Clark reached Jersey City, found a phone to call his house and report that he was alive. Then he caught a train to his station, and from there, drove home. In front of his house, he leaned on the horn, long and loud, a blaring fanfare to declare life as loud as he could. He was smothered in the embrace of his wife, then all the family and friends who had come to console her.

Having survived a plane that flew almost directly into his window, Stanley Praimnath, a devout man before September 11, became a speaker much in demand at churches and with religious groups who wanted to see the man who saw the plane coming. As his story became known, his autumn weekends were soon booked, and he told audiences about the divine love that he believes carried him to safety.

The planning, and the bickering, over what should be done with the trade center site began before the sixteen acres had been cleared of the twisted steel and powdered concrete. Filling the void became a pressing and difficult matter. Years passed and the slow pace in settling on a blueprint, in honoring the dead, in laying some kind of foundation for a new, brighter, safer future, seemed conspicuous, in part because so much else in Manhattan seemed to revive.

When the PATH station, the remnant of the Hudson Terminal train line on which the trade center had been built, was reopened in November 2003, many found themselves for the first time in the very pit where the towers and satellite buildings once stood. Among the remnants of the old complex was a bank of escalators that had carried streams of New Jersey commuters from the PATH station into the trade center. Now the train platform, once invisible to the world and from which it was hard to see anything, was, startlingly, wide open, at the center of the remains. Everything that once sat above and around the train station had disappeared. Trains rolled in and out, but the platform, swept every moment by wind and memory, could never be merely a place to catch a train. On her way to an appointment in New Jersey, Tirsa Moya, one of the people who had escaped from the 89th floor, finally returned to the site in the spring of 2004. As she rode the escalator down to the PATH platform, she wept. She felt as though she were going to her grave. Her boss distracted her, and she completed the trip. On her return from New Jersey, however, she found herself again buried in history, in loss, in the moment of escape. She cried all the way home.

Across the street from the towers, at the Millenium Hilton, where the breakfast dishes had been fossilized in soot, the building was cleaned and ready for guests by May 2003. A year later, after making do in temporary offices, Cantor Fitzgerald, the bond trading firm that lost 658 people at the top of the north tower, found a new, permanent home, four miles uptown, in the lower floors of an East 59th Street skyscraper.

Yet even as New Yorkers resumed old rhythms or struggled to shape new ones, much of what had happened that morning remained inconceivable, the depth of the disaster so stunning it took on the dreamlike quality of myth. Efforts to reconstruct a solid version of what had happened inside the towers had to navigate through the fog of pain, politics, and fear. In fact, the answers to some questions had disappeared with those who had been lost in the collapses.

Why had only eighteen people in the south tower been able to escape using stairway A, the only effective route out of the imperiled upper floors in either of the buildings?

Had others found the stairwell but were still descending when the south tower fell?

How did Battalion Chief Orio Palmer come to understand that Channel 7, the radio frequency that had been specially designed to work inside the towers, was not completely out of service, as he and other fire commanders originally thought? For much of the morning Palmer had been able to use that channel to talk to his commander in the south tower lobby, even as he climbed, floor by floor, into the higher reaches of the building to rescue the injured. Such a line of communication would have been invaluable in the north tower where the escape of so many firefighters had been impeded by poor communications.

How many people had actually jumped from either of the towers? And in many of the cases was "jumping" an accurate depiction of what bodies at 98.6 degrees do reflexively when confronted by 1,000-degree heat?

Even after the report of the 9/11 Commission, the studies by management specialists, and the sifting of evidence by investigators, journalists, and family members, the precise shape of the disaster and the texture of the final moments of many men and women remained unknown.

In 2005, though, rich new sources of information became available that sharpened some perceptions, offered fresh insights, and filled out incomplete chapters in the sprawling chronicle of the morning. In June, the National Institute of Standards and Technologies released its final draft report, a three-year engineering study primarily designed to make the next generation of skyscrapers safer.

The document amounted to a 10,000-page autopsy of the trade center's collapse: the efficacy of the fireproofing, the adequacy of the original design, the efficiency of the emergency response and the evacuation that followed. In one section, the analysts found that the towers should have had four exit staircases under the 1968 New York City building code, not just the three that were in each building. The planes' impact had destroyed those three escape stairwells in the north tower, and two of the three in the south tower. Although the Port Authority, as an interstate agency, was not bound by local codes in constructing the trade center, it had publicly pledged to "meet or exceed" the city codes. The investigators found that to have met even the newly liberalized 1968 code, the builders should have installed the fourth staircase, one specifically designed to accommodate the 1,000 people who would use the large public meeting rooms at the top of each building: the restaurant in the north tower and the observation deck atop the south tower.

"Once you go over 1,000 people on a floor, you need to have a fourth stairway," said Richard W. Bukowski, a senior engineer with the institute. Of course, the location of that additional staircase in each tower would have determined whether they survived the crashes, and ultimately, whether they might have been useful as escape routes for the people trapped on the high floors.

The Port Authority said it believed the institute was mistaken and noted that New York City building officials, who reviewed the trade center plans in the 1960s and after the 1993 terrorist bombing, had not raised any questions about the missing staircase.

Nevertheless, the city Buildings Department in 2005 had no doubts: A fourth staircase was unambiguously required by the code, its officials said.

At the same time, the institute offered additional evidence that the Port Authority had indeed been eager to reduce the amount of space devoted to stairs in the buildings. One of the documents included in its report was a September 29, 1965, letter from Malcolm P. Levy, the authority's chief planning engineer, to Minoru Yamasaki, the architect, in which the agency noted that it would be using the new, less restrictive building code then being drafted.

"It is my understanding that the present drawings have been prepared to permit rapid conversion to the new code," Levy wrote. "The tower core should be redesigned to eliminate the fire towers and to take advantage of the more lenient provisions regarding exit stairs." A few years later when city building officials took exception to those plans, arguing that they did not meet the 1938 code that was still the law, Levy and others at the Port Authority said they had decided that the buildings would comply with the less-stringent code, then in draft form, but on the verge of being enacted. The NIST investigators also located notes showing that the Port Authority saw advantages in the new code because it required fewer exits and less fireproofing.

On the question of building code compliance, the federal report had a significant, and possibly stinging recommendation: government agencies such as the Port Authority that were exempt, by law, from building code enforcement should not escape all outside scrutiny. The federal report said those agencies should not be permitted to "self-certify" that they had met the codes. That was the approach that had been used by the Port Authority in building the trade center—its own engineers and experts decided if the buildings met standards, and when they were entitled to take an exception. Now, the federal authorities suggested, even in cases where a government agency was exempt, an independent third party should review the procedures to determine if they were consistent with the code.

Asked if the Port Authority—an agency whose executives were appointed by the governors of New York and New Jersey—would now subject its building safety standards to the scrutiny of an outside expert, a spokesman replied: "It is an interesting proposal and we will consider it."

Two months later, in August 2005, the City of New York released hours of audio tape from emergency dispatchers who had directed the Fire Department's response, as well as 12,000 pages of transcribed interviews with 503 firefighters, fire officials, and emergency medical workers who had been at the towers that morning. The interviews had been ordered in the fall of 2001 by Fire Commissioner Thomas Von Essen, who sought to preserve accurate recollections before they were refashioned by collective memory.

The department later made no effort to analyze the information, however, and when *The New York Times* asked to see the material in February 2002, the city refused to release it, saying it would interfere with the prosecution of a man accused of plotting with the September 11 hijackers. A federal judge ruled that most of the records had no bearing whatsoever on the trial. Later, city lawyers claimed that the firefighters had been promised confidentiality, but ultimately withdrew that assertion. The city finally argued that much of the oral histories were opinions and not public records. The newspaper sued, under New York's freedom of information law, and in April 2005 the Court of Appeals, the state's highest court, ordered that the materials be released.

The interviews provided searing, vivid testimony, uncensored by protocol. Firefighters recalled the confusion of the day and their frustrations and struggles against the surging fire in highly personal accounts that resonated with their own residual disbelief at what had occurred. All were recorded at a time when the whereabouts of hundreds of people had yet to be determined. In many cases, the interviewers asked for any sightings of colleagues, many of whose remains had yet to be found.

Particularly informative were the accounts of 200 emergency medical technicians, paramedics, and their supervisors, whose response had been vital but whose perspective had been largely overlooked in the retellings of the day. The Emergency Medical Services, which became a division within the Fire Department in 1996, had deployed en masse to the incident and, almost from the start, had difficulty coordinating an orderly response. Crews had trouble finding supervisors. Radio communications were spotty. Each unit was forced to fend for itself. Efforts at triage were scattershot. Isolated and without clear lines of command, each crew made its own judgments and set its own priorities.

Paramedics shepherded crowds away from the towers, bandaged people inside a bank lobby, and packed their ambulances with the dazed, the bleeding, and the burned. At one point, a group of the medical chiefs met, in part by chance, at the Embassy Suites Hotel in the World Financial Center and sat down to configure a new plan. Gathered in the lobby, they began to work out the details over a tabletop and then, distracted by the arrival of more people needing care, moved into a back corridor where they fashioned a strategy to regain some semblance of order over the disaster. When they emerged, however, they found they could not communicate the plan to the entire force because their own radios could not contact the dispatchers.

Joseph Cahill, a paramedic, said the experience felt like being in an infantry unit that had been overrun. "We are scattered everywhere," he said. "Nobody knew where anybody was. Nobody knew who was in charge. It really felt for a moment that I was in *Apocalypse Now*, where Martin Sheen goes, 'Where is your C.O.? Ain't that you? No. Uh-oh.'"

Several medical technicians had family in the burning buildings—a father, a wife, a fiancé, a close friend. Manuel Delgado, a paramedic, was standing on Church Street with another paramedic, Carlos Lillo, treating several critically injured people when Delgado noticed that Lillo was crying. It was an overwhelming moment, Delgado understood, but Lillo was a seasoned veteran.

"I go to him, 'Carlos, what's the matter? What's going on?'"

"My wife's in there," Lillo responded, indicating the north tower.

Cecilia Lillo worked as an administrator for the Port Authority on the 64th floor. She ultimately survived after escaping with the other people from her floor. Her husband, who went looking for her, did not.

Two emergency medical technicians, Richard Erdey and Soraya O'Donnell, recounted how they were on the scene only a few moments when they were directed to help a firefighter, Danny Suhr. He had been hit by the body of a woman who had fallen from one of the towers and, after loading him into the ambulance, his condition was immediately clear: He had no vital signs and his injuries were catastrophic.

Erdey was certain the firefighter was dead, but two of the firefighter's colleagues from Engine 216 had climbed into the ambulance with them for the ride to Bellevue Hospital Center. "They kept yelling, 'Danny, Danny, Danny!'" Erdey said. He was struck by how intently they were staring at him. "I'm saying, should I tell them? Should I not tell them? How can I tell them tactfully?"

As they continued the hopeless resuscitation efforts, Erdey finally warned the firefighters there was only a small glimmer of hope for their friend. Indeed, Suhr was pronounced dead when they arrived at the hospital. Minutes later, as the crew began preparing to return to the towers, they were approached by two people from the hospital, an emergency room doctor and an Anglican nun, Sister Cynthia Mahoney. They wanted to go along to help.

Erdey looked at the nun, unsure if she knew the magnitude of what she was volunteering for. "You understand, ma'am, we might not come back from this," he said. She understood, Sister Cynthia said, and the pair from the hospital climbed in for a trip back to the towers. When they arrived, the chaos had intensified. The towers had fallen and as they approached in their ambulance they encountered a fellow medical technician wandering, disoriented, through the smoke, holding his helmet.

"Where is your partner?" O'Donnell asked.

"I'm looking for my father," the technician responded. "He was in the World Trade Center."

"Why don't you get in the back with us," O'Donnell called out to him. "We had the nun in the back with us," she said. "We figured she could talk to him."

The oral histories from the firefighters presented fresh evidence of how deeply unaware firefighters in the north tower had been of their own peril after the south tower collapsed. The bleak picture provided in the accounts is in stark contrast to the depiction by public officials—most particularly, Mayor Michael R. Bloomberg and former Mayor Rudolph W. Giuliani, in submissions to the 9/11 Commission—that firefighters were broadly aware of the dangers they faced but stayed in the building to carry out their rescue duties.

In actual fact, of the fifty-eight firefighters who escaped the north tower and gave oral histories, only four said they knew that the south tower had fallen.

Lt. William Walsh of Ladder 1 said he had heard the order to evacuate when he was around the 19th floor. Yet he did not know that a plane had struck the other building or that it had already collapsed, and as he descended he encountered firefighters who had significantly less sense of what was going on than he did.

"They were hanging out in the stairwell and in the occupancy and they were resting," Walsh said. "I told them, 'Didn't you hear the Mayday? Get out.' They were saying, 'Yeah, we'll be right with you, Lou.' They just didn't give it a second thought. They just continued with their rest."

Long after September 11, long after studies had identified breaches in New York City's preparedness for a mammoth disaster, city officials struggled to mend the gaps. The inherent difficulty of using a small, hand-held radio in a high-rise setting was addressed by issuing new Command Post radios to chiefs, twenty-two-pound devices that a fire captain had designed using an old marine radio and a battery taken from his daughter's Jet Ski. They were carried to the upper floors of a large building and were effective at establishing clear communications with commanders below.

The protocol of police and firefighters sharing one set of helicopters as response and reconnaissance aircraft was also resolved, and the two departments resumed training flights together. The need to establish a single, joint command post and to share information was embraced, at least in concept.

Some problems, however, could not be solved with battery power and bandwidth. The enmity between New York's fire and police agencies did not seem to dissipate, even if it resembled the animosities of divorce within some families—dreadfully apparent but still not spoken about. Years after the disaster, New York was still working to install radios that would allow firefighters and police to talk to each other on the same frequency in special situations. And when the city unveiled a new emergency response protocol for disasters in the spring of 2005, the police were assigned primary responsibility for biological and chemical attacks, an adjustment that provoked open bitterness in the Fire Department ranks. Chief Peter Hayden, who had been the commander in the north tower, responded to the city's decision by telling a reporter for *The New York Times:* "If the question was posed today—would the response at a terrorist incident be different than it was on 9/11?—the answer would have to be no. Now if that isn't a recipe for disaster, I don't know what is."

———

The next major disaster that New York responded to was not man-made and it was far away, in New Orleans, where 650 firefighters and police officers arrived in September 2005 to help bail out a city that had disappeared beneath flood waters. Some of the firefighters drove down in a pumper truck that the people of New Orleans and Louisiana had given to a Brooklyn firehouse in December 2001 to replace one destroyed on 9/11. The truck was called "The Spirit of Louisiana."

In the days after the towers collapsed, a group of New Orleans firefighters had traveled north to help out, cooking and cleaning at firehouses while the New Yorkers searched for lost colleagues in the rubble. Now the New York crews were in the south riding to calls with a fire force that had been depleted by the hurricane. Bill Butler of Ladder 6. Sean Halper of Engine 279. Liam Flaherty of Rescue 4. Many of the firefighters were veterans of the towers and the pile, repaying a debt, offering lessons learned, losing themselves and finding themselves in someone else's catastrophe.

On the morning of September 11, 2005, the Spirit of Louisiana was parked on the lawn of Our Lady of Holy Cross College, near the buildings where the firefighters were staying, in the Algiers section of New Orleans, which had not been flooded. At 8:30 A.M. eastern time, a quarter hour before the time the first plane had hit, Father Peter Weiss, a Brooklyn native, began an outdoor Catholic Mass in observance of the anniversary. Hundreds of firefighters stood on the field in front of the administration building, a red brick Georgian colonial that had lost one of its white columns to the storm. The lawn was edged with twisted oaks and magnolias, some with branches that hung limp or lay on the grass. "We are here today with another community devastated by another tragic event," said New York's Assistant Fire Chief Michael Weinlein. "We feel your pain and understand your frustration. It may take some time, but I promise you from personal experience, things will get better."

At 9:35 A.M., as the Mass wound down, word of a house fire nearby came in over the radios. Firefighters from Maryland, Illinois, and New York ran for their trucks parked along the road in groups of five and six. A company from Chicago pulled its truck out of a formation of rigs that had been arranged around the altar. Firefighters, who a few minutes before had waited in line for communion, now stood along Woodland Drive, hurrying to pull on their gear.

With the passing of years, the emotions of the day no longer surged with the same force. Still, they retained unique power.

Esmerlin Salcedo, thirty-six years old, worked the afternoon shift as a security guard at the trade center, often stationed in a basement command center where he monitored the elevator intercoms and other emergency gear. Since his workday did not begin until 3 P.M., he was not present when the planes struck; he was not down in the basement, on the B-1 level, when the first, urgent calls came from the elevators or by phone from the people upstairs, seeking guidance. In fact, he was just a block or so away, taking a computer class at the Chubb Institute, a business school. Those in the command center had no time to think of who was not there: The cries for help were raining on them, unceasingly.

"People were calling from the elevators, from the floors, pleading with us to get them out," Roselyn Braud, a member of the staff, recalled. She fell apart, thinking of her children at home. Suddenly, a door opened. Esmerlin Salcedo had arrived.

"He came flying down here, threw his book bag on the ground, and started answering phones," Braud said. She was too upset to continue. Salcedo said he would escort her upstairs. "We linked arms, and he came up with me," Braud said. He led her to a door near Church Street.

"He told me to 'Run, run for your life,' and that was the last I saw of him." A moment later, Salcedo was seen helping another security guard shortly before the south tower collapsed.

Off-duty, he was paid nothing; on-duty, his salary was $10.51 an hour, on which he supported his wife and four children.

In September 2005, the case of a belligerent, disrespectful teenager from Atlanta, Georgia, was put before a television judge.

The girl wanted to be adopted by another family; she hated her own parents, she said. The judge fashioned a television solution. She sent the young woman to meet another sixteen-year-old girl in New York City.

They met at Ground Zero—the girl from Atlanta, and the other sixteen-year-old, named Melody Salcedo. She explained who her father was: Esmerlin Salcedo. And she warned the other girl of learning too late the value of loving the people who cared for her.

Postscript

The firefighters from Ladder 6 carried Josephine Harris again on a wintry morning in January. They moved slowly, as they had nearly ten years earlier. But this time there was no worry that the walls around them might crumble as they moved Harris's blue steel casket toward the steps of St. Joseph's Church in Greenwich Village.

The entrance to St. Joseph's, two miles north of the trade center and six miles from Harris's Brooklyn apartment, was framed by Doric columns and had a simple, unadorned look, unusual in a Catholic church. The nine pallbearers—eight firefighters and Lieutenant Dennis Lim of the Port Authority Police Department—wore their dress uniforms, the fire officers in white hats. Each rested one hand on the casket, the other on his heart.

Many of them had seen a lot of Harris in the years since the attacks, since the painfully slow walk down stairway B in the north tower's final minutes, the pleading procession with Harris and her fallen arches that had left them in a precise place when the building fell, the only stub to survive as the tower dissolved around them.

Harris had been to Sal D'Agostino's wedding and had flown down to Florida with Jay Jonas to speak to retired firefighters. The men would meet with her several times a year and when Jonas was picked to lead a firefighters parade in upstate New York, Harris rode behind him in a silver convertible, waving to the crowd.

The men of Ladder 6 regarded Harris as a guardian angel, a blessing who had arrived very much in disguise when speed down the stairs had seemed the safer choice. Instead, her halting descent had given them all an opportunity to continue on with their lives.

Most of the men were still on the job.

Jonas had been promoted from captain to deputy chief and was now responsible for a large swath of the Bronx and upper Manhattan.

Billy Butler and Matt Komorowski were now lieutenants, serving in the Bronx and Brooklyn.

Tommy Falco and Mike Meldrum of the company had retired, as had Mickey Kross from Ladder 16, who had been with them in the stairwell.

Lim, the Port Authority K-9 officer, had also been promoted, and his dog, Sirius, a yellow lab who died in the attacks, had been remembered with a monument in Canada and a dog run in lower Manhattan.

Josephine Harris had died nine days earlier, at age sixty-nine, of a heart attack. She called 911 from her apartment at 2:20 a.m. on Wednesday, January 12, 2011, but the Fire Department medics could not revive her. Her life, like those of the others, had not been frozen by the calamity. For all their impact, the attacks were powerless to stop a future that swept forward with fresh moments of joy and achievement, as well as new encounters with panic and sadness and illness, like the heart condition that eventually felled her.

After the attacks, Harris, a widowed bookkeeper for the Port Authority, had briefly returned to work, but she did not follow in 2004 when her job was transferred to Newark. She lived alone, somewhat reclusively, surviving on disability assistance as her financial and health problems mounted. Papers found in her apartment indicated she had recently filed for bankruptcy.

Six months earlier, though, she had been energetic during an interview for a new TV show, *Miracle Detectives,* which recounted the story of the stairwell survivors.

"Somebody was with us," she said. "Somebody was watching over us."

Inevitably, time drained color and details from memories of the day. For many, it became difficult to recall just how shaken, how apocalyptic everything had seemed in the days and weeks after the attacks.

Had there really been a morning when just the sound of an airplane engine could send New Yorkers screaming down the street? Who were those people who hoarded bottled water in their basements, or asked their doctors for radiation sickness pills, or flew American flags from the antennas of their cars?

Needless to say, many people confronted—in some cases embraced—lives that had been completely reshaped by the catastrophe, and searched for ways to make lasting answer to those 102 minutes.

The family of Peter Alderman, the Bloomberg employee who could not escape a breakfast conference at Windows on the World, used funds they received under a federal compensation program to create a foundation that helps the victims of terrorism and mass violence cope emotionally with the trauma. The impulse to build something enduring—gardens, parks, literacy programs, cross-cultural learning opportunities, scholarships funded by golf outings and road races—was a common response by the surviving families.

About a hundred survivors refused compensation grants because they would have had to surrender their right to file civil lawsuits against the public and private parties they believed bore some responsibility for actions, and inactions, that exposed airline passengers, office tower workers, and the country to the attacks. The power of subpoena in a lawsuit could compel answers under oath. Among those filing suits were Monica Gabrielle, whose husband,

Richard, was injured and trapped on the 78th floor in the south tower while waiting for an elevator, and Beverly Eckert, whose husband, Sean Rooney, had found doors locked when he tried to get onto the roof in the same building.

They were part of a determined band of 9/11 family members whose gaze fell on everything from building codes that left the skyscrapers without enough stairways for emergency evacuations, to a system of national intelligence that seemed to have a hard time passing e-mail messages from one agency to another. Their status gave them general—though hardly absolute—immunity from accusations that they were seeking partisan advantage, or that by asking questions about what went wrong they were subverting a president leading a war in one country and preparing for an invasion in a second one. At a meeting in the White House, senior officials explained to the family group that a far-reaching inquiry was too risky for a country at war, as it might lay bare the failures of national defense.

"Are you going to stand here and look me in the eye and tell me we are not going to have an investigation into the death of my husband and the relatives of all the other people in this room?" Beverly Eckert asked.

Well, no, as it turned out. The 9/11 Commission was reluctantly created by Congress and the president, and it would often be hamstrung by delays and evasions at all levels of government. Nevertheless, due in large part to the doggedness of a Family Steering Committee, scholars believe that the 9/11 Commission cut more quickly and deeply into the secrets of two presidential administrations than did earlier commissions that studied national calamities like Pearl Harbor, the assassination of John F. Kennedy, and the Iran-contra affair. Yet many of those who had fought for the creation of the commission felt that it had left important questions unanswered. They believed that the commission's declaration that the attacks had not been prevented because of "a failure of imagination" had shielded many senior officials from being held responsible. New systems without true accountability, Monica Gabrielle and others argued, would leave the country as vulnerable as ever. On Christmas Day 2009, a Nigerian man who months earlier had been identified as a terrorist threat by intelligence agents—and by his own father—was able to board a flight to Detroit and ignite plastic explosives stitched into his underwear. He was subdued by another passenger. The United States was spending $75 billion annually on national security intelligence. None of it had stopped him.

On the morning of September 11, 2001, the U.S. military had fewer soldiers, sailors, marines, and aviators in its ranks than at any time in the previous sixty years. American governments had been engaged in overt and covert wars almost nonstop since 1941, and at the beginning of the twenty-first century the United States was still enjoying a peace dividend from the end of the Cold War. The 9/11 attacks roused a spirit of service and duty that had been embodied that day by the valor of firefighters, medics, and police officers. Military recruitment surged. Over the next decade, two million members of the U.S. armed forces would be deployed to Iraq and Afghanistan. Among them was Christian P. Engeldrum. He had already served in the U.S. Army from 1986 to 1991 and completed his obligations as a reservist in the Army National Guard. By 9/11, he was working as a firefighter in New York City. He had responded to the trade center attack and spent days there, experiences that his family said had prompted him to reenlist. In 2004, he was one of thirty New York City firefighters on active duty in the military, and he arrived in Iraq on November 2 of that year. Before the month was out, he and another soldier were killed by a roadside bomb. Firefighter Engeldrum was the first of fifteen emergency responders who survived 9/11 but died in Iraq or Afghanistan. He was thirty-nine years old, the father of two sons, and his wife was expecting their third child at the time of his death. His eldest son, Sean, said in a eulogy, "He was brave and courageous all the time, but able to cry over a sick dog."

Sister Cynthia Mahoney, the nun who jumped into the city ambulance to volunteer after the attacks, later developed crippling respiratory ailments. One of the first civilians to join the rescue workers, she had ridden back to the collapsed towers with Richard Erdey and Soraya O'Donnell, two emergency medical technicians who worked for the Fire Department. Months later, the nun was still there, showing up day after day to comfort families and bless remains as they were pulled from the debris.

Sister Cynthia, a member of the Anglican Order of St. Helena, had moved to New York from South Carolina only a few weeks before the attacks. Her convent was near Bellevue, the hospital where the ambulance crew had taken Danny Suhr, the firefighter who died after being hit by a falling body.

When she approached Erdey and O'Donnell in the hospital parking lot, the crew had been direct with her: the dangers at the trade center could not be minimized.

"Oh, I understand," Sister Cynthia replied. She had been an emergency medical technician herself in South Carolina before leaving that job to join the religious order.

As it turned out, the threats she faced were never as obvious as fire and falling concrete. Years later, more than 60,000 people who had worked in the buildings or had participated in rescue and recovery efforts would sign up for health monitoring or treatment programs because they feared the lasting effects of the foul soup of dust, ash, and smoke they had inhaled after the collapse. Sister Cynthia, a nonsmoker, developed asthma and lung disease after her work at the site.

She died, at age fifty-four, in November 2006, from respiratory ailments. By that time, the rubble she had worked amid was long gone, but many viewed her death as another casualty of the day.

Sean Rooney would have turned fifty-two years old on February 15, 2003, and his widow, Beverly Eckert, marked the day by taking the train from Connecticut to New York and joining an ocean of people that stretched for nearly two miles along the east side of Manhattan. It was a bitterly cold Sunday, but hundreds of thousands of people turned out for a rally to protest the invasion of Iraq, which was then a month away. Another woman who had been speaking against the war was Rita Lasar, whose brother, Abe Zelmanowitz, had died while standing by his wheelchair-bound friend Ed Beyea, on the 27th floor of the north tower. Days before the attacks, Zelmanowitz had gone to a Sabbath lesson where the rabbi spoke about sacrificing oneself for the love of God. "You speak of the great historical heroes, like Rabbi Akiva and Rabbi Shimon Bar-Yochai," Zelmanowitz asked the rabbi, "but how can a simple Jew like myself show his love of God?" He answered his own question on the morning of 9/11.

Now it was Rita, on a journey born in the embers of that day, who found her way to Afghanistan in early 2002, shortly after American and allied troops arrived. There, she met people who had also lost loved ones. Her trip had been arranged by Global Exchange, an advocacy and human rights organization. Like her brother, she said, the dead Afghan civilians were filed under the category of "collateral damage."

The war in Afghanistan, launched a month after the 9/11 attacks, had broad support in the United States and internationally. The enemy had a face and a name: Osama bin Laden, leader of Al Qaeda, the network of Islamic radicals that had carried out the plans to kill thousands of innocent people. On a videotape of a celebratory meal that was released a few weeks after the attacks, bin Laden—a tall, thin man with flowing beard and robes—laughed and said that they had expected the hijacked planes to destroy only a few floors in each tower. An international coalition joined the United States to hunt down Al Qaeda and to uproot the Taliban, the fundamentalist Islamists who controlled Afghanistan and had given sanctuary to bin Laden and his organization. The Taliban were quickly heaved out of power and regrouped as insurgents. Bin Laden, however, eluded the manhunt. Not long after the invasion of Afghanistan, military planners in the United States began preparations to invade Iraq and depose Saddam Hussein, that country's dictatorial ruler.

As with any issue involving thousands of people, a monolithic "family" view of either war was out of the question. Quite a few families spoke in favor of one or the other as a necessary act; artifacts of the 9/11 attacks—flags, pictures, bits of steel—were packed off with American troops who were being deployed overseas. Polls showed that the country was uncertain about the Iraq invasion, and the demonstrations of February 15, 2003, with millions of people gathering in cities around the United States and the world, put faces on the numbers. As the wars were prosecuted in three presidential terms, covering the administrations of George W. Bush and Barack Obama, support for them waxed and waned. Backers defended them as well-meaning missions to export democratic principles to the Middle East and maintained that they had reduced American vulnerability to terrorism by transferring the theater of battle overseas. Opponents argued that the wars were killing people who had nothing to do with the 9/11 attacks, and were fueling violent anti-American sentiment. From whatever perspective, the toll in money and lives had been profound: as of the spring of 2011, the wars had cost more than a trillion dollars, and the lives of tens of thousands of Iraqis, Afghans, and Americans, as well as soldiers from the international coalition led by the United States.

For her part, Beverly followed with equal diligence the high-profile inquiries, like the 9/11 Commission, and the barely visible ones, like a special panel assigned to look into the handling of weapons of mass destruction. Long after the television lights had been switched off, she would fly across the country for meetings where she and others would ask how many recommendations from these studies had been put into effect.

Only after Congress passed the first wave of intelligence reforms recommended by the 9/11 Commission did the day begin to loosen its grip on her life. "Somehow," she wrote early in 2005, "I feel more at peace with Sean's death, having had the opportunity to help change our government—hopefully, for the better." She met an avid sailor, Shawn Monks, on a visit to Block Island, off the coast of Rhode Island. They became a couple. Aboard a catamaran called "Never Land," they sailed from Florida to Connecticut, and she used e-mails to keep family and friends updated on the journey. At one point, her thoughts turned to her husband and to the man who had ordered his death, Osama bin Laden. That July, she wrote:

> As we entered NY Harbor, we passed the Statue of Liberty and then the section of Manhattan where the World Trade Center towers once stood. Sean is always with me in spirit, and he felt especially near at that moment.
>
> It's always painful to be at Ground Zero, but sailing past the location of the attacks while standing on the deck of my own boat, knowing that in contrast, bin Laden was hiding in a cave, made me feel something of a sense of triumph over terrorism.

After parts of New Orleans were crushed by Hurricane Katrina, she and Shawn volunteered with Habitat for Humanity, helping to build houses. In 2008, she began working as a tutor in the school system near her home in Connecticut.

This quieter, private life was not a return to slumber after a political awakening. She remain keenly interested in seeing those accused of plotting the attacks brought to justice, particularly Khalid Shaikh Mohammed, who faced charges of mass murder as a key organizer. He had given detailed confessions to a long list of crimes against civilians in the United States and around the world. It also emerged that he had been waterboarded 183 times during interrogations. Months passed, then years, as the courts, the executive branch, and Congress wrestled over the appropriate administration of justice for Mohammed and people like him, all classified as enemy combatants. Should they be tried before military commissions or in the civilian courts? Most of them were being held in a military detention center at the U.S. base in Guantánamo Bay, Cuba. During Barack Obama's campaign for president in 2008, he promised to bring them quickly to trial in American civilian courts, and he said he would close the Guantánamo facility, the subject of intense criticism at home and abroad. It would be a symbol of change, a point of unmistakable departure, from the policies of his predecessor, George W. Bush. He also declared that he would make it a priority to find Osama bin Laden. And on his second day in office, President Obama suspended the military tribunal process and announced that Guantánamo would be closed within a year. At the president's invitation, Beverly and other 9/11 family members met with President Obama on February 6, 2009, to hear his plans for the detainees, and to let him know what they thought; Beverly believed that criminal trials were long overdue, but just as with the two wars, there were many views among the family members on the wisdom of closing Guantánamo and shifting away from military tribunals.

By then, Beverly was no stranger to speaking truth to power. That didn't mean she was jaded about going to the White House. Leaving the meeting, she picked up a souvenir: a paper napkin embossed with the presidential seal that had been under President Obama's water bottle.

That same week, Sean's birthday was rolling around again. It would have been his fifty-eighth. Beverly planned to join his family in Buffalo, New York, and to present a scholarship at his alma mater, Canisius High School, the Jesuit boys school he was attending when they met at a dance in a gym as sixteen-year-olds. She flew from Newark aboard Continental Flight 3407; about five miles from the airport, the jet lost speed. An investigation would find that the overtired pilot did not use the right procedures to fly out of a stall. All forty-nine people on board were killed, as well as one person on the ground. In the months afterward, Beverly's sisters helped to organize the families of that calamity to lobby Congress and the Federal Aviation Administration for a range of safety reforms.

Later that year, in November 2009, Attorney General Eric Holder announced plans to implement the president's orders to close Guantánamo and to begin civilian trials for as many detainees as practical. The administration would bring Khalid Shaikh Mohammed and other high-level Al Qaeda detainees to trial at the federal courthouse in lower Manhattan, a few blocks from the World Trade Center site. The whole effort quickly became a contentious political issue.

Although New York's mayor, Michael Bloomberg, initially hailed the courthouse as a "fitting" venue for the cases, his administration later maintained that the trials would incur security costs of as much as a billion dollars, and would paralyze lower Manhattan. Congressional opposition from Republicans and Democrats was considerable as well, and continued through 2010. Near the end of the year, Congress passed a military spending bill that included a provision barring the use of funds to transport Guantánamo detainees anywhere in the United States. President Obama reluctantly signed it, effectively reversing his decision to close the detention center. On April 4, 2011, as the tenth anniversary of the attacks approached without a single person accused of direct involvement having faced charges in any forum, the attorney general announced that the Justice Department was dropping plans for criminal trials. Mohammed, the highest ranking Al Qaeda figure in captivity, would be presented as an enemy combatant to a panel of military officers who would decide his fate. Guantánamo would remain open indefinitely.

May 1, 2011, was a pleasant spring Sunday in Washington, D.C., and reporters assigned to weekend duty covering the White House were glad to hear that the "lid" had been put on at 2 P.M.—meaning that the president was home for the day, and they didn't have to hang around for any kind of public appearance. That meant they could grab a few extra hours of personal time away from their hectic beat. It also cleared the White House of people who might notice that the building was humming at a strikingly high pitch for a Sunday afternoon. The secretary of state, Hillary Rodham Clinton, was there. So were senior counterterrorism and military officials. And, of course, the president himself. He may not have left the house that day, but he was busy. Near 10 P.M., reporters got an e-mail from the White House with a simple message: Get back to work.

At 11:30 P.M., President Obama appeared on television. "Tonight," he began, "I can report to the American people and to the world that the United States has conducted an operation that killed Osama bin Laden, the leader of Al Qaeda, and a terrorist who's responsible for the murder of thousands of innocent men, women, and children."

After months of surveillance on a compound in Abbottabad, Pakistan, a team of U.S. commandos raided the house and killed bin Laden. "The American people did not choose this fight," the president said. "It came to our shores and started with the senseless slaughter of our citizens."

A few days later, President Obama visited a firehouse in midtown Manhattan that had lost fifteen members on 9/11, among them Chief Ed Geraghty, who had worked his way up the south tower behind Chief Orio Palmer. He had been one of the voices crackling across the radio that morning, all business, facing all chaos. "What floor should we try to get up to, Orio?" Chief Geraghty had asked.

The president's session in the firehouse included handshakes all around, a meal from the kitchen, and a short speech about the death of bin Laden and the unspent force of memory. "When we say we will never forget, we mean what we say," he said.

By the time Josephine Harris died, in 2011, the new skyscraper at the trade center site, the Freedom Tower, had risen 50-some stories, en route to its final height of 104. No one can recall that Harris ever ventured back to the trade center site after 9/11. But for the men who had rescued her, seeing her was among the many triggers that could close the distance from the day. The deafening sound, the impenetrable dust, the furious wind, the wait in the dark crevices to be dug out.

"I can close my eyes and re-create the collapse," Jay Jonas said.

The men of Ladder 6 had given Harris a shiny green baseball jacket that read "Our Guardian Angel," and they hung it in the vestibule of the church during the funeral service. An image of an angel was embroidered into the lining of her casket, holding hands with a firefighter.

The funeral arrangements were paid for by Peter DeLuca, the owner of the Greenwich Village Funeral Home, a local businessman who felt a special affection for firefighters. In 1987 they had worked feverishly to save his thirteen-month-old son, Peter Jr., who died when the family's Manhattan townhouse collapsed.

Cardinal Edward Egan, the retired archbishop of New York, celebrated the funeral Mass with Monsignor John Delendick, the Fire Department chaplain who ten years earlier had given everyone general absolution as they ran from the towers. In his homily, Monsignor Delendick spoke of how the firefighters had been saved, not by speed but by compassion, by their belief in a set of values that did not waver even as the walls did.

"Interesting," he told the church about Harris and the firefighters, "how both groups accuse each other of saving the other. I think that's the best part."

After the service, Harris's neighbors from Brooklyn climbed into a Fire Department van, and the procession rode off behind the hearse to Cypress Hills Cemetery in Brooklyn, where Harris's husband, Frederick, had been buried in 1993.

There had been a storm the night before, and the snow was still fresh on the ground near the gravesite. Friends and relatives gathered around the casket. The firefighters saluted.

"Eternal rest grant unto them, O Lord," said Monsignor Delendick, as he prayed for Josephine and all the dead who had gone before her.

And let perpetual light shine upon them.
May they rest in peace.
May their souls and the souls of all the faithful departed,
Through the mercy of God, rest in peace.
Amen.

Lost

Among the 2,753 who died in the attacks on New York, 131 in this account did not survive:

In the north tower: Peter Alderman, Ezra Aviles, Ed Beyea, Ivhan Carpio, Stephen Cherry, Caleb Arron Dack, Carlos DeCosta, Frank De Martini, Brendan Dolan, Doris Eng, Garth Feeney, James Gartenberg, John Griffin, Christopher Hanley, Emeric Harvey, Charles Heeran, Patrick Hoey, Joe Holland, Steve Jacobson, Howard Kane, William Kelly, Stuart Lee, Neil Levin, Jan Maciejewski, Peter Mardikian, Patricia Massari, Tom McGinnis, Damian Meehan, Pete Negron, Jeffrey Nussbaum, Christine Olender, Pablo Ortiz, Jim Paul, Patricia Puma, Judith Reese, Andrew Rosenblum, Tony Savas, Tony Segarra, Stephen Tompsett, Martin Wortley, Elkin Yuen, Abe Zelmanowitz.

In the south tower: J. J. Aguiar, Jack Andreacchio, Brett Bailey, Joseph Berry, Shimmy Biegeleisen, Ed Calderon, Roko Camaj, Bobby Coll, Kevin Cosgrove, Frank Doyle, Eric Eisenberg, Ed Emery, Bradley Fetchet, Tamitha Freeman, Richard Gabrielle, Alayne Gentul, Dianne Gladstone, Manny Gomez, Karen Hagerty, Phil Hayes, Ron Hoerner, Howard Kestenbaum, Ed Mardovich, Jose Marrero, Robert Gabriel Martinez, Bob Mattson, Ann

McHugh, Ed McNally, Greg Milanowycz, Stephen Mulderry, Vijay Paramsothy, Rick Rescorla, Francis Riccardelli, Paul Rizza, Sean Rooney, Esmerlin Salcedo, Herman Sandler, Thomas Sparacio, Michael Stabile, Keiji Takahashi, Yeshavant Tembe, Brian Thompson, Rick Thorpe, Doris Torres, Diane Urban, Brad Vadas, Sankara Velamuri, Dave Vera, Kevin York.

In the Marriott Hotel: Joe Keller, Abdu A. Malahi.

From the Fire Department of New York: Chief of Department Peter Ganci; Deputy Chief Donald Burns; Battalion Chiefs Ed Geraghty, Orio J. Palmer, and John Paolillo; Fire Marshal Ron Bucca; Captains William Burke Jr. and Fred Ill; Lieutenants John Fischer, Joseph Leavey, Bob Nagel, Kevin Pfeifer, and Mike Warchola; Reverend Mychal Judge; Firefighters David Arce, Michael Boyle, Robert Evans, Tom Kelly, Robert King Jr., Scott Kopytko, Scott Larsen, Joseph Maffeo, Keithroy Maynard, Douglas Oelschlager, Michael Otten, Christian Regenhard, Danny Suhr, David Weiss.

From the New York Police Department: Sergeant Michael Curtin; Officers John D'Allara, John Perry, Moira Smith.

From the Port Authority Police Department: Inspector James Romito; Officers Christopher Amoroso, Dominick Pezzulo, Antonio Rodriguez.

From New York City Emergency Medical Services: Paramedic Carlos Lillo.

Notes

Portions of *102 Minutes* draw on interviews conducted by the authors for this book, for a 1994 book on the World Trade Center, and for several articles that appeared in *The New York Times;* the citations include interviews for those articles by *New York Times* reporters Ford Fessenden, James Glanz, and Eric Lipton.

Authors' Note
Page

xxii *North tower hit first:* The times here are those established by the National Institute of Standards and Technology (hereafter NIST).

xxii *Beyond the hijackers' designs:* Osama bin Laden, the leader of Al Qaeda, said in a taped interview that was discovered a few weeks after the hijacking that they had not expected the entire buildings to collapse, only that there would be localized collapses.

xxiv *2,753 people died:* The official count of people identified as dead by the Office of the Chief Medical Examiner of New York City as of May 2011.

xxiv *Estimation of the dead:* An analysis by NIST in July 2004 is the source for the numbers of passengers and the number of first responders who died; the estimate of 600 people on the floors where the planes hit is by the authors, using the span of impact as described by NIST, and the number of people who worked on those floors and did not escape.

Prologue
Page

1 *First into the office:* Interview with Dianne DeFontes by Jim Dwyer, August 25, 2003.

2   *... one of 14,154 people:* The number of people in the towers has been consistently and substantially overestimated, often merged with the total population of all seven buildings in the complex, along with the commuters who passed through the concourse coming or going from one of the six train lines that connected to the complex. The average turnstile count was provided by Alan Reiss, former director, World Trade Department, Port Authority of New York and New Jersey; surveys of the actual building population on the morning, performed by the *New York Times* and *USA Today,* are consistent with that figure. In July 2004, NIST estimated the total population of the towers as no more than 17,400.

2   *Another 940 were registered:* Kathy Duffy, Marriott, interview by Jim Dwyer, June 2002.

3   *On 88, Frank and Nicole De Martini:* Nicole De Martini, interview by Jim Dwyer, August 26, 2003.

3   *... his colleague, Jim Connors:* Mak Hanna, interview by Jim Dwyer, August 25, 2003.

4   *Alan Reiss ran world trade department:* Alan Reiss, interview by Jim Dwyer, April 30, 2002.

4   *Most of the 91st floor:* Mike McQuaid, interview by Ford Fessenden, May 2002.

4   *Tom McGinnis, who normally worked:* Iliana McGinnis, interview by Jim Dwyer, May 2002.

5   *... the firm's managing director, David Kravette:* David Kravette, interview by Joseph Plambeck for the authors, July 13, 2004.

8   *Yasyuka Shibata had arrived:* Yasyuka Shibata, interview by Jim Dwyer, February 26, 1993.

8   *The pursuit of bombers:* Jim Dwyer, David Kocieniewski, Dee Murphy, and Peg Tyre, *Two Seconds under the World: Terror Comes to America* (New York: Crown Publishers, 1994).

10   *Not long after the bombing:* NIST, *Progress Report on the Federal Building and Fire Safety Investigation of the World Trade Center Disaster,* Gaithersburg, Md., May 2003.

10   *The structural engineer explained:* Leslie E. Robertson, interview by Jim Dwyer, February 27, 1993.

11   *As Liz Thompson arrived:* The description of the morning at Windows on the World is based on interviews by Kevin Flynn in 2002 with Liz Thompson, Geoffrey Wharton, and Michael Nestor, as well as with relatives of people who died, and with members of the restaurant staff who had not yet arrived that morning.

12   *A few strides behind:* The compelling story of the last elevator out of Windows on the World was first reported by Lisa DePaulo in "The Last Day of Windows on the World," *Talk* magazine, December 2001.

Chapter 1: "It's a bomb, let's get out of here."
Page
13 *A bomb, Dianne DeFontes thought:* Dianne DeFontes, Walter Pilipiak, Akane Ito, Rob Sibarium, interviews by Jim Dwyer, May 2002 and August 2003.
13 *Mike McQuaid, the electrician:* Mike McQuaid, interview by Ford Fessenden, May 2002.
14 *In the lobby, David Kravette:* David Kravette, interview by Joseph Plambeck for the authors, July 13, 2004; *The Early Show*, CBS News, September 19, 2001.
14 *She dropped the phone:* Louis Massari, Laurie Kane, Abigail Carter, interviews by *New York Times* staff members, October 2001–May 2002.
15 *At another breakfast:* Alan Reiss, interview by Jim Dwyer, April 30, 2002.
16 *As soon as Gerry Gaeta:* Gerry Gaeta, interview with Jim Dwyer, August 2003.
16 *Down the hall, Nicole De Martini:* Nicole De Martini, interview by Jim Dwyer, August 2003.
17 *A window washer named Jan Demczur:* Jan Demczur, interview by Jim Dwyer, October 4, 2001.
18 *In fact, its lower wing cut the ceiling:* NIST, "Progress Report on the Federal Building and Fire Safety Investigation of the WTC Disaster," June 2004, Gaithersburg, Md., p. 5.
18 *Aviles worked for the Port Authority:* Ezra Aviles, transcript of voice mail, Port Authority of New York and New Jersey, September 11, 2001.
18 *Then he phoned his wife:* Mildred Aviles, interview by Jim Dwyer, April 2002.
18 *In the police bureau:* Reiss, interview.
20 *Flight 11 had hit 1 World Trade Center:* NIST, "Progress Report," p. 5.
20 *The plane itself was fractionalized:* Federal Emergency Management Agency (hereafter FEMA), *World Trade Center Building Performance Study*, May 2002, pp. 2–30.
20 *The impact registered:* From the website of Lamont-Doherty Earth Observatory of Columbia University, report on the World Trade Center disaster, noted at http:// www.ldeo.columbia.edu/LCSN/Eq/20010911_wtc.html.

Chapter 2: "It's going to be the top story of the day."
Page

21 *The 1993 bombing:* Jim Dwyer, David Kocieniewski, Dee Murphy, Peg Tyre, *Two Seconds under the World: Terror Comes to America* (New York: Crown Publishers, 1994).

22 . . . *a company that handled $200 billion a day:* Garban ICAP website, www.icap.com.

22 *Sheehan ran Nemeth down:* Michael Sheehan, interview by Jim Dwyer, December 5, 2003.

23 *He left a voice-mail message:* Tape of voice mails provided by Beverly Eckert, April 2002.

24 *Richard Fern neither heard nor saw:* Richard Fern e-mail to Eric Lipton, May 2002.

24 *On the trading floor:* Patricia Emerson, interview by Jim Dwyer, December 26, 2003.

24 *The place was crammed:* Pictures of the Euro Brokers office at 2 WTC posted at www.ebi.com.

25 *Mardovich and nine others:* Emerson, interview.

25 *More fire wardens appeared:* Brian Clark interview by Jim Dwyer, August 5, 2004; interview by Eric Lipton, May 2002.

25 *These wardens, like Jose Marrero:* Mike Hurley, fire-safety director, World Trade Center, interview by Jim Dwyer, April 10, 2002.

25 *After fires in two new skyscrapers:* Comments on proposed building code revisions by O'Hagan in 1966 to the 1968 code were provided by Tom Lally, who oversaw building code issues for the Fire Department. O'Hagan served simultaneously in the 1970s as both the fire commissioner, a position appointed by the mayor, and as chief of department, a civil service title.

25 *But when it came to complying:* Michael Goodwin, "Trade Center Getting Sprinklers at $45 Million Cost; Only One Major Fire; Noncompliance Is Rampant," *New York Times,* March 13, 1981, p. A1.

26 . . . *the fitful role fire-safety issues:* Mike Hurley, interview by Jim Dwyer and Kevin Flynn, February 2004.

26 *A private contractor:* Graham Rayman, "Sky Lobby Questions; Could Safety Officers Have Helped Towers' Evacuation?" *Newsday,* April 11, 2002, p. A4.

27 *Instead he contacted his counterpart:* Port Authority of New York and New Jersey, transcript, World Trade Center, Channel 17, September 11, 2001.

27 *The messages had been delivered:* Michael Otten, interview by Lauren Wolfe for the authors, December 11, 2003.

28 *For Stephen Miller:* Stephen Miller, interview by Lauren Wolfe for the authors, December 8, 2003.

29   *Perhaps more important:* Otten, interview.

30   *Joined by a group:* Katrina Brooker, "Starting Over," *Fortune,* January 21, 2002, p. 50.

30   *They began operations:* Christian Murray, "To Honor Those Who Have Died," *Newsday,* September 8, 2003, p. F6.

30   *On the morning of September 11:* Gorsuch account from Murray, "To Honor Those Who Have Died"; yachts, description of Sandler, from Brooker, "Starting Over."

31   *But one of his partners:* Brooker, "Starting Over."

31   *Nearly 200 feet below:* John Duffy and Mary S. Schaeffer, *Triumph over Tragedy* (New York: John Wiley & Sons, 2002), pp. 5–38, 132.

32   *The board of KBW:* Duffy and Schaeffer, p. 36.

32   *A veteran of the 1993 bombing:* Linda Perry Thorpe, interview by Jim Dwyer, May 2002.

32   *Vadas had just called:* Kris McFerren, interview by Ford Fessenden, May 2002.

33   *Will De Riso, a salesman:* "Former ND Athlete Sprints down Tower," *South Bend Tribune,* September 13, 2001.

33   *Two women from the information technology:* Duffy and Schaeffer, p. 62.

33   *He heard other traders:* Duffy and Schaeffer, p. 54.

33   *Bradley Fetchet, a twenty-four-year-old:* Audio tape played at the 9/11 Commission hearings on March 31, 2003.

33   *Of the eight Mulderry children:* Peter Mulderry, interview by Jim Dwyer, May 2003.

Chapter 3: "Mom, I'm not calling to chat."
Page

36   *Gerry Wertz, a purchasing manager:* Gerry Wertz, interview by Joseph Plambeck, June 3, 2004.

36   *The worker in McQuaid's crew:* Mike McQuaid, interview by Ford Fessenden, May 2002.

36   *Eugene heard his brother put down the phone:* Eugene Meehan, interview by Jim Dwyer, October 2001.

37   *Garth Feeney did not work in the trade center:* Judy Feeney, interview by Kevin Flynn, April 2002.

37   *Actually, the restaurant was well above:* NIST, "Visual Data Collection and Analysis," December 2, 2003.

37   *Doris Eng, who had spent the first part of the morning:* Lisa DePaulo, "The Last Day of Windows," *Talk,* December 2001.

37   *. . . emerging in billowing, ghastly clouds:* NIST, "Progress Report on the Federal Building and Fire Safety Investigation of the WTC Disaster," June 2004, Gaithersburg, Md., p. 29.

25

38   *During the first ten minutes after the crash:* NYPD statistic, hearing of Federal Communications Commission, November 16, 2001, Brooklyn, N.Y.

38   *Officer Steve Maggett answered one of the lines:* Transcript of phone conversation, Port Authority Police Department, September 11, 2001.

40   *The wind load on an ordinary day:* Thomas Eagar and Christopher Musso, "Why Did the World Trade Center Collapse? Science, Engineer and Speculation," *JOM*, 53 (12) (2001): 8–11.

40   *In the instant after the plane struck:* James Glanz, "In Collapsing Towers, a Cascade of Failures," *New York Times*, November 11, 2001.

40   *It looked as if the structural engineers:* Leslie E. Robertson, interviews by Jim Dwyer, February 28, 1993; March 1994; see also, James Glanz and Eric Lipton, *City in the Sky* (New York: Times Books/Henry Holt, 2003).

40   *So they did what humans do:* Jim Dwyer, Eric Lipton, Kevin Flynn, James Glanz, Ford Fessenden, "Fighting to Live as the Towers Died," *New York Times*, May 26, 2002. A comprehensive survey by the *Times* of post-impact communications from the two towers found that while hundreds of people probably died on the 15 floors impacted in the towers (94 through 99 in the north tower, and 77 through 85 in the south), that was less than half the area where people were trapped, which included the top 19 floors of the north tower and the top 33 of the south tower. Virtually all 658 employees of Cantor Fitzgerald who died survived the initial impact, as did 69 people in Carr Futures; 66 in Sandler O'Neill; and many of the 176 who died from Aon.

41   *A friend of Kelly's:* Colleen Kelly and Maureen Donegan, interviews by Kevin Flynn, April 2002.

41   *Alderman heard from a colleague:* Copies of e-mail provided by Liz Alderman.

41   *Greg Trevor, an authority spokesman:* Trevor detailed his experience in a written account provided to the authors.

42   *At a stairway landing:* Details of Beyea's and Zelmanowitz's relationship and their movements that day are based on interviews by Kevin Flynn and Lauren Wolfe with Beyea's nurse, Irma Fuller, and his mother, Janet Beyea; Zelmanowitz's brother, Jack Zelmanowitz; Beyea's wife, Paulinita; several rescuers who saw them that day, including Fire Capt. Jay Jonas and firefighter Rich Billy, Port Authority police officer David Lion; civilians in the building, including Keith Meerholz and Patricia Cullen.

Chapter 4: "We have no communication established up there yet."

Page

45 *In the lobby of the north tower:* Lloyd Thompson, interview by Ian Urbina, *New York Times,* May 2004.

45 *His message went nowhere:* Timing and futility of the evacuation order over the public-address system is a finding of the National 9/11 Commission, Statement 13, May 2004.

46 *Even the simplest advice:* Jim Dwyer, Eric Lipton, Kevin Flynn, James Glanz, Ford Fessenden, "Fighting to Live as the Towers Died," *New York Times,* May 26, 2002.

46 *Several blocks away at the Court Officers Academy:* Joseph Baccellieri, interviews by Kevin Flynn, May 2002 and November 2003.

47 *The fireball of exploding jet fuel:* National 9/11 Commission, Statement 13.

47 *He had heard Flight 11 screeching:* Jules Naudet, video footage.

48 *His first message began at 8:46:43:* Time of Pfeifer transmission from Manhattan dispatch tape 432, September 11, 2001, job 1-44. Time of impact from National Institute of Standards and Technology, "December 2003: Public Update on the Federal Building and Fire Safety Investigation of the World Trade Center Disaster," Special Publication 1000-4, p. 13.

48 *Ninety seconds after the plane struck:* Manhattan dispatch tape.

48 *The brothers had become regulars:* Jonathan Storm, "Surprise Witness," *Philadelphia Inquirer,* March 10, 2002.

48 *The routine made for hearty fellowship:* CBS TV documentary, *9/11,* March 10, 2002.

49 *More than 225 fire units would go:* McKinsey and FDNY statistic, McKinsey Report, August 2002.

49 *In the brave, pell-mell rush:* Deputy Fire Commissioner Stephen Gregory, testimony to Federal Communications Commission, November 16, 2001.

49 *Among them were seventeen rookies:* from www.ChristianRegenhard.com.

49 *They were both low-key commanders:* Details of the brothers' lives were reported in "Portraits of Grief," by Jim Dwyer, *New York Times,* November 25, 2001, and in "'He Was a Quiet Guy Who Made a Difference,'" by Jennifer Smith, *Newsday,* November 18, 2001.

49 *Kevin didn't say much in reply:* Joseph Pfeifer account to *Firehouse,* April 2002.

50 *They could not handle what confronted them:* Deputy Chief Albert Turi, chief of safety, FDNY, interview by Kevin Flynn, May 2002.

50   *Each hose could shoot 250 gallons:* Deputy Chief Vincent Dunn (ret.), interview by Kevin Flynn, January 2002.

50   *So the three chiefs in charge:* Chief Joseph Callan, Fire Department of New York, oral history, November 2, 2001.

50   *Still others were assigned floors:* The operational details for the first few minutes were derived from several interviews with Pfeifer and Deputy Chief Peter Hayden, including those published by *Firehouse* magazine, April 2002, and conducted by the FDNY, as well as their statements as captured in footage shot by the Naudet brothers.

51   *Among the most experienced chiefs:* Donald J. Burns, "Operations in Tower 1," *The World Trade Center Bombing: Report and Analysis, United States Fire Administration,* 1994.

51   *With the guests herded onto the lower floor:* Owners and managers of the restaurant, including David Emil and Glenn Vogt, interviews by Kevin Flynn, April 2002.

52   *People farther away were to leave:* Port Authority of New York and New Jersey, *Fire Safety Plan for the World Trade Center,* New York, 1997.

52   *The operators for the 911 system:* National 9/11 Commission, Statement 13.

52   *Ivhan Carpio, a worker at the restaurant:* Andrew Jacobs, "Things Were Going So Well," *New York Times,* September 26, 2001, and Dwyer, Lipton, Flynn, Glanz, Fessenden, *New York Times,* May 26, 2002.

52   *Christine Olender now called the police desk:* Port Authority police transcript, September 11, 2001.

53   *The console at the fire command desk:* Oral histories, New York Fire Department, October–December 2001.

53   *Few departments equal the rigor of New York City's:* A Naval War College study, conducted two months after September 11, 2001, concluded: "As a function of command and control, it was evident that the Fire Department has no formal system to evaluate problems or develop plans for multiple complex events. It was equally evident that the Fire Department has conducted very little formal planning at the operational level." Cited in "Fatal Confusion: A Troubled Emergency Response; 9/11 Exposed Deadly Flaws in Rescue Plan," *New York Times,* July 7, 2002, p. 1.

53   *Though the FDNY rarely lacked for resources:* Citizens Budget Commission, "Financial and Service Indicators, 1990–2002," available at www.cbcny.org, shows that expenditures for the Fire Department increased from $858.6 million in fiscal 1992 to $1.1 billion in fiscal 2002. In constant 2002 dollars, this represented an increase

of 29 percent, or $253 million. The numbers of fires in the city declined by 46 percent during that period, from 100,429 to 54,327.

54 *The New York Police Department had figured this out:* Testimony of Chief Ari Wax of the NYPD to the Federal Communication Commission, November 16, 2001.

55 *. . . where buildings seldom topped six stories:* Chief Vincent Dunn and Fire Chief Nicholas Visconti (ret.), interviews by Kevin Flynn, 2002.

55 *. . . a department that resisted technological change:* One of those who acknowledged that the agency has not always embraced change was Office of Emergency Management commissioner Richard Sheirer, a former FDNY dispatcher.

55 *. . . Fire Department had also issued new handheld radios:* This synopsis of the FDNY history of using portable radios was derived from interviews with Motorola officials and with retired Chief Vincent Dunn, by Kevin Flynn, January 2002; and from Chief John T. O'Hagan, *High-Rise/Fire & Life Safety* (Saddle Brook, N.J.: Pennwell Publications, 1977).

56 *. . . the new radios were pulled from service:* This debate ended when the new digital radios, reprogrammed to work in the more familiar analog mode, were redistributed to firefighters in 2003 and did not generate significant complaints.

56 *It had been tested only a few months earlier:* Synopsis of communication improvements to WTC are based on interviews with Alan Reiss, a PA official, by Jim Dwyer, in 2002, and FDNY records of radio tests within the buildings.

56 *. . . police officers summoned at 8:56:* McKinsey and Company report to NYPD, 2002, provides chronology for dispatch of officers to the scene.

56 *. . . about 1,000 officers would be responding:* Deployment total from 9/11 Commission, Statement 13.

57 *Some teams did check in:* 9/11 Commission, Statement 13.

57 *They did not bicker:* In May 2004, a staff report from the 9/11 Commission stated that police and fire commanders did not coordinate their activities. In an interview with the *New York Times*, published July 7, 2002, Fire Commissioner Thomas Von Essen stated, "That day, the police did not hook up with the Fire Department. I don't know why." Former police commissioner Bernard Kerik, however, testified at a 9/11 Commission hearing that he saw a police sergeant serving as a liaison to the fire command post. No witnesses corroborate Kerik's account. The sergeant is dead and no fire officer, including those at the command post, say that they saw

any coordination between the departments. An hour after the first plane hit, one police commander, Chief Thomas Purtell of the Emergency Service Unit, did try to make his way to the fire command post, according to an oral history by his aide, but the south tower collapsed before the chief could get there.

57 *No one from the Fire Department:* The account is based on interviews with NYPD and FDNY officials, including commanders who were at the scene and pilots who flew that day, and conclusions reached by McKinsey and Company in its studies for New York City.

58 *... the group was disbanded in 1994:* Communication from Michael Rogovin, former deputy counsel to Queens borough president, and representative of the Aviation Emergency Preparedness Group.

58 *... though none that involved an airliner:* Testimony, Richard Sheirer, former commissioner of OEM, 9/11 Commission, May 2004.

59 *... Guy Tozzoli told a legislative hearing:* Graham Rayman, "Crash Scenario Foretold in '93; WTC Official Wanted Plan for Jet Disaster," *New York Newsday,* November 12, 2001, p. 6. In his 1993 testimony before a state legislative committee, Guy Tozzoli referred to a replicated plane disaster staged in the 1970s. The authors could not find newspaper accounts of such a drill. However, there was a drill similar to the one he described in November 1982.

59 *... the city did not organize a single joint drill:* Interviews with Office of Emergency Management director Richard Sheirer; Port Authority deputy police chief Anthony Whitaker; World Trade Center fire director Michael Hurley; Fire Department deputy commissioner Frank Gribbon, by Jim Dwyer and Kevin Flynn, January–June 2002.

60 *... it served as an occasional backdrop for Giuliani's meetings:* Dan Janison, "Mayor's Snow Time/Rudy Uses City's Emergency Center to Show His Command," *New York Newsday,* February 19, 2000, p. A3.

60 *... dozens of these radios had been distributed:* Battalion Chief Charles Blaich, interview by Kevin Flynn, June 2002; testimony by Jerome Hauer, former director of the Office of Emergency Management, 9/11 Commission, May 19, 2004.

60 *... but the talks had broken down:* Interviews by Kevin Flynn, with officials involved in the negotiations.

60 *Thompson began fiddling with something:* Jules Naudet, video footage.

61 *But before being used:* Chief Joseph Pfeifer, interview by Kevin Flynn, May 2004.

61 *Palmer could not hear Pfeifer:* Pfeifer and Palmer remarks were captured on an audio tape of Channel 7 that was later recovered from the rubble.

61   ... *Orio Palmer was among the most knowledgeable:* Article Palmer
      wrote for the FDNY newsletter gives Palmer's educational credentials.
61   *It did not seem to work, either:* Account of developing radio recep-
      tion problems is based on oral histories provided by firefighters
      and chiefs, Joseph Pfeifer account to *Firehouse,* transcripts of fire
      radio transmissions, the tape of Channel 7, and transcripts of Port
      Authority radio transmissions.
62   ... *losing touch with the ascending companies:* Jules Naudet, video
      footage.
62   *If there was an answer:* Chief Callan's oral history interview with
      FDNY, November 2, 2001.

Chapter 5: "Should we be staying here, or should we evacuate?"

Page

63   *Stanley Praimnath and seventeen others:* Stanley Praimnath, inter-
      views by Eric Lipton, April 2002, and by Jim Dwyer, August 2004.
64   *All the technical literature on high-rise fires:* Fire Department, City of
      New York, *Firefighting Procedures, Volume 1, Book 5,* January 1, 1997.
      Paradoxically, fire scientists who have studied human behavior in
      fire report that panic very rarely occurs, and that it is far more com-
      mon for large groups to conduct an orderly self-evacuation. Inter-
      views with Guylene Proulx and Jake Pauls, 2004.
65   ... *only people on the same floor as the fire:* Glenn Corbett, profes-
      sor of fire science, John Jay College, testimony before 9/11 Com-
      mission, November 19, 2003.
65   *The Port Authority had adopted this strategy:* Port Authority of New
      York and New Jersey, *World Trade Center Fire Safety Plan,* 1995.
65   ... *stairways actually could be made narrower:* Steve Berry, Mitchell
      Landsberg, and Doug Smith, "A New View of High-Rise Firefight-
      ing," *Los Angeles Times,* September 24, 2001, p. 6.
66   ... *the Port Authority's promotional literature:* Port Authority of
      New York and New Jersey, *The World Trade Center: A Building Proj-
      ect Like No Other,* February 1990.
67   ... *refused to vouch for the floors to withstand fire:* NIST, Interim
      Report, May 2003, p. 20.
67   *The Port Authority has no records:* In May 1963, Malcom Levy, chief
      of the planning division for the world trade department of the Port
      Authority, instructed the architect to comply with the New York
      City Building Code. NIST, Interim Report, May 2003, p. 60. In
      1969, the architect would protest that Levy had rendered some of
      its specifications "meaningless" by lessening the fireproofing require-
      ments. Also James Glanz and Eric Lipton, *City in the Sky* (New
      York: Times Books/Henry Holt, 2003).

67   *... the fire rating of the floor system could not be determined:* NIST, Interim Report, May 2003, p. 20.

67   *The fire damaged portions of the ninth through sixteenth floors:* John T. O'Hagan, *High-Rise/Fire & Life Safety* (Saddle Brook, N.J.: Pennwell Publications, 1977), p. 43.

68   *Also in 1969, an architect from Emery Roth noted:* NIST Interim Report, May 2003, p. 70.

68   *... the Port Authority refused to permit natural gas lines:* Frank Lombardi, chief engineer, Port Authority of New York and New Jersey, interview by Jim Dwyer, February 9, 2004.

68   *... had to cook using electricity:* Charles Maikish, interview by Jim Dwyer, March 1994.

69   *The Port Authority would pick up the cost:* Lombardi, interview.

69   *To one officer, who understood that the trouble:* Brady conversations are from Port Authority of New York and New Jersey, World Trade Center, Channel 8, September 11, 2001. Maggett conversations are from Channel 9.

72   *... heard a familiar voice:* Brian Clark, testimony before 9/11 Commission, Statement 13, May 2004; interview by Jim Dwyer, August 5, 2004. No recording of this announcement has been located, but the accounts of multiple witnesses are consistent on the gist of it.

72   *The announcement most likely was made:* Michael Hurley, fire-safety director, World Trade Center, interview by Jim Dwyer and Kevin Flynn, February 2004.

73   *... did not know about the hijacking of Flight 11:* Port Authority of New York and New Jersey, transcripts of La Guardia tower, September 11, 2001.

75   *She was among the forces that began driving people:* Jack Gentul, interview by James Glanz, April 26, 2002.

76   *Hutton counted about ten people:* Steve Bates, "Above and Beyond: An HR Director's 'Sense of Duty' Saved Co-workers' Lives at the World Trade Center," *HRMagazine*, December 1, 2001.

76   *Ed Emery, another of the voices shepherding:* Stephanie Koskuba, interview by James Glanz, April 28, 2002.

76   *The Fiduciary group looked to Emery:* Koskuba, Anne Foodim, interviews.

76   *Stephanie Koskuba turned to look for Emery:* Koskuba, interview.

77   *... he would meet up with Alayne Gentul:* Jack Gentul, interview.

77   *Marissa Panigrosso and Sarah Dechalus:* Marissa Panigrosso and Sarah Dechalus, interviews by Joseph Plambeck, June 4, 2004; Eric Lipton, April 2002.

77 *She also met Tamitha Freeman:* Phil Reisman, *The Journal News* (Westchester County, N.Y.), September 10, 2002.

77 *She pondered for a couple of minutes:* Dechalus, interview.

77 *She turned back upstairs:* Marissa Panigrosso, interview.

77 *Her elevator, which could hold fifty-five people:* Dechalus and Panigrosso, interviews.

78 *It was, after all, their complex:* The Port Authority, which had built the center, existed to improve trade in the region, and was controlled by the governors of New York and New Jersey. The agency's police department had a broad portfolio: the New York airports, among the busiest in the world, the ports in New Jersey and New York, and of course the trade center. Even though the Port Authority had turned over the operation of the trade center to a private real estate concern a few weeks earlier, the agreement called for the PAPD to continue providing security there.

78 *... Capt. Anthony Whitaker, the commander:* Anthony Whitaker, interview by Jim Dwyer, May 2002.

78 *A moment after DeVona issued his order:* Excerpts from transcript made by the Port Authority of Channel 26, Channel W, PAPD.

79 *... Charles Maikish, then the director of the trade center:* Jim Dwyer, David Kocieniewski, Dee Murphy, and Peg Tyre, *Two Seconds under the World* (New York: Crown Publishers, 1994), pp. 61–62.

79 *... Michael Hurley caught the attention of Chief Pfeifer:* Pfeifer, Hurley, interviews by Kevin Flynn and Jim Dwyer, May 2004.

Chapter 6: "Get away from the door!"
Page

80 *The jet fuel probably was spent within a few minutes:* FEMA, *World Trade Center Building Performance Study,* pp. 2–21.

81 *His nephew had moved the company: Der Spiegel,* reporters and editors, *Inside 9-11—What Really Happened* (New York: St. Martin's Press, 2001).

81 *Damian Meehan, a half century younger than Cava:* Eugene Meehan, interview by Jim Dwyer, October 2001.

83 *Where the elevators had been were now gaping holes:* Mak Hanna, Gerry Gaeta, interviews by Jim Dwyer, August 25, 2003.

83 *... the man who had just wheeled cartons of documents:* Hanna, interview.

83 *A few others stood with Elaine Duch:* Joanne Ciccolello, affidavit, June 14, 2002.

83 *... this exchange was taped:* Transcript, Port Authority Channel 25, Radio Channel B, Electrical and Mechanical.

84   . . . *De Martini's eyes were red:* Anita Serpe, affidavit, June 14, 2002.

84   *"Okay, I found a stairway":* Dorene Smith, e-mail to Nicole De Martini, May 20, 2002.

84   *Judith Reese, accompanied by Jeff Gertler:* Hanna, interview.

85   *The stairway below was fine, Gaeta yelled:* Gaeta, interview.

85   *Between twenty-five and forty people:* Estimates based on interviews with eight people who were on the floor. No precise head count was possible.

85   *Walter Pilipiak, the company's president:* Walter Pilipiak, interview by Jim Dwyer, August 2003.

86   *Stephanie Manning from MetLife hung up:* Rob Sibarium, interview by Jim Dwyer, April 2002.

86   *Ridiculous, he thought:* Rick Bryan, interview by Jim Dwyer, August 26, 2003.

86   . . . *Bryan stood with his fire extinguisher:* Sibarium, interview.

87   *Suddenly, a muffled voice called out:* Nathan Goldwasser, interview by Jim Dwyer, August 27, 2003.

87   *Pablo Ortiz pushed the door open:* Some of the people rescued from the 89th floor believed that De Martini was the one to open the door, but Mak Hanna, a friend of De Martini's, said that Pablo Ortiz actually pried open the door. De Martini stood with Hanna a few steps away.

87   *Ortiz walked to the law office:* Dianne DeFontes, interview by Jim Dwyer, August 25, 2003.

87   *He thought he saw them continue up:* Pilipiak, interview.

87   *Anne Prosser had gotten to her office:* Anne Prosser interview, by Sherri Day, September 11, 2001; also Anne Paine and Adriane Jaeckle, "Nashville Native Makes Long Descent to Ground," *The Tennessean,* September 12, 2001.

87   *On the 86th floor, Louis Lesce:* Louis Lesce, interview by Jim Dwyer, April 2002.

Chapter 7: "If the conditions warrant on your floor, you may wish to start an orderly evacuation."

Page

89   *Now a different message was being broadcast:* Tape of voice mail provided by Beverly Eckert; digital audio enhancement by Paul Ginsberg, Professional Audio Labs, Spring Valley, New York.

90   *Scott Johnson, an analyst at Keefe, Bruyette & Woods:* Voice mail recording provided by Ann Johnson, enhanced by Paul Ginsberg, Professional Audio Laboratories.

91   *The realization slammed into his mind:* Michael Sheehan, interview by Jim Dwyer, November 2003. The itinerary, as it turned out, was

not for either of the planes that crashed into the towers, but for a USAir flight to Los Angeles. Sheehan suggested it could have been blown off a desk as easily as fallen from one of the jets.

91   *At the south tower's 44th-floor sky lobby, Michael Otten:* Michael Otten, interview by Lauren Wolfe for the authors, December 12, 2003.

91   *A big group from the New York State Department of Taxation:* Ling Young, interview by Jim Dwyer, August 2, 2002.

92   *. . . Cowan pushed the button for the 97th floor:* Donovan Cowan, interview by Ford Fessenden, May 2002.

92   *Silvion Ramsundar and Christine Sasser:* Christine Sasser, interview by Eric Lipton, April 2002.

92   *Howard Kestenbaum, another Aon colleague:* Judy Wein, interview by Eric Lipton, April 2002; interview by Jim Dwyer, August 2, 2002.

93   *He dived under his desk, screaming:* Stanley Praimnath, video statement and testimony before 9/11 Commission, May 2004; interview by Eric Lipton, May 2002.

93   *The time was 9:02:59 A.M.:* The times used here for both plane crashes are those established by the NIST, which based its readings on the moment power was lost to television broadcasters working on the top floor of the north tower. The NIST times are five seconds later than those established through seismographic records at the Columbia Lamont-Doherty Station in Palisades, New York. From the seismographic time, the moment of impact was calculated based on how long it should have taken the waves from the impacts to travel twenty-two miles to the station. The NIST times, while lacking the elegant arithmetical acrobatics, have the virtue of being directly fixed by the moment the broadcasters lost power.

93   *. . . across nine floors, from 77 through 85:* NIST, Interim Report, December 2003, p. 14.

93   *The wing of the jet was jammed into a door:* Praimnath testimony, 9/11 Commission, May 2004; interview.

95   *It was filled with people:* Michael Otten, interview by Lauren Wolfe, December 11, 2002.

95   *The plane's speed was 545 miles per hour:* The speed of both airplanes is given in the interim report of NIST, June 2004.

95   *Donovan Cowan, one finger poised at the button:* Cowan, interview.

95   *. . . anothter twenty people were alive:* Wein, interviews.

96   *Reyher crawled across them:* Reyher account is drawn from the interview by Eric Lipton, April 2002, and Dennis Cauchan and Martha Moore, "Inches Decide Life, Death on 78th Floor," *USA Today*, September 3, 2002.

96   *Ling Young, who worked in the state tax department:* Young, interview.

96   *A sixth colleague, Mary Jos, had been knocked cold:* Mary Jos, interview by Ford Fessenden, April 2002.

96   *Ed Nicholls, thrown to the ground, saw a fire:* Ed Nicholls, interview by Jim Dwyer, August 2, 2002.

97   *. . . Michael Sheehan had been gazing at the airline itinerary:* Sheehan, interview.

97   *On the 81st floor, where part of the wing was lodged in the doorway:* Praimnath, interview.

99   *They retreated to the stairs and began to head down:* Brian Clark, interview by Eric Lipton, May 2002; interview by Jim Dwyer, August 4, 2004.

99   *Above them, Ron DiFrancesco had caught up:* Ron DiFrancesco, interview by Eric Lipton, May 2002.

Chapter 8: "You can't go this way."
Page

101   *Now that he was in the stairs, nothing would slow him:* Richard Fern, e-mail, September 2001, provided by Mr. Fern.

101   *Fern would navigate this line down the next 1,512 steps:* E-mail correspondence with Alan Reiss, January 15, 2004. There were nine steps per flight, two flights per story, with occasional deviations from this pattern as the staircase neared the lobby.

102   *Puma spoke to a reporter:* Conversations with James Gartenberg and Patricia Puma, by Jim Dwyer, September 11, 2001.

103   *"The time and place to ensure life safety in high-rise buildings":* Chief John T. O'Hagan, *High-Rise/Fire & Life Safety* (Saddle Brook, N.J.: Pennwell Publications, 1977), p. 243.

104   *The first plans for the trade center:* James Glanz and Eric Lipton, *City in the Sky* (New York: Times Books/ Henry Holt, 2003).

104   *. . . the trade center would be built according to the city code:* Richard Bulowski, "Analysis of Building and Fire Codes and Practices" (presented at meeting of National Institute of Standards and Technology, December 2, 2003), minutes of meeting.

105   *. . . The New York Times* noted that the trade center was an example: Glenn Fowler, "Broad Revisions of Building Code Proposed to City," *New York Times,* July 9, 1965, p. 1.

105   *. . . it would make the trade center much cheaper to build:* Ada Louise Huxtable, "A Code for the 20th Century," and editorial, "A City Is for Building," *New York Times,* July 9, 1965, p. 12.

106   *"The proposed code more accurately evaluates the hazards":* Harold Birns, address to the Board of Governors, New York Building Congress, January 28, 1965.

106 *An article in the* Times *took note of the flexibility:* Glenn Fowler, p. 1.

106 *. . . the new code significantly lowered the requirements:* H. S. Lew, Richard Bukowski, Nick Carino, Dat Duthinh, "Analysis of Building and Fire Codes and Practices," National Institute of Standards and Technology, December 3, 2003.

106 *. . . it forced buildings to be far sturdier and heavier than needed:* Dudley Dalton, "Savings Expected in Building Code," *New York Times,* March 15, 1964.

107 *"After fighting high-rise fires in midtown Manhattan":* Vincent Dunn, "Why Can't the Fire Service Extinguish Fires in High-Rise Buildings?," *Fire Engineering* magazine, December 1995.

107 *"The antiquated towers of commerce will fail":* Joseph P. Fried, "Building Code Expected to Spur Change in City's Appearance and Dimensions," *New York Times,* October 27, 1968, p. R1.

107 *That was worth about $1.8 million annually in 1968:* "Low Sees Savings under New Code," *New York Times,* October 20, 1968, p. 64. The Pan Am building, just north of Grand Central, later was renamed the MetLife building after the airline fell on hard times.

107 *The previous generation of skyscrapers:* New York City 1938 Building Code.

108 *The image of young girls, leaping to their death:* David Von Drehle, *Triangle: The Fire That Changed America* (New York: Atlantic Monthly Press, 2003).

108 *In January 1912, the Equitable Building:* Chief John T. O'Hagan, *High-Rise/Fire & Life Safety* (Saddle Brook, N.J.: Pennwell, 1977).

108 *The* Titanic *had space in its lifeboats for fewer than half:* Michael Davie, *Titanic: The Death and Life of a Legend* (New York: Alfred A. Knopf, 1987); Tom Kutz, ed., *The Titanic Disaster Hearings: Official Transcripts of the 1912 Senate Investigation* (New York: Pocket Books, 1988); Walter Lord, *A Night to Remember* (New York: Holt, Rinehart & Winston, 1955).

108 *Not only the fire towers disappeared:* NIST, "Progress Report on the Federal Building and Fire Safety Investigation of the World Trade Center Disaster," June 2004, Gaithersburg, Md., pp. 55–61.

110 *. . . "as remote from the others as is practicable":* NYC Building Code, Subarticle 602.0, effective December 6, 1968.

110 *Although the lifeboats had space only for about half:* Davie, *Titanic.*

110 *That was 21 percent higher than the best yield:* Peter Tyson, "Towers of Innovation," Nova Online, http://www.pbs.org/wgbh/nova/wtc/innovation2.html.

112 *Since then, the Port Authority had spent $2.1 million:* Alan Reiss, testimony before 9/11 Commission, May 18, 2004.

112 *One of these detours ran from the 82nd to the 76th floors:* This was
first reported by Dennis Cauchon and Martha T. Moore in "Machinery Saved People in WTC," *USA Today,* May 17, 2002. It was also
described by Alan Reiss, former director of the world trade department for the Port Authority, in April 2002 and August 2003, in
interviews with Jim Dwyer.

113 *A few floors down, most likely on the 82nd floor:* Richard Fern,
e-mail correspondence with Eric Lipton, April and May 2002. At
first, Fern recalled leaving the stairway at the 78th floor, but later
said he was unsure, and that it might have been higher. Stairway A
shifted at the 82nd floor.

114 *He thought he would collapse:* Fern, e-mail correspondence.

114 *Keating Crown of Aon:* Keating Crown, interview by Eric Lipton,
April 2004.

117 *A 911 operator typed up a summary:* Brian Clark, testimony, contained in 9/11 Commission, "Emergency Preparedness: Staff Statement No. 13"; interview with Jim Dwyer, August 4, 2004.

117 *Brian Clark and Stanley Praimnath departed for the lobby:* New York
Police Department, "SPRINT summary," 911 phone calls, September 11, 2001. (SPRINT is a computer system that logs 911 phone
calls.)

117 *. . . three stairways were not sufficient to accommodate:* Glenn Corbett, testimony before the National Commission on Terrorist
Attacks upon the United States, November 19, 2003.

117 *Chief Donald Burns had noted in a report:* United States Fire Administration, *The World Trade Center Bombing: Report and Analysis,*
1994 report, p. 55.

118 *Nat Alcamo, a fifty-six-year-old former Marine:* the accounts of
descending the stairs from Alcamo, Richard Jacobs, Edgardo Villegas, Robert Radomsky, Sean Pierce, Louis A. Torres, Louis Lesce,
Norma Hessic, Richard Wright, and others are from interviews
conducted on September 11, 2001, by numerous members of the
New York Times staff, including Joseph Treaster, Denise Grady,
Lynda Richardson, Jennifer Steinhauer, Rosalie Radomsky, Jennifer Lee, Felicity Barringer, and Stuart Elliot.

118 *Steven Salovich had been herded off Euro Brokers' 84th floor:* Steven
Salovich, written account provided to Eric Lipton, May 2002.

119 *Terence McCormick, who worked for Kemper:* Terence C. McCormick,
statement submitted to the Smithsonian Institution's Museum of
American History exhibit, "September 11: Bearing Witness to History" (www.americanhistory.si.edu/september11/collection).

120 *Sharon Premoli, an executive with Beast Financial Systems:* Sharon
Premoli, interviews by Kevin Flynn, April 2002, January 2004.

120 *Elaine Duch, who had been burned on the 88th floor:* Gerry Gaeta, interview by Jim Dwyer, August 25, 2003.

122 *Another ailing person from the 88th floor:* Jeff Gertler, interview by Jim Dwyer, January 13, 2004.

123 *John Labriola came down from the 71st floor:* John Labriola, statement submitted to the Smithsonian Institution's Museum of American History exhibit, "September 11: Bearing Witness to History" (www.americanhistory.si.edu/september11/collection).

123 *Theresa Leone, who worked in a law firm:* Theresa Marino Leone, "Rosary Beads and Sensible Shoes," as told to Roy Peter Clark, Poynter Institute, www.poynter.org, September 13, 2001.

123 *Michael Benfante and John Cerquiera:* Michael Benfante and John Cerquiera, interview by Joyce Wadler, September 11, 2001; interview by Jim Dwyer, November 2001.

124 *... Hoey called the Port Authority police desk in Jersey City:* Port Authority radio transcripts, Central Police Desk, Channel 24, September 11, 2001.

Chapter 9: "The doors are locked."
Page

126 *At 9:05 A.M., Peter Mardikian called his wife:* Corine Mardikian, interview by Kevin Flynn, May 2002.

126 *In the south tower, Sean Rooney began climbing:* Information about the trips to the roof collected in interviews by Jim Dwyer and others from the *New York Times* with family members, 2001 and 2002.

127 *Heeran had called his father:* Bernie Heeran, interview by Joseph Plambeck, May 2004.

127 *The rig crawled down the towers along tracks: Engineering News Record,* November 5, 1970.

128 *This order briefly touched off a snit:* James Glanz and Eric Lipton, *City in the Sky* (New York: Times Books/ Henry Holt, 2003), p. 114.

128 *... Camaj had become part of the trade center's folklore:* Biographical information about Roko Camaj compiled from *New York Times* interviews with family and from www.Warnerbros.com.

128 *Los Angeles was one of the few American cities:* Scott Paltrow and Queena Sook Kim, "Could Helicopters Have Saved People from the Top of the Trade Center?" *Wall Street Journal,* October 23, 2001.

128 *In Las Vegas, during the fire at the MGM Grand Hotel:* Glenn Puit, "MGM Grand Fire: The Pilot," *Las Vegas Review-Journal,* November 19, 2000.

129 *... most experts did not view the roof:* Information about firefighting tactics derived from interviews with Chief Vincent Dunn (ret.) in 2004.

129 *Despite the aversion to aerial rescues:* 9/11 Commission staff investigation.

129 *At mandatory fire drills held in the tenant offices:* Information about fire-safety policies at the WTC derived from several interviews, in 2004, with Michael Hurley, the fire-safety director for the complex.

129 *During the Triangle Shirtwaist Factory blaze of 1911:* David Von Drehle, *Triangle: The Fire That Changed America* (New York: Atlantic Monthly Press, 2003).

130 *Bob Mattson, a banker with Fiduciary Trust International:* Elizabeth Mattson, wife of Bob Mattson, interview by Kevin Flynn, January 2004.

130 *This was nothing like 1993:* Greg Semendinger, interviews by Kevin Flynn, December 2003, May 2004.

130 *Semendinger and Ciccone had arrived about 8:54 A.M.:* Helicopter arrival times from NIST, Interim Report, June 2004.

130 *They had barely stopped talking when Hayes spotted United Flight 175:* Tim Hayes, interview on Abcnews.com, November 8, 2001.

131 *They pulled up quickly and the plane shot beneath them:* Police account to *New York Newsday,* September 8, 2002.

131 *Trapped inside one of the offices that February day:* Details of the rescue of Matut-Perina taken from *Newsday* accounts by Duggan, February 11, 2003, and McQueen, February 28, 1993.

132 *She was the first of several dozen people:* The number of people rescued by helicopter after the 1993 bombing remains a matter of some debate. The Police Aviation Unit, which operated the helicopters, said it has no record of the number. The police commander in charge that day has said the number was thirty-five. Port Authority officials have put the number as low as twelve. Emergency Medical Service officials in a 1994 report for the federal government, *The World Trade Center Bombing: Report and Analysis,* said that twenty-eight people needing medical treatment were removed from the two roofs. Interviews with people who participated in the rescues, and were on the rooftops that day suggest that the number was roughly several dozen, split roughly equally between the two towers.

132 *When the commander of the Aviation Unit later recorded the events:* Capt. William Wilkens, commander of the Police Aviation Unit, in an account given to Nycop.com.

133 *. . . Hurley led the shivering throng back down:* Mike Hurley, interview by Kevin Flynn and Jim Dwyer, February 2004.

133 *. . . the New York City Fire Chiefs Association:* William Murphy and Joseph W. Queen, "Derring Don't: Firefighters Blast Towers' Copter Rescue," *New York Newsday,* April 10, 1993, p. 3.

134 *The fire commissioner, Carlos Rivera, said:* William Murphy and Joseph W. Queen, "A Failure to Communicate?" *New York Newsday,* April 11, 1993, p. 46.

134 *There would be joint training runs:* Many of the details of the city's use of helicopters in an emergency were first reported in Paltrow and Kim, *Wall Street Journal,* October 23, 2001.

134 *As Captain Fred Ill of Ladder Company 2:* Jim Dwyer, "More Tapes from 9/11: 'They Have Exits in There?'" *New York Times,* August 17, 2006.

135 . . . *Chief Pfeifer told his aide to write the words:* Chief Joseph Pfeifer, interviews by Kevin Flynn, in April 2004 as well as his oral history and an account he gave to *Firehouse* magazine.

135 *But Pfeifer couldn't find the radio he needed:* Pfeifer, oral history.

135 *He figured that the commanders outside:* Pfeifer, interview.

135 *The police aviation team had been anticipating a call:* Conversations of the pilots were recorded by the Police Department.

135 *At 9:08, he had spoken over the police radio:* NYPD radio transmissions, September 11, 2001.

136 *On the 110th floor, Steve Jacobson:* Allison Gilbert, Phil Hirschkorn, Melinda Murphy, Robyn Walensky, and Mitchell Stephens, eds., *Covering Catastrophe: Broadcast Journalists Report September 11* (Chicago: Bonus Books, 2002).

137 . . . *Richard Smiouskas could see that not everyone:* Richard Smiouskas, oral history to the FDNY, November 27, 2001.

138 *Since most of the space was open:* NIST, fact sheet, "Key Findings of NIST's June 2004 Progress Report," June 18, 2004 (www.wtc.nist.gov).

139 *He did not mention that people were falling:* Jim Dwyer, Eric Lipton, Kevin Flynn, James Glanz, Ford Fessenden, "Fighting to Live as the Towers Died," *New York Times,* May 26, 2002.

140 *But Semendinger held out some hope:* Greg Semendinger, interview.

141 *"Open the goddamn doors":* Port Authority transcript, WTC Channel 25.

141 *Now he couldn't fathom why the doors would not open:* Sean Rooney's account was provided by his wife, Beverly, during several interviews by Kevin Flynn and Jim Dwyer, 2002 to 2004.

141 . . . *the operators typed shorthand versions:* Quotation from the city's 911 dispatch tape.

142 *The Port Authority had decided to lock the doors:* Details of how the roof doors operated came from interviews with Port Authority officials, including Mike Hurley and Alan Reiss.

142 *Marie Refuse, one of the security officers:* Port Authority tapes, Channel 27.

142 ACCESS DENIED, *the screen blared:* Graham Rayman, "Control Center Chaos," *New York Newsday,* September 11, 2002, p. 8.

143 *A deputy security director, George Tabeek, led a team:* Port Authority transcript.

143 *Roko Camaj, the window washer:* Vinny Camaj, interview by Jim Dwyer, May 2002.

143 *Perhaps Camaj and the others had gotten as far as the 110th floor:* The A and C stairways were the ones that carried all the way up to the 110th floor. Stairway B ended at the 107th floor.

143 *Camaj used his radio to call down:* Port Authority transcripts of the conversation.

144 *Most of them were dialing not into the basement command center:* National Commission on Terrorist Attacks upon the United States, *The 9/11 Commission Report* (Washington, D.C., 2004), p. 286.

144 *Frank Doyle and some of the other traders:* Kimmy Chedel, interview by Jim Dwyer, April 2002.

144 *Stephen called Peter again:* This account of the conversation related by Peter Mulderry to Jim Dwyer, May 2002.

144 *A few minutes later, the phone was passed to Rick Thorpe:* Based on accounts given by family members to the *New York Times,* spring 2002.

Chapter 10: "I've got a second wind."
Page

146 *In a riot of sound, Frank De Martini's voice was calm:* Port Authority transcript, Channel X, September 11, 2001, 9:11 A.M.

147 *Drohan was at ground level:* Gerard Drohan, interview by Jim Dwyer, August 22, 2003. There is no transcript of De Martini's radio transmissions; the account here is based on Drohan's recollection.

147 *The drywall had been knocked off parts of the sky lobby:* Greg Trapp, Summit Security guard stationed on the 78th floor, interview by Jim Dwyer, January 14, 2004, and February 8, 2004.

149 *. . . he arranged to ship a 14,000-pound steel brace:* Leslie E. Robertson, interview by Jim Dwyer, March 1994.

149 *. . . when he was interviewed for the History Channel documentary:* "World Trade Center: In Memoriam," The History Channel, 2002.

150 *Fifteen minutes after his first warning, De Martini broadcast:* Port Authority transcript, Radio Channel 25, Y, Maintenance and Electric, September 11, 2001, 9:18 A.M.

151 *Savas loved coming to work, rising at 5:45:* Steven Greenhouse, "Refusing to Retire," *New York Times,* November 9, 2001.

152 *Out came Savas:* Trapp, interview.

153 *The lobby doors shot off their frames:* Alan Reiss, interview by Jim Dwyer, April 30, 2002.

153 *. . . the carrier of devastation:* These circumstances were first and most emphatically documented by Dennis Cauchon and Martha T. Moore in "Elevators Were Disaster within Disaster," *USA Today,* September 11, 2002.

154 *In 1854, Elisha Graves Otis was hoisted by a rope on a platform:* James Glanz and Eric Lipton, *City in the Sky* (New York: Times Books/ Henry Holt, 2003), p. 22.

155 *. . . there were fifteen miles of elevator shafts in the towers:* Cauchon and Moore.

155 *After the 1993 bombing, the United States Fire Administration:* FEMA, *1993 World Trade Center Report,* p. 27.

156 *On the single-file descent, someone teased Demczur:* Jan Demczur, interview by Jim Dwyer, October 6, 2001; Shivam Iyer, George Phoenix, interview by Jim Dwyer, October 8, 2001; John Paczkowski, Al Smith, interviews by Jim Dwyer, December 2001. Mike McQuaid, interview by Ford Fessenden, May 2002.

156 *An instant before Flight 175 hit the south tower:* The most thorough exploration of the elevators on September 11, and the experiences of individuals in them, can be seen in Cauchon and Moore.

157 *Her fall was broken by a beam in the shaft:* John Duffy and Mary S. Schaeffer, *Triumph over Tragedy* (New York: John Wiley & Sons, 2002), p. 13.

158 *PAPD Officer Thomas Grogan—radio transmission:* WTC police transcript, Channel 9, September 11, 2001.

158 *She remembered being hoisted by a "human ladder":* Smith account in Duffy and Schaeffer, p. 68.

158 *Another message went out over the radio:* WTC police transcript, Channel 9, September 11, 2001.

158 *Hoerner summoned James Flores:* James Flores, interview by Jim Dwyer, February 2004.

159 *Flores watched as one of them, a man with powerful arms:* In interview with Dwyer, Flores stated that he saw the firefighter with the pry tool. Later, recovery workers said they found a pry tool at the elevator bank. Smith account.

159 *The elevator mechanics who worked at the trade center:* Cauchon and Moore.

160 *The mechanics planned on reentering:* Port Authority transcript, Radio Channel Z, September 11, 2001.

160 *Mike McQuaid, the electrician, heard the voices:* Mike McQuaid, interview by Ford Fessenden, May 2002.

160 *He sent a radio message to the command center:* Port Authority transcripts, Vertical Transportation Channel, September 11, 2001.

161 *Some people trapped in the cars managed to get calls:* Emergency Medical Services job log, 911 call center, September 11, 2001; call logged at 9:33 A.M.

161 *On the 71st floor of the north tower:* Frank DeMola, interview by Jim Dwyer, October 2003.

162 *DeCosta apparently changed his mind:* Port Authority transcript, WTC Channel 29.

163 *... the Port Authority had installed alarm bells:* Alan Reiss, former director of the world trade department, e-mail correspondence, February 7, 2004.

163 *One of the Port Authority workers turned to the security guard:* Trapp, interview.

163 *After some consultations, the dispatcher came back to Trapp:* Port Authority transcript, Channel 27. In it, Trapp's name is rendered erroneously as Greg Trevor, a Port Authority official who was already leaving the building.

164 *The evidence suggests that Tony Savas:* The remains of Savas and Griffin were discovered in staircases near the bottom of the building.

Chapter 11: "I'm staying with my friend."
Page

166 *... Stephen Miller glimpsed the outside world again:* Stephen Miller, interviews by Lauren Wolfe and Kevin Flynn, December 2003.

166 *One Port Authority officer thought he saw thirteen people jump:* Port Authority police officer Michael Simons, written memo, March 5, 2002.

168 *He felt like clapping his hands, and so he did, rhythmically:* Miller, interview.

170 *The stairwells had twists and turns:* 9/11 Commission study determined that the stairwell arrangement had confused many evacuees because they did not know the configuration.

170 *A windowpane covered in blood:* Recollection of window from Port Authority police officer Roger Fernandez, written memo, January 4, 2002.

170 *Cops at the top of the escalators:* Recollection of panic from Port Authority police officer Anthony L. Croce, written memo, January 28, 2002, and others.

171 *He had pulled up in a Ford Explorer:* NYPD Deputy Inspector Timothy Pearson, interview by Kevin Flynn, March 2004.

171 *Sue Keane, a Port Authority police officer:* Port Authority police officer Sue Keane, written memo, March 4, 2002.

4

171 *Ken Greene, the Port Authority's assistant director of aviation:* Some details of Greene's account were gleaned from an interview he did with CBS News that was broadcast on *48 Hours,* October 19, 2001.

171 *Nelson Chanfrau, a risk manager for the agency:* Sources for the account of Chanfrau's activities that day include written memo of Port Authority inspector Timothy Norris, interview with Jim Dwyer, October 2001.

171 *Perry was an activist and an actor:* Sources for aspects of this account include Pearson interview, an interview with Officer Perry's mother, Patricia, on March 4, 2004, and John Tierney in "A Policeman for Starters, and at the End," *New York Times,* November 16, 2001.

172 *Perry and a few others picked her up:* Details are taken from the Fernandez memo and interview with Pearson.

172 *Instead, many people were directed south:* Details are based on interviews of Rich Fetter, resident manager of the Marriott Hotel, by Jim Dwyer, May 2002.

172 *Most of the seventy-five stores had closed:* The closing of the stores is recounted by Port Authority police officer A. Greenstein, written memo, December 9, 2001. Water recounted by Steven Charest of May Davis Group, interview by Kevin Flynn, March 2004.

173 *These were demolished and turned into corridors:* Alan Reiss, e-mail, May 25, 2004; Reiss testimony before the 9/11 Commission, May 18, 2004.

173 *... five Port Authority police officers, wheeling a canvas laundry cart:* The account of Sergeant McLoughlin's team was taken from *New York Times* interviews of Port Authority police officer Will Jimeno, Port Authority police chief Joseph Morris, and various written memos of police officers, including those of Lt. John Murphy and Sgt. William Ross. Although both Murphy and Ross recall that a Port Authority officer, J. D. Levi, was part of the original group that went with McLoughlin to find the equipment, he somehow was assigned to other duties and Amoroso joined the group instead.

174 *... crowd scurrying in all directions:* Alan Reiss, interview by Jim Dwyer, April 30, 2002.

174 *... Leclaire had to pull them off pay phones:* Port Authority police officer David Leclaire, January 29, 2002.

174 *Sgt. Robert Vargas of the Port Authority police:* Port Authority police Sgt. Robert Vargas, written memo, January 31, 2002.

175 *Firefighter Michael Otten of Ladder 35:* Michael Otten, interview by Lauren Wolfe, December 12, 2003.

175 *Steve Charest, a broker from May Davis:* Charest, interview.

176 *Maffeo always carried tuna to a fire:* Linda Maffeo, interview by Elissa Gootman, *New York Times,* December 2001.

176 *Capt. William Burke Jr. of Engine 21:* Jean Traina, interview by Lauren Wolfe, January 2004.

176 *Sharon Premoli, the financial executive:* Sharon Premoli, interview by Kevin Flynn, March 2004.

176 . . . *reports of firemen having chest pains:* Lt. Gregg Hansson, interview by Ford Fessenden, July 2002.

176 *Engine 9. Squad 18:* Specific citations of the other units that suffered chest pains is listed in an oral history by Capt. Jay Jonas of the Fire Department of New York that was published in the *Times Herald-Record,* September 8, 2003.

176 *At the 19th floor, dozens of exhausted firefighters:* Interview with Capt. Joseph Baccellieri of the Court Officers by Kevin Flynn, July 2002 and 2003. An alternative explanation for the large collection of firefighters on the 19th floor is offered by Dennis Smith, the author and retired firefighter, who notes that a battalion chief had been sent to the 23rd floor to set up a command post, and the firefighters may have used the 19th floor as a mustering point.

177 *On the 31st floor, a dozen firefighters slumped in the hallway:* This account is based on radio transmissions and an interview with David Norman, June 2004.

178 . . . *a firefighter told them to stuff wet rags underneath the doors:* Capt. Joseph Baccellieri, interview.

178 *"No, I'm staying with my friend":* Anthony Giardina, who witnessed the conversation, interview by Kevin Flynn, April 2004.

178 *Now, as he approached 27:* Keith Meerholz, interview by Jim Dwyer, January 2004.

180 *Martin and her fellow passengers had tried pushing the alarm buttons:* Ian Robb, Judith Martin, Mike Jacobs, Chris Young, interviews by Joseph Plambeck, May 2004.

181 *Just before 9:30, a new note of alarm:* The scene in the lobby was reconstructed based on footage shot by Jules and Gedeon Naudet, accounts in the McKinsey Report, and oral history recollections of firefighters and others present, including Chiefs Pfeifer, Hayden, and Callan.

181 *In the skies above the trade center, Greg Semendinger:* Semendinger's words and those of other helicopter radio transmissions are taken from a Police Department transcript of traffic on the channel used by its Special Operations Division.

182 . . . *thousands of planes were still in the air across the country:* Information about the number of flights in the air at the time and the

timing of the shutdown of New York airspace is from an interview with Laura J. Brown, a spokesperson for the FAA.

182 *Air controllers did not realize that at that moment:* Port Authority transcripts, La Guardia Airport channels; Jim Dwyer, "Takeoffs Continued until Second Jet Hit the Trade Center, Transcripts Show," *New York Times,* December 30, 2003.

182 *A strike by a third plane:* Hayden's recollections are contained in his oral history obtained by the *New York Times* and an interview with *Firehouse* magazine, April 2002.

182 *Some police officers who had been preparing to go inside paused:* Ross memo as above, March 6, 2002.

182 *. . . just looked at one another and kept working:* Port Authority police officer A. Greenstein, written memo, December 9, 2001.

182 *. . . cleared out of the lobby, relocating to West Street:* McKinsey Report.

183 *Later, he would cite the order as a mark:* Sheirer's account is based on footage by the Naudet brothers and an interview with Jim Dwyer, March 2002.

183 *No one answered his call:* McKinsey Report states that no one responded to Callan.

Chapter 12: "Tell the chief what you just told me."
Page

185 *Andreacchio had even started downstairs:* Jessica Carucci, niece of Andreacchio, interview by Lauren Wolfe, January 28, 2004. She learned this information at his memorial service.

185 *Now, he was stuck with Manny Gomez:* Carucci, interview. He told her that he was with five people. She spoke with him several minutes before Bramante.

185 *Bramante talked him through the options:* Anthony Bramante, interview by Lauren Wolfe, January 28, 2004.

186 *. . . the city's emergency response program had no mechanism:* Bernard B. Kerik, former police commissioner, testimony before 9/11 Commission, May 18, 2004.

186 *At 9:19, Vadas left a message:* Kris McFerren, interviewed by Ford Fessenden, May 2002.

186 *Mulderry, the former college basketball star:* Peter Mulderry, interview by Jim Dwyer, May 2002.

186 *Five floors above them, Greg Milanowycz:* Joseph Milanowycz, interview by Eric Lipton, April 2002.

187 *At the main post, across West Street:* Thomas Fitzpatrick, FDNY, oral history, October 1, 2001.

Notes

187 *At the same post, Lt. Joseph Chiafari:* Joseph Chiafari, FDNY, oral history, December 3, 2001.

187 *His boss, Deputy Assistant Chief Al Turi, began to think:* Al Turi, oral history, FDNY, October 23, 2001.

188 *In one potentially critical area:* Years after September 11, the precise reason why the firefighters had such trouble communicating by radio that morning remains a matter of significant debate. Much of the debate centers on the performance of the repeater, or amplifier, that was designed to boost the radio signals of the small handheld radios so that firefighters could communicate through the multiple floors of a high-rise. The repeater was operated through a console that looked like a phone set and sat at the fire-command desks in each of the towers. The 9/11 Commission staff reported in May 2004 that the repeater had worked properly but that, in the stress of the morning, fire chiefs mistakenly thought otherwise. The investigators said the chiefs had not noticed that the button that activated the phone handset on the repeater console had not been depressed. The investigators concluded that when the chiefs could not hear through the handset, they mistakenly believed that the equipment itself was not working and prematurely abandoned it. Actually, it was just the handset that had not been turned on, they said. Fire chiefs in the north tower then relied simply on the unaided signal of their small handheld radios to communicate. The chiefs have insisted that the handset button was correctly pushed and that testing in the lobby showed the repeater was not working properly. Lloyd Thompson, one of the fire-safety directors in the north tower lobby that morning, told the commission that he saw that the handset button had been correctly depressed. As of June 2004, investigators had yet to determine who actually activated the repeater that morning or who might have touched any of the buttons. Chief Palmer subsequently decided to use the repeater channel, Channel 7, when he responded to the south tower. It is not clear how he came to realize that the repeater was working, at least partly. He had been one of the chiefs who had initially tested the repeater in the north tower lobby that morning and concluded it was not working. It is clear that at some point when he arrived at the south tower he tuned his radio to Channel 7, the channel amplified by the repeater. A tape recording of his radio transmissions and those of other firefighters over Channel 7 that morning was later recovered from the rubble. None of the transmissions gives a sense of how Palmer came to realize the repeater was working. The recording also does not contain transmissions from many of the other firefighters who were operating in the south tower. Fire officials have said the low

320

number of transmissions is evidence that the repeater did not work properly. Investigators have said the low number is more likely explained by the fact that so few firefighters were told to operate on that channel.

189 *Here, too, Palmer was ready:* Debbie Palmer, interview by Jim Dwyer, January 2004.

190 *Mary Jos crawled across the ground:* Mary Jos, interview by Ford Fessenden, May 2002.

191 *Young had not seen Jos on fire:* Ling Young, interview by Eric Lipton, *New York Times,* April 2002; interview by Jim Dwyer, August 2, 2002.

192 *Despite being battered:* Judy Wein, Ed Nicholls, interviews by Eric Lipton, April 2002; interviews by Jim Dwyer, August 2002.

194 *From the 88th and 89th floors came calls:* 9/11 Commission staff reports, May 2004; interviews with Peter Mulderry, Kimmy Chedel, Kris McFerren, by the *New York Times* staff.

194 *Of the eighty-seven people:* Work figures from Sandler O'Neill.

194 *Around this time, Alayne Gentul:* Jack Gentul, interview by James Glanz, April 2002.

194 *Another Fiduciary employee on the 97th floor:* Marion Biegeleisen, David Langer, Jack Edelstein, interviews by Lauren Wolfe for the authors, December 2003.

195 *Ed McNally, the director of technology for Fiduciary:* Liz McNally, interview by James Glanz, April 2002.

195 *Over the radio, the fire dispatcher:* FDNY response tape, 9:35 A.M. All quotes of firefighters in chapter 12 were taken from this tape.

196 *He quietly lobbied:* Frank Gribbon, FDNY, interview by Jim Dwyer, February 20, 2004.

197 *The director of Morgan Stanley:* James B. Stewart, *Heart of a Soldier: A Story of Love, Heroism, and September 11th* (New York: Simon & Schuster, 2002).

198 *Not far behind them were Judy Wein:* Judy Wein, interview by Jim Dwyer, August 2002.

199 *The firemen looked at them:* Ed Nicholls, interview by Jim Dwyer, August 2002.

200 *Firefighter Tom Kelly struck people:* Biographical details from Maureen Paglia, Dennis Kelly, and Tommy Patchel; interviews by Lauren Wolfe for the authors, December 2003–January 2004.

202 *The city's 911 operation:* Jim Dwyer and Ed Wyatt, "Bloomberg Plans Overhaul of Creaky 911 System," *New York Times,* April 13, 2004, p. A1.

203 *Peruggia summoned an emergency medical technician:* John Peruggia, oral history, FDNY, October 25, 2001.

207 *The 83rd floor appeared to be draped across windows:* NIST, "World Trade Center Investigation Status," December 2003.

207 *Kevin Cosgrove from Aon:* Matthew Walberg, John Keilman, Mickey Ciokajlo, and Ted Gregory, "Small Things Remind of Huge Loss," *Chicago Tribune,* October 15, 2001, p. 10.

207 *The voices from the 105th floor:* New York Police Department, "911 Sprint Run," September 11, 2001. (SPRINT is a computer system that logs 911 phone calls.)

208 *Calling from the 93rd floor:* Marcia De Leon, interviewed by Eric Lipton, May 2002.

208 *On the street, Rich Zarillo had arrived:* Steve Mosiello, oral history, FDNY, October 23, 2001.

208 *After thirty-three years in the Fire Department:* Ganci had been in the Fire Department for thirty-one years when he was named chief.

209 *A few months earlier, Robert Gabriel Martinez:* N. R. Kleinfeld, "A Niche for Helping," *New York Times,* December 31, 2001.

210 *"They're trying":* Transcript, Port Authority Radio Channel 27 (security), September 11, 2001.

210 *At that moment, at the command center:* Steve Mosiello, Albert Turi, FDNY, oral histories, October 23, 2001.

Chapter 13: "We'll come down in a few minutes."
Page

211 *"What was that explosion?":* Arlene Nussbaum, interview by Jim Dwyer, April 2002.

212 *Stockpiled in the south tower:* Steve Ashley, "When the Twin Towers Fell," *Scientific American,* October 9, 2001.

212 *It was so strong, the earth shuddered:* Won-Young Kim, research scientist, Lamont-Doherty Earth Observatory of Columbia University, e-mail, March 24, 2004.

212 *It found Sharon Premoli just as she ascended from the concourse:* Sharon Premoli, interviews by Kevin Flynn, April 2002, January 2004.

213 *Mak Hanna, from Frank De Martini's crew:* Mak Hannah, interview by Jim Dwyer, August 2003; Patricia Cullen, e-mail correspondence, January to February 2004.

214 *By 10:01, two minutes after the south tower:* New York Police Department radio transmissions, Special Operations Division channel, September 11, 2001.

215 *The radio that captured those messages:* Chief Joseph Pfeifer, interview by Kevin Flynn, June 2004.

215 *A moment or two after the shudder:* Steve Modica, interview by Michelle O'Donnell, June 2002; Modica, oral history, undated, fall 2001.

216 *In the middle zone, the building:* Joseph Baccellieri, interview by Kevin Flynn, November 2003.

217 *Warren Smith had fought fires in Manhattan:* Warren Smith, oral history, FDNY, December 4, 2001; in his oral history, Smith puts himself on the 31st floor, but other survivors, including people Smith described, uniformly say they were on the 35th floor, not the 31st.

218 *A moment later:* In Smith's oral history, and in an interview with Hansson, both describe hearing this message through the chief's radio. However, in the film by Jules Naudet broadcast on CBS, Chief Joseph Pfeifer does not use the term "mayday" in giving his evacuation order. It is possible that another chief also issued an evacuation order and did use the term "mayday."

218 *While some firefighters in trouble gave mayday calls:* The National Commission on Terrorist Attacks upon the United States, *The 9/11 Commission Report* (Washington, D.C., 2004); 307.

218 *In any event, Chief Picciotto:* In *Last Man Down*, a bestselling book by Picciotto, he maintains that no one communicated with him from the ground to order an evacuation, with or without a mayday, and that he ordered the evacuation on his own initiative. Other dramatic aspects of his account have been directly challenged by other firefighters, and Picciotto has said in newspaper interviews that he no longer makes one of the central claims of the book—that he directed the rescue of a particular woman.

218 *No one among that group knew the other building:* Warren Smith, oral history.

218 *Robert Byrne, a probationary firefighter:* Robert Byrne, oral history, December 7, 2001.

218 *Hansson and his men went to stairway A:* Gregg Hansson, interview by Ford Fessenden, June 2002.

219 *Billy recognized Captain Burke:* Rich Billy, interview by Michelle O'Donnell for the authors, January 2004.

220 *Forty-six years old, he had worked for twenty-five years:* Constance L. Hays, "Rendered by the Flame," November 11, 2001.

220 *The elevator door was moving as he pushed it:* Chris Young's account is based on interviews with Dennis Cauchon of *USA Today* and ABC News in 2002 and subsequent interviews with Joseph Plambeck, on behalf of the authors, in May and June 2004.

221 *At the collapse of the south tower:* Frank DiMola, interview by Jim Dwyer, January 2004.

221 *Romito's search crew was at least the fourth agency:* National Fire Administration report on 1993 bombing.
222 *Once again, duplicative searches:* Descriptions of multiple sweeps by, among others, PAPD Sgt. Conrad Krueger, memorandum October 1, 2001, which records that he met NYPD ESU officers in tower 1 who wanted to sweep each floor.
222 *The word to leave finally got to Steve Modica:* Steve Modica, interview by Michelle O'Donnell, July 1, 2002.
223 *"About fifteen floors down from the top, it looks like it's glowing red":* NYPD tape, Special Operations Division, September 11, 2001.
223 *For more than eighty minutes:* The Port Authority transcripts show that Hoey was directly told to stay in the office by the Port Authority police desk. The transcripts also show that later, a colleague of someone on the 64th floor called the police from outside the building, seeking information on their behalf; he was told they should evacuate. A spokesman for the Port Authority says that this colleague did convey this instruction to the people on the 64th floor, although the agency would not make the person available for an interview.
224 *They found a door that was open:* Port Authority commendation for Pasquale Buzzelli, 2002.
224 *Hoey called the police desk first:* Port Authority transcripts, sergeant's desk, Central Police Desk, September 11, 2001, 10:12 A.M.
224 *The message to leave spread fitfully:* Smith, oral history.
225 *Then Hansson walked onto the 19th floor:* Gregg Hansson, interview by Ford Fessenden, June 2002.
226 *They could scarcely believe their eyes:* Andrew Wender, interview with Kevin Flynn, June 2002.
226 *Baccallieri and Moscola took in the scene:* Al Moscola, interview with Kevin Flynn, June 2002; Baccellieri, interviews with Kevin Flynn, June 2002, January 2004; Baccellieri, interview with Jim Dwyer, September 2002.
227 *Hayes, in police helicopter Aviation 14:* NYPD Special Operations Division Channel, tape, September 11, 2001.
227 *Fred Ill, the captain of Ladder Company 2:* Jim Dwyer, "More Tapes from 9/11: 'They Have Exits in There?'" *New York Times*, August 17, 2006.

Chapter 14: "You don't understand."
Page
229 *Spent, Reese sat on the stairs:* Jeff Gertler, interview by Jim Dwyer, February 2004.
229 *For much of the morning, the hotel lobby had served:* Rich Fetter, interview by Jim Dwyer, June 2002.

232 *"Sound off!" the sergeant, John McLoughlin:* Will Jimeno, interview by Jim Dwyer, October 29, 2001.

234 *A bolt of fear ran through Cerquiera:* John Cerquiera, interview by Jim Dwyer, November 2001.

234 *John Abruzzo, a quadriplegic:* Port Authority awards citations.

235 *That sounded like madness to Gertler:* Jeff Gertler, interview by Jim Dwyer, January 2004.

235 *Bill Spade, who eventually found two police officers:* Bill Spade, interview by Ford Fessenden, July 2002.

236 *As the two cops, Curtin and D'Allara:* Spade, interview.

238 *Over time, the flames had spread:* Video review of WTC footage by Eric Lipton.

238 *It was 10:26:* Iliana McGinnis, interview by Jim Dwyer, May 2002.

239 *Lucas would remember:* NYPD officer Patrick Lucas, "September 11, 2001," memorandum, December 10, 2001.

239 *Upon meeting this latest crisis:* Gregg Hansson, interview by Ford Fessenden, July 2002, described seeing Kelly with the man.

239 *Hansson and James Hall:* NYPD officer James E. Hall, "Events Occurring during the World Trade Center Attack," memorandum, November 2, 2001.

240 *The building was unstable:* Hall, memorandum, p. 2.

240 *... aluminum skin of the building that seemed to float:* Robert Byrne, oral history, winter 2001.

240 *"It's clear," D'Allara yelled:* Spade, interview.

241 *Jay Jonas, the captain of Ladder 6:* This account is drawn from an interview with Jay Jonas, January 27, 2004, by Lauren Wolfe for the authors; Gerald M. Carbone, "The Miracle of Ladder 6 and Josephine" (four parts), *Providence Journal,* September 11, 2002; and Dennis Smith, *Report from Ground Zero: The Story of the Rescue Efforts at the World Trade Center* (New York: Viking Press, 2002).

242 *"Then I'm giving general absolution":* John Delendick, oral history, FDNY, December 6, 2001.

Epilogue
Page

246 *Some time later, Will Jimeno found himself buried but alive:* Will Jimeno, interview by Jim Dwyer, October 29, 2001.

247 *Those historic currents, and others:* 9/11 Commission, Staff Statement 17, "Improvising a Homeland Defense," June 17, 2004.

248 *At scores of funerals for firefighters and police officers:* See, for example, New York *Daily News* in 2001: October 3, October 26, November 4, December 30; also *Newsday,* October 6, 2001.

250   *The interagency radios were sitting:* Jerome Hauer, former director of the Office of Emergency Management, testimony before the 9/11 Commission, May 19, 2004.

250   *It is likely that as many as 200 firefighters were inside:* An analysis by the *New York Times* in July 2002 of eyewitness accounts of locations of the 343 dead firefighters placed 97 in the south tower; 34 in the Marriott Hotel; 13 outside any building; and at least 121 in the north tower when it collapsed. The locations of 78 could not be determined, but most of them had been assigned to the south tower. However, it is likely that they went to the north tower because they were unfamiliar with the complex, as many surviving firefighters reported. A radio tape released in November 2002 in response to a lawsuit by the *Times* provided additional support for this theory. It showed that very few companies made it into the south tower, and the commander in the building was calling for additional companies some forty minutes after the second plane struck. By inference, the tape suggests that fewer than 97 firefighters were in the south building. Given that 121 of the dead are known to have been in the north tower, that 78 are unaccounted for but most likely were also in the tower, and that the figure of 97 in the south tower appears to be high, it is clear that a majority of the firefighter deaths took place in the north tower.

251   *Nearly all of the 6,000 civilians below the impact zone:* An overwhelming majority of civilians who died in the north tower worked on high floors, either above the crash zone or just below it, and were trapped. Approximately 110 people who worked below the 92nd floor died; few were in a position to be helped by firefighters. Approximately 26 were trapped in their offices in the 80s, where many doors jammed, or were trying to help other people free those doors. They are not known to have had contact with the firefighters. Another 14 were Port Authority employees who left their offices on the 64th floor at 10:08. They were moving without assistance. An unknown number were trapped in the tower's ninety-nine elevators. At least one person from the north tower was killed in the concourse during the collapse of the south tower, and others are believed to have died there. See also Dennis Cauchon, "For Many on September 11, Survival Was No Accident," *USA Today,* December 20, 2001, and NIST, "WTC Victims' Locations," July 20, 2004.

252   *Even so, when questions were raised in 2004:* Thomas Von Essen, Bernard Kerik, Richard Sheirer, Rudolph W. Giuliani, testimony before 9/11 Commission, May 18–19, 2004. Also, Stephanie Gaskell, "Commish's Fury—Scoppetta Fires Back at Sept. 11 Panel," *New York Post,* June 3, 2004.

255 *"On the morning of September 11, 2001, the last, best hope":* 9/11 Commission, Staff Statement 13, "Emergency Preparedness and Response," May 18, 2004.

261 *His old paramedic shirt torn, he plodded north:* Account of the rescue of Will Jimeno based on interviews with Jimeno, Dave Karnes, Scott Strauss, and Chuck Sereika, by Jim Dwyer, October 2001.

Afterword
Page

262 *Injured to go home:* Deborah Mardenfeld interviews, *Dateline,* NBC, August 31, 2003, and count of the injured from the federal claims filed as reported by Agence France Presse, "Sept. 11th Compensation Fund Expects to Pay Out $6 Billion," Catherine Hours, June 15, 2004.

263 *They immediately picked out Pablo Ortiz:* Alan Reiss, interview by Jim Dwyer, April 30, 2002.

263 *And Mak Hanna, who had accompanied:* Mak Hanna, interview by Jim Dwyer, August 25, 2003.

263 *When the Ortiz children held a memorial for their father:* Tirsa Moya, interviews and e-mails with Jim Dwyer, August 2003–August 2004.

264 *The accounts of Frank De Martini's valor:* e-mail from Enrico Tittarelli to Jim Dwyer, April 3, 2005.

265 *Brian Clark and Stanley Praimnath:* Brian Clark, interview by Jim Dwyer, August 4, 2004.

265 *Having survived a plane:* Stanley Praimnath, interview by Jim Dwyer, August 24, 2004.

266 *On her way to an appointment in New Jersey:* e-mail from Tirsa Moya to Jim Dwyer, August 17, 2004.

266 *East 59th Street skyscraper:* Karen Matthews, Associated Press, "Manhattan Hotel Damaged in 9/11 Attack Re-opens," May 5, 2003, and Charles V. Bagli, "Firm That Lost 658 in Towers Finds a New Home on 59th Street," *New York Times,* July 27, 2004.

267 *The document was a 10,000-page autopsy:* National Institute of Standards and Technology, "Final Report of the National Construction Safety Team on the Collapses of the World Trade Center Towers (Draft)," June 2005.

268 *In one section, the analysts found:* Jim Dwyer, "Towers Should Have Had One More Staircase, Report Finds," *New York Times,* June 24, 2005, p. B7.

268 *One of the documents:* H. S. Lew, Richard W. Bukowski, Nicholas J. Carino, "Design, Construction, and Maintenance of Structural and Life Safety Systems," NIST, p. 195.

269 *Asked if the Port Authority:* E-mail from Steve Coleman, spokesman, Port Authority of New York and New Jersey, June 23, 2005.

270 *The interviews provided searing, vivid testimony:* Jim Dwyer and Michelle O'Donnell, "9/11 Firefighters Told of Isolation Amid Disaster," *New York Times,* September 9, 2005, p. A1.

270 *Particularly informative were:* Jim Dwyer, Kevin Flynn, Ian Urbina, and Michelle O'Donnell, "Vast Archive Yields New View of 9/11," *New York Times,* August 13, 2005, p. A1.

270 *When they emerged:* Oral history of Emergency Medical Service Chief Zachary Goldfarb, October 23, 2001.

270 *Joseph Cahill, a paramedic:* Oral history, October 15, 2001.

271 *Manuel Delgado, a paramedic:* Oral history, October 2, 2001.

271 *Two emergency medical technicians:* Oral histories of Richard Erdey and Soraya O'Donnell, both October 10, 2001.

272 *The oral histories from the firefighters presented fresh evidence:* Dwyer and O'Donnell, "9/11 Firefighters Told of Isolation Amid Disaster."

273 *They were carried to the upper floors:* Eric Lipton, "Fire Department Gets Better Radios, but Needs Much More," *New York Times,* May 30, 2004.

273 *Some problems, however, could not be solved with battery power and bandwidth:* Michelle O'Donnell, "New Terror Plan Angers Fire Dept.," *New York Times,* April 22, 2005, p. A1.

274 *The next major disaster that New York responded to:* The account of the memorial service in New Orleans is based on interviews with Deputy Fire Commissioner Francis X. Gribben, Assistant Fire Chief Michael Weinlein, and *New York Times* reporter Al Baker by Kevin Flynn, September 2005, as well as accounts of activities in New Orleans by Erin McClam of the Associated Press, "NY Cops, Firefighters Help in N.O.," September 10, 2005, and Patrice O'Shaughnessy of the New York *Daily News,* "Hero Calls WTC Duty Therapy," September 12, 2005.

275 *With the passing of years:* Roselyn Braud interview by Jim Dwyer, September 2001; Melody Salcedo, on "Judge Hackett Show," Sony Pictures Television, September 12, 2005.

Postscript
Page

277 *Each rested one hand on the casket:* Jay Jonas, interview by Kevin Flynn, February 2011.

278 *Harris rode behind him in a silver convertible:* Jonas, interview by Flynn.

278 ... *a monument in Canada:* Jim Algie, "New Star in Beautiful Joe Park," *Collingwood Enterprise Bulletin,* May 14, 2002.

278 ... *recently filed for bankruptcy:* Al Baker, "Mourning a Woman Who Shared a 9/11 Escape," *New York Times,* January 17, 2011.

280 *At a meeting in the White House:* Carol Ashley, interview by Jim Dwyer, February 13, 2009.

280 ... *often be hamstrung by delays and evasions:* See, for instance, John Farmer, *The Ground Truth: The Untold Story of America Under Attack on 9/11* (New York: Riverhead, 2009), an account of the commission's struggle to get truthful information about the FAA and the deployment of air defenses on the morning of 9/11. The author, John Farmer, was senior counsel to the commission. See also Jim Dwyer, "Captain of Silence," *New York Times,* October 26, 2003, and Jim Dwyer, "Errors and a Lack of Information in New York's Response to Sept. 11," *New York Times,* May 19, 2004.

280 ... *due in large part:* Jim Dwyer, "Families Forced a Rare Look at Government Secrecy," *New York Times,* July 22, 2004.

281 *The United States was spending:* Dana Priest and William M. Arkin, "Top Secret America," *Washington Post,* July 19, 2010.

281 *On the morning of September 11, 2001, the U.S. military:* Stephen Daggett and Amy Belasco, *Defense Budget for FY 2003; Data Summary,* Congressional Research Service, March 29, 2002, p. 16.

281 *Over the next decade:* Sydney J. Freedberg Jr., "The Army's Growing Pains," *National Journal,* September 19, 2009.

281 *Among them was Christian P. Engeldrum:* Sean Engeldrum, interview by Jim Dwyer, 2009.

281 *Firefighter Engeldrum was the first:* Susan Edelman, "Grim Toll of 9/11 Casualties Keeps Rising," *New York Post,* September 12, 2010.

282 ... *had moved to New York from South Carolina:* David Worby, attorney for Sister Mahoney, interview by Kevin Flynn, March 2011.

282 *Sister Cynthia replied:* Oral history of Richard Erdey, October 10, 2001.

283 *Days before the attacks, Zelmanowitz:* Baruch Kra, "Twin Towers Saint Laid to Rest on Jerusalem's Mount of Olives," *Ha'aretz,* August 5, 2002.

284 *"I feel more at peace with Sean's death":* E-mail from Beverly Eckert to Jim Dwyer, February 2005.

285 ... *waterboarded 183 times:* Scott Shane, "Waterboarding Used 266 Times on 2 Suspects," *New York Times,* April 19, 2009.

286 *Leaving the meeting:* Kathleen Delaney, interviewed on "Larry King Live," CNN, February 13, 2009.

288 *The funeral arrangements:* Baker, *New York Times,* January 17, 2011.

289 *. . . even as the walls did:* Monsignor John Delendick, interview by Kevin Flynn, February 2011.

Acknowledgments

This work was supported and guided by a cast of hundreds—by people who escaped the buildings, family members of those lost at the trade center, our colleagues at *The New York Times* and other newspapers, the editorial staff in the Times Books division of Henry Holt and Company, many past and present public servants, interested citizens, friends, and our own families. In the fabric of September 11, there are many to mourn and much to admire; we regret that we could recount only a fraction of the day's struggles in these pages. We are grateful to all who told us of what they saw, heard, and did.

Scores of people provided voice mails, e-mails, and their recollections of conversations with loved ones inside the trade center and trapped on the upper floors. Many families were insistent that the history be told straight. We thank Nicole De Martini, Nina De Martini, Rosemary De Martini, and other members of the De Martini family, Debbie Palmer, Edna Kang Ortiz, Sally and Al Regenhard, Monica Gabrielle, Beverly Eckert, Jimmy Boyle, Iliana McGinnis, Steve and Liz Alderman, Beth Tipperman, Irma Fuller, the Eng family, the Olender family, Maureen Paglia, Lori Kane, Rita Palacios, Glenn Voght, Jim Smith, George and Mary Andrucki, Lynn Udbjorg, Dennis Kelly, Tommy Patchel, Michael and Peg Meehan and their family, Ann Johnson, Maureen Foo-Van Natten, Bernie Heeran, Jill Rosenblum, Arline Nussbaum, the Beyea family, the Zelmanowitz family, Judy Feeney, Colleen Kelly, Maureen Donegan, Peter Mulderry, Dorry Tompsett, Laurie Carter, Mary Maciejewski,

Marion Biegeleisen, Elizabeth Mattson, Linda Perry Thorpe, Mary
Fetchet, Kimmy Chedel, Corine Mardikian, Jessica Carucci, Vinny
Camaj, Patricia Perry, Cristy Ferer.

In early 2002, a team of reporters at the *Times* traced the events
on the upper floors of the towers and aspects of the emergency
response. We drew on that research for this book, and on the
insights of Ford Fessenden, James Glanz, and Eric Lipton. We were
honored to share bylines with them. Anyone interested in the history of late twentieth–century New York City can turn to *City in the
Sky*, a masterful account of the trade center's rise and fall written by
Jim and Eric. Ford and Eric helped create a framework for cata-
loging the research, and it has stood up well, thanks to a database
designed by Tom Torok. It has been an essential and durable tool in
piecing together a narrative from thousands of fragments of information. Others who worked with us on the initial newspaper projects or provided essential veins of research for this book include
Alain Delaqueriere, Michelle O'Donnell, Michael Pollak, Lauren
Wolfe, Joseph Plambeck, David Dunlap, Ian Urbina, Leslie Eaton,
and Aron Pilhoffer. They have our thanks.

With careful reporting and illuminating artwork, visual journalists at the *Times*—Steve Duenes, Archie Tse, Mika Gröndahl, and
James Bronzan—captured both the shape of the moment and the
form of the buildings. We are especially grateful to Steve, who
refined the graphics for this book.

Joe Sexton, editor and friend, read all the documents and
tracked each sentence in our newspaper stories; we are better in
every way because of him, his passion, his demanding intelligence,
and the occasional late-hour refreshments. Paul Golob, the editorial director of Times Books, edited this manuscript with great
vigor, rigor, and clarity; any writer would be fortunate indeed to
have Paul's sharp eyes on the page and wise hands around the book.

Over a period of three years, two metropolitan editors at the
Times, Jon Landman and Susan Edgerley, made sure that these
stones were told. We could not ask for better bosses.

This work began with the unbridled support of Howell Raines
and Gerald Boyd, then executive editor and managing editor of the

Times, and continued with similar backing from their successors, Bill Keller, Jill Abramson, and John Geddes. John Sterling, president and publisher of Henry Holt and Company, provided critical early guidance and support. The former editorial director of book development at the *Times*, Susan Chira, championed this book when it was only a couple of sentences, mumbled across a cup of coffee, and continued her efforts until she took over the world as the newspaper's foreign editor; her successor, Alex Ward, contributed keen observations about the manuscript and marshaled graphics and many of the pictures that appear in these pages. We thank, as well, Bill Schmidt and Jennifer Preston, for their assistance.

A number of public officials believed that the history of the day, as recorded in city records, belonged in the public domain, and used informal channels to make vital material available to us. We thank them by not naming them in these pages.

In federal and state courts in New York, New Jersey, and Virginia, David McCraw, *New York Times* counsel, has been a resourceful, principled, and determined advocate for access to public records concerning September 11. Among other things, his advocacy led to the release of the sole radio recording of firefighters inside either building, a tape that not even the Fire Department had listened to until David argued that it was a public record whose release would not jeopardize any fights against terrorism. From it emerged the account of Orio Palmer's race to the 78th floor of the south tower, and important revelations about the working of the radio system. David was assisted in New Jersey by another diligent lawyer, Bruce Rosen of McCusker, Anselmi, Rosen, Carvelli & Walsh, who brought an action in Superior Court that ultimately forced the Port Authority to release 2,000 pages of radio transcripts and police memoranda. In addition, Norman Siegel, a civil rights attorney in New York acting on behalf of a group of people lost at the trade center, has also been a determined advocate for the release of public records.

Paul Ginsberg, the president of Professional Audio Laboratories, enhanced certain Port Authority tape recordings and significantly improved the reliability of the transcript.

Others who played key roles in getting this book ready are

Michael Pollak, Brianna Smith, Robin Dennis, and Rita Quintas. We thank our agent and friend, Flip Brophy, and her assistant, Cia Glover, and for legal advice, Louise Sommers.

At the Port Authority of New York and New Jersey, important information about the buildings and the events of the day was provided by Alan Reiss and Mike Hurley. We were also assisted by Greg Trevor, Allen Morrison, Peter Yerkes, Kevin Davitt, Steve Coleman, Frank Lombardi, and Christopher Hartwyk. We also thank Patricia Cullen, Mak Hannah, Gerry Gaeta, Gerry Drohan, George Phoenix, Shivam Iyer, Anthony Whitaker, Al DeVona, David Lim.

We thank John Auletta of Summit Security, along with John Nolan, James Flores, and Greg Trapp.

Among those who provided information about their experiences inside the trade center are Brian Clark, Dianne DeFontes, Tirsa Moya, Walter Pilipiak, Michael Sheehan, Jan Demczur, Al Smith, Tim Pearson, Joseph Baccellieri, Will Jimeno, Dave Karnes, Chuck Sereika, and Sharon Premoli. Many other people who also were generous with their time and recollections are cited in the notes section. In particular, Roberta Gordon, an attorney and friend of Frank De Martini's family, shared with us a thoroughly researched profile of De Martini and a moving narrative of his actions. We are very grateful.

We received help on technical issues from many experts, including Nicholas Grecco, the retired chief engineer of the New York City Department of Buildings; Glenn Corbett, professor of fire safety at John Jay College of Criminal Justice of the City University of New York; retired fire chiefs Vincent Dunne, Charles Blaich, Bernard Lally, and retired firefighter and author Dennis Smith; John McFadden of Motorola and New York radio expert Eric Lustig; Greg Semendinger, a retired NYPD pilot; former officials with the city's Office of Emergency Management, Frank McCarton, Richard Sheirer, and Jerome Hauer; the current building commissioner, Patricia J. Lancaster, the buildings department spokeswoman, Ilyse Fink, and former building commissioner Rudolph Rinaldi; on the 911 system from Gino Menchini; Charles Brecher of the Citizens Budget Commission; on evacuation issues, Jake Pauls and Robyn Gershon; Won-Young Kim of the Lamont-Doherty

Earth Observatory of Columbia University; Shyam Sunder and Michael Newman of the National Institute of Standards and Technology; and Jack J. Murphy of the Fire Safety Directors Association. We also thank George Taylor, Bernie Patton, Martin J. Steadman, and Darlene Dwyer for their assistance.

At the Fire Department, Deputy Commissioner Frank Gribbon and former First Deputy Commissioner Michael Regan, former Deputy Commissioners Thomas Fitzpatrick and Lynn Tierney; Chiefs Joseph Pfeifer and Peter Hayden, and Chief Fire Marshall Louis Garcia were among those who were generous with their time. Former Commissioner Thomas Von Essen provided his perspective, thoughtfully and candidly. At his initiative, the FDNY took oral histories from more than 500 firefighters. The city has refused to make those documents public, but we were able to review about 100 of them, and not surprisingly, they provide essential views of what happened that day.

At the Police Department, among those who helped were Commissioner Raymond W. Kelly, former Deputy Commissioner Michael O'Looney, Deputy Commissioner Paul J. Browne, Deputy Inspector Joseph Galluci, Deputy Chief Michael Collins, and Sam Katz of the Detectives Endowment Association.

From the National Commission on Terrorist Attacks upon the United States—also known as the 9/11 Commission—we thank John Farmer, Al Felzenberg, and Jonathan Stull.

The distinguished work of Dennis Cauchon and Martha Moore, reporters at *USA Today*, fundamentally shaped the understanding of the events of the day; they were generous, too, with advice and leads for this book. The brave documentary film made by Jules and Gedeon Naudet serves as a source document for all who study the firefighting operations. The staff of *Der Spiegel* produced *Inside 9/11*, a useful reconstruction of the morning's events. At the other New York area newspapers, we turned to the work of, among others, Patrice O'Shaughnessy, Michele McPhee, Russ Buettner, Joseph Calderone, Michael Daly, Dennis Duggan, Sean Gardiner, Bill Murphy, Graham Rayman, and Michael Kelly. We also thank Philip Wearme and Niall O'Dowd for their help, and Deirdre Maloney of Bloomberg L.P. Many others are cited in the notes; our thanks to them, as well.

We thank Karen Preziosi and Janice Brooks for their help with Euro Brokers photographs.

At *The New York Times*, many of our colleagues provided help and leads. Here is the short, and certainly not complete, list of those we thank: Carla Baranauckas, Jacques Steinberg, Kirk Johnson, David Halbfinger, Joyce Wadler, Corey Kilgannon, David Barstow, Michael Cooper, Anthony DePalma, Sarah Kershaw, Chris Drew, Elissa Gootman, Lynette Holloway, Michael Wilson, Melena Ryzik, Marcos Mocine-McQueen, Geoff McGhee, Steve Greenhouse, Jeff Roth, Donald Parsons, Nancy Weinstock, Bill O'Donnell, Sherri Day, Dan Barry, Nina Bernstein, Ed Wyatt, Jennifer Steinhauer, Jan Hoffman, Janny Scott, Dean Murphy, Chris Chivers, Al Baker, Willie Rashbaum, Wendell Jamieson, and Anne Cronin.

All of this help has, we believe, drastically reduced our margin of error but not eliminated it; we alone are responsible for any mistakes in these pages.

We thank Rick Atkinson, Pete Hamill, Robert Kurson, and Richard Ben Cramer for their kindnesses.

From Kevin: I would like to thank my brother, Jim, for his clearheaded advice in so many matters that arose while writing the book and my mother, Margaret, for her constant support and encouragement. Finally, I would like to thank my wife, Mary, for her boundless patience, insight, and compassion. She and my children, Maggie and Kevin, afforded me the clearest perspective on what others had lost.

From Jim: As this book was getting started in the fall of 2003, Carol Rigolot, Tony Grafton, and David Kasunic of the Council on the Humanities at Princeton University, along with other staff and a keen group of students, made a visiting journalist welcome to the campus. Friends and family, in one way or another, pitched in and kept me company; a short, if incomplete, list includes Julie Talen, Margaret Scott, Ray Schroth, Kevin Doyle and Mary Sullivan and their family, Bob Muir and his people, and the Jorisch family. Thanks, again, to Cathy Cipressi and her family, my parents, Phil and Mary Dwyer, and my brothers Pat, Phil, and John and their families. And first and last, Cathy, Maura, and Catherine, not only give me my daily bread, but forgive me my fairly frequent trespasses.

Index

Entries in *italics* refer to diagrams and captions.

About the Authors

JIM DWYER and KEVIN FLYNN, native New Yorkers, veteran newspaper reporters and winners of many awards together and separately, now write in *The New York Times*. Dwyer is coauthor of *Two Seconds under the World*, an account of the 1993 effort to knock down the trade center, and of *Actual Innocence: Five Days to Execution and Other Dispatches from the Wrongly Convicted*. He is also the author of *Subway Lives: 24 Hours in the Life of the New York City Subway*. Flynn, a special projects editor at the *Times*, was the newspaper's police bureau chief on September 11. He previously worked as a reporter for the New York *Daily News*, *New York Newsday*, and the *Stamford Advocate*.